Cinema and the Shoah

THE SUNY SERIES

HORIZONSⁿCINEMA

MURRAY POMERANCE | EDITOR

Also in the series

William Rothman, editor, *Cavell on Film*

J. David Slocum, editor, *Rebel Without a Cause*

Joe McElhaney, *The Death of Classical Cinema*

Kirsten Moana Thompson, *Apocalyptic Dread*

Francis Gateward, editor, *Seoul Searching*

Michael Atkinson, editor, *Exile Cinema*

Bert Cardullo, *Soundings on Cinema*

Paul S. Moore, *Now Playing*

Robin L. Murray and Joseph K. Heumann,
Ecology and Popular Film

William Rothman, editor, *Three Documentary Filmmakers*

Sean Griffin, editor, *Hetero*

Cinema and the Shoah

An Art Confronts the Tragedy of the Twentieth Century

Edited by

Jean-Michel Frodon

Translated by

Anna Harrison
and
Tom Mes

Le cinéma et la Shoah: Un art à l'épreuve de la tragédie du 20ᵉ siécle
© Éditions Cahiers du cinéma, Paris, 2007

Published by
State University of New York Press, Albany

© 2010 State University of New York

For information, contact State University of New York Press, Albany, NY
www.sunypress.edu

Production by Ryan Morris
Marketing by Anne M. Valentine

Library of Congress Cataloging-in-Publication Data

Cinéma et la Shoah. English
  Cinema and the Shoah : an art confronts the tragedy of the twentieth
century / Jean-Michel Frodon, editor ; translated by Anna Harrison and
Tom Mes.
      p. cm. — (SUNY series, horizons of cinema)
  Includes bibliographical references and index.
  ISBN 978-1-4384-3027-0 (hardcover : alk. paper)
  ISBN 978-1-4384-3026-3 (pbk. : alk. paper)
  1. Holocaust, Jewish (1939–1945), in motion pictures.   2. Holocaust, Jewish
(1939–1945)—Influence.   I. Frodon, Jean-Michel.   II. Title.

  PN1995.9.H53C5514 2010
  791.43'658405318—dc22   2009022994

10 9 8 7 6 5 4 3 2 1

Contents

Introduction

THIS BOOK ASPIRES TO HELP CREATE a better perception of the ways in which the Shoah, a tragic historical event, left a unique mark upon its century and decisively influenced all manner of representation—above all the cinema. This "influence," or rather this radical questioning, started happening as the event itself was taking place and has not ceased ever since. Although its effects are much more far-reaching than the cinema, we believe it is through the cinema that the question must be posed. Why the cinema? Because it is a documentary tool that has played a decisive role in the building of knowledge for this period, with great effect in terms of historical education, the building of ethical criteria, and political strategy. And because at the same time it is a process of fiction that builds our visual and auditory imaginative faculties, which in turn configure our knowledge, our ethics, and our commitment. Because the cinema, as a mass-media pastime, is a means of diffusion of these representations, both real and imaginative, and this has tremendous impact. And finally—perhaps above all—because the cinema is an art form, and as such it is a source of emotions felt by each of us and a challenge to all of our established representational systems. Cinema therefore creates a possible questioning of our world vision and our self-image. This has a bearing upon the phenomenon of genocide. And thanks to *Survival in Auschwitz* and *The Human Race* by Primo Levi and Robert Antelme, we know to what extent genocide affects the world.

Our book is both collective and plural. Its plurality is in the manner of enunciation (essays, conferences, interviews, group discussions, visual archives, documented descriptions, and filmography), in the range of geographic origins (France, Germany, United States, Israel), and in the various professional points of view (philosophers, filmmakers, historians, film critics, art historians, teachers, and archivists).

The purpose of this book is to make these different approaches resonate to the reader. One of the common threads throughout these chapters is the historical accuracy of the topics discussed.

Cinema and the Shoah was conceived and produced from 2004–07, based on an idea that came about during preparations for the celebration of the sixtieth anniversary of the liberation of Auschwitz on January 27, 2005. This idea, formulated by Annette Wieviorka, Sylvie Lindeperg, Jacques Mandelbaum, and Jean-Michel Frodon, was initiated by the Foundation for the Memory of the Shoah, which has since supported the book project. We wish to express our thanks to the Foundation now. To remember these origins and these dates is, in a way, to say that if this type of book had been developed fifteen years ago it would have been an entirely different project, and that its very spirit makes it possible for others in the future to challenge and rethink it.

This book is divided into six parts. Although deliberately heterogeneous, it nonetheless follows a logical evolution. Beginning with a theoretical, philosophical, and critical discussion (in the sense of artistic criticism), this work progresses toward a more historically focused reflection, in view of the perspectives revealed in the first part of the book.

The first chapter ("Intersecting Paths," by Jean-Michel Frodon) aims at clarifying the overall project, the spirit in which the book was conceived, and the factual and theoretical backdrop upon which it centers.

The section "Milestones" undertakes to mark out more specifically three possible approaches, and each of the pieces in this chapter offers a particular focus regarding the entire issue. The first approach is philosophical ("The Shoah as a Question of Cinema," by Marie-José Mondzain), defining the very nature of the question as well as the methods of thought and formulation that it engages. A second approach, an aesthetic one from a film critic's perspective ("Recovery," by Jacques Mandelbaum) reveals the recurrence of certain forms of narrative, both visual and auditory, within a vast body of films that do or don't refer explicitly to the Shoah, and that question our relationship to what is true and false, to what is visible and invisible, regarding the radical crisis created by the Shoah. A third approach, again an aesthetic one but this time with an art history angle ("A Cinema No Longer Silent," by Hubert Damisch), reveals the stature and validity of "statements" (verbal, scriptural, iconic) as films relating to the Shoah reconfigure them, specify them, or challenge them.

"Three films" attempts to demonstrate the proportions and complexity of the questions surrounding representational procedures through three exemplary works, which also relate to more contemporary audiovisual productions. "Fatal Rendezvous" (by Jean-Louis Comolli) revisits the British film *Memory of the Camps*, which remained unscreened for forty years, in order to review the manner of stating reality and cinematic models, properly speaking, of certain representations. Thanks to the rigorous historical records of the conditions in the making and diffusion of Alain Resnais' film, "*Night and Fog*: Inventing a Perspective" (Sylvie Lindeperg) clarifies the constituting of visual archetypes and the unstable fate of the filmed image, recycled according to the perceptions and strategies of various periods and different situations; incorporated into this long-term study is the debate on the existence and legitimacy of "images of the Shoah" as it was formulated. *Shoah*, by Claude Lanzmann, played a decisive role in building our modern comprehension of the genocide, and holds a prominent place in the history of modern cinema. The coherence between these two aspects is the very principle of this book. The interview with Lanzmann covers the nature and meaning of the technical and artistic choices made in the creation of this film.

"Conversations at the Mill" took the form of a discussion between five participants (historians Sylvie Lindeperg and Annette Wieviorka, philosopher Marie-José Mondzain, filmmaker Arnaud Desplechin, and film critics Jean-Michel Frodon and Jacques Mandelbaum), an exchange fueled by having watched three films together: Ernst Lubitsch's *To Be or Not to Be*, Resnais' *Night and Fog*, and Michelangelo Antonioni's *L'Avventura*. The transcript of these two days spent together at the Moulin d'Andé, away from our daily routines, is an attempt at challenging the different approaches, the methodologies and formulations of the participants, distinct in their various fields but sharing the same concerns and commitments.

"Cinematography Put to the Test" examines how references to the Shoah in the cinema of three different countries have affected their systems of collective representation and thus contributed to clarifying the evolution of people's mentalities. This is less a question of "measuring" if, and in what quantities, this cinematography has referred to the Shoah, than of making an attempt at understanding, by formulating a specific question to each of the three, how these representations, silences, and symbolisms have played out. Aside from France, discussed at great length elsewhere in the book, the three countries in question—the United States, Israel, and Germany—are those for which the relationship to the theme of the Shoah is the most instructive. Bill Krohn discusses prevailing tendencies, much more differentiated than is commonly thought, in the approaches of the American cinema during the period of the growing threat of extermination, and then when it had occurred ("Hollywood and the Shoah, 1933–1945"), notably the strategies used by various studios, and the often paradoxical behavior of those involved, depending upon their positions in the community or their political ties. With the Israeli cinema, Ariel Schweitzer talks about the rapport between modes of reference to the Shoah and the ideological statute of Zionism as an ideological concretization for the country ("Forgetting, Instrumentalization, and Transgression: The Shoah in the Cinema of Israel"). And finally, Ronny Loewy uses the significant example of producer Artur Brauner, who sought for several decades to encourage reference to the camps and the extermination in mass-market German cinema ("'The Past in the Present': The Films of Producer Artur Brauner and the Dominant Narratives on the Genocide of European Jews in German Cinema").

"Tools for History" offers two critical approaches to cinema practices in historical research of the Shoah. As the author of the book *The Era of the Witness*, Annette Wieviorka reveals in her chapter, "The Filmed Witness," the complicity in strategies elaborated around the personality of witnesses and the unique challenges represented in the act of filming witnesses and using the gleaned images. Stuart Liebman, a specialist in audiovisual documentation regarding the Shoah, questions certain effects in the discourse that has come to accompany historical research concerning films about the Shoah, and the inherent risks of impeding or instrumentalizing it, in his chapter, "Historiography/Cinema of the Holocaust: Challenges and Advances."

"Resources": It would have been flippant and even irresponsible to attempt to "illustrate" a book in which the use of images is precisely the object of a complex and disquieting examination. On the other hand, it did appear useful for us to assemble, in the chapter entitled "Referent Images," those images that from the forties until the present time have fueled debates more or less closely centered on the Shoah. And with the intent of making information about films available to everyone (teachers, researchers, programmers, etc.) we put together the most complete "Filmography" possible to date of films dealing with the Shoah. Prepared thematically and not analytically or critically, this filmography obviously does not mention all of the films referenced in preceding chapters. And finally, we asked Ronny Loewy to present a project that has no existing precedent, entitled "Cinematography of the Holocaust," which he developed at the Fritz Bauer Institute in Frankfurt. Our sole objective was to offer a well-balanced archival record, available to anyone interested, of all audiovisual documentation linked to the Shoah.

Many people contributed to the production of this book. We would like to thank, in particular, Alain Bergala, Pierre Billard, Caroline Champetier, Anne Chaussebourg, Agnès Devictor, Jean-Claude Laureux, Annette Michelson, Dominique Trimbur, as well as Suzanne Lipinska, Fabienne Aguado and the entire team at Moulin d'Andé for all their help.

The translation required still more in the way of contributions, and we owe gratitude to Charlotte Garson, Anna Harrison, Bill Krohn, Tom Mes, Claudine Paquot, Emilie Saada, and Caroline de Salaberry, and Ian Dahlman, as well as to the thoughtful staff of the State University of New York Press, including James Peltz; Ryan Morris, production editor; Anne M. Valentine, marketing manager; Amanda Lanne, editorial assistant; Alan Hewat, copyeditor; Amane Kaneko, cover designer; and Sue Morreale, typesetter. Without the generosity and consideration of Matthew and Natalie Bernstein, Elliot L. Bien, Michael W. Bien, Ralph D. and Liliane U. Bien, David Edelberg, and the Lucius Littauer Foundation, this book could not have appeared for English readers. Grateful acknowledgment is also made to Ryerson University and its president, Sheldon Levy, for providing funds for the indexing of this book. Finally, we must thank Murray Pomerance, without whose enthusiasm and uncompromising and demanding support this English version of the book would simply not exist.

Translated from the French by Anna Harrison

legal, and administrative organization, and at the same time because of the position, both strategic and appalling, granted to it by the highest-ranking political heads of Germany until the very final days of the Nazi regime. The extravagant combination of these heterogeneous factors constitutes an unfathomable and monstrous enigma, which exceeds and will continue to do so the descriptions and explanations that we are capable of giving, while *at the same time* being a sequence of events subject to description, study, and reflection. This double nature makes the Shoah, with its multiple dimensions, a unique event, laden with meaning and questions, a cardinal catastrophe in a time already not lacking in other immense dramatic events and atrocities.

The cinema, on the other hand, is born of nineteenth-century technology. It configured the collective imagination on a planetary scale during the first two thirds of the twentieth century, before losing this prominent status to television, which has in turn been challenged by new communications technologies. Although it has become a minority practice, the cinema has not disappeared and will not do so. It corresponds to a manner of articulation between individual and collective reality and imagination that, since its inception, established its pertinence for human beings. That pertinence continues into the twenty-first century.

These two phenomena are historically dated: the Shoah (brief but of extreme intensity) and the cinema (several decades long in its role as the "art of the century"). But they affect more than just the periods of time that contained them. They are heterogeneous but of the same era, and are not confined to the exact same period; they belong to the same state of human civilization, that of the Western world as defined at the turn of the nineteenth century, a state that has spread its influence over the entire world. Technology, organizations focusing on an industrial model, the Great War as the founding tragedy of the twentieth century, and the methods used in the construction of the collective imagination that characterize that particular time frame also constitute some of the principal conditions of existence both of the cinema and of the Shoah; they designate the relationships, more or less direct, between these two events. These relationships can at times be complicit, as in "the aestheticization of politics," denounced by Walter Benjamin as a characteristic of fascism, that will have been practiced widely on a cinematic model (one need only observe the Nuremberg ritual, directed by Goebbels and filmed by Riefenstahl, to be convinced of this). These relationships can also at times be in opposition to each other: the cinema that warned of the terror to come also attempted, in vain, to combat it. Those who would love the cinema the most later on would say that its very reason for being, its "historic mission," would be to render the extermination impossible.

To a great extent, these relationships connect around what is visible: the cinema is the device of making real bodies appear in time, the machine that shows men to themselves having recorded the marks they have made in four dimensions. The Shoah was not only an operation of annihilation of real bodies, killed and then burned, but also a procedure of erasing that very device of annihilation itself, a machine that did away with humanity as well as every trace of it. *The Shoah is a tragedy of humanity in its relationship to the visible, and it is as such that it fundamentally concerns the cinema.* The Shoah is not the only horrific event that marked the twentieth century. But the dual crisis that it opens upon—the denial of what is human, the denial of the image—and even more so the manner in which the ideology and the practices of mass extermination perpetrated by the Nazis solidify these two denials, make the Shoah the event that questions the cinema itself in the entirety of these terms of aesthetic and social existence.

The stakes that will be discussed herein are those that largely exceed the limits of factual time. They are those of long-term history, the stakes of ongoing modern History—therefore, also, those of the present time.

The Shoah has left its unique mark on the history of mankind. The cinema, as a unique material and imaginative device, reconfigures the relationship of men to themselves and to the world. These two assertions, which give such great importance to both phenomena, state at the same time that they are *in History;* that it is not a matter here of making either essential; that however extreme the Shoah was, and to a great extent incomparable to other horrific events committed by men, however specific the procedures of cinema are, the question here is not to give either an absolute character. Neither the Shoah nor the cinema are ideas, or at least not Ideas. They are fact. But such facts challenge our manner of being within the world, in any case since the forties, based on terms previously unknown that remain active to this day.

The decisive relationship between these two phenomena is still at work in the one that endures: the cinema. One of the characteristics of the cinema is that it only exists in symbiosis with its time, and to redistribute, with more or less impact and more or less explicitly in real life, what is modeled in its bosom. This book is therefore a "book about the cinema" in the sense that it is about the cinema as it has been worked, transformed, and challenged to its very depths by the Shoah—depths that existed prior to the extermination, but that were perceived only in the black light of the industrialized racial prejudice perpetrated by the Nazis.

However, because there is filtration between the cinema and the real world, this work within the cinema engendered by the Shoah also has many effects on practices, mores, laws, individual and collective behaviors, and our manner of reflecting and debating upon it. While this book is in fact, in its approach and its references, a book about the cinema, its scope is hence not limited to the sole field of cinematography.

There are a number of ways of approaching this intersection of the phenomenon of cinema and the phenomenon of extermination. We believe these approaches have a lot to offer to each other, and therefore to all of us. It is possible to draw up a schematic list of these approaches: the cinema as archive; the cinema as material for historical research; the cinema as material for constructing one or several realms of imagination; the cinema as method of investigation and/or revelation; the Shoah as the subject of film; the Shoah as a backdrop to films whose "subject" is or appears to be something else; the Shoah as a question mark on an ethic of representation or of narration; the Shoah as a test of the limit to the possibility of representing things, as a threshold to the possibility of the image.

The classical distinction between documentary and fiction, which should be made with caution, reveals itself in this case as manifestly problematic. There are archives that turn out to be fiction (fabrications which are not admitted as such: propaganda films, for example, those of the period as well as more recent ones such as the manipulated footage of the Eichmann trials done by Sivan and Brauman in their film *A Specialist* [1999]) and other fictions that are invaluable documents for historians; there are documents recording reality but in which staging entirely recreates actual reality (for example, *Triumph of the Will* [1935] by Leni Riefenstahl) and there are scrupulous recordings of reality that tell a story, even a tragic saga (for example, *Shoah* [1985] by Claude Lanzmann) and of course other films that deliberately work at mixing genres, such as *Drancy Avenir* (1997) by Arnaud Des Pallières. There are works of fiction, which explicitly or in a roundabout way interpret the characters and situations of reality and of fantasy that were those of the Shoah, from *To Be or Not to Be* (1942) by Ernst Lubitsch to *L'Avventura* (1960) by Michelangelo Antonioni. There are also films—and this is most often the case—that have recourse to fiction or romance, without taking into consideration the radical and particular nature of the Shoah or its powerful questioning of the very process of filmed fiction. This questioning is pushed to the extreme by the fact that the film is in relation to the extreme and particular event that is the Shoah, but it opens or at least intensifies the possibility of questioning the very process of all cinematic fiction: critical questioning that involves no condemnation of principle, which would again be an abusive closure to conclude the impossibility or the indignity of all fiction regarding the extermination, and why not, of the impossibility or indignity of fiction "in general." It is a matter of daring to think, when faced with this horror, of refusing both the effects of being staggered and the lazy despicableness of passing it off to the profits and losses of History. It is a matter of attempting to bring out the positive idea that the Shoah will have not only inspired a great number of films (as is also the case for many other historic events) but above all reworked the manner in which we make films and the manner in which we watch them and speak of them.

The (too) famous phrase, "How to create poetry after Auschwitz?" applies to the cinema as well, but taken to the letter: not in the thought that it would be impossible from that point onward to make films, any more than poems, but in the question of "how." In Auschwitz, at the same time this extreme blind spot in the relationship of humans to humans and to the very idea of humanity—as Primo Levi, Robert Antelme, Elie Wiesel, Paul Celan, or Jean Améry have always clearly specified—resides also the question of representation of men by themselves, the manner of telling stories, of seeing the world. It is certainly not a question of saying that explicitly or in a suggested manner there must be a reference to the Shoah in each cultural production, and notably in each film, but that the great questions of what humanity is, that are by nature at the heart of all work (not only all great books, or all great visual works of art, or all great musical works, but at the very least of any popular song, just as of the least artistic film), have been underlyingly affected by the Shoah.

This is true of all cultural production, but more so in the field of representation. We live, in the Western world, in a place where images are a moral issue. They are subject to questioning and often condemnation, for the sake of dividing what is True from what is False or Good from Evil, under the influence of the two great sources of our conception of the world, the monotheistic theologies and Greek philosophy. These stakes were formulated based upon the question of figuration, in other words, based upon nature and the intensity of the real presence of what is presented in its representation. The taboo in the "images carved" by Deuteronomy, the allegory of Plato's cave, the philosophical thought of the mime, of the diaphanous, of the catharsis and the political role of Aristotle's theatre, the Christian dogma of incarnation, the clashing of church fathers on the representations of God, the vigor and complexity of the banning of images in Islam and the diversity of its implementations constitute the great milestones of this long history. They have been reprised subsequently by art history—figurative arts, painting and sculpture, but also the performing arts—at the heart of the philosophic category of aesthetics. Why is this issue a "moral" one? Because it has always involved a reference to a *norm*, beyond what is personal between the image[1] and the one who created it, as well as the one who is seeing it. This norm can be absolute, in the case of religion (Evil is at work in the figurative process and that which it inspires in he who observes it) or of relative nature, in the case of Greek philosophy and its long descent (images fool you, they are in the realm of illusion, humanity will progress as it detaches itself from them in order to approach the truths of the world). In all these cases, what is at stake is morality, in the sense that one must refer to a norm intended to regulate individual behavior and relationships between humans and to a certain ethic, wherein this reference guides choices, practices that are autonomous to each of us—makers of images and observer of images—and wherein these choices engage the rapport with others.

This moral and ethical question, fundamentally linked to imagery, will have carried over into the visible world through the invention of analogue recording technologies, specifically photography and then the cinematograph. The moral questioning with regard to the effects of the cinema began at its inception. It was frequently denounced as immoral, pornographic, and blasphemous by nature and in its essence by religious authorities and virtue leagues from all denominations, whether for the way in which it reproduced reality (it "would compete with the Creator") or for its power of fascination over people. It would take much longer for people to begin to question what was being challenged, with regard to ethics, in the actual creation—in other words, the direction—of cinematic images.

What do we mean, in this context, by "with regard to ethics"? We mean that the specific methods used to create films bring about new ethical stakes. We see on the screen not the actual world, but pieces of the world, and in particular, human beings. For this to happen, it means that the person who organized the recording of these "pieces of the world" makes a great number of very real choices—imposing one's self in the real world on those one is filming. Such choices are more or less emphasized, colored, or sidestepped by what happens after filming: the combination of processes that we designate by the generic name of post-production.[2] These choices, as they are configured once the film is finalized, bring about in turn considerable relationships for the viewer with what he is seeing (the characters, the twists and turns of the action), but also with regard to the real world of which the pieces of every film are more or less, at least in part, an assembly.

This is why, while all representation is "a matter of morality" (and especially a matter of ethics), and while any visual work of art is subject to ethical questioning with regard to the means that it uses to move the viewer, the cinema, as a piece of reality, is particularly a matter of morality, and above all, of ethics: it involves the personal practices of those who make the film and those who observe it. When Jean-Luc Godard states his now famous assertion, "The tracking shot is a matter of morals,"[3] he is really stating that beyond what is at stake in all representation, the techniques of filming (and sound recording and editing) in the cinema are all the more laden with ethical questions. What questions? Basically they can be boiled down to two: how should we depict something? What effect are we looking to have upon the viewers? There are ways of showing things, and above all people, with contempt, with condescension, with hatred; these methods are ethically reprehensible. There are ways of showing images and telling stories that subjugate the audience, remove their objectivity, manipulate them, and these means are ethically reprehensible. While these "means," otherwise known as choices of form (in the cinema, they are about directing), are always defined by the medium in use, what is at stake is common to all modes of representation. But they take on a particular gravity with regard to the cinema because real people were filmed, and we see their images on the screen. The indignity in the manner in which they were filmed, like the act of using them to limit the freedom of viewers, is particularly obscene and disgraceful.

These two questions (How to depict? What effect are we looking to have upon the viewers?) are considered connected by critics and modern cinema. They are the singular means of the cinema that can cause an increase of oppression or alienation, or that on the contrary can open spaces of liberty, of affective and intellectual autonomy. The opposition between these two realms—oppression or liberty—is similar to that which opposes art to industry, and they remain the two key active ingredients or principles in the cinema. Art is an opening; it is a call to each of us, by aesthetic means, to venture outside of himself, to encounter the world, other people, and any other experience possible. Industry is production, including by aesthetic means (pretty images, pretty sounds, pretty stories, etc.) of objects that seem different but that are only desirable, in other words consumable, as reproductions of the same thing. The consequence of industry is the commercialization of desire (which exists in all of us), the opportunity to take refuge in the consummation of that which has already been tried, in the manner of regressive pleasure. The cinema is always both art and industry, which is what its impure nature is based upon. But it is art and industry in proportions than can vary a great deal, on an arc in which each film occupies its own specific position.

These theories were to a great extent developed thanks to André Bazin, and with him the *Cahiers du cinéma* (of which Godard and Moullet are members), even though they have roots just as well in an older history of theory, alongside Jean Epstein and Elie Faure, and in certain artistic practices, the films of Jean Vigo, Jean Renoir, and Italian neorealism. This approach confers a decisive role upon the moment of filming and the so-called "documentary" content (the recording of reality) in all films. It is in the name of this approach that the essential of what is proper to the cinema from the point of view of the ethics of representation[4] plays out.

Among the critical texts that demonstrate this concern regarding the ethics of direction, a short article by Jacques Rivette became a reference. Entitled "Abjection," it was published in *Cahiers du cinéma* 120 (June 1961). This text did not draw too much attention when it was published; it was only fifteen years later that it would begin to function as the basis of a requirement from which Serge Daney would build his essential theoretical architecture. But it is remarkable that Rivette's text was inspired by a film, *Kapò* (1959) by Gillo Pontecorvo, whose story takes place in a concentration camp. When Rivette writes that the director "only deserves his deepest contempt" for obtaining a spectacular effect—where a prisoner (Emmanuelle Riva) commits suicide by throwing herself on an electrified wire fence—through constructing a tracking shot that ends with a reframing of the hand, the fact that this is about a film whose subject is tied to Nazi terror is completely secondary in his mind. He seeks to share a requirement regarding the direction which could just as well have applied to a tragic scene coming from an entirely different context, and he implies that his condemnation does not only concern the aestheticization of a death scene. The critical (ethical) demands concern all forms of direction, to judge all methods employed in order to produce emotion: laughter, compassion, anger, and so forth.

On the other hand, the rapport between the subject of the film that provided the basis for Rivette's text and the ethical stakes of direction is taken into consideration by Serge Daney when he makes it the cornerstone of his critical judgment, as he would much later in an article that would become a major reference, "The Tracking Shot in Kapo," published in *Trafic*'s fourth issue (Autumn 1992) and reused as the opening of the book *Perseverance* (POL, 1994). In the meantime, a number of events in the critical discourse of the cinema took place. The question of the ethics of cinematic direction and its political corollary was developed and deepened, particularly by Godard, the Straubs, Pasolini, Eustache, and Fassbinder. *Cahiers du cinéma*, at the end of the sixties and throughout the seventies, gave it a great deal of reflection. This ethical and political questioning relies to a great extent upon the updating of a paradox: it is a documentary dimension, therefore the recording of what is visible, that defines the impact of the cinema and the particular moral demands that this impact imposes upon it, but at the same time all its beauty, its interior richness, and its artistic nature are based upon what it brings up that is invisible, through visible means. The art of cinema is the art of giving the most in feeling and in understanding what we cannot see (the real world, feelings, ideas, the supernatural, God, etc.) thanks to the recording of what we do see. And notably, following the works and writings of Robert Bresson,[5] it is once again Serge Daney who made the strongest opposition, to denounce the obscenity of what he calls the "visual," in other words the saturation of what is visible, which in fact hides the invisible, the crushing of the freedom of the image beneath what it shows, the enslavement to the "message" of what makes its open richness unlimited. This horror for which the cinema is so often guilty is the very principle of publicity, in which the image must be entirely controlled by its objective (to sell the object), and also characteristic of television, a means of communication that is theoretically "without remainders," without loss, whereas art, precisely, only exists through loss or excess, is born of loss. And it is in this loss, through subtraction or excess in this unmastered area of artistic representation, that the viewer's freedom is played out, as well as the respect for the complexity of the world. The ethical thought of the cinema will have been to a large extent the thought for the invisible.

And then a cinematic event that came out of a different conceptual universe took a historic turn: the release of *Shoah* by Claude Lanzmann, in 1985.

From the point of view of its genealogy, *Shoah* belongs in another filiation, that of "films about the camps." We must briefly recall here that the specific history regarding the evocation of the Shoah is connected to numerous parameters, beginning with the constitution of the extermination of European Jews as an autonomous event, against essential practices—historiographical, commemorative, militant, and so forth—of the period immediately following the war. The concentration camp phenomenon will primarily have been perceived through literary works based upon lived experience (by Primo Levi, David Rousset, Robert Antelme, Elie Wiesel, etc.), without allowing a clear distinction between the horror of the concentration camps (comparable to what is committed, alas so frequently, for reasons of war, foreign or civil, for colonization, for oppression) and the exceptional particularity of the process of systematic extermination. It would take the solitary and titanic work of the historian Raul Hilberg, *The Destruction of Europe's Jews*[6]; it would take the turnaround of Eichmann's trial and the instauration of a "policy of remembrance" by the State of Israel in the service of its specific objectives, in order for the issue of the Shoah to be created as such.

As it referred to the event that was the Shoah, the cinema unavoidably accompanied this process, with an imprecision and confusion that seem retrospectively shocking but that corresponded to the state of knowledge and comprehension of the time. We know that the word "Jew" is only pronounced once, and only incidentally, in *Night and Fog* (1955) by Alain Resnais, whose title, significantly, was originally to have been *Resistance and Deportation*. And while the film justifiably represents a founding cinematic work on the subject, it is certainly not the first film to be mentioned. An enormous image documentation was produced and distributed, often creating both its own directorial rhetoric and new uses of filmed imagery, notably in a legal context or mass reeducation—where the shown images are never those of actual extermination but documents from the "ordinary" camps, where the atrocity serves as metaphor (and therefore also as mask) for even worse things. Fiction also mentioned the Nazi camp atrocities very early on: *The Criminal* by Orson Welles (1947), *The Last Stop* by Wanda Jakubowska (1948), and *Distant Journey* by Alfred Radok (1949) referred to it clearly, and the episode of the collective film *Return to Life* (1949) directed by André Cayatte evoked it as well.

The fact that it was Alain Resnais, one of the modern greats of the cinema from the fifties on, who took on the first great cinematic work dealing with the abyss that was the Nazi camps and the Shoah, is not a coincidence. *The Passenger* (1963) by Polish director Andrzej Munk; *Memory of Justice* (1976), an American film by French director Marcel Ophuls; *Mr. Klein* (1976), a French film by American director Joseph Losey; *Hitler: A Film from Germany* (1977) by the German director Hans-Jürgen Syberberg; more indirectly the work of Samuel Fuller; and of course the films of Rainer Werner Fassbinder, are milestones in the parallel paths of the history of the Shoah and the modernization of the cinema. These two paths, that of the construction of the particular place of the extermination of the Jews by the Nazis and that of the modern adventures of the observation of the world by the cinema, would take a long time, forty years to be exact, to reach their exact point of convergence. This point of convergence is the film entitled *Shoah*.

There is a before and an after *Shoah*, both for History and individual and collective perception of the extermination event itself, and for the history of the art of cinema. And this is something that is stated immediately by a great number of texts of varying origins and focus that followed the release of this film.

The principal choices in direction taken by Lanzmann were based upon his recording of live witnesses, his refusal to use any archival images, his wanting to connect present day sound (the present voices of the victims, the executioners, the witnesses) and the locations as they exist today, with traces as well as lack of trace, forgotten places haunted by those who were to be forgotten and whom Lanzmann summons for what they are: dead, ghosts. *Shoah* is not a film about the camps, but about the immense enterprise of convening something that no longer exists, something that was erased several times over: the men, women, and children who were assassinated, their bodies reduced to dispersed ashes, and the machines that were used to kill them, also destroyed. Precise, complex, combative, and very well documented, the strategies used in making this film aim at infinitely opening each person's spirit to the immeasurable horror of this crime, in "seeing through" the survivors and their testimonies as stated by Soshana Felman.[7] These direction choices were inspired in Lanzmann by his thoughts and feelings toward the extermination itself, but they have a great bearing upon the questioning of the modern cinema in ethical terms about film directing. The crisis of story, subject, and character, the disjunction of sound and image, the reciprocal challenge of fiction and documentary, the impact of perceiving the invisible through the most fierce attachment to the reality of the locations, bodies, voices, and temporalities: Bresson and Rossellini, Antonioni and Godard, Resnais and Buñuel, Ozu and Cassavetes, Rohmer and Straub, Pialat and Welles are present. Their aesthetic decisions, their directing biases put to the test of classical representations of the world through fiction and documentary, find not only a translation legitimized by the imperious ethical demands that carry all directing decisions in filming *Shoah*, but also their paroxysmal accomplishment.

When the question regarding the non-appearance, the invisible within the visible, was posed, first by Lanzmann's film and then by his statements, a number of cinema critics were willing to hear and pick up this discourse based on its own progression. And the film *Shoah*, born of an approach built upon a rapport with the subject—the extermination of Europe's Jews in the oblivion of visibility chosen and obtained by the Nazis—will have crossed paths with, and become the major example of, not only a crisis of the visible at the heart of the cinema but of the art of cinema confronted with the onslaught of "modern" visuals, that of publicity and the media.

It is therefore at the intersection of these stakes which are contradictory but which do not cancel each other out, that one hopes—based on the power of imagery, particularly recorded imagery, and based in that decisive importance, for all forms of representation and in particular those that have to do with art (because they deal with the invisible, the invisible as a principle of their reason to be, as opposed to propaganda, publicity, and communication)—that the cinema will find itself confronted with the Shoah. It is therefore logical that questions of film criticism—in which criticism is justified in intervening, including in the offensive, when it discovers the effects of crushing, of visual influence—have managed to point in a particularly engaged manner that can be spotted in the media, to films whose subjects are linked to the Shoah, particularly *Schindler's List* (1993) by Steven Spielberg and *Life is Beautiful* (1997) by Roberto Benigni. And it is just as logical that critics, whose work is based upon the ethical and political concerns of the visual, and Claude Lanzmann, whose reflection and directing strategies come from other sources, find themselves side by side struggling with such instrumentation of the abyss of the Shoah in order to produce spectacular effects—with the best intentions.[8] If a debate (in our opinion biased and artificially bitter) later opposed Lanzmann and Godard, it must be reiterated that in a letter that is a veritable testament of what he considers his political failure as a filmmaker, Jean-Luc Godard states as being at the top of the list the fact that he was incapable of preventing Steven Spielberg from reconstructing Auschwitz in order to film *Schindler's List*.[9] Godard situates himself very clearly here in connection to his assertion that "the tracking shot is a question of morality" and to Rivette's critique of *Kapò*.

After the release of Claude Lanzmann's film, it would take time for this fundamental convergence with the aesthetic and ethical questions of modern cinema to be completely recognized, because of the gigantic importance of the "subject," the extermination of the Jews of Europe. This film that marks a summit in the history of art is also, and in a more visible manner, a turning point in the history of the extermination and how it is perceived by society. *Shoah*, this masterpiece at the height of modern art, is also a stroke of thunder, less in the domain of History in the strict sense, in spite of the imposing historian's work accomplished by Lanzmann, than in History in the proper "political" sense, wherein ideational power struggles are developed. The film will play an essential role in recognizing the particularity of the event, notably in at last imposing a distinction between Nazi crimes taken as a whole and the specific project of industrially exterminating a people responsible for a metaphysical function, possessing an attribute marked off by an absolutely negative sign, an attribute conferred from the outset, by law, to each individual reputed to be part of this people.

One of the most visible effects of the film will have been to name the event, or rather to impose in a part of civil society and scholarly circles (not all of them) the Hebrew word *Shoah*. Very logically, following this film and the decisive role it played, *Shoah* will be the preferred term in this work. This preference was not the general rule, however: some auteur filmmakers refused to use the word, for two types of reasons. Some reject it as a perceived gesture, an act of appropriation of such an event, in Lanzmann's claim to name it; others remain attached to the use of another word, "Holocaust," whose usage is of Anglo-Saxon origin. It is noteworthy that another method of direction and imagery, an American television series[10] that did not pose *any* ethical directorial questions regarding the depiction of extermination, was also in the position of naming the event. In this manner, it would be only one film, the one made by Claude Lanzmann, and a television miniseries that will have been at the origin of the two words accepted from that point forward to name this major event.[11] And now we return to the very heart of the present work.

This book is born of the conviction that contribution to the thought of the Shoah as a real event and as an event of representation cannot presume to establish a *doxa*, a body of rules and precepts. This would require several inscriptive clauses in vaster compilations. It would require precise nomenclature and intimate emotion. It would require reference to political violence, to art history, to the history of philosophy, to the effects of meaning within national cinematographies. It would require the difference in sensibilities engendered by belonging to different countries and cultures. This book will therefore deliberately be lacking in what has so often accompanied contemporary thought regarding the representational stakes of the Shoah: the verbosity, the invectives, the posturing and demonstrations of rhetorical strength. The very lesson of contemporary art, such as it will have been affected by the Shoah, and in particular the art of the cinema as *the* art of that period—a period that is still, sixty years after the liberation of the Auschwitz camp, *our* period—this lesson is precisely the reformulated demand that we reject any closed system, any totalitarian or linear pretension. Crisis and disjunction are necessary in order to be, as much as possible, worthy of such an event, in its double nature: brief history (the 1940 to 1945 extermination) and long-term history, that which is still ours at the present time. The divergences summoned here *in the name of a shared ethic* are not only part of the very basis of this work, they are its criteria.

Translated from the French by Anna Harrison

Notes

1. These complex questions bring up a number of further developments, which have no place in this context. But we must mention nonetheless that when we speak here of "image," we are obviously speaking of images "created by the hand of man," and having recourse to elements that are materially visible, and not to the whole of perceptive representations, and even less to the imagination or so-called acheiropoiete images, in other words those that were not created by man.

2. Post-production involves mainly the editing of the film, and often post-synchronization (the adding on of re-recorded dialogue), then the mixing (the arranging of the various components of the soundtrack) and the calibration (the color and lighting corrections).

3. This phrase was a play on words, while underlining and specifying the meaning of a symmetrical phrase used by Luc Moullet, "Morals are a matter

of the tracking shot," to attest that it is in the choices of the direction that the ethics of a film are played out.

4. It must be noted here how much this history, this approach to the cinema, this demanding nature toward it, which is the quid pro quo of a love for films and the hope in the political possibilities of cinematic form, has been essentially a French history—or one under a French influence. The resources of other great schools of critical discourse—Germany, Russia, the United States, and to a lesser degree Italy and Japan—have for the most part worked according to different approaches, with other stakes at hand.

5. *Notes on the Camera* (Paris: Gallimard, 1975).

6. Although pioneers like Leon Poliakov, who wrote *The Breviary of Hate* in 1951, and Gerald Reitlinger, who wrote *The Final Solution* in 1953, contributed tremendously to creating awareness of the genocide.

7. "In the Age of Testimony," *On the Subject of the Shoah* (Collectif. Belin, 1990).

8. See notably the interview granted by Lanzmann at the release of *Schindler's List*, entitled "Holocaust, the Impossible Representation" (the unfortunate title was chosen by the newspaper *Le Monde* [3 March 1994]).

9. "Letter to an American Friend" in *Jean-Luc Godard by Jean-Luc Godard*, Vol. 2 (Cahiers du cinéma, 1998). We very deliberately chose not to reprint the debate between Godard and Lanzmann, one which also involved, in terms very unlikely to promote further thought, in our opinion, contributions from very high-quality intellectuals such as Georges Didi-Huberman and Gérard Wajcman. In a typically media-driven manner, in which this debate focused upon "short sentences," Lanzmann stated that if he were to find a film that recorded a group killing in a gas chamber he would destroy it, Godard having said that he was sure that such a film existed and that he could find it if he were given the means. All parties took these statements out of context and beyond their interrogatory value and trouble, in order to make of this, in bad faith, slogans. Readers interested in this discussion can find the key points in the interview with Lanzmann in *Le Monde* (see note 8, above); the Godard interview in *Les Inrockuptibles* (October 21, 1998); Gérard Wajcman, "Photographic Belief," in *Modern Times* (Spring 2001); "Saint Paul Godard versus Moses Lanzmann?" (*Le Monde* [3 December 1998]); Georges Didi-Huberman's *Images In Spite of Everything* (Editions de Minuit, 2003).

10. The "Holocaust" miniseries, broadcast in 1978 in the United States on the NBC channel, contributed a great deal to commemorating, or revealing to Americans, the history of the extermination. Even during the scenes of extermination, the episodes were interrupted every fifteen minutes by advertisements. The series was also broadcast widely all over the world, and it is estimated that it was viewed by 220 million people in all.

11. The television miniseries did not create the usage of the word "holocaust," but it is what popularized it and instated it for researchers. The extermination was also named in the language of its victims, Yiddish, as *Khourbn*.

Milestones

The Shoah as a Question of Cinema

Marie-José Mondzain

THIS ESSAY FINDS ITS ORIGIN IN a conference on the role of culture and art in the transmission of what we call the Shoah.[1] We owe a great deal to Claude Lanzmann for the clarification brought about by this term. Even though it has a Hebraic connotation that might suggest only one specific historical tragedy that devastated one specific community, it has since lent its authority to the questioning of all the threats to mankind. That, too, we owe to Lanzmann's film and the universal resonance of the way it dealt with that one specific genocide.

This assessment forms the basis of this chapter, since it deals with questioning the methods of transmission, the forms of collective memory in sharing an ordeal of which there will soon be no more survivors. This is not merely a case of collecting every document and every testimony that could help build knowledge and pass on information. Whether or not archives are conclusive, they remain lifeless if they do not actively communicate. Questioning culture or the whole of symbolic operations, questioning art or the forms of emotion that accompany these operations, means demanding of culture and art that they find ways to become political. Political here does not refer to the exercise of power but is an appeal to the strength of the bonds that make up a community, a city—in the sense of the Greek word *polis*.

During the conference mentioned above, I argued that in order to speak of art in the face of the Shoah, we should stop looking at the issue as a problem. Philosophy is by nature cautious in its use of words and it is worthwhile to distinguish *questions* from *problems*. The relation between

17

the Shoah, transmission, and art should be regarded as a question and not as a problem. The question is open and troubling, and acknowledges its own historical evolution and the relativity of suggested responses. A question is shared and knows no final word. A problem always begs a solution and is all the more satisfied with solutions when they are proposed by experts—or at least those who seem most competent. In our case there is no solution to be found, there are no experts who can put a stop to the rupture of memory. On the contrary, we need to tirelessly build upon the question in the way our concern is kept alive, in the way we work for the future, in the way one pleads endlessly for freedom. This is not to be confused with a sophisticated exploitation of the question by pretending that the lack of answers proves its vitality. A question has no solution, but it nevertheless listens to answers because it forms an appeal to the ties that bind those who share it. Which means that everything must remain open in such a way that the quality of the exchanges depends on each person's conviction that no individual holds the solution but that it is the very nature of the interaction that lends every proposition its merit.

The Shoah is a historical and political question that appeals to the ethical dimension of our memory and the political responsibility of its transmission into the future. It sets the very definition of humanity wavering, since we now know that humanity is not a stable, real substance occasionally betrayed by barbarians. Its barbarism has made us understand that humanity is a work in progress and an endless creation. Humanity as such is a quality of the world and not the reality of a state or a creed. What we call mankind is nothing but a fragile system, a product of history and therefore of time, susceptible to disappear at any moment. Paul Valéry gave us his famous declaration on the mortality of civilizations, but what he spoke of was the deciduousness of everything we create rather than of an ontological disaster. Valéry takes melancholy note of the fantasy of immortality. To say on the contrary that mankind is mortal does not mean its components are subjects of death, but that this world's consistence, the transmission of meaning between generations is under threat. Mankind may not be immortal, but it can be threatened by what Spinoza called its eternity, in other words what it constitutes against, and in the face of, death. The Shoah dealt a crippling blow to this eternal fragility of meaning.

To become human is an art that has always come up from a nonhuman underground. For centuries we believed that this nonhuman underground was no more than matter: marble, earth, language, color, sound. That nonhumanity is also known as nature, which art can use to its own ends. Yet artists are aware that they have to deal with not only the nonhuman but also the inhuman: suffering and evil. With what might be called "diabolical"—a term acceptable only if it has been stripped of all religious connotations and reduced to its true meaning: that which cannot be symbolized. In this way, art makes human that which is not: the inhumanity of evil, of crime, and of death. If dealing with the Shoah were merely this, making human that which is not, then the Shoah would be a problem and not a question. Humanizing, moralizing, and aestheticizing can all be solutions that soften our fear of the inhuman. Some films have approached it in this manner, as a problem for which they presented a formal and soothing solution. Other films avoided the question to solve the problem, thus fitting into the market for comfort more smoothly. To state that handing down the Shoah is a question is precisely to deny that art makes human what is not, to deny that it is necessary to make the intolerable bearable and to create hope where there is only desperation. In that case, inhumanity is not something behind us that we remember by dressing it up and masking it, nor is it a rigid, petrified object of worship like a relic of the horrors. It is before us as a constant, insistently menacing presence that can't be humanized. Like death, one might say. Well, no, because death is a mystery at the heart of what defines every living thing, whereas the Shoah is a question at the heart of what defines a human being whether he is alive or dead. It is the meaning of the word *man* as it flows so gravely from the pen of Primo Levi.

To say, as we hear all too often, that the Shoah should be "contemplated or re-contemplated at a time when memory becomes history" is not enough, because it mistakes the nature of passage. It is not so much the passage of memory into history (and what would the latter be without the former?) as a two-way passage: that which was present becomes past; and that which comes from the past reemerges in all its urgency into our current lives. The present that unites us around a theme such as this, survives by its concern for the future. By which I mean to say that handing down the Shoah is about not simply its solemn and terrible entry into the realm of history but also, and if not more, its continued presence today in the irreducible form of an appeal to vigilance and the resistance of all humanity in the face of a threat that comes from inside itself.

Subsequently, to say that the Shoah must be taught is a reductive and even misleading expression, since we are talking about an ordeal and not a fact simply given as information. The Shoah is no one's exclusive domain, not of science or literature. It does not belong to the historians, or to the moralists, or to the psychoanalysts. They are all free to speak about it, but since the Shoah defies the existence of the human at the heart of what constitutes an independent individual, it is in art and in art alone that we can offer responses to the anguish provoked by the question. This anguish that confronts each of us with the violence of our impulses can find a constructive outlet only in art and creation. This is where we turn our most destructive emotions into something that can be shared, in other words, this is where we give it a political dimension. In whatever domain, the function of art is not to teach but to touch, to create an emotion that is not undergone but constituent. It thus contributes to the dignity of its audience as independent individuals capable of feeling and free to choose for themselves. The question, then, is rather this: What forms, what shapes should a work of art take in order for the emotions it provokes to contribute to an independent judgment and point of view of that terrifying historical ordeal? What space do we allow other people's eyes and ears, how do we touch their bodies and their sensibilities while respecting them as mature, thinking human beings capable of independent judgment? No passion should be taboo.

We could say and think that art and culture express the noblest aspects of man. It would be a statement of intent or a pious wish, and this is precisely where the problem lies—for it is indeed a problem. I would express it like this: since the beginning of the twentieth century and more precisely since the Shoah, art and culture have been the arena for all possible forms of uninhibited fantasies and violence. I would even go so far as to suggest that the Shoah has been an excuse for countless artists and dilettantes to give free reign to their most barbaric fantasies, to the connection of pleasure with cruelty, to the eroticization of all kinds of exposure and nudity. Perversion wears the mask of revolution by reducing it to a catalogue of provocation. The most flagrant theater of symbolic collapse of the twentieth century has been the world of art and culture, where the cult of the impulse masquerades as freedom and has become a market in which communication is in the service of consumption. Who hasn't seen advertising in which a beautiful young woman, her hand and feet bound, lets herself be whipped in exchange for a piece of chocolate or dessert? To this impulsive idolatry the media connects a promise to hide nothing, to bare all. This is the programming of the new totalitarianism, the visual dictatorship so typical of what we call democracy. He who seeks pleasure can do with others as he wishes, without limit or taboo. This is how the Shoah has inspired the worst eroticization of violence and pornography. Paradoxically, there is a clear continuity between those who eroticize violence and those who moralize history and humanize the Shoah. The link between the manufacturers of comfort and those of pleasure is created by the market of visual consumption whose goal is to deprive each and every one of its users of their freedom and civility. We have gone directly from industrialized murder in the camps to industries that annihilate all their consumers and all they consume. It is for this reason that we must reflect on the Shoah if we want to reflect on our current history.

This is why, in the face of the ordeal of barbarism and the perverse temptation to derive pleasure from its exposure in the name of truth, I believe it crucial to question the conditions for symbolization today. In other words, what are we not allowed to see or show, and why? When someone asks, "Do we have the right to write poetry after Auschwitz?," echoing Adorno's famous declaration, I do not believe it useful or right to talk in those terms, for two reasons. The first is that the art of language, images, and sounds was not interrupted after Auschwitz, and its creators never experienced this as a question of legitimacy but continued to compose within their ethical demands. The second and more important reason is that if art is a measure of our freedom and the political destiny of our emotions, then it must take into account the most dramatic threats to that freedom and to the emotive nature of our shared lives.

When we assume that it is impossible to tell or express anything about an ordeal that destroyed all means of expression because it is the ordeal of, as some have stated, "absolute negativity," we create a double deadlock: producing a culture of silence—which is a contradiction in terms—or producing an untouchable and unique object that allows no other form of transmission. The two deadlocks are the consequence of some people's incapacity to lend this ordeal its universal dimension. Yet, it is this dimension that opens it up to art. All is found here. If the Shoah is defined as pure negativity, or more precisely as absolute, then we make this ordeal that touches the entire world into something theological. And nothing is more dangerous than turning suffering and tragedy into theology. Instead of creating a symbolic fertility through transmission, we build a terrified memory, transmitting terror and provoking further violence. When the object is absolute, the intrinsic inadequacy of all expression paralyzes every gesture, every sign. This is the death of all hope and all freedom. Finally, to turn the Shoah absolute and rigid would render absurd the very idea of transmission and the importance the event holds for the whole of human history. Its radically historical character does not need to cast doubt on its nature as an example; on the contrary, the example should be a shield against terrible dictatorships that are the inevitable result of violently enforced symbolic impotence. The expression Hannah Arendt borrowed from Kant, that of a *radical* evil, becomes infinitely more powerful and more open when we wonder how to express the past in the present with the intention of protecting future freedom. The question of inhumanity and evil does not start with the Shoah, but the Shoah takes the question out of its metaphysical and theological context, rendering it historical and purely human. For this very fact it demands that we dispense with language that is sanctimonious ("holocaust") and steeped in theology ("the absolute").

Let me remind the reader that cinema is the same age as the deployment of the barbarisms that have marked the twentieth century. It accompanied the ravages of World War I and echoed the warnings and the hopes between the two wars. It was in the wake of World War II that the communications industry got its hold on events across the world. And it was during this same period that cinema's historical responsibility came into question. Its archives are visual, and visual documents are interpreted as proof precisely when visual production becomes a part of the market for communication, belief, propaganda, and publicity. The image is truth, the image is lie: both suggestions are false, since images need those who fabricate and receive them to give them the validity and meaning they wish to share. History is henceforth envisioned in terms of images, scenarios, and roles; and the writing of history is seen in terms of archives, documents, and fiction. It also seems increasingly accepted that politicians create for themselves an imaginary platform meant to establish the dignity of their symbolic strength. In this social and cultural landscape, film and television have provided the lion's share of the narrative potential of information and transmission. But cinema and television are inseparable from the industry that supports them and the commerce that provides the conditions for their very capacity of expression. In other words, it is not just the story of the Shoah whose truth and dignity are threatened, but the whole of what passes through our dominant modes of expression and distribution. Cinema and television increasingly address their viewers as consumers of information and as customers paying to receive pleasure. This situation makes one fact tangible: it is not the object of the story, the Shoah, that demands unique treatment, but the spectator who has the right to demand what position he or she has been assigned with regards to the cinematic or televised object. There is no doubt that the eradication of this position of independent subject is all the more dangerous because the question itself is of a unique gravity. Fundamentally, however, the problem posed by the Shoah is only the paradigm and the extreme form of a general problem: What is at stake for our future and our freedom in the things we show and explain? Which also means that the right question is not, "How do we teach the Shoah?" but, "What has the ordeal of the Shoah radically changed in the conception of representation, transmission, and education?"

Filmmakers, historians, thinkers, curators, and teachers—each in his own way—assume their historical responsibility toward the future as well as their loyalty and respect for the field of creation. We all need to acknowledge that our position is not that of the knowledgeable teacher but that of the civilian who must, as either creator or intermediary, justify what we awaken or what we let lie, what we set free and what we control. And in this context, the question turns itself around one more time. It is not how the cinema and television "must transmit" or "must teach" the Shoah, but rather how the ordeal of the Shoah has completely shaken up cinematic forms of cruelty and rendered crucial the position of the receiver of all that is shown. Neither demonstrations nor visual evidence, the Shoah is a call to testify in the sharing of concern, in the production of a certain vigilance. If art is invoked, it is because we believe in the poetics of responsibility, or, if you prefer, in the ethics of passion. In this light we hope to reflect together in order to grasp something we do not grasp very well yet, especially having regained the strength we all need to resist the clear and daily threat of a return to barbarism.

Translated from the French by Tom Mes

Notes

1. Symposium "Enseignment de la Shoah et création artistique," organized by the European Counsel in Strasbourg, October 15–18, 2002.

Recovery

JACQUES MANDELBAUM

T HE TWENTIETH CENTURY WAS not only the century of the cinema but also that of the worst disasters in human history. The experience of the camps during World War II, and more specifically the Shoah, changed the relationship of humans to their own history, just as it did for the cinema and the world that it was responsible for depicting. While this assessment is based today upon an established history of the cinema that explicitly ties modern cinema to this historical disaster, the question nonetheless remains open, as much on the basis of ongoing debates that surround the event as on the rehashing of the common vulgates. To connect the cinema to the experience of the genocide requires further analysis, at the risk of losing sight of what is truly contemporary and discovering an aesthetic confusion that alters, and no doubt exceeds, conventional barriers.

We will deliberately depart from a theory that hangs by a hair, adapting throughout this chapter the majestic exegesis done by André Bazin on Charlie Chaplin's *The Great Dictator*. The premise of that argument, if not the actual text from which it is drawn,[1] is well known: Hitler, a mythical swindler in politics, stole his mustache from another, cinematic, myth, namely Charlie Chaplin. Chaplin has taken revenge in retrieving what was his and creating the character of Hynkel in the figure of whom is revealed "Hitler's oblivion." "This ontological robbery," states Bazin, "is based, in the final analysis, upon the theft of the mustache," since, for Hynkel to be defeated, the character must derive from both Chaplin and Hitler. Beyond this specific instance, the issue of the *postiche*[2] (i.e., the fake mustache or hairpiece) seems particularly productive, both

25

as a theme and as a recurring device that enables the cinema to face the new challenges created by representation of the genocide.

As a theme, take the utilization of what is designated by the common noun: hairpiece, mustache, beard, and all other subterfuge-enabling disguise. As a procedure, have recourse to what is suggested by the broader definition of the adjective, as defined by the Robert dictionary: "Done and added after the fact, that which by nature is not part of a whole." This pathetic allowance, this modest accessory drawn from the ancient magic box of spectacular representation, ties into the means by which certain films, connecting with the long history of the representational arts, foresee, accompany, or challenge the unique reality of the genocide: that of a project that enacted, on an industrial scale, the simultaneous disappearance of the bodies and all trace of their extermination. Unable, by definition, to show visibly what there is no trace of, the cinema must make visible the process of disappearance itself, by revealing the baroque nature of film directing and, if need be, completely inventing the steps in a process that, in so doing, it appropriates. It is a matter of "asserting a negation,"[3] as Gerard Wajcman said about Claude Lanzmann's *Shoah* and as is illustrated in the work of artist Jochen Gerz. We shall call this act, specifically, "recovery," a word whose ambiguous etymology illustrates our intention: on the one hand the act of recovering, on the other the act of retrieving.

This definition also calls to mind the archaic function of the mask as an illusion intended for revelation, which Greek tragedy inherited from more ancient cultures. The most well-known mask—that of the Gorgon, who petrified anyone who looked at her—comes from a creature touched on by Primo Levi to define the Mussulman, one of the living dead of the camps, that is, someone who had seen the Gorgon. The philosopher Giorgio Agamben would fine-tune this image: "The Mussulman doesn't see or know anything—aside from the impossibility of seeing or knowing. And this is why speaking for the Mussulman, trying to contemplate the impossibility to see, is not an easy task."[4] Perseus decapitated the Medusa without looking at her, thanks to the shield he used as a mirror; the cinema will have to do something similar, faced with the monstrosity of the anti-face,[5] with a descent into darkness, an oblique confrontation with oblivion, an initiation rite of drawing from the terror of something that has no face the very means of imagining it. It is through the dual act of recovery—an act that recreates the gesture of erasing while simultaneously designating—that the cinema will attest, more or less deliberately, to its proximity to the disaster. And not only this disaster, whose blind spot would be Auschwitz, but also Hiroshima and its traced-out bodies, and more generally the disaster of a technological evolution of war in which, as Paul Virilio brilliantly demonstrated, the extension of the domain of perception is paradoxically associated with the derealization of a world now governed, through radar and sonar, by ghosts:

> The assault arsenal is equipped with new organs, prostheses of a conflict in which optical illusion and motor illusion have merged into delirium, a cinematic delirium of lightning war, a war of speed of the propagation of objects, images and sounds, as we await a nuclear blast.[6]

In this respect, our hypothesis relies less upon the Bazinian creed of cinematic realism—on the basis of which Serge Daney wrote a canonical article, derived from what he calls the "anti-fiction" of Alain Resnais' *Night and Fog*, on the question of the link between the Shoah and the modern cinema[7]—than upon the "strength of artifice" at work in it at the time, according to Gilles Deleuze.[8] Going from Orson Welles to Jean Rouch, what Bazin the philosopher reveals here is now based—exceeding what is real and what is fiction by redefining the cinema—upon the power of art to make things happen and to qualify characters under the auspices of their own transformation. This is not too far a distinction from the primordial function of the mask, through which man, in reestablishing his connection with the spirit world, becomes what he is disguised as. Thus, "the cinema can be called cinéma-vérité, all the more because in order to become the creator, the producer of truth, it will have destroyed all model of truth: it is no longer the cinema of truth but the truth of cinema." We will finally see to what extent the question of speech, and beyond that the use of sound, intervenes in an often determinant manner in the emergence of this cinematic truth, associated with the plays on appearance, the law of metamorphosis, and the exhaustion of what is visible.

The Postiche as Accessory

In the history of the cinema, three great classics would herald this change in the system, in what one can be tempted, at the risk of being interpreted as teleological, to liken to the presentiment of catastrophe. *The Great Dictator* (1940) was an excellent testament of this process. There is nothing to add, per se, beyond Bazin's impeccable analysis, except to emphasize Charlie Chaplin's ultimate misfortune in becoming the Jewish barber in the ghetto, a condition and profession that specifically refer to the question of appearances and representation. Everything in the film plays upon the rival strengths of the little Jew and the great dictator, just as between the cinema and politics. Another crucial point deserves mention: *The Great Dictator* was Charlie Chaplin's first talkie, and he exerted his prerogative by becoming literally a body with two voices: that of Hynkel vociferating in a Teutonic hodgepodge, and the voice of the barber, so tenuous that it appears practically nonexistent. When, disguised as Hynkel, the barber makes his final speech at the tribune to an assembly of Nazis, the sudden fusion of both characters creates a chimerical figure that supersedes the two of them in order to better voice, through Chaplin's humanitarian plea, "what speaking really means." From this expression, writer Michel Leiris would derive the title of a sumptuous text published immediately after the liberation, in which he evokes the ordeal that Nazism was for language—the manifest expression of humanity—thereby distancing the responsibility that is incumbent upon the writer as a result.[9] Hence, it is the filmmaker Chaplin, "acting out" in his first articulated cinematic discourse, who brutally disrupts the double play on appearances and by accomplishing his transformation affirms the authority of his art. Deleuze would have stated it in this manner: "If the future is the power of what is false, then the good, the generous, the noble is what raises the false to the 'nth' power, or the will to become an artist."

When the barber's escape partner, seeing his friend's hesitation to speak, exhorts him to do so in order that their lives may be saved and they won't look like fools, we hear him urging: "You must speak; it's our only hope." It is one of the great heralds of change that would occur from that point forward in the history of the cinema, in the shadow of catastrophe. This change would lead Jean-Luc Godard to say later on that we owe "the invention of cinéma-vérité to Chaplin's final speech in *The Great Dictator*."[10] What is at play in the final passage of Chaplin's talkie is also the mutation of his cinema through the progressive disappearance of the Tramp, an immortal character who would nonetheless not escape the mounting barbarity. In this process, *The Great Dictator* occupies a central role. Crushed by the mechanization of a world on the verge of dehumanization, from the insides of which Chaplin had made his voice heard for the first time through the unarticulated words of a song (*Modern Times*, 1936), the character had to be merged with Hitler and then the two had to dissolve so that, on the other side of the looking glass, and in the unrecognizable faded finery of a serial killer, a monstrous burner of cadavers, a voice, so long delayed it was now tragically in tune with his time, could come to us from beyond the grave to be reborn (*Monsieur Verdoux*, 1947).

Severely criticized when it was released, *Verdoux* had one notable defender in Jean Renoir, for whom "By ridding himself of the worn-out shoes, the bowler hat and the cane of the little guy in rags whose pathetic face broke our hearts, Chaplin deliberately enters into a world that is more frightening because it is closer to where we live."[11] Renoir made a film called *The Rules of the Game* in 1939, which is part of the turning point mentioned above. It is again Michel Leiris, by the way, who used this same title at the end of the war for his large work dedicated to the autobiographical exploration of this elusive identity as, through the labyrinth of the subjective etymology of the world, it becomes the ultimate truth of his poetic art. Few films during this time will have given, as did Jean Renoir's, the feeling of a universe governed by appearances, of a society that reduces men to puppets and a world that is preparing for that very reason to be pushed into horror. *The Rules of the Game*, like Chaplin's *Monsieur Verdoux*, comes much too close to this horror for the audience—which does not recognize itself—to grasp the very troubling proximity.

It is not just the choice of the play that inspired *The Rules of the Game* that bears testimony to this poetic premonition of the threatening disaster: *The Moods of Marianne* by Alfred de Musset, a poet with a changing face if ever there was one, holds a position in the French theatre comparable to the one held by *The Rules of the Game* in the French national cinema. It attests to a mutation that marked the movement from the eighteenth-century comedy of intrigue (Marivaux) to romantic drama sealing the death of innocents. Showing the encounter of the classical trio (husband, wife, lover), this film drifts slowly along, from the robot concert to the costumed ball, all the way to the fatal accessory error (one coat is mistaken for another) that causes the death of Jurrieu. To the old adage—all the world's a stage—we must add the conscience of the mortal mechanism that (like the macabre dance that figures in the film) will carry the divertissement forward. The truth of this theatre of appearances, in which no one is what he appears to be and in which one lives or dies depending on what one is wearing, was brilliantly created in the great outdoors scene that reveals both what is being hatched in the palace and the era that is approaching—an organized hunt, in preparation for the slaughterhouse. The merciless montage of animal carnage in broad daylight brings to mind the night scene in which Jurrieu, the pure-hearted lover, will be shot like a rabbit in the woods. Jurrieu does not die as a result of his change in appearance, but is assassinated because of his incapacity to change and blend into the human community from which he is excluded. That community will logically end up eliminating him in order to preserve its cohesion. As clearly as is possible, *The Rules of the Game* heralds the regime that would very soon begin in occupied France.

Easy passage across the frontier between the theatre stage and politics is at the heart of Ernst Lubitsch's *To Be or Not to Be* (1942) (just as unsuccessful at the time), a film that troubles these borders with regard to elaboration through the story of the resistance of a theatre group in occupied Poland. Pretense becomes the principal value. Only one character is removed, the way Jurrieu was, from this incessant faculty of transformation, and that is the Jewish actor in the troupe, who is always just an extra, and whose alienation is revealed even in his actor's dream: to play the role of Shylock onstage. Regarding this devastating device that will allow Lubitsch to beat Hitler hollow, let us simply mention one scene in which the use of the postiche is a determining choice. The situation is this: the Warsaw theatre actors have killed a Nazi spy, and one of them has taken on his appearance (glasses and a false beard) in order to have people believe that the man is still alive; in this way they hope to retrieve a list of names that might otherwise jeopardize the Resistance. Meanwhile, the Nazis have discovered the body and summon the usurper in order to expose him.

There follows a scene in which the Nazis place the cadaver on a chair and bring in the actor whom they now know is a usurper, counting upon his surprise to betray him. Alone with the body, and caught in the striking effect of duplication in the situation, the actor improvises his rescue with a redirected sign of duplicity: he cuts off the cadaver's beard and then glues it back just as it was. Now, nothing has changed in the way things appear. In this simple gesture of props, the situation has been reversed: it is no longer the deceased who catches the living person, but the living person who defies death. When the Nazis come back into the room, the situation is reversed in the tone of the language: the actor challenges them—absurd!—to tug on the dead man's "real" beard in order to waylay them before they tug on his false one. All poetic license afforded to the mad fantasy of the screenplay aside, we can also assume that the cadaver's beard remaining in the dumbfounded Nazi's hand is nothing more than a harbinger of what the real Nazis are preparing to do to their victims: to camouflage the dead in order to write them off, retrospectively, as living.

These tragic comedies and light-hearted dramas that precede the catastrophe will be followed after the war by other works that pay a debt to terror, again using the renewing prop of the false hairpiece or beard. It is hardly coincidence that Samuel Fuller, who was a soldier in the liberation of the camps, would go on to produce one of the most striking figurations in the opening scene of *The Naked Kiss* (1964). Filmed in close-up and in a montage of alternating forward and backward tracking shots, we see a prostitute making her pimp recoil by lacerating his face with her spiked heel. In so doing, the woman loses her wig, revealing that her head is completely shaven, a detail that brings the savagery of the scene to its absolute depth and unites the tormentor and victim in the same process of disfigurement. This is a scene that precedes the film credits and is set two years before the true beginning of the story—in a desire to change her life, once her hair has grown back, she goes to live in a small town that will soon after reveal, to the insistent melody of Beethoven's "Moonlight" Sonata, the depravity of the American dream. It implicitly anchors its action into a historical matrix—that of a barbarism that reduces human beings to a state of merchandise—and Fuller never ceases to question whether or not we have emerged from it. Forty years later, in *Promised Land*, the Israeli filmmaker Amos Gitaï, a great admirer of Fuller's, would renew this invisible thread that binds Nazi madness to the derailment of market economy, through the merchandise/character of the prostitute.

Regarding this fragile division that separates civilization from barbarism: in a fateful lesson learned from World War II and Fuller's great theme, what film better offers testimony, albeit in a diametrically opposed style, than *Sleuth* (1972) by Joseph Mankiewicz, the grand master of trompe l'oeil and labyrinths? In this behind-closed-doors drama (adapted from an eponymous play by Anthony Shaffer), we rediscover the universe of theatre, with all its tricks and effects and false beards and mustaches. It is about a duel to the death between an English nobleman (Wyke) and the Italian upstart (Tindle) who is his wife's lover: a struggle between two men whom everything separates, beginning with their origins. If we believe that truth lies in detail, we can allow ourselves to think that *Sleuth* is a remake in disguise of *The Great Dictator*. The two men are simply fighting over a woman rather than a mustache. Mankiewicz even made Tindle a hairdresser and Wyke a man who, on a whim, purposely speaks English with a guttural German accent when asking the other character if he is Jewish.

While this type of element is present throughout the film, the essential point remains the strangeness of its dramatic art. First, a racist who is very full of his superiority humiliates his wife's lover by pretending to kill him. Then, the victim returns to the scene of this crime which has supposedly not taken place, unrecognizably disguised as a police inspector, but not without having previously placed the evidence that attests to the crime's existence. Next, after removing his disguise, he challenges his executioner to find this evidence before the arrival of the real police, whom he pretends to have truly alerted. Finally, outsmarted and humiliated himself, Wyke really does kill his adversary, putting an end to the game and to the film. In passing, one brief dialogue gives us the reason for which this admirable work transcends the traditional enigma film: to the protestations of Wyke, an author of crime fiction who prides himself on his knowledge and refuses to play the game, arguing that there is no body, Tindle answers, "What need do we have for a body?" Thus, *Sleuth* can be considered as a film whose police intrigue is sparked off by a false crime and whose poetic needs consist in precisely making a crime happen. The dramatic function of the postiche—which marks the return to the stage of the Italian hairdresser disguised as an English policeman—is not limited in this sense to that of a disguise used as a trick, but crystallizes the turning point of the film where only artistic transfiguration allows the cadaver to be incarnated.

As suggested by philosopher Jean-Luc Nancy, there is a dimension of absence that enters just as much in defining victims of the genocide as in all true images. The extermination of the Jews by a totalitarian system that aspires to be everything to its followers supposes that "to show the most terrible images is always possible, but to show what kills all possibility of an image is impossible, except in recreating the act of murder."[12] It is to this formidable vocation that the work of Claude Lanzmann seems to respond. *Shoah* (1985) is unique in that it enables the concealed event that he names to finally take place. The representation is precisely what allowed it to happen, in the genesis (the excess, the relentlessness, the insanity that were required for Lanzmann to carry out his project) and in the method (the mixture of persuasion, violence, and cleverness exhibited by the auteur in order to obtain testimonies). Incessantly incited to remember the most minor details, to relive them in the present of one's imagination, the actors in the film are in fact called upon to recreate together the act of murder—whether the administrative precision of the camp officers, the terror of the Jewish child singing, or the intact sadism of the Polish locomotive conductor. Rithy Pahn conveniently remembered this lesson in order to evoke the Cambodian genocide in his beautiful film *S-21* (2004).

The most remarkable scene is no doubt the one in which Lanzmann asks the camp escapee Avraham Bomba to talk about his previous profession. He is a retired Israeli hairdresser, and since the director places him in situ he must both cut a customer's hair and evoke the task that his membership in the *Sonderkommando* required of him at the heart of the extermination process. The powerful genius of Lanzmann is to have grasped in this case that these two tasks were connected, in the guise of cosmetic transformation. The simulation of the Nazis in wiping out the bodies of their victims—but not without having first removed all recyclables (dental metals and hair)—is responded to by Lanzmann by way of another simulation, a false haircutting which has the effect of unmasking survivor Avraham Bomba for what he is: one too many in the bodies of the world. And when, strangled by sobs, he can no longer utter a word, how can we not hear the incredibly moving order given by Lanzmann, "You must speak, Avraham!" as an echo of the intense moment of truth that is the final speech in Chaplin's *The Great Dictator*?

It is also with the ambiguous hallmark of recovery and the dialectic between speaking and silence that one of the strangest scenes of Lanzmann's *Sobibor, October 14, 1943, 4 p.m.* (2001) is played out. Based upon the account of one Yehuda Lerner, a survivor of Sobibor who participated in the revolt there, the film notably evokes the function assigned by the Nazis to a flock of geese raised there: that of sound camouflage intended to muffle the screams of camp victims. Lanzmann cuts back to this part of the story twice by giving full close-ups of a flock of geese: the first time when screams saturate the soundtrack, and the second with a deliberate cut in the soundtrack. In appropriating this sensory illusion used by the Nazis to mask horror, and then technically altering its function, the filmmaker does much more than point out, in his own terms, the "struggle" between the cries of the geese and the words of Lerner: he turns the subterfuge inside-out like a glove and makes the voiceless cries of the victims literally scream in the mute whiteness of the fowl filling the shot.

In the history of the cinema, at least two films utilize the dramatic suspension of sound with such efficacy. In each of these cases we are brought back to the borderline situation of theatrical representation, that of an actress "going blank" as she is confined to psycho-sensory vertigo. These are obviously *Persona* (1966) by Ingmar Bergman and *Esther Kahn* (2000) by Arnaud Desplechin. These two masterpieces—one narrating the abrupt psychological collapse of a stage celebrity, and the other the conversion to Catholicism of a young Jewish actress who breaks with her tradition—are each a testimony to the gulf over which the power of incarnation exerts itself and that each woman has a vocation to serve. With a basis in the tragic repertory (*Electra* by Sophocles for the one, *Hedda Gabler* by Ibsen for the other), these two works borrow the vehicle of theatrical representation in order to better convey the dimension of absence and the threat of being erased that affects any cinematic body through the historical catastrophe of genocide (evoked between the lines in both these films).

The Postiche as Character

Given the specific vocation of the actor, we see how the notion of the postiche can just as well expand to that of a character. In the chapter of his book about "the power of what is false," Gilles Deleuze admirably characterized this regarding Fritz Lang, defined as the filmmaker of appearances par excellence:

> For Lang, it seems, truth no longer exists, only appearances do. The American Lang has become the greatest filmmaker of appearances, of false images. . . . Everything is appearance and yet this new state of being transforms the judgment system rather than replacing it. In fact, appearance is something that betrays itself. . . . As a result, it becomes possible to create new appearances in relation to which the initial ones will be judgeable and judged.

The *Dr. Mabuse* series of films demonstrated this phenomenon—in which a body disappears leaving a voice that spreads evil like a virus—during the passage from silent films to talkies and during the time of the growing threat of Nazism; but the world would have to await *Hangmen Also Die* (1943) to see the creation of a character whose sole vocation consisted in doing away with others as a profession. The action in this political film takes place in Prague, under Heydrich's regime. Svoboda, a member of the Czech resistance, assassinates him and takes refuge during his escape in the home of Professor Novodny. Novodny is soon arrested by the Nazis, who kill great numbers of hostages every day as they await the surrender of the murderer. Meanwhile, the resistance network to which Svoboda belongs has just realized they have a traitor in their midst. They decide to turn him in as the murderer and gather some contrived evidence and damning eyewitness accounts. From this machination is born a false character, whose function of recovery serves to create a false criminal for the Nazis while doing away with the real one.

The fact that this false criminal is a real bastard, morally speaking, and that the real criminal is a hero will surprise no one. After all, this filmmaker was trained in the chiaroscuro of the Weimar Republic. This, and the duplicity that would swallow it up, he prefigured in his horror films. Like no other filmmaker he confounded the realms of truth and lies through the cinema. Was Lang a pessimist? He was lucid, at the very least in tune with the reality that made his last German film before his exile, *The Testament of Dr. Mabuse*, a scathing anti-Nazi statement and won him a ban on the part of Goebbels and a concomitant proposal to become the head of German cinema. In the same manner, the filming of *Hangmen Also Die* in English, according to convention, required that immigrant Jewish actors, whose accents were more appropriate, be hired for the portrayal of Nazi roles and actors who were Anglo-Saxon play the Czech resistance characters.

This film—actually Lang's entire body of work, beginning with *M*—is all the more interesting because it formalizes the issues that run implicitly in each analysis: the question of directing as an exercise of manipulation and power, and the relativity of that which ensures its legitimacy. In other words, in what measure can art retrieve its due (Charlie Chaplin's mustache) without necessarily being stained by the abomination of totalitarian misappropriation? Representation becomes a more obscure zone and less innocent than ever. Two films will push this paradox to its furthest extremes: *Beyond a Reasonable Doubt* (1956) also by Lang, in which someone who is against the death penalty entraps a reputable judge by rearranging evidence of his guilt to appear as proof of his innocence, before revealing himself in the end as the real criminal; and *A Touch of Evil* (1958) by Orson Welles, in which a megalomaniac policeman who is revolted by the impunity of evil (portrayed, of course, by Welles himself) has no qualms about fabricating false proof to incriminate his suspects.

This detour through film noir, like a convulsive adieu to the innocence of the cinema, is necessary, the golden age of the genre having been inaugurated in the immediate postwar period by resuscitating the spell of English gothic and German expressionism. In between these two terms is precisely where the historical ghost of the genocide resides, a locus to which the two main figures of the genre—the flashback and voiceover—seem to incessantly return. As Noël Simsolo wrote, "In film noir, shadow and light follow beings who struggle in a funereal no man's land. . . . To depict this, one must evoke a collective subconscious favoring, in a given period, the sublimation of subjects by the loss of focused vision due to the loss of identity."[13] In this regard, we cannot help noticing the number of stories that situate a character more or less deliberately usurping the place of a deceased person or one supposed to be deceased: *Laura* (1944) by Otto Preminger, *The Body Snatcher* (1945) and *The House on Telegraph Hill* (1951) by Robert Wise, *My Name is Julia Ross* (1945) by Joseph H. Lewis, *Golden Earrings* (1947) by Mitchell Leisen, and of course *Vertigo* (1958) by Alfred Hitchcock. *Dark Passage* (1947) by Delmer Daves, which implies resurrection after the plastic surgery of a falsely accused criminal (Humphrey Bogart) whose face we don't see for the first hour of the film, or *Sunset Blvd.* (1950) by Billy Wilder, in which the narration is done by a character whose voice comes from beyond the grave, are two spectral variations of this genre.

In fact, film noir is linked with fantasy films that gave it new energy when it was in decline. As he often did, Alfred Hitchcock turned out to be the man of the hour when he directed the terrifying *Psycho* (1960). Norman Bates, the killer played by Anthony Perkins, is literally possessed, a being inhabited by his mother, whom he murdered. His very personality is little by little dissolved to the point of being erased by the spirit of her ghost speaking through his voice. The entire film is built upon the principal of this deadly exchange which advances the story through successive withdrawals, based upon the commerce of bodies reduced to devalued matter (the mother stuffed with straw, the possessed killer, the sliced victims, the drowned cadavers). Marion, en route to the appropriately named Phoenix, brings us to Norman (whose victim she becomes), himself the victim of an assassinated woman who will in turn be discovered by Marion's sister.

In this regard, we could essentialize *Psycho* as the trajectory of a voice separate from its body, trying, through the discordant mishaps in the story, to incorporate itself into an emitting organ. Michel Chion suggests this in fact, when he writes that this voice is "condemned to roam on the surface" attesting to an "impossible embodiment,"[14] just as a ghost, by coming to haunt the living, attests to an impossible return to earth. In fact, the murdered mother's voice is heard throughout the film, but only offscreen, which leaves us to presume the character exists until we are finally confronted, once the enigma is resolved, with the image of the arrested son, whose lips remain obstinately sealed. This passage from the offscreen to the onscreen voice is less a sign of the resolution of a problem than a real issue: that of the impossibility of reconciling (except in a spectral mode) the synchronization between sound (voice) and image (body) that characterizes modern cinema. We find this just as much with narrative disjunction, as with the brutal disappearance of a main character in the first third of the film (which is also the case in *L'Avventura* by Michelangelo Antonioni, made that same year). Is this eclipse of what is "in" not at the heart of the crime—just like graphic offscreen elements—as soon as we realize that the first names of the victim (Marion) and the executioner (Norman) are quasi-anagrams?

With its credits spelled out in stripes and its mortal voyeurism (Bates watches his victim undress through a secret peephole hidden behind a painting), its crime scene in the shower, its recycled and buried cadavers, its impossible path to Phoenix, *Psycho* presents itself as a film powerfully affected by reminiscence of the genocide. One of the key elements of this is the status of the lead character, Bates, who turns out to be a literal zombie. Borrowed from Haitian animism and voodoo rituals, this concept, which implies a taking over of the spirit of the victim, whose body becomes simply an envelope, attests to this absence of soul. Of all the ghostly creatures depicted onscreen, the zombie, entirely fated to this visibility of disappearance that we call recovery, is the one that demonstrates with the most acuity the effect of the return of the genocide in the history of the cinema. The chronology of its expression in a fantasy genre generally speaking conducive to the exhumation of the subconscious, is significant: specifically on one hand, the periods immediately preceding or following World War II, with poetic terror films such as Victor Halperin's *White Zombie* (1932), Michael Waszynski's *The Dybbuk* (1937), and Jacques Tourneur's *I Walked with a Zombie* (1943); and on the other, the sixties, which carried with it—just at the moment when, starting with the Eichmann trials, the specificity of the genocide emerged in the collective consciousness—a frenetic resurgence on both sides of the Atlantic, with British director John Gilling's *The Plague of the Zombies* (1965) and U.S. director George Romero's *Night of the Living Dead* (1968). Then came the surge of gore that would soon affect the genre in Italy, followed by its exploitation in Hollywood.

The questionable commerce between the dead and the living that followed in the shadow of the genocide affected the destiny of modern cinema all the more, not just in the devitalization of its rapport to the rules of classic cinema but also through its neurotic fascination with dual characters and its predilection for characters who seem to exist only by virtue of their own disappearance. We mentioned *Persona* by Bergman and *L'Avventura* by Antonioni, but *Hiroshima mon amour* (1959) by Alain Resnais, *A Man Vanishes* by Shohei Imamura (1967), *The Legend of Lylah Clare* (1968) by Robert Aldrich, *F for Fake* (1975) by Orson Welles, *The Green Room* (1978) by François Truffaut, *Zelig* (1983) by Woody Allen, *New Wave* (1991) by Jean-Luc Godard, and the recent *A History of Violence* (2005) by David Cronenberg also attest to this phenomenon.

Among all these films, *Mr. Klein* (1976) by Joseph Losey brought the possible roots of this evil to the light of day. As Jean-François Burié suggested subtly in a text falling under the auspices of *The Purloined Letter*,[15] the plot evokes that of Alfred Hitchcock's *North by Northwest* (1959) transposed to Occupied France. In both cases, a man is mistaken for another. With *North by Northwest*, a quiet advertising man is taken for a fictitious agent of American counterespionage; in *Mr. Klein*, an art merchant from Alsace is taken for a Jew in hiding who has the same name. From Kaplan to Klein we see the same ghostly quality of the referent character, the same visible transformation of a man into his double, the same risk of death threatening the one who enters more or less voluntarily into the destiny of someone who turns out to be the nightmarish opposite of himself: Kafka's Joseph K. is not far off. The great difference between these two films, aside from their endings, is that the first does away with the mistaken identity situation by exposing the plot behind it, whereas the second is steeped all the way to the end in the opacity of the fateful misunderstanding.

What *Mr. Klein* reveals to us is the subterranean rapport between the postiche/future of the movie character and the disappearance of the Jewish body from the European scene. A constant link ties the two devices in the film. The Jewish body, little by little reduced to nothing through the racial anthropometry exam, the anti-Semitic caricature of the Parisian cabaret, and the lottery that designates him for deportation, corresponds to that of the lead character, whose protestations of innocence regarding his Jewish name make it paradoxically more and more evident. This destines him to the fate that is none other than disappearance. So it is the issue of representation that Joseph Losey questions in this moving film, by making the primary condition, that of visibility, the basis for the unsuspected reversibility and guilt.

The Postiche as Film

While the introduction of the postiche often takes place through directing the creation of a character in the cinema, certain films attest to the fact that this process can also affect the film as such. The recourse to the theatrical device, through archival images or a literary corpus, exceeds the framework of intrigue or investigation to give birth to hybrid works that resemble, beyond documentary and fiction, the essay. In his film entitled *Hitler: A Film from Germany* (1977), Hans-Jürgen Syberberg has recourse to all theatrical resources as an illusion-producing machine in order to establish a back-to-back connection, at times questionable, between Hitler and contemporary kitsch. Make-up, transparency, projections, puppets are thus utilized in this film as so many exhibits, thanks to which the filmmaker devises a completely new charge against Hitler: for the assault that his regime and he himself perpetrated against the spirit of art, art all the way to the bodies and words of this film. In this sense, Syberberg is offering us his own *Hitler: A Film from Germany*, after and against Germany as Hitler's film. The consequences of this oppressing device—which we could compare to a Baroque in-camera gathering in which for seven hours a struggle to the death between two concepts of representation is played out and places the viewer in a strange position—are defined by Serge Daney: "We are not just asked to judge Hitler (in general, already done), but to verify that Syberberg is cinematically victorious over him as well."[16]

Also from Germany—and perhaps this is no coincidence—came the film that Romuald Karmakar called *Das Himmler Projekt* (2000), presented as a recovery experiment that is just as radical. Actor Manfred Zapatka, placed in a neutral setting and seated at a table, reads for three hours straight a speech given by Heinrich Himmler to his SS officers in the utmost secrecy on October 4, 1943. Again, the intent is to expose a disappearance, not only by filming a secret speech, not only in retrospectively citing the disaster caused by its contents, but also—and in this Karmakar joins Syberberg by other means—in retrieving a national gift corrupted by the Nazis, the German language itself. The film is in fact the word for word repetition of Himmler's interminable speech, but by removing it from its context and depriving it of all affect, he simultaneously reveals all its perversion and insanity. Thus neutralized, the Nazi rhetoric is revealed for what it is: a monstrosity drawn from the common lexicon, as demonstrated by other means by philologist Viktor Klemperer and philosopher Jean-Pierre Fay.[17]

In his film *In Memory*[18] (1993), American filmmaker Abraham Ravett had recourse to a similar method, applied to photography. This remarkable *found footage* short uses silent archival material filmed by military cameramen in the Lodz ghetto and follows it with a long black shot during which we hear the vibrant phrasing of the Jewish prayer for the dead, giving the passage the power of resurrection. Entirely composed of images that the executioners had already seen, this film is now available to us in a variation that is tenuous but in reality has vast range, consisting of shots ripped from their original abject source. The film is given time and space to sediment in the collective memory, the victims that inhabit it are finally given the possibility to have existed, and the viewers who discover it are given the freedom to grieve.

In Memory is a sepulchral film, created from the strength of oblivion recovered in extremis through artistic method. It could be the definition of *(Hi)Stories of the Cinema* by Jean-Luc Godard, which captures in video the conjugated history of the twentieth century and of the cinema in the manner of light given off by a dying planet, or the definition of *Drancy Avenir* (1996) by Arnaud des Pallières, which establishes a brand new pact between the absence of the genocide in the visible world (deliberate eclipse of the event, weakening of the memory, disappearance of its witnesses) and the insistent presence of the voices and literary texts that haunts the devastating beauty and the infinite calm of this film. This is neither filmed archive nor commentary, nor written dialogue, nor the slightest trace of what actually happened. The work is built upon bronze materialism, shoots only what really exists, records a perpetual present at last revealed—through the tectonic movement of quotations and connections, words and locations—and the hallucination upon which it is based: the continued presence of the extermination.

What better words to describe this film than those of philosopher Jacques Rancière: "It is a matter of representing a negation of humanity, of putting inhumanity in relation to humanity."[19] The films mentioned here (as well as many others) made use of this artistic process by employing, in varying degrees, the ambivalent device of the postiche. As though the cinema, in order to pursue this inhumanity mentioned by Rancière, were forced to necessarily recompose itself around one of the founding images of concentration camp horror, that of the horrible mass of human hair taken from victims, in order to replace this terrifying still life in movement and go in search of new bodies. With these bodies the modern cinema, putting itself ahead of digital technology, has not ceased to suggest for half a century that it shares the same horizon of absence.

Translated from the French by Anna Harrison

Notes

1. "Pastiche et postiche ou le néant pour une moustache," an article published in *Esprit* magazine, 1945.

2. *Postiche*: a French term for an imitation, a counterfeit, particularly used of an inartistic addition to an otherwise perfect work of art. A postiche is anything added after something has supposedly been completed, for example, a hairpiece or artificial hair used for disguise or adornment. The French word was adapted from the Italian *posticcio*, from Latin *positus*: placed, added.—Trans.

3. *L'Objet du siècle* (Ed. Verdier, 1998).

4. *Ce qui reste d'Auschwitz* (Bibliothèque Rivages, 1999).

5. Siegfried Kracauer uses the same mythological reference in his *Theory of Film: The Redemption of Physical Reality*, with a different focus. See, farther along, Stuart Liebman's text.

6. *Guerre et cinéma, la logistique de la perception* (Ed. *Cahiers du Cinema*, 1991).

7. "Le Travelling de Kapo," *Trafic* 4 (Autumn 1992) POL.

8. Gilles Deleuze, *L'image temps* (Ed. de Minuit, 1994).

9. "Ce que parler veut dire," *Les Lettres françaises*, October 28, 1944.

10. Special issue of *Cahiers du Cinéma*, on the American cinema, 1964.

11. *Non, Monsieur Verdoux n'a pas tué Charlie Chaplin!*, initially published in *L'Écran français*, July 15, 1947, and republished in *Écrits (1926–1971)* (Ed. Belfond, 1974).

12. 'La représentation interdite in *L'art et la mémoire des camps*," *Le Genre humain* 36 (December 2001), published by Seuil.

13. *Le film noir, vrais et faux cauchemars*, published by *Cahiers du Cinéma*, 2005.

14. *La voix au cinéma*, published by *Cahiers du Cinéma*, 1982.

15. "L'hypothèse du film volé," *Cinéma* 10 (Fall 2005).

16. *L'État-Syberberg* in *La Rampe* (Petite Bibliothèque, *Cahiers du Cinéma*, 1996).

17. *LTI, la langue du IIIe Reich* (Albin Michel, 1996) for the former; *La déraison antisémite et son langage* (Acte Sud, 1993) for the latter. Klemperer's work inspired Stan Neumann's inspiring film, *La Langue ne ment pas* (2004).

18. The creation of original work, using documentaries truly or fictitiously recovered, imposed itself as a cinematic genre.

19. "La constance de l'art," *Trafic* 21 (Spring 1997) POL.

A Cinema No Longer Silent

HUBERT DAMISCH

There was a sign,
just a small sign, at Treblinka station
I don't know
whether it was at the station or just before.
Along the track where we were waiting,
there was this sign, very small:
Treblinka.
I'd never heard of Treblinka
because nobody knew it. It's not a place,
not a town, not even a small village.

The Jews have always dreamed.
Their lives, their messianic wait,
revolved around dreaming
that one day they would be free.

More than the dream,
the hope the dream sustained.

> —Pan Falborski (Kolo) in
> Claude Lanzmann's *Shoah* (1985)

WHAT HAS CINEMA LEARNED from the ordeal of having to measure itself against the images from the death camps? It never had a problem with producing images in direct competition with photography. In this manner, cinema was present at the liberation of the camps, while the witnesses were still in the dark about the fact that the hell of the deportation and the concentration camps went hand in hand with a genocide carried out in what truly were extermination camps, with the objective of eliminating the Jews of Europe—a genocide of which the perpetrators systematically sought to erase all visual traces. A handful of exceptions notwithstanding—such as Orson Welles who, as early as during the Nuremberg trial, at a time when such a discourse was far from widespread, very subtly linked the concentration camp system and anti-Semitism[1]—it would take ten to fifteen years before the thing began to take shape and a first differentiation was made within the images of a horror until then indistinct. Retrospectively we may ask, what common ground exists between the belated contributions of such auteurs as Alain Resnais, Jean-Luc Godard, Claude Lanzmann, and a few others, and the accomplishments of men as diverse—at least in age and military rank—as George Stevens (then head of U.S. Army Cinema Services) and a lowly G.I. by the name of Samuel Fuller, when they had to face a still nameless horror and record it, then and there?

Although we have no images of the extermination camps, images of the concentration camps should be enough to stamp out any pathos, apparently irrepressible where commemorative rhetoric rules, and to demand that we use our imagination in an attempt to approach, however little, an experience recorded by only a few very rare texts. For documents, all we have are *non-images*, to borrow Serge Daney's term (non-images the way Treblinka was a non-location until Claude Lanzmann's excavations turned it into one of the lynchpins of what we call memory). Their weight, their excess of reality, is such that their opacity renders it impossible to deny what they describe: the way an image, even one as seemingly immaterial as a photograph, can deny the reality of what it depicts—something Sartre saw as the fundamental condition of any image—while at the same time being devoid of any aesthetic tendency. But if no one ever came back from the gas chambers and if as a result all identification with the victims is excluded, then logically the same cannot be said of the reactions of the American, Russian, British, or French soldiers when they discovered the camps. In much the same way that no one can predict his behavior under torture, since the capacity of our imagination is limited, the images recorded by some of the witnesses to an effectively unimaginable reality offer us enough material for at least projection if not identification. All that's required is a gaze, the same gaze that brought these films to light: that any observers watching these photographs and films should be placed in the position of witnesses, even if only to their own unwilling bodies.

Such is the effect of these documents that, while they can be incorporated into a work of fiction—which required the political intelligence of Orson Welles in *The Stranger* (1946) and, fifteen years later, the force of conviction of Richard Widmark's prosecutor in Stanley Kramer's *Judgment at Nuremberg* (1961)—they leave no room for the imagination and impose themselves as unmodifiable pieces of reality. For a start, let us take the film shot at the behest of his captain by a young Samuel Fuller at Falkenau in 1945, which managed, at that precise place and time in history, to rise to truth and achieve through the fact (I initially wrote "by the grace") of cinema an epic tone. It must have been a moment close to apocalypse that these soldiers experienced—overpowered by the discovery of the horror of the camps but obstructed, by Germany's unconditional surrender, from executing the Nazi torturers on the spot, as the first American troops who entered Dachau had done with the help of the prisoners themselves there. The aftermath of that massacre was filmed several hours later by a crew led by George Stevens, who had been dispatched into what could well be seen as a tragic road movie by Eisenhower in person, under whose direct command they operated—this when they were just getting ready to film the discovery in the Ruhr area of large underground factories and the emergence of the workers who had been reduced to living like troglodytes, blinded by the light of day. For Samuel Fuller and his comrades at arms the moment of judgment came when they forced the dignitaries and inhabitants of the nearby village to dig up and wash the corpses of the deported (as those who were sent to the camps came to be called—Trans.) in order to bury them in their own nightwear and bed linen—acts that needed to be captured, recorded, fixed onto celluloid in a way that cannot with any decency be considered "amateurish," even if that was the nature of the camera Fuller's mother had sent him so he could bring back some images from the war. See Fuller's comments in Emil Weiss's documentary *Falkenau, vision de l'impossible* (1988)—in which he returns to the same spot fifty years later to survey, Lanzmann-like, the remains of a wall emerging from the grass—on the sequence that, in a single uninterrupted shot which (as he emphasizes) made manipulation impossible, shows how near the village was to the camp, no matter how obstinate the denials of the inhabitants: "You knew nothing? You didn't see anything? You didn't hear anything? You didn't smell anything?"—"No, nothing."

Are we capable of articulating the problem posed, in cinematic terms, by the images of the Shoah—whatever the term means—and do we have the right? And how do we pretend to use them, when it is obvious that these images are also using us, in a different way and with different results than we find with a few rare works of literature and cinema?

Under what conditions can these images be given a word that pretends to give them a meaning, as Walter Benjamin said of a caption under a photograph? These questions force us to consider more closely the relationship between *saying* and *showing*, or the ties that can be created between the frame, the shot, and the context of a supposedly "talking" cinema. They are anything but straightforward, these Wittgensteinian words that I consider it permissible to borrow, with polemical intentions, from the Lanzmann of *Shoah* ("What we cannot show, we must say"). They coexist uneasily with what François Truffaut, along with Hitchcock, considered a fundamental law of cinema: "Everything that is *said* instead of *shown* is lost to the audience."[3]

Aesthetically speaking, the validity of this law needs no *illustration*: "The cinema is not a technique of exposing images, it is *the art of showing*. And showing is an act that forces one to see, to watch. Without this act, there is only imagery. But if something was shown, someone *must* acknowledge reception."[4] To Serge Daney, joining *Cahiers du Cinéma* meant, in his own words, choosing realism, with the consequence, as he was to discover, of developing a certain disdain for the imagination, though within this context: "To Lacan's 'You wish to watch? Then watch this,' the answer was 'It was recorded? Then I must watch it.' Even and especially when 'it' was uncomfortable, intolerable, or downright unwatchable."[5] In the same way it must have been uncomfortable, intolerable, or downright impossible for the accused at the Nuremberg trial to watch those images recorded at the liberation of the camps (and presented to them in one compact sitting), whose opacity excluded any argumentation and left space for only "non-images" whose unimaginable horror left one speechless. Yet, "it is the voice that counts" in the end: the voice that says, "This took place, we watched a film that showed it." Daney's voice and what it said are all the more important to our case because this "son of cinema" saw, retrospectively, in the bodies of *Night and Fog* (1955) and those of the opening moments of *Hiroshima mon amour* (1959) two years later, the starting point of the means which the cinema that was born with him gave him to name his "history" and to declare himself its "subject." (He dubbed it "modern," this wise, mature cinema, cruel as Anna Magnani's death by gunfire in *Rome, Open City* [1945], the same sequence that made Ingrid Bergman decide to leave Hollywood and join Roberto Rossellini.) But Daney took the time to realize that this particular cinema could not be separated from the *knowledge* of the camps, which he believed changed "the way to make cinema" (with a side note from him to the effect that while he was writing this, a page was turned):[6] knowledge of the camps, but also of course of Hiroshima. "No, you saw nothing in Hiroshima." And yet it was not for lack of watching.

But is "knowledge" really the proper term at a time when research on the Shoah constantly brings about new developments, with all the risks of institutionalization or even instrumentalization that this entails? We still need a voice, one that can find the words expected of it without using them as an a excuse to denounce the prevalence accorded to language: as if the arguments that occupy historians were echoed in a frame in which images have an entirely different status and obey an entirely different rule, have an entirely different destiny than those they are meant to judge within their own domain. The thoughtless use of the very term *image* can only add to the confusion, as Daney was the first to notice. If nevertheless I had to express how a certain knowledge of the camps (and Hiroshima) has contributed to changing the ways cinema is made, as Daney again said, I would firstly cite that which seems to flow, in the very terms of knowledge, from the awareness, more than a quarter of a century after the fact, of what it meant and implied for the cinema to begin to speak. And what do we actually know about the camps in their various guises but what came and continues to come to us, in competition with those "images" that have lost none of their power or their unbearable nature, through what witnesses have been led to say and what the camera has been able to capture and the cinema to show of the circumstances and the methods of all these exclamations, while communicating some of the accompanying *noise* that blurred its meaning?

These witnesses come in several guises: first, those who have lived through the camps, perpetrators or victims. Some of whom, such as Primo Levi, only survived because of the driving need to testify. Others would never have testified had they not been constrained or reduced to doing so after being trapped in interviews and all the other ploys Claude Lanzmann used so masterfully and without any qualms in what remains, as Pierre Vidal-Naquet noted, the most important historical initiative undertaken in France on what was until then known as the Holocaust. One needs to think merely of the ordeal to which the only two survivors of the final period of Chelmno subjected themselves, which from *Shoah*'s opening moments sets the tone for the entire work: the "singing child," found in Tel-Aviv, whom Lanzmann convinced to join him in returning to the place where he first arrived at the age of thirteen and where his entire youth was filled with visions of the dead and of corpses; and the other, who went through that hell like a dead man and who wished nothing more than to live, and to forget.

The history of cinema would no doubt have had a different course if film hadn't had to wait until the late 1920s to begin to speak, an event which gave the disciples of silent film enough time to invent forms of expression in keeping with modernist ideology, which expected all forms of art to display its foundations and to stick rigidly to its competence and its specific quality. Hitchcock, to name one example, spoke of the nostalgia evoked by silent films, which he saw as the purest form of cinema: "The only thing missing from silent films was obviously the sounds coming from people's mouths and the noises. But this imperfection in itself didn't justify the great changes the introduction of sound has brought about. I mean to say that silent cinema lacked little besides natural sound. We shouldn't have abandoned the techniques of pure cinema the way we did when sound came along."[7]

But for all this, what Hitchcock called "the language of the camera" was not born from the need to find a substitute to missing words. Cinema had started to talk a lot earlier, in intertitles, handwritten or typed texts that allowed audiences to read what the silently moving lips of the actors were suggesting. The fact that the masters of the silent cinema, and the best of today's filmmakers who continue to claim its heritage, make it a point to stick to purely visual means of expression, is proven by a few illustrious examples, such as Murnau's *The Last Laugh*, cited by Hitchcock,[8] in which the filmmaker to whom we owe the famous phrase from *Nosferatu* ("And no sooner had he crossed the bridge than the ghosts came to meet him") prohibited himself from resorting to intertitles at all. This confers almost experimental dimensions upon this ultimate production by one of the great masters of silent film. But cinema, silent or otherwise, could not be reduced to similar problems as plagued painting. Dealing with time as well as movement, it could introduce, by way of editing and framing, principles of articulation *sui generis* in which it only had to set the limits for affirming its uniqueness, if not its "purity," in keeping with modernist ideology.

Cinema could never speak as painting pretended to, which inspired in Claudel the expression: "The eye listens." The spoken word did not come to cinema as a supplement, in the style of what purported to be a "talking architecture," whose surface finish made no fundamental change to the basic structure. Would it have sufficed for cinema to adapt to this new gift (for it received speech rather than taking it), at the price of the difficulties that numerous silent film actors suffered and that generated a good many comedies? Or should we admit that this idea of a pure cinema was merely an illusion, that the voice was just another means at the disposal of a fundamentally hybrid and composite art form, and that its introduction did nothing more than add to an already existing confusion of signs and genres? At the very least, didn't intertitles and other writings which silent cinema employed in order to be heard already undermine its supposedly "visual" essence? The problem that sound and speech posed to the supporters of the silent aesthetic was that they made cinema no longer appeal exclusively to the eyes but also to the ears, with all the possibilities this introduced: the eye had listened, now it was up to the ears to *see*.

"My instinct is purely visual," Hitchcock liked to say. And while he cared little for style in literature, he had the strictest ideas about what cinematic style should be, in opposition to what he considered filmed theater. It was without doubt Orson Welles who did most to rid us of the late-nineteenth-century cliché so dear to Freud, that individuals come in two forms, those who think predominantly in images and those for whom words weigh more strongly. In this light it is remarkable that Truffaut mentions precisely *The Stranger* as an example of Hitchcock's influence on "the only visual temperament" Hollywood had produced since the advent of the talkies.[9] Welles certainly was "visual" and he recognized the importance, if not the predominance, of this aspect in his approach to cinema. But he was also a man of words, a man of many words in fact, like so many other directors and actors who came from the stage and never severed their roots. To which we can add his experience working in radio, from which Welles said he had learned more in the years leading up to *Citizen Kane* than from the cinema.

All this means that if a transmission did take place between the silent and talking periods of cinema, as well as between what appear to be two distinct moments of talking film, it appeals to a division in periods as well as to a point of view that is radically different, itself the consequence of the shake-up of the relationship between saying and showing, the visible and the legible that produced, along different lines, the best of contemporary cinema. Everyone is free to suggest names— from Welles to Godard, from Bergman to Cassavetes, or from Imamura to Hou Hsiao-hsien—that will only form additional markers or signs of an activity that would gain its full meaning only a posteriori, thanks to Lanzmann's venture. It is as if, after the duly literary experiences of Alain Resnais' *Night and Fog* and *Hiroshima mon amour*, in which the word was the exclusive domain of authors, we had to wait for *Shoah* to be able to grasp the full meaning of a cinema that is spoken. The importance resides less in the content of the words that are offered voluntarily than in what manifests itself without the speakers realizing it, or even without them wanting to say it, unwillingly and while they speak. All while the form, the conditions, and the circumstances under which this happens are absolutely clear, in keeping with the stance and the fundamentally cinematic style that is, and remains, that of Lanzmann in *A Visitor from the Living* (1997) or *Sobibor* (2001).

"When telling a story in film, one should only resort to dialogue when it's impossible to convey things otherwise," said Hitchcock.[10] To say nothing of monologues or, worse still, voiceover narration. When a story seems little more than white noise and leaves nothing more to tell, it is the *style* of the words that becomes important. But what role can we give history, and what types of histories, in every sense of the word, after

Auschwitz? (The Dziga Vertov emulators asked themselves the question just after the revolution, from a different, strictly *silent* perspective.) In Claude Lanzmann's *Shoah*, a truth gradually tries to manifest itself not through dialogue but through an ordeal that could take place at no other location and on no other stage—a truth that rings in our ears with a heartrending noise, while we can no longer separate what is word and what is image. Not to dodge the question: To what does spoken cinema owe being the art form it is, while at the same time being an unparalleled instrument in overturning the obstacles that prevent the subconscious from taking part in the writing of history?

Ingmar Bergman learned that lesson and tells it without hiding the sympathy he once carried for the national socialist ideology, even for Hitler himself: "When the testimonies about the concentration camps arrived to hit me in the face, my mind at first could not accept what my eyes were seeing. Like many others, I considered these images lies orchestrated by propaganda. When the truth finally broke down my resistance, I felt desperate and my self-loathing became unbearable."[11] This complements well what the director of *The Silence* (1963) said about cinema: "When it isn't a documentary, a film is a dream."[12] A dream at risk of turning into a nightmare, with all the lessons that can be learned from it regarding the respective stature and regime of image, words, and sound. The invention of the talking picture may well be reduced to the addition of sound and noise to the panoply of means at cinema's disposal: the savage and painful episode of the barber in *Shoah* essentially revolves around a truth that its protagonist cannot bring himself to express, bound as it is to its very incommunicability, bound to that other truth he was not allowed to tell his family members and townsmen when he saw them arrive, stripped of their clothing, in the cloakroom where he was supposed to shave their heads, if he was not incapable of telling: the knowledge that what awaited them was not a shower but the gas chamber from which none of them would emerge alive. Should he have warned them? Could he have? The scene plays as if the unanswered question turned this man into the custodian of the truth about the gas chambers. That truth and the truth about what today could be called history; a truth that, through its very utterance, goes far beyond the legal notion of evidence. There is probably no better example of what "talking" can mean, under these conditions, in reference to cinema. Which in no way excludes the fact that Lanzmann used any means at his disposal, without worrying about being original or about what constituted the specific nature of his art form, but with a completely assured sense of style and effect. This also goes for the Vertov-like forward dollies between two seemingly endless chains of freight cars, until the locomotive stops at a location identified—without any need for sound or noise—by a simple sign that reads: TREBLINKA.

Translated from the French by Tom Mes

Notes

1. This text follows on the one published in *Cahiers du Cinéma* 599 (March 2005), entitled "Montage du désastre," which talks about Orson Welles's *The Stranger* (1945), the first fiction film in which images of the camps taken from the footage projected by the prosecution at the Nuremberg trial appear. In the film, the Nazi hunter played by Edward G. Robinson knows that he has found his man when he hears him remark that Marx was not a German but a Jew.

2. Emil Weiss, *Falkenau, vision de l'impossible* (Paris, 1988).

3. *Hitchcock/Truffaut, édition définitive* (Paris: Gallimard, 2003 [1986]), 12.

4. Serge Daney, *Persévérance* (coll. Essais) (Paris: POL, 1994), 78–79.

5. Ibid., 30.

6. Ibid., 54.

7. *Hitchcock/Truffaut*, 47.

8. Ibid., 21.

9. "Where silent cinema gave us such great visual temperaments as Murnau, Eisenstein, and Dreyer, the talkies only created one, one single filmmaker whose style is recognizable from three minutes of film and his name is Orson Welles," François Truffaut.

10. *Hitchcock/Truffaut*, 47.

11. Ingmar Bergman, *Laterna magica* (Paris: Gallimard, 1987), 167.

12. Ibid.

Three Films

Fatal Rendezvous

Jean-Louis Comolli

THE FOLLOWING TEXT WRITTEN by Jean-Louis Comolli centers around a film, entitled *Memory of the Camps*, that would have an unusual destiny. It was made in 1945, at the request of the Supreme Headquarters Allied Expeditionary Force, using elements filmed by the Allied forces upon the liberation of concentration and extermination camps. Sidney Bernstein was put in charge of the creation of this film. He was chief of the "cinema" section of the Psychological Action Division of the SHAEF. He was to use material filmed by the British, American, and Russian armies. The initial objective of the project was to make three versions of the film, one intended for Germans still in Germany, one for imprisoned Germans, and the third for the general public. According to Bernstein, it was a matter of shaking up and humiliating all Germans and showing them that they were all—not just those who were in the SS or those who were Nazis—responsible for crimes against humanity. This six-reel film was never released as intended, since the new priorities of the emerging Cold War were to minimize the culpability of the German people and to interrupt collaboration between Anglo-Americans and the Soviet people.

In 1952, five reels were transferred from the British War Office to the Imperial War Museum in London, accompanied by a typed manuscript commentary (the sixth reel, which contained footage filmed by Russian cameramen, had vanished). The museum gave this material the title *Memory of the Camps*. It was acquired by the BBC television program "Frontline" in 1985, whereupon the commentary was added, narrated by actor Trevor Howard, and the film was at last broadcast on May 7, 1985.

The British and American armies did not liberate any of the extermination camps—they were all located in East Germany, in the zones taken over by the Red Army. The images in *Memory of the Camps*, notably those of the liberation of camp Bergen-Belsen by British army troops, therefore do not show a true location of the Shoah. But these images, which were all screened repeatedly at the time, with various editings, are unquestionably one of the elements in the construction of how we now imagine the Shoah, in other words the manner in which it is present in our minds today. This visualization has continued to develop ever since, and the strange forty-year delay of the arrival of *Memory of the Camps* is but one element of it.

J-M.F.

One

Two stories overlap—and they are perhaps but one. There is a technical element in the cinematography of the liberation of the Nazi concentration camps: the history of cinematic techniques intermingles with that of the representation of military actions and situations tied to the state of war. It is within the articulation of these that we understand to what point the limits of each technique configure the parameters through which one or the other gesture of representation takes and gives shape; for example, the long poses still required by photographic emulsions led to many of the images produced between 1860 and 1880, precisely "taking a pose," which ritualizes—theatricalizes—situations and also models the look of similarity in the images of the time, as if the historic moment were crystallized in one or another type of imagery and the result ended up conforming to our idea of the past.

Let's take the Paris Commune (1871). When it is photographed, the barricade functions as a set, the soldiers look like actors frozen in evocative poses. Anything that is furtive, accelerated, instantaneous exceeds what it is possible to record and therefore cannot be accessed through photographic representation. The moment lived in its transience, the gesture, the act, the assault or combat, the lightning of the event are absent in photographs: one might say that they are technically obscured or that they can only figure fictitiously, retranslated, reformulated in this language of pose which is not really their own. When photographed, the Commune appears (primarily) in the form of the barricade held in the expectation of an assault of which the photograph cannot and does not say if it will be bloody. What can be photographed becomes the representative image of the situation or the moment, discharging older forms of figuration, drawings, engravings, paintings; and that which is not (yet) photographable (and therefore still belongs to the realm of these older techniques) tends to be outside of the frame of what is visible, since it is not photographed. Prints, engravings, drawings, and paintings therefore belong to the vast realm of imaginary representations tied to stories, to literature, to the theatre.

There is, however, one exception: the very well known photograph of dead Communards in their coffins. Death is there before us, photographed directly, and the photograph reproduces the exhibit of the corpses in barely deferred time. The dimension of death is born here through the photographic gesture itself, through the viewing of death,[1] since the dead body lends itself perfectly to the photographic pose, a very early complicity between photography and the exhibiting[2] of cadavers in funeral rites as the aftermath of combat or massacres. In Richard Dindo's film, *Che Guevara, The Bolivian Diary* (1994), we see—and it is both terrifying and macabre—the American advisors to the Bolivian army taking pictures of the dead body of El Che. And when this same body is filmed, when Dindo combines a series of these bits of film, the trembling of the photogram, the rustling of the film itself raises, absurd and yet irresistible, the promise of rebirth. And, a few moments later in the film, a clumsy hand has scrawled these words on a yellow wall: "You are still alive."[3]

Two

We know about how New York photographer Mathew B. Brady engaged in a large-scale project to document the Civil War, gathering a troop of traveling photographers and sending them to all fronts—no small feat when one remembers how cumbersome view cameras were.[4] Brady worked both as an agency manager and as a collector. He collected negatives, preserved them, bought others from independent photographers, printed, and published them. And perhaps for the first time in history, he exhibited his collection of photographs of the battle of Antietam (1862) showing piles of dead Confederate soldiers, in his New York gallery under the heading "The Dead of Antietam," a shocking exhibit that confronted visitors, the curious, and passersby who were his audience at this premiere (?) photographic representation of death en masse.[5] Whereas the most terrifying images of the disasters of war had always been well known, from Jacques Callot to Francisco Goya, here was a supplement of horror that was due precisely to the supposed link of representation with its reference in reality. Once photographed, the death of soldiers brings us into the violence of battle.

How should we interpret the *New York Times* phrase that says that horror has been brought home to us—that is, *into our homes?* The *us* implies the *familiar*, tied—*between us, we contemporaries*—to the sharing of implicit knowledge from our act of looking. We know implicitly that there is a gap between a drawing or engraving and photography. We know implicitly that the photograph has passed through the mechanical eye of the photographic chamber; that to the *machine* was added the human element of looking, which turned it into a *different type of look.* This implicit knowledge creates a place for the *desire for truth* within the *desire to see.* It is a matter once again of *being able to believe* in something. And it is certain that this desire to believe (or this need to believe) is based upon the mechanical production of the analogue dimension of the photographic image, which is at play in spite of all that separates it from duplication of the observed scene in the strictest sense (framing, the grain of the photo, focal length, black and white).

Three

We could say, paraphrasing the words of Roland Barthes: "What is represented is not real—*but it bears the mark of reality.*" Conceptually, photography works by definition and as a condition of existence, if not for its destiny, to attest to the reality of what it records. The image represents the world. "This was." One moment, one instant was recorded. The image is the record in the present of each observation. The mechanical image is validated by its very means of creation: its light, its form, its substance, its frame, its subject, its figures or the forms it represents are all determined by a certain *state of the world.* Itself a part of this state of the world, the machine records. The scene to be photographed determines the photo, quite as though it might have been prepared by the photographer. There is a dependency, a reciprocity, between the situation and the representation of the situation. The representation is part of the situation.

Something happens when photography is only attributable to the machine: not only is the resistance of matter no longer man's business, not only does matter (light) deal with matter (lenses, emulsions), but there is *a sharing of time.* No matter what it is, the length of the pose, long or brief, creates this sharing. The machine conjugates in its very mechanism a fragment of time synchronous with that of the action, of the situation, of the person being photographed. The act of recording in the moment. Let's say that this photographic trace of the world, so as to neither be loyal to it nor conform to it, is nonetheless a bearer of truth—what Serge Daney called the inscription of truth. The very truth of recording is a sharing of a common moment in time through the uncoiling of a situation and the revelation of the lens in the exposure of the plate—or with regard to the cinema, synchronous with the uncoiling of the film in the camera or the tape recorder.

Four

As we know, World War II was filmed from beginning to end and from all sides. It became the first mass cinematic worldwide event. The Allied Forces filmed it. So did the German army, the Nazis, and of course, the Japanese. It was a triumph of 16mm film.[6] Perfectly suited to the amateur market (the network of Kodak stores allowed the purchase and development of 16mm film just about everywhere), this film was also perfect for filming exteriors, and as such was very suited to the war. An ironic fact: the amateur market allowed U.S. and German firms to develop tools and techniques that would be used to film the war and its massacre of civilians from close up, in a different way. Cameramen filmed everything. Their manner of making films was closer to that of amateur filmmakers than to that of studio technicians. These people were professionals, some of them filmmakers (George Stevens, for example), others journalists (Samuel Fuller), but the very conditions of war cinema—the urgency, the impromptu nature, the danger, the speed—like the 16mm tools they used, led them to face constant challenges. Filming war is obviously risking finding death, which can be interpreted both as dying or as filming the real death of others. What happened in the middle of April 1945 in Bergen-Belsen is distinct from both of these categories.

Five

On April 15, 1945, British soldiers liberated the Bergen-Belsen camp. This camp was called a "transit" camp, and also a "death chamber." Here, groups of male and female prisoners of extremely diverse origins stayed for more or less lengthy periods of time and were discovered in varying degrees of starvation. Cadavers were everywhere, tens of thousands of bodies strewn among the survivors.[7] During the trial of the SS officers in charge of this camp, which took place in Luneburg before a military tribunal, Glyn Hughes, a British officer in the health service, gave his first impression:

> The condition of the camp was truly indescribable. No recounting, no photograph could give an adequate impression of the vision of horror that was this camp; and the images we saw inside the

barracks were even more horrific. In many places in the camp,
bodies were piled up in stacks, more or less high. . . . Human bodies were rotting everywhere in the camp. The sewage ditches were
filled with bodies, and in the barracks as well, there were innumerable bodies, at times lying near people who were still alive, on the
same pallet. . . . That was the overall impression.

Hughes said it well: no recounting, no photograph . . . What did he discover? A different type of reality, too powerful, he thought, to be able to
be translated or reduced by the taking of photographs, a reality before
which a recounting or a photograph seemed insufficient. As I've said,
wars and massacres have been photographed for the past eighty years,
and the feeling of horror that these photos manage to convey can no
longer, without having become banal, be considered unbearable. The
culture of war photography, the culture of death, on film and on glossy
paper, was already well ingrained. All sorts of magazines have published
these images of great battles and the troop landings. But in this case?
This was something different, for which we have no other example.

Six

America, Great Britain, and Russia sent photographers and cameramen
to accompany their troops. The Bergen-Belsen liberators had some great
British photographers, among others George Rodger, in charge of covering this event. Here is what he said about his arrival at Bergen-Belsen:

I took the first few shots, I saw a bunch of people lying under the
trees, pine trees, and I thought they were sleeping, rolled up in
blankets. It looked like a nice peaceful scene. I took some photos; I
still have one. It was the first thing I shot there, my first look inside
the camp, my first impression. But then, immediately after that,
when I got closer to them, I realized they weren't sleeping at all,
they were all dead. Under the pine trees, dead people lying on the
ground, not just two or three, not dozens, but thousands of them.
It was terrifying. Little children leaning their head on their rotting
mother's corpse. They didn't even have the strength to cry.

Rodger had photographed (for *Life* magazine) the bombing of London;
the war in Asia; the African, Sicilian, and Italian campaigns; the landing
in Normandy; the liberation of Paris; and German operations. But what
he saw at Bergen-Belsen made him change the way he looked at things
and changed his life.[8] He had discovered, he said, "the ultimate degree
of human degradation."

When you look into the eye of the camera, you forget the horror and you shoot automatically, without thinking. . . . And then I
realized that I had arranged hundreds of Jewish bodies to create a
nice photographic composition.[9]

What I want to convey in what is said here is the emergence of a new
type of reality: living people mixed in with the dead to this degree.
Beyond exhaustion, most of them skeletal and haggard, the living we
see here are frightening. But it is their life among the dead that makes
the image unbearable. It is this that cannot be embellished. Irresistibly,
photography attempts to embellish death, and framing itself is removing,
centering, trimming. The difficulty faced by the photographers and cameramen working at Bergen-Belsen is paradoxically that of the improb-
able but possible photographic beauty of the dead body.[10] On the one
hand, the bodies are everywhere, death is everywhere, it overflows, it
takes over the shot. On the other, there is a deep connection between
the body frozen in death and the body frozen in photography. Photographing corpses is not photographing the living. Redundancy removes
photographic distance. And it is perhaps for this reason that the living
amongst the dead bodies, the conjunction of both, seems such a scan-
dalous abomination: hence the child (one of the first photos taken by
Rodger) who walks along a road lined with hundreds of bodies lying on
the embankment, some naked, others partially dressed.

Seven

The British cameramen (of the British Army Film Unit) filmed what
Rodger had photographed. Their reels of film were sent to London,
where Sidney Bernstein, a cinema manager and distributor, a friend and
associate of Alfred Hitchcock, put together a film on the liberation of
the Nazi camps for the Psychological Warfare Division of the Supreme
Headquarters Allied Expeditionary Force. *Memory of the Camps*, quickly
edited,[11] is a testament to the extent of the horror of the Nazi crimes
first of all in Germany itself, just liberated, and beyond it throughout
the world.[12]

The filmed footage from Bergen-Belsen arrived in London. Immediately the question of its credibility was posed. Would German viewers,
the primary audience intended for the film, believe these images? Would
they not suspect trickery? Once filmed, does horror of this degree seem
believable, can it be believed possible? How to believe these images that
show what has never yet been seen, never before been shown? But also:
Can these images be considered proof? To quote Sidney Bernstein, "I
asked that anything that could one day prove what had really happened

be filmed. It would also be a lesson intended for all of humanity, and especially the German people, for whom we would screen this film. In fact, most of them said they knew nothing of the camps, and we wanted the film to be the proof of what we wanted them to see."[13]

Filming was not enough. The project would have to be directed. However, it had already been directed: the Allies themselves (upon the horrific discovery of the massive crime) had forced the German neighbors of the concentration camps, where any trace of the crimes had not been erased, to see for themselves what had happened practically under their noses for years and that they had preferred not to look at. The German town or village notables from areas near Bergen-Belsen, men and women who surprise us wearing their Sunday best among the soldiers' uniforms and the survivors' rags, are led to come look at the communal graves, where bodies transported by the SS have been thrown. Like the Americans in Falkenau, the British directed this confrontation in Bergen-Belsen. It is exactly what is filmed. The panorama is imposed upon the cameramen: on one side the living, on the other the dead, and in between, the act of looking. The confrontation was therefore directed twice: in situ, and then cinematically.

And it is here—for this redirection—that Hitchcock intervened. He suggested that at the editing stage the sequential shots and the filmed panorama should be preserved as much as possible. Here is what the second editor of the film, Peter Tanner, said:

> The essential thing that Hitchcock brought to the project was to make the film as authentic as possible; it was important above all that the audience, and especially the German people themselves, be able to believe that these horrors had really taken place. And I remember him pacing the length of his room at the Claridge and saying, "How can we make this convincing?" We tried to edit the shots in the greatest length possible, using the camera movements, so there would be no way of cheating. By panning from a group of notables and church people to the dead bodies, we knew that no one could say the film was tricked.[14]

The sequence shot was intended to attest to the presence of these spectators before the mass graves. The direct effect of the panning shots was to connect the look of these spectators to what they were seeing: to materialize the look and therefore to inscribe the look as movement from one to the other, from the subject to the object, from the "me" to the "not-me," in other words to represent the act of seeing itself as a material and temporal liaison, a form, a figure of style.

Eight

Spatio-temporal continuity of true inscription, no doubt. The same filmic unity combines the elements of time, of locale, and of action. Trickery is forbidden, to paraphrase André Bazin regarding the forbidding of editing. But that's not all. What happens in these panning shots that connect the piles of naked and emaciated corpses to the looks of the spectators gathered there—different types of spectators: some forced to be there, such as the German officers, but also the SS camp guards; and others, the witnesses: soldiers, officers, and British chaplains—what happens is precisely the conjunction in one recording of the looks of the living and the subject of their looks, the dead bodies. The film audience will see the spectators in the film seeing what they see themselves. To see another person seeing and to see what he is seeing doubles the effect and attests to the reality of seeing, establishing at the very least the possibility of believing what one sees, that there is seeing in the look, in the same shot which makes it indisputable proof, which it would be absurd not to believe. For the audience to believe in what is filmed would begin the acceptance that the spectators in the film also believed what they were seeing, preceding us on the path to belief, marking it, and validating it. Here, the doubled act of seeing is the key to the sequential shot. It is not, in this sense, exactly the same version of what Bazin said: it is not about having the hunter and the hunted in the same shot, but rather having the spectator and the spectacle, and offering to the viewer the framework of a filmed act of seeing with which to connect his own seeing. The sequence shots in *Memory of the Camps* situate a framework device and the confirmation of what is being seen by the supposed spectators in the film. (We call this setting up of the spectators' looks, *direction*.)

The other effect of articulating in one panned shot the look of the spectators to what is—literally—at the other end of their line of sight, in other words, death in the shape of the emaciated, piled up, bulldozed bodies, is not just to attest to the very possibility of the situation (since they are seeing it) but to give to the dead the weight of being viewed by the living. Rodger said: the living mixed in with the dead no longer paid any attention to them. It is this *attention* that the British demanded from the German civilians brought to the scene of the crime. The connection—which never existed before—between the dead and the living. The place of the film audience is changed as a result. I mentally connect to the relationship that the panning sequence shots inscribe materially on the screen. The living and the dead belong to the same world. The cinema gives me the sensible form of that, and I am obliged to connect both parts of the shot, the corpses, the living, the victims, the executioners and their accomplices. Sequence shots and panning shots become political figures.

The dilemma in which the film's auteurs found themselves gives us an idea of the extraordinary dimension of what was filmed at Bergen-Belsen; but it is just as telling of the essential ambivalence of the cinematic gesture, the gesture that tries to connect what is real and what is virtual, the thing itself and its representation. Doubt does not vanish when we pose the question of whether or not to believe (see, again, all of *To Be or Not to Be* [1942] by Ernst Lubitsch). The doubt is there, it is present, even when it is not allowed, even when the process of direction tries to obliterate it. How to be rid of it? It will be the effect, to a lesser degree, of the great trials (Nuremberg, Eichmann) and more than that of the lengthy work of historians (Raul Hilberg, Annette Wieviorka, and so many others).

Nine

To bring the dead back among the living. But also to bring the camp, the territory of a horror that has reached the limits of the unspeakable and the limits of what can be represented, back to the familiar folds of the living. The second suggestion that Hitchcock made, a rather subtle one, was to enlarge the scope, the field of vision, by filming a few moments of daily life in Nazi Germany during the time of the death camps.[15] Thus we see, in *Memory of the Camps*, a few nice shots of cows grazing in a meadow, orchards, and lovers holding hands along a misty lake. Postcards and mass graves. The Nazi death machine is even more terrible when it is seen in comparison to "normal life," to the world of men, to the place where there is also peace, desire, and love.

Ten

In the mass killings of previous wars, in the terrible images of the Armenian genocide, what was "missing" (if I may use the expression) were the essential parameters of ideology, of organization, or of any idea of a system, a desire for power, a contempt for the weak, a cult of power, and a taste for death, that led to the attainment of the appalling intensity of mass killing of which the Nazis were the authors and directors. All the work of the film (if only all that remained was a promise in the unfinished work of this project) was to attempt to take the responsibility for filming something that had never been filmed, had never been imagined, for which what was missing was the image: the never before experienced event in cinematography. Never before, in the cinema project, in the invention of the cinema, in the utopia that was created in the form of cinema, had such situations been filmed or even imagined. Perhaps the Nazis were aware of the absolute novelty of the spectacle that death represented to the living, and perhaps this is one of the reasons for their ultimate attempt to erase all trace of their crimes—to make them literally *invisible*.

What was filmed in Bergen-Belsen was done without knowing or comprehending the very proportions of the filmed event itself—the Shoah. People didn't know, didn't really want to know what had happened to the Jews in the camps. Those who made *Memory of the Camps* filmed and edited it without realizing the full breadth of the elements they were putting together. Filming without knowing, filming without comprehending. Filming to see, later on, in the aftermath of history. There is an urgency to filming, even if we don't know the meaning that it can have. Filming in order to give meaning that has not yet been defined, that is not yet possible, but that is already written without our knowing it, in what has been filmed—as if there were a direct dialogue between the event and the film, in anticipation of the work of historians. The confusion felt and described by the makers of this film attests to an as yet unresolved (but nonetheless filmically documented) opacity, as though there were promise of meaning still to come. The film contains a meaning that is not yet defined.

Eleven

While the cinema can be defined as the temple of the filmed body and the filmed body as the apotheosis of the human body—two examples among a hundred thousand others: *Tabu* by Murnau (1931) and *Gertrud* by Dreyer (1964)—this dimension of the exaltation of the body is removed from the images of Bergen-Belsen. The film is a catalogue of bodies and the condition of bodies of which very few other films in the history of the cinema give example, but it is at the cost of discomfort, of great repulsion, that we are made to consider these bodies as having anything to do with our own. The dialogue of the bodies that characterizes the cinema (the body of the viewer projecting itself into the body of the actor) is formidable here. The emaciated bodies are hard to look at because of the destruction they demonstrate of all that radiates from the human body, the destruction of the humanity that belongs to the human body, the destruction of the identity linked to the uniqueness of the body. All that is confounded by the repetition of physical deterioration, dismemberments, confounded by the mass in which there are no more faces, no more names. As for the spectators shown in the film, these German neighbors who come, summoned by the victors of the war, to look at—in other words to become consciously aware of—the terrifying spectacle of the burial of thousands of corpses in mass graves: these spectators see as we are seeing, no doubt, but in a different history than ours. It is as accomplices that they are inscribed through the direction of these victors of war, doubly involved, confirmed, formalized in the panned sequence shots. Their horror, their tears at times no longer moving to us: they didn't want to see, let them see! "They" are not "us," even though their place and ours are mirror images. They are even less "us" because they are forced to see. For them, seeing is not a free act. In this sense, they are separate from the viewers of the film who are free to see and to not see, to put a hand in front of one's eyes like a child. The forced look of the filmed spectators is in opposition to the unforced look of the film's viewers. The representation of the force exerted on the filmed spectators renders them foreign to us. Here again there is ambivalence. How can we not recognize these others as "one of us"? And how can we recognize ourselves in them if not as part of the same species (the *Human Race* given both as norm and limit by Robert Antelme and by Primo Levi—*If This Is A Man*)? The anthropological dimension of the cinema gives us no choice; the historical dimension of the process of direction (of films) lumps us all in the same history—there is no other—but this history is contentious. *Memory of the Camps* makes us confront the other that is us, or inversely: we must *choose sides*, with and against the cinema.

Twelve

The worst is kept for last: the long minutes, again in panned shots and sequence shots, in which we see the imprisoned SS, threatened by bayonets and forced to pick up the corpses of their victims, forced to carry them in their arms, to throw them into trucks that will take them to the mass graves, and there, forced again to pick the dangling bodies up in their arms to throw them into the grave. During the course of this transport, in a sort of "danse macabre," the living and the dead are in each others' arms, the corpses with skin stretched over their bones held closely against the living bodies of the SS guards. Through the extraordinary reversal through which war becomes the director, the executioners and the victims find themselves in an embrace. The Nazi wanted to destroy the bodies, the spirits, the identities, the filiation of the Jews of Europe: and now here he is, holding in his arms these dead who have come back to embrace (embarrass) him.

Beneath the concept of "redemption" that could be perceived through these after-death embraces (the executioners forced to connect their bodies to those of their victims), we see, filmed and visible, the assembling of living body with dead body. It is to the very principle of the cinema that we owe the impact of this embrace: the cinematic act is born and is carried out as a passage from "alive" to "dead." This is what, for example, we see in *Man with a Movie Camera* (1929): life is captured by the machine, but frozen in time in each photogram; the film holds images that are *stopped movement* and we must make this ribbon of film move for the movement of the images to resume. The synthesis of movement is created by projection, while the previous stages of the cinematic work (filming, editing) are situated more on the side of analysis. The scientific work done by Étienne-Jules Marey focused on this analysis of movement: stopping life's movements in order to make them visible, by stopping and cutting a series of photographs that are already photograms of a man walking, a cat jumping, the flight of a bird, or curls of smoke. The Lumière brothers, making this series of photograms move by projecting them, reconstitute the relative invisibility of the phases of living: life as something that defies vision.

In the shots of *Memory of the Camps* in which we see SS men lift and carry the dislocated bodies, it is as though, for once, analysis and synthesis could coexist. In one same shot, the violent contrast: the connectedness, the smoothness, the build of the living body, and the disconnected, the broken, the roughness of the dead corpse. The macabre dance is created by this opposition of moving forms: smooth and continuous on the side of the living; jerky, bumping, decomposing on the side of the dead. We know that the SS men used the term *Figuren* for their prisoners: "characters," "figures," "silhouettes" . . . but it can also mean "statuettes" or "figurines" or "marionettes." The disarticulated bodies move like broken puppets. In the movement of images, the jolting corpses; and under the movement of images, the steadiness of the photograms. There is—and it is heart rending—something of an ultimate attempt to rewind the dead body, to ward off the rigidity of death, to shake the corpse so that it will take off again in a parody of movement. This horror that defies representation paradoxically reminds us of the intimate economy of the cinema, its secret, in the very word of its magic. To give to what is photographically dead the movement of life, the air of life. What the cinema is not meant to film, death as such, as if unsurpassable, is filmed here. Violence has been done to the cinema by death. The cinema—the medium of life—takes on this challenge because through it, through analysis, death is at work.

Translated from the French by Anna Harrison

Notes

This text is a development of the transcript of a seminar held in November 2005 at Belo Horizonte, Federal University of Minas Gerais (Brazil), to which we were invited by Ruben Caixeta de Queiroz and Cesar Guimaraes. Words cannot express how much I owe to the work done by Sylvie Lindeperg: *Les Écrans de l'Ombre* (*The Screens of Shadow*) (CNRS, 1997), *Clio de 5 à 7* (CNRS, 2000), and also with her help, the transcription of a workshop held at Inathèque entitled "Use of New Technologies in the Social Sciences," June 2002, as well as the collective volume published by Al Dante (1997).

1. We will see it again a little farther on in *Memory of the Camps*. This living/dead montage is very present in what Samuel Fuller filmed at the liberation of the Falkenau camp (reprised and commented on by Fuller in Emil Weiss's film *Falkenau, A Vision of the Impossible*). Under the eye of the liberators, local German notables, imprisoned German guards, the caring of the dead is carried out on the skeletal remains of the victims by the executioners themselves. See "Falkenau 1945. Ouvrir les camps, fermer les yeux," by Georges Didi-Huberman (conference given at the Collège de Philosophie, published in the *Annales* review, issue no. 5, 2006).

2. The death mask becomes a photographic subject. Molding, sculpture, give way to two-dimensional image. There is nothing of this complicity in the case of "filmed death." There is antipathy between the cinema and real death. When it comes to death simulated by actors of fiction, it is never taken for reality. The documentary role of the cinema dislikes filming real dead people, and yet this is the lot of war photographers, which may explain the discomfort they experience. We are familiar with the debate over the well-known photo by Robert Capa showing a Republican soldier at the moment when he is shot. See the rapport of photography and death in the book by Susan Sontag entitled *Regarding the Pain of Others* (Picador, 2004): "The suspicion that the Capa photograph, *Death of a Loyalist Soldier during an Assault at Cerro Murioano*, does not show what it purports to show (according to one hypothesis it was a training exercise near the front) continues to haunt debates on war photography. In photography, we tend to accept anything we see verbatim." See also Marcel Ophuls's *The Troubles We've Seen: A History of Journalism in Wartime*.

3. On this point, and more generally, see two books by Susan Sontag: *On Photography* (Picador, 2001) and *Regarding the Pain of Others* (op.cit.).

4. Two photographers worked together to take a picture: the first mixed the chemical solutions and placed them onto a perfectly clean plate of glass. Then this solution was made receptive by immersing it in water, in absolute darkness. The plate of glass thus prepared was introduced into the camera chamber, which the second photographer had placed, correctly positioned and aimed at the subject. Exposing the picture took several minutes. Then the plate of glass had to be developed as quickly as possible. All this took place on the battlefront. (Library of Congress, *American Memory: Selected Civil War Photographs*).

5. The *New York Times* wrote that Brady "had brought home to us the terrible reality and earnestness of war."

6. Sixteen millimeter film was developed by Kodak in the 1920s and the first Bell and Howell cameras came out around the same time. Sixteen mm sound was technically ready shortly before the war. And yet most of the footage filmed during the war had no sound, although some had sound effects and ambiance added after the fact.

7. For most of the information in this chapter, I used the following sources: *The Shoah Memorial; Jewish Memory and Education*; the *Multimedia Encyclopedia of the Shoah*/United States Holocaust Memorial Museum; Centre Régional Résistance et Liberté; Centre de Documentation de Bergen-Belsen.

8. After Bergen-Belsen and the Luneberg trial, Rodger gave up photojournalism and took part in the creation of the Magnum agency and went on a photographic journey around the world.

9. Quote taken from the "Sur la pellicule" ("On Film") section of the Web site of the Montaigne School in Bordeaux. Rodger's comment on the "Jewish bodies" is no doubt an afterthought about the moment of discovery: the awareness of the gigantic dimension of the extermination of the Jews of Europe was very little known when the camps were liberated.

10. The film commentary, as narrated by Trevor Howard in 1985, speaks of the torsos and faces of corpses filmed as if "sculpted in marble"; and in fact there are in this film a few shots (only a few) in which we see something akin to the striking beauty of death, the face of death frozen in Baroque ecstasy.

11. One of the film's editors, Stewart MacAllister, oversaw the making of the film with Sidney Bernstein. Alfred Hitchcock was called in as "treatment advisor." He also played the role of advisor in the organization of the filmed material, along with journalists Colin Wills and Richard Crossman (of the *London News Chronicle*) and editors Peter Tanner and MacAllister. The initial project was to make three versions of the film, one intended for the German public, another for the German prisoners of war, and a third for the general public "perhaps specialized" in other countries. Bernstein had clearly stated his purpose: to shock and humiliate the Germans, to prove without a doubt that the crimes against humanity were the work of the Germans, and that the German people as a whole were responsible for them, not just the Nazis and the SS.

What was filmed at Bergen-Belsen is the essential part of the film; other brief scenes enlarge the scope of the film at dozens of other concentration camps. The distinction between extermination camps (Auschwitz, Belzec, Majdanek, Sobibor, Treblinka, etc.) and concentration camps was not clearly made.

12. The shift in rationales for supporting "denazification" in favor of another plan, that of urgently combating the Soviet threat, made Bernstein's project inopportune, and the unfinished film remained in the War Office archives.

13. Taken from Sylvie Lindeperg's "Usages des nouvelles technologies en sciences socials" ("Usage of New Technologies in Social Science"), op. cit.

14. Sylvie Lindeperg, op.cit. Some specific points about Hitchcock's London visit are elaborated upon on the "Frontline" website (the BBC program that broadcast *Memory of the Camps*): "Sidney Bernstein, the film's director, persuaded his friend Alfred Hitchcock to leave Hollywood and come to England to collaborate for several weeks in the making of the film. Hitchcock arrived in late June,

after the Belsen material (the first three reels of the film) had been assembled. He left in late July, two months before work on the film appears to have stopped. According to Bernstein, Hitchcock would not take a fee for his work."

15. According to Sidney Bernstein, Hitchcock, using a map of Germany, "traced a circle around each concentration camp, showing the villages around each one and specifying the number of inhabitants who lived near the camp: '. . . We must realize they exist, otherwise how can we situate the camp, it could be anywhere in the world, a thousand miles from civilization . . . .'" The juxtaposition of what is familiar with what is horrible is one of the great Hitchcock themes. (see "Frontline" site, op.cit.).

Night and Fog

Inventing a Perspective

SYLVIE LINDEPERG

"'AUSCHWITZ IS A PART OF FILM history now.' she tells me, and her words sound terrifying. Still, the despondency and the terror are right there, so far from Auschwitz spatially and ever further from Auschwitz time-wise, yet forever near, in Alain Resnais's film *Night and Fog*. Gabriela's grandparents, like my parents, lost their lives there, in the places shown in the film—more precisely, *in the film itself*." To the protagonist of Alain Fleischer's novel *Les Angles morts*, visiting Auschwitz means above all "seeing the places where *Night and Fog* was shot":[1] the film becomes a portable memorial, a substitute for the site itself. Film as mausoleum. All that remains of *Night and Fog* (1955) in Alain Fleischer's novel are its full-color tracking shots across the grounds of the Polish camps.

However, *Night and Fog* also made a decisive contribution to the way we regard the concentration camp system, while apprehensively inventing a gesture of cinema in order to face it. By assembling archival footage—some of it known, some of it revealed to French audiences for the first time—Resnais shaped our image of the camps.

It's through *Night and Fog* that certain images, notably that of the bulldozer in Bergen-Belsen, have become part of the collective consciousness and have been handed down through time to the present day. Other shots from the film have gone on to live a life of their own, such as the photograph by the Birkenau *Sonderkommando*, used by Resnais while he was still unaware of its singularity. *Night and Fog* accompanied yet other images (the Westerbork train convoy, the child of the Warsaw ghetto) on their way to iconic status. All of these are thanks to the film's lengthy shelf life at home and abroad but also to the use of extracts, to re-edits, and to the film's absorption into other French and foreign films.

To come to grips with this double movement of fixation and displacement of perspectives, we shall start by opening the black box of the film's creation, which reveals a level of historical knowledge and memory but also the nature of the social and symbolic interactions of the images from the camps with the period when the film was made, so different from ours. We will then follow the film's legacy and look at the various ways it has been used and reinterpreted as well as at the fates and journeys of some of its individual components.

Through interlocking perspectives *Night and Fog* has transcended decades, and its instability has provided a picture of the changes in our complex rapport with the "images from the camps."

I

In 1945, on the occasion of the first exhibit on "Hitler's crimes," the French public discovered *Les Camps de la mort*, a film made by Actualités Françaises and composed of footage shot at the liberation of the western concentration camps. In November 1954, historians Henri Michel and Olga Wormser opened the "Resistance, Liberation, Deportation" exhibit at the Musée Pédagogique in the rue de l'Ulm in Paris, by announcing the start of production on a film on "Germany's concentration camp system." At the origin of this initiative are the Comité d'histoire de la Deuxième Guerre mondiale (World War II Historical Committee) and the Réseau du Souvenir (Memorial Network), an association founded in 1952 to further the memory of the deportation.[2]

Instigated by both organizations, the documentary is intended as a follow-up to previous efforts by the two historians, who would work in close conjunction with the director: their collective anthology of eyewitness accounts *Tragédie de la déportation* (*Tragedy of the Deportation*) would provide the narrative structure for the screenplay, while the documentation gathered by Wormser for the exhibit (photographs of the liberation of the camps plus objects and drawings that belonged to the deported) would serve as a source of archival material.

Resnais and his two collaborators were not content to limit themselves to the material already gathered, and set out on an ambitious quest for imagery that started in the spring of 1955, around the same time as the writing of the first versions of the script.

After immersing themselves in the photo archives of the Centre de Documentation Juive Contemporaine (Center for Contemporary Jewish Documentation, abbreviated as CDJC), the Comité d'histoire de la Deuxième Guerre mondiale, and the memorial organization Amicale de Mauthausen, they viewed the footage of the liberation of the camps gathered by the Actualités Françaises in the spring of 1945, as well as various fiction and documentary films. But the Service Cinématographique des Armées refused Resnais permission to use a number of shots and London's Imperial War Museum forbade entry to its archives.[3] Instead, Resnais and his collaborators turned to the Dutch Institute for War Documentation in Amsterdam.

In Holland, Resnais, Wormser, and Michel discovered copies of the footage shot by the British at the liberation of Bergen-Belsen. They also found sequences from Westerbork (Holland's equivalent to the Drancy camp), whose existence was still unknown to the French.

The images selected by Resnais show the boarding and departure of a deportation transport that left the Dutch camp on May 19, 1944. We see the preparations for the convoy: a crowd of men and women carrying their belongings, huddled together on a platform full of luggage. Stars of David can clearly be seen on their jackets and overcoats. Members of the *Ordnungsdienst* (the Jewish order-keeping regiments) hold watch in front of carriages full of people. Impassive and haughty German officers consult documents and give a few instructions. Finally, soldiers and order-keepers close and lock the wagon doors. Some faces remain visible behind the gaps between the wooden planks. The convoy begins to move. Hands stick out through the narrow openings while the officers mount the steps and grab the handrails of the front carriages.

What is striking about this scene is the calm and orderly nature of the boarding process. There are no signs of violence and outwardly all is serene: a couple almost distractedly exchanges a fleeting kiss near the platforms; a man already on board talks to the member of the *Ordnungsdienst* who has come to lock his wagon; another lends a hand in closing the door. The same oddly serene atmosphere can be found in the now famous photographs in the *Auschwitz Album*[4] (one of which was used in *Night and Fog*) that show the other end of the journey. The two series of images were made with the endorsement of the executioners and would end up being used against them: through the violence hidden underneath and the relationship of the images with the horrid events that happened offscreen.

The recordings at Westerbork were made at the behest of camp commander Albert Konrad Gemmeker, with the aim of using them in a propaganda film about life in the camps to be written by "Heinz Todtmann, a baptized Jew, member of the *Ordnungsdienst*, and close aide to Gemmeker."[5] Between March and May 1944, two other detainees, photographer Rudolf Breslauer and his assistant Karl Jordan, filmed the activities of the inmates (workshops, theater performance, sporting events). These scenes are reminiscent of the well-known film shot in similar conditions at Theresienstadt (derisively titled *Der Führer schenkt den Juden ein Stadt [The Führer Offers the Jews a City* (1944–45)]). Yet, as Ido de Haan notes, the images of the latter film are "more thoroughly filtered of any embarrassing information."[6] At Westerbork, after all, what is filmed is the arrival of prisoners at the camp and the departure of the convoy of deportation.

Alain Resnais was partially aware of the history of these images. In the shooting script for *Night and Fog* they are described as "Holland. Film shot at Westerbork and at the station by the deported at the order of the Nazis." The filmmaker shows the boarding in a continuous sequence accompanied only by Hanns Eisler's musical score. He does however incorporate a cutaway shot, of Polish origin, of an old man slowly advancing across a station platform with three small children in tow. By adding this image, the director creates a disturbance in the tranquility of the Westerbork scenes; as if to allow the world that was kept offscreen to intrude, he introduces a foreign element found in Warsaw, that symbol of the persecution and extermination of the Jewish people. In the decades that followed, one of the images from Westerbork visible in *Night and Fog* as well as in Ervin Leiser's *Mein Kampf* (1960) would go on to acquire the status of "icon of the Shoah." This shot begins with the inscription "74 persons" on the side of a train carriage, then pans up to frame a child's face wrapped in a veil staring out from the doorway and into the lens. During the 1980s, this image was used many times over in films and on television. However, the instatement of this picture of the young girl as symbol of the extermination of the Jews would encounter yet another movement, which sought to re-singularize the fates of the victims through the double gesture of identification and the reconstruction of personal trajectories.

In 1997, a group of researchers launched an inquiry with the aim of finding this girl's identity. Much to their surprise, they discovered that the truth was quite different from what the image symbolized. The girl's name was Anna Maria Steinbach. She had been born in 1934 in the south of the Netherlands and was assassinated on the night of August 1, 1944, at Birkenau. However, she was not Jewish. She was part of the only convoy of gypsies sent from Westerbork to Auschwitz.[7]

Beyond the anecdotal, this tendency toward identification is symptomatic of a change in our interaction with these images. It is part of a wider phenomenon of giving names to the anonymous victims whose identities had remained buried under the crushing weight of numbers, as a general and abstract apprehension of the extermination. This movement was initiated largely by Serge Klarsfeld and his association, which researched and published, convoy by convoy, the names of the Jews deported from France. More recently, this imperative gesture has extended to images used in anniversary publications, memorials, and museum spaces. The 2002 American edition of *The Auschwitz Album*, for example, contained the names of almost two hundred people identified from photographs. We find a similar wish to link names to faces in the concept of the French pavilion at Auschwitz, on the sixtieth anniversary of the liberation of the camps.[8]

Let us return to Poland, where the crew of *Night and Fog* continued its research during the shooting. In the collections of the Institute for Jewish History, Resnais, Wormser, and Michel discovered the picture of the "child of the Warsaw ghetto," a number of photographs from the *Auschwitz Album*,[9] several images of camp construction, and photographs of executions carried out by the *Einsatzgruppen*. At the Documentary Film Studios in Warsaw they viewed films and excerpts selected for them by filmmaker and former deportee Wanda Jakubowska: clips from Soviet and Polish newsreels, footage shot by the Russians at the liberation of Auschwitz, shots of roundups in Polish cities and ghettos.

The final steps of documentary research took them to collections of the ghetto museums, of Majdanek (the Lodz children's column) and especially of Auschwitz where they learned of the existence of four photographs taken in secret by members of the Birkenau *Sonderkommando* and of the images of Himmler's visit to Auschwitz in July 1942. The insertion of these images into *Night and Fog* marks an important scansion in the narrative. As I've pointed out previously,[10] in studying the various drafts of the script one finds a noticeable hesitation that speaks from this break represented by 1942—a hesitation about how much emphasis to put on two related events: the concentration camp system that forms the main subject of the film commissioned from the director; and the extermination of Europe's Jews uneasily integrated into this film without being entirely excluded from it. In the anthology *Tragédie de la déportation*, which posits the univocal model of a generic camp whose characteristics are largely borrowed from the concentration camps, Olga Wormser had already made incidental mention of the genocide of the Jews. She takes the same approach to the script of *Night and Fog* by evoking, in a

somewhat confused manner, the moment when the two systems congre-
gate, during the summer of 1942 at Auschwitz-Birkenau. A transitional
version of the screenplay thus mentions, in the same breath, the use
of the deported as forced labor in service of the war economy and the
establishment of the "final solution to the Jewish problem." This explicit
mention would later disappear from Jean Cayrol's narration.

Getting back to the historical documentation, we can note a dual
movement in the work of the three filmmakers: in addition to assembling
familiar documents in order to illustrate an already largely preplanned
narrative, there is the unexpected discovery of new material that changes
existing perceptions of events and that in some cases would influence the
structure of the film.

Nevertheless, Resnais long retained a painful feeling of incompleteness about their tireless research: "I had the terrible feeling that we
needed another year of research, that there were other documents in existence. But we were up against a deadline, so we had to stop. . . . What's
more, we didn't have enough money to go to Germany and a lot of
other places, even to simply look for documents."[11]

This reminiscence doesn't quite do justice to what was achieved
in spite of limitations, thanks to the team's ambitions and the decision
to expand the research to Poland, which would have a great effect on
the final result.

Whereas the documentary *Les Camps de la mort* consisted simply of
a montage of newsreel footage supplied by Western allies, *Night and Fog*
was the fruit of a genuine investigation that complemented the research
already accomplished for the Wormser-Michel exhibition.

The film *Les Camps de la mort* furthermore limited itself to images
filmed at the liberation of the western camps while the images chosen for
Night and Fog widened the view in terms of both time and space, allowing
for the emergence of an additional strand of history: the deportation of
Europe's Jews. This event had largely been obscured after the liberation
and played no more than a very marginal role in public debate during the
1950s. The Réseau du Souvenir and its backers (particularly the Ministry
of War Veterans) preferred to project the image of the resistant deportee
by sanctifying both his struggle and his status as a "martyr." This is the
edifying image they wished to see dominate the film, which was initially
entitled *Resistance and Deportation*.

Within the context of this memorial policy, the extermination of
the Jews was not an issue. Yet, the search for imagery in Holland and
Poland allowed the filmmakers to bring it to their audience's attention.
The editing showed the consecutive steps in the persecution of the Jews
(establishing ghettos; arrests; internment; deportation—which preceded

their extermination in the death camps). The narrative logic and the generalizing tendencies of the narration obscured its singularity.

Thinking of Resnais' comments, we could posit that his "bitterness" and dissatisfaction might have been due to an overestimation of the wealth and variety of existing documentation. It is true that the crew had very limited access to American archives of the liberation of the western camps.[12] It is also true that all they could see from Soviet sources were images of the liberation of Auschwitz. Still, it is very unlikely that another year of research and an extra financial boost would have fundamentally altered the shape of the film, for two opposing reasons.

First, the scattered corpus of photographs would not be catalogued, reassembled, and annotated until the surge in interest in imagery from the camps during the 1980s. Then, as far as the specific question of the death camps is concerned, the filmmakers had, without realizing it, already laid eyes upon the only existing records to have been made around the gas chambers during the Nazi reign: the as yet scattered pieces from *The Auschwitz Album* and the four clandestine photographs taken by the Birkenau *Sonderkommando*. They simply weren't capable of perceiving the rarity of these items, which was the result of the Nazis' policy to keep the genocide unseen. We should interpret the editor/ director's gesture within the context of this vacillation between feelings of incompleteness and the period's gaps in knowledge of the extent of iconographic sources.

II

What interests us here about the recording that took place in Auschwitz, Birkenau, and Majdanek in September and October 1955 is Resnais' decision, in accordance with his prescribed tasks, to shoot black and white footage (later assimilated into the film's "archive" material) to fill one of the film's three requirements. Resnais' contract in fact stipulated that his documentary had to encompass three cinematographic elements: "an iconographic part based on documents, supported with animated graphs or objects that form authentic reminders of the Deportation"; "a 'montage' part composed of footage culled from French and foreign film archives whose historical importance is beyond question"; "a part with material newly recorded at key locations of the Deportation."[13]

The first technique was to be an extension of the exhibition, which would serve as a source of objects and documents to be integrated into the film. The director was asked to complement them in Poland. Once he was on location, Resnais, who shot in color at Birkenau and around the barracks of Auschwitz I, decided to use black and white to film objects and the interiors of the museum (the pan through the kapo's room, uniforms, insignias, and service numbers, etc.)—a choice intended to minimize the risk of creating an atrocity exhibition such as the newsreel footage shot at the liberation of the camps in 1945 had offered. This also made it easier to integrate the shots with the documents supplied by the exhibition and the Comité d'histoire (cloth covered in writing by Germaine Tillon, Jean Cayrol's metal box, the Mauthausen register, the poster "Un pou c'est ta mort"/"One louse means death"), and the two sequences borrowed from Wanda Jakubowska's fiction film *The Last Stop* (1948).

This black and white visit to the barracks of the camp-turned-museum, which would also haunt the prologue of *Hiroshima mon amour* (1949), did not exclude all emotion; think of the "terrifying sweetness"[14] of the panning shot along the mountain of women's hair preserved in block 4. But where the Réseau du Souvenir's intention was to "transform memory into monument," Resnais and Cayrol agreed that *Night and Fog* should not become a museum piece. It should be neither a memorial nor a relic.

The extremely rigorous editing would help meld all the disparate elements into a whole and, in the eyes of the film's original audience, harmonize the assembled mass of "archives of the past." The distinguishing principle revolved around the sole opposition defined by the narration as well as the rhythm of the editing and the shifts in color: "sweeping and wide" movement for the color sequences identified as the present; "pillaged and chopped" for the monochrome shots referring to the Nazi past.[15] No distinctions were made within the assembled "icons of horror," represented as a single entity and kept at arm's length by Cayrol's critical meditations on the present time.

However, our view (specifically that of historians) of this "archival" section of the film has changed in recent years: today we know much more about "images of the camps" and this knowledge has almost instinctively made us want to pick apart the filmmaker's assemblage. What we have gained in knowledge we have lost in innocence. Boosted by this recently acquired knowledge, some believe they have the right to judge and condemn a film that by any standard was conceived with exceptional rigor for its day.

Instead of feeding this debate or trying to silence it, let us look at the editing of *Night and Fog* from the point of view of this gap between two eras of reading and perceiving images. Though we can't reconstruct the editor's gaze upon the camp archives with any degree of certainty, at least we can determine the questions he asked himself and, more importantly, those he didn't but which we pose ourselves today.[16]

Looking at the central part of the film today, the part devoted to the workings of the concentration camp system, it is easy to detect the mixture of two generations of images: those made during the Nazi regime and those recorded by the Allies upon the liberation of the camps. The considerable effort devoted to photographs from the camps over the past decade and a half renders this juxtaposition of different periods noticeable.[17] Pictures of the construction of the camps, of visits from Nazi dignitaries, of the Auschwitz orchestra, and of the deported put to work in the *kommandos* or the underground factory; the anthropometric photographs; and the "snapshots" of the camp commanders are shown side by side with images of the liberation. Notable examples include a shot of the deportees lying in their bunks, taken by the Americans at Buchenwald; that of the "Mussulman," taken by the British at Sandbostel; the picture of a man supported by his comrades, made by the Americans at Wöbbelin; or the image of a dying man staring straight into the lens, photographed by Germaine Canova on April 13, 1945, at Vaihingen camp.

The use of images from the liberation obviously becomes more systematic when it comes to filmed material. With the exception of a tracking shot along a line of rounded-up Polish citizens, a sequence from Jakubowska's film of a truck leaving at night and lit by the flames of the crematorium, and the monochrome footage recorded by the film crew themselves, all moving images utilized in the central part of *Night and Fog* were shot by Allied cameramen.

If some material was mistakenly identified as having been recorded by the Nazis, other shots had already been identified and documented as dating from the liberation. We can therefore suggest that while Resnais, Wormser, and Michel perhaps underestimated the amount of liberation-era material employed in the central part of the film, they nevertheless consciously decided to use some of it to evoke the daily lives of the deported.

Keeping in mind Resnais' feelings of incompleteness, it's not inconceivable that the filmmakers considered it necessary sometimes to use certain images for what they "symbolized" (the lives of prisoners of the concentration camps) at the expense of what they "documented" (the liberation of the deportees). But we might just as easily assume that they never openly posed themselves this question in the first place; knowing the origin of an image does not automatically mean making a reasoned distinction between these two types of imagery.

The different point of view we have of the images today can only be understood in the light of the fifty years that have passed since the film was made. It should be considered as the convergence of new knowledge

of historical facts and the recent uses of archival imagery. The com-
memorations of the fiftieth and sixtieth anniversaries of the liberation
of the camps, both of which had various richly documented scientific
publications devoted to them, have been a major factor in delineating
quite clearly the distinction between photographic imagery from the
Nazi period and from the liberation of the camps. Despite the short
time frame that separates them, the two are no longer seen as interchangeable. Aside from documenting two very separate events, they also
oppose two radically different perspectives of the camps: those of the
executioners (sometimes those of their victims) and those of the witnesses
who arrived on the spot belatedly (and after the fact). Those two points
of view now strike us as irreconcilable in the same visual context, in the
same way that we make the distinction between photographs taken by
the Nazis and those taken by the deported during the period leading up
to the camp system.

Let us examine another effect of montage that has come under
criticism from historians: the "annihilation" sequence. Opening with
Himmler's visit to Auschwitz in July 1942, it is constructed as follows:
images of raids and convoys; the train of corpses discovered by the
Americans at Dachau; a photograph from the *Auschwitz Album* showing the selection process on the platform at Birkenau; six photographs
of men, women, and children nude or forced to strip, taken just before
their execution; a fixed shot of Zyklon gas canisters; a color sequence
of the gas chamber.

This montage seems symptomatic of the ambiguities in the script
and the final version of Jean Cayrol's narration. Making no mention of
the Final Solution, the voiceover lists the various ways of administering
death and implicitly presents the gas chamber as one of the modes of
extermination used against all deportees. Aside from the image of the
train of corpses recorded during the liberation of Dachau, however, all
the archival material used to make up this sequence relates to the extermination of Europe's Jews. Based on the exact same sequence of images,
a different narration could have addressed the specific fate of the Jews
exterminated in the gas chambers after the phase that Poliakov refers to
as the "chaotic exterminations": the executions of Jews from the Soviet
Union by the *Einsatzgruppen* and the liquidation of the Polish ghettos.
The six photographs of victims mentioned above depict sporadic executions by firing squad.[18] The fourth image, showing a number of naked
women huddled together in a ditch (some carrying their babies in their
arms), is widely known today—we know that these were Jewish women
and children from the ghetto of Mizosc in Ukraine, photographed before
their execution in October 1942. This image, reproduced countless times

since the 1980s, has often been the subject of misuse rightly deplored by Clément Chéroux: "This well-known image . . . has for a long time and in many history books been presented as 'the entry into the gas chamber' [*sic*]."[19]

Night and Fog has been the subject of similar criticism: some viewers interpret the six photographs as depicting victims about to enter the gas chamber. Critical attacks about this are not entirely justified. One can debate the logic of the montage, which places these images immediately after a photograph of the selection at Birkenau while the narrator refers to the fate of those considered "unfit" for labor. However, Cayrol's voice immediately adds, in reference to these same images, that "manual killings take time"—thus correcting the false first impression that these were victims of the industrialized gas chambers. These contradictions between text and visuals create a somewhat confused narrative that seems indicative and symptomatic of the hesitations that surfaced during scriptwriting.

It is important to understand why this selection of imagery of massacres is the subject of such sensitive attention today, so different from the approach of the filmmakers in 1955. If the misinterpretation of the shot from Mizosc comes across as the gravest of misuses, as signaled by Chéroux, this is because it lies at the heart of the controversy over the "missing image" that began during the 1990s in the wake of Lanzmann's *Shoah* (1985).

In the late seventies, the rise of negationism and the subsequent countermovement organized against it contributed to focusing more attention on the gas chamber as a murder weapon. A few years later, *Shoah* profoundly changed our views of the event and the way it should be represented. As we know, the question of the "invisibility" of the extermination of the Jews lay at the heart of the filmmaker's approach. In the death camps, the Nazis achieved their desire to render the genocide invisible by manipulating language, banning photography, destroying material evidence, and disposing of the corpses that formed the ultimate proof. *Shoah* established the singular event of the annihilation of Europe's Jews—until then an issue absorbed into the larger matter of the deportation and the concentration camp system—as an occurrence that was not captured on film while it happened. Refusing to use archives and documents out of context, Claude Lanzmann made the full extent of this organized absence of images felt. He put a spotlight on the repeated misuse that had been made of documentation until then: photographs from the concentration camps employed to "illustrate" the genocide, thus creating an imagery that is wholly inappropriate. The filmmaker's approach permitted an entire generation of spectators, historians included, to face what had until then only been suggested (notably by Serge Klarsfeld): the radical difference in visibility between the extermination camps ruled by the law of secrecy and the concentration camps where photography, with or without permission, was a relatively common occurrence.

   Shoah provoked a lengthy period of analysis, debate, and controversy, all of which reach far beyond the factual issue of the use of archival material, which is what interests us here. We should specify, however, that this issue came to play a part in a parallel debate of a more philosophical nature, regarding the impossibility of reconstructing, representing, and imagining. Lanzmann's refusal to resort to footage from archives was initially interpreted as confirmation that no "images of the Shoah" exist, a statement oft repeated since. The value of this declaration obviously depends on how we define the event concerned.[20] We can agree that a large amount of photographic and filmed material exists, which was recorded by the Nazis during the phases of the persecution leading up to the mass exterminations in the gas chambers: images from the ghettos and their "liquidation," shots of roundups and executions by the *Einsatzgruppen*, and so on. But these serve to underline the lack of images recorded in the death camps, with the previously noted exceptions of the *Auschwitz Album* and the four shots taken at Birkenau by members of the *Sonderkommando*. Those two series come as close as possible to the real blind spot, that of the murders in the gas chambers of which to this day no images are known to exist.

   The extreme and radically imageless nature of this event would form the lynchpin of a dispute that arose in France in 1994, in the wake of the release of *Schindler's List* (1993). In an interview with *Le Monde*, Lanzmann confided that, had it existed, he would have destroyed any footage filmed by the SS that portrayed "how 3000 Jews, men, women, children, died together, asphyxiated in a gas chamber of crematorium 2 at Auschwitz."[21] The debate was reignited by comments made by Jean-Luc Godard in the weekly *Les Inrockuptibles* in 1998. Arguing from the basic premise that the Nazis "recorded everything obsessively," the filmmaker declared that "images of the gas chamber" must exist and that he would probably find them if he was given "twenty years" to search for them in the company of "a good investigative reporter."[22] Having previously covered the dispute elsewhere,[23] let me limit myself here to noting that Godard's comments turned what Lanzmann considered "nonexistent" images into "missing" images. More than a mere semantic shift, these words opened up a new breach, turning the search for such documents into a sort of sacred quest, lending them a dangerous power of attesting to reality, and making their discovery a pressing and necessary matter. The "opportune" reemergence of the four pictures taken in the summer of 1944 by a member of the *Sonderkommando* assigned to crematorium V at Birkenau, for the 2001 exhibit *Mémoire des camps*, is a direct result of this new atmosphere of expectation.[24] None of these images known since the Liberation show the inside of the gas chamber during the period of its activity. They document what our knowledge of history allows us to identify as a "before" (naked women in the woods at Birkenau) and an "after" (members of the *Sonderkommando* burning a heap of corpses out in the open air). The present assessment is by no means intended to minimize the importance of this unparalleled series of photographs; rather, it is meant to emphasize the fact that the four *Sonderkommando* photographs do not refute Lanzmann's claim that there are no images in existence that show the extermination of Jews in the gas chamber.

However, refutation is what Clément Chéroux suggests by framing the documents within the context of the headline-grabbing dispute:

> These images that "would show the prisoners enter and the state in which they re-emerge" (Godard), are precisely those that were taken during the summer of 1944 by members of the Sonderkommando and the Polish Resistance at Auschwitz around—but also seen from inside—the gas chamber of crematorium V at Birkenau. These images can be *shown*, and they have been shown since the end of the war without any *ban or restriction* placed upon them. They were not made from the point of view of the Nazis, but of the deported. They have value not only as *evidence*, but also as documents. They are far from *useless* and there is no question about *destroying* them. They must be studied as historical documents that will allow us to deepen our knowledge of the events they depict.[25]

It is a peculiar form of argumentation by which this champion of the "positivist" cause (which advocates, not without reason, restoring every photograph of the Nazi camps to its original documentary purity) hands these images over to the domain of science after first weighing them down with a symbolic heritage that allows him to declare to his readers: see here, the images Godard was looking for . . . [26] Lanzmann claimed they didn't exist and could not be shown, but they can and must be shown because they contribute to our knowledge of history and are a testimony from the perspective of the victims.

Far from closing the debate, this magic act instead relaunched it. Readers can catch up on the latest chapters in this ongoing discussion if they so desire.[27] What concerns us here is exclusively the manner in which the debate contributed to changing the way these photographs, which have been published and exhibited regularly since 1945 and of which one was used in *Night and Fog*, are regarded.

At the Auschwitz Museum the crew initially selected two images, the only ones useable within the context of the documentary: a photograph of the women of Birkenau can be found in one of the reels of rushes not used in the final edit; one of the cremation of gassed bodies[28] was incorporated into the film with the following commentary: "When the crematoria don't suffice, they resort to bonfires." The storyboard contains the handwritten reference, "*Sonderkommando* clandestine photograph Schmouleski [*sic*] Auschwitz museum,"[29] under the description "photograph of corpses burned by hand."

The discreet presence of this shot in *Night and Fog* and the confirmation that Resnais was more or less aware of its clandestine origins demonstrates the scansions that are part and parcel of this complex history of perspectives—a history that is shaped by a specific configuration consisting of the progression of historical knowledge, shifting priorities in memorializing the extermination of the Jews, and the changing symbolic and social demands made of these images.

Even if it is not entirely certain that this photograph will one day allow us to deepen our understanding of the events, we cannot deny that it is from our progressively expanding historical knowledge that it derives much of its current value. The concentration camp system and the Jewish genocide needed to be regarded both for their convergences and for their radical differences before this series of four photographs could finally surface from an indistinct mass of visual materials and look us straight in the eyes.

What distinguishes this series of photographs are the conditions under which they were taken, their existence "in spite of it all," our interest in the "point of view" of the victims, and the fact that the images form a resistance to the policy of invisibility which the Nazis applied to the death camps.

On the contrary, it is because the specific nature of the Jewish genocide still needed to be properly established (even though it had already been partially written down, notably by Poliakov) and because images of it were not yet considered "lacking" or even "nonexistent" that Alain Resnais was incapable of appreciating the unique nature of this photograph considered so rare today. He chose it for what it showed: an outdoor pyre that allowed him to evoke the final destination of the deported. He associated it with both the image from the *Auschwitz Album* and the images of corpses and mass graves that ends the sequence, mixing them with footage shot by the Soviets in Poland and by the Allies in the western camps.

That this miscellaneous assemblage imposed by a shortage of images that the crew considered contingent with their unfinished research should be the subject of criticism today as a result of new understanding of the very reasons behind this lack, is a paradox.

There is no such archival diversity in the final part of *Night and Fog*. In many ways, the film's ending suspends the principle of alternating montage: the footage of the liberation of the camps is not mixed with the color tracking shots.[30] With the exception of the photo taken at Dachau of a prisoner lost in thought, this entire section is made up of filmed material essentially culled from the footage shot by British cameramen at Bergen-Belsen.

The history of this shoot is well known today. Let us simply reiterate that it was meant to provide "proof through imagery" as well as to accuse the German people. It was at Belsen that the shot was taken of a bulldozer pushing a pile of dead bodies into a mass grave—now part of our collective conscience largely thanks to *Night and Fog*. Both photographers and cameramen recorded this horrible operation that the British troops were faced with due to the atrocious sanitary conditions of the camp they had just liberated, and their recordings were used in the press and in newsreels. Struck by the horror of the scene, many were those who in 1945 believed that the material had been recorded by the Nazis themselves. Attributed to the Germans, the bulldozer became the very symbol of the industrialized dehumanization and destruction imposed by the torturers of the Third Reich.[31]

In *Night and Fog*, however, these same images from Belsen, chosen by Resnais for their "cinematic power," are clearly marked as dating from the liberation and introduced by Cayrol's famous phrase: "When the Allies open the gates."

Different readings and uses of the film would nevertheless change their meaning.

III. Migrations

Upon the film's Parisian release in the spring of 1956, rare were the reviews that did not mention the scene of the bulldozer at Belsen. From among so many, it was this shot that was singled out and held up without further precision (of either date or place) as a symbol of the horror of the concentration camps.

In 1974, one of the two East German versions of *Night and Fog* consciously severs the text from the original edit and moves these images back in time once again. This odious "pirated" translation of Cayrol's narration was the product of East Germany's politics of memory, which sought to condemn capitalism in the same breath with fascism. In this regard, the East German commentary over the aerial shots of the Buna-Monowitz factory emphasizes the collusion between Nazism and capital. The images of the bulldozer at Belsen were integrated into this sequence, which takes as its theme the workings of the Nazi machine, accompanied by the following narration: "Once more, the butchers produce mountains of corpses under which they crumble." Cayrol's line, "When the Allies open the gates," is relocated to the end of this montage, over the shots of the arrest of the executioners of Belsen. Removed from their context and reattributed to the Nazis, these scenes become a metaphor for the industrialization of death in the camps under the control of the fascists and the capitalists.

A few years later, in West Germany this time, Margarethe von Trotta chose those same images from Belsen as a framework for *Night and Fog*'s exposure to Germany's postwar generations. Made in 1981, *The German Sisters* (*Die Bleierne Zeit*) is based on the life of Gudrun Ensslin and her role in the Red Army Faction. Seeing Resnais' film at a very young age is a seminal experience that will guide Gudrun's future political choices. Didn't Ensslin state the impossibility of speaking "to those who created Auschwitz"? Within this metonymic movement, German viewers of *Night and Fog* and the director of *The German Sisters* associate the scenes from Belsen with Auschwitz, the camp that had come to exemplify the Jewish genocide. The West German version of the narration, established by Paul Celan, aided this reinterpretation through several changes to Cayrol's text, notably by mentioning the largely absent issue of the extermination of the Jews.

This change of historical referent would take place in France in successive steps until becoming dominant in the late 1980s.[32] *Night and Fog* became the subject of a new and widespread usage in service of public debate on the Nazi era, which now centered on anti-Semitism, state collaboration, and the Jewish genocide. TF1 and Antenne 2's collective decision to interrupt their scheduled programming to show *Night and Fog* on May 14, 1990, after tombs had been desecrated at Carpentras cemetery, forms an early archetypal example. Two years later, after the case against Paul Touvier was dismissed from court, Minister of Education Jack Lang organized a screening in high schools across the country.

With *Night and Fog* paradoxically reinterpreted as a film about the Shoah,[33] the scenes from Belsen once again emerged as images from the extermination of the Jews.[34] The bulldozer sequence used in 1956 as a symbol of "the horror of the concentration camps" came to be associated with mass murder in the death camps of Poland. Belsen's mass graves became a dramatic and inappropriate substitute for the missing images of the massacre of old people, women, and children who were led straight into the gas chambers upon disembarking from their convoys.

The United States was even quicker to transform *Night and Fog* into a film on the "Holocaust" and led the way in turning Alain Resnais' film into archival material.

In 1959, the production company Argos met with the polite refusal of American distributors to release *Night and Fog* in the United States. This situation changed in 1960, from the moment David Ben-Gurion announced the capture of Adolf Eichmann; in the month that followed, producer Anatole Dauman received offers from several New York-based exhibitors.

Around the same time, *Night and Fog* was shown in fragmented, reordered form on a peculiar television program directed by Arnee Nocks for the Metropolitan Broadcasting Corporation. This hybrid show on the atrocities committed in the Nazi camps was broadcast on July 18, 1960, under the title "Remember US."

Contrary to *Night and Fog*, this television program focused largely on the extermination of the Jews (although the issue was placed in a Cold War context). Within this framework, Nocks reedited two-thirds of *Night and Fog* and delivered an approximate translation of the narration, which constituted the second half of his program. The treatment of the sequence on the extermination speaks volumes: the American text follows Cayrol's[35] but adds an extract from the confessions of Rudolf Höss that radically changes its referent. Over the *Einsatzgruppen* photographs, the narrator recites the famous passage in which the former Auschwitz commander describes how the executions of Jewish women and children were carried out in the camp. The American text thus removes the veil of indecision Cayrol placed over this set of images. It reestablishes and prolongs the script's original intentions, but at the same time it establishes the misuse of these photographs, which through the combined effect of text and editing are turned explicitly into images of entry into the gas chamber.

The first part of the broadcast is very enlightening about how the stature of the various images that make up *Night and Fog* has changed. It consists of three components: studio, montage of archive footage, and eyewitness reports by Jewish survivors (of the Warsaw ghetto and the Polish camps). Here, Nocks shows four extracts from *Night and Fog* in order to "illustrate" the witnesses' words. Notable is the use of the sequence from Westerbork that is used to "support" the testimony of a Jewish deportee named Gisela Perl, who describes the transport to Auschwitz. Shown along with the opening moments of the next shot originating from Jakubowska's *The Last Stop*, the sequence is brought back to pure archival material where Resnais' gesture to recut it and include the shot from Poland was to turn it into a "tertiary source." By neutralizing this action, the American director attempts to objectify these fragments from *Night and Fog* and give them the status of primary source, fit to be recycled into his own edit.

Later during the same broadcast, to accompany a further appearance by Perl talking about the selection, the role call, the cold, and the bullying guards and kapos, Nocks shows several sequences shot by Resnais in the Polish camps in color: the latrine sequence, the dolly in front of the women's camp, the exterior of the Majdanek shower compound, the bird's eye view from the Birkenau watch tower, the long opening sequence of *Night and Fog*, and others. Shown here in black and white, these images from 1955 find themselves chronologically recontextualized and transformed into generic "archive material."

The effect created by Arnee Nocks's methods is to confound documents from the period (complemented with shots of the museum) and tracking shots from 1955 into the same regime of the visible, where Resnais' intent had been to dialectically oppose them. The temporal gap thus filled, each component of the film becomes archival, at the cost of a leveling of the original film's various strata and their reduction into a single, unequivocal function.

The same process also took place in West Germany around the same time. In March 1960, the Cologne-based production company Brevis Film was preparing a documentary on the *Krystallnacht* and contacted Dauman to negotiate the use of four sequences from *Night and Fog*, including both archive footage (Westerbork again) and Resnais' tracking shots (the sequences in front of the barracks of Auschwitz and the Majdanek crematorium).

From the 1960s onward, *Night and Fog* would serve as a "catalogue of images" for film and especially television producers, in Germany and France alike. For decades, Alain Resnais' film alongside others (notably Ervin Leiser's *Mein Kampf* in Germany) became a benchmark of the state of documentary research about the deportation. In France as well as Germany, this use of *Night and Fog* as stock and inventory of archive material would gradually die down as the demand for "new images"[36] grew stronger, particularly around the fiftieth anniversary of the liberation of the camps.

Although *Night and Fog* is most definitely a part of film history, as Alain Fleischer's protagonist states, its status is a paradox: the power of the intelligence that made it into a work of cinema assured its life span; its documentary dimensions—inevitably dated since it was the product of the historical and memorial preoccupations of its time—have given it a legacy for which it was not necessarily intended and which no other film of the immediate postwar decades attained. Its longevity has also been the source of its fragility and the attacks that have been launched upon it. However, at the risk of physically losing its artistic integrity (screenings of the film in black and white, reedits, tampering, abusive translation, etc.), this film-turned-document gained a multitude of uses and readings, which have now become as much a part of its history as it is a part of ours.

Translated from the French by Tom Mes

Notes

1. Alain Fleischer, *Les Angles morts* (Paris: Le Seuil, 2003), 378.

2. Like an intermediary between the logic of historiography and that of memory, Henri Michel held the post of secretary general at both organizations.

3. Cf. Interview with Alain Resnais, in Richard Raskin, *"Night and Fog" by Alain Resnais. On the Making, Reception and Functions of a Major Documentary Film* (Aarhus: Aarhus University Press, 1987).

4. Published by Al Dante and the Fondation pour la mémoire de la Shoah.

5. Ido de Haan, "Vivre sur le seuil. Le camp de Westerbork dans l'histoire et la mémoire des Pays-Bas," in *Génocides. Lieux (et non-lieux) de mémoire, Revue d'histoire de la Shoah*, CDJC 181 (July-December 2004), 37–60.

6. Ibid.

7. There were 245 gypsies in the convoy of May 19, 1944.

8. *The Auschwitz Album. The Story of a Transport* (Yad Vashem Institute and Auschwitz State Museum), 2002.

9. They retained photograph #24 showing a step in the selection process.

10. Sylvie Lindeperg, *Nuit et Brouillard, Un film dans l'Histoire*, Odile Jacob, 2007.

11. Interview with Resnais by R. Raskin, op.cit, 53.

12. The images filmed by the Americans were found mostly in French newsreel archives.

13. Letter of engagement dated May 24, 1955 (Argos archives, Institut Lumière).

14. To borrow François Truffaut's expression.

15. Vincent Pinel, Idhec filmographic record #163.

16. On the gaze applied to painting see Daniel Arasse, *Le Détail. Pour une histoire rapprochée de la peinture*, Paris: Flammarion, 1992 (republished 1996), 206–207; and *Histoires de peintures*, Paris: Denoël, 2004, 21, 194.

17. To mention a few examples: the pioneering book by Marie-Anne Matard-Bonucci and Edouard Lynch, eds., *La Libération des camps et le retour des déportés* (Brussels: Editions Complexe, 1995); C. Chéroux, ed., *Mémoire des camps*.

Photographies des camps de concentration et d'extermination nazis (1933–1999) (Paris: Editions Marval, 2001); *Allemagne, avril-mai 1945 (Buchenwald, Leipzig, Dachau, Itter). Photographies d'Erich Schwab*, op.cit.; and the very recent catalog of the Mauthausen exhibit "La part visible des camps. Les photographies du camp de concentration Mauthausen."

18. Three of these shots (2, 3, and 6, in the order of the editing) were published from 1945 onward in a Polish publication entitled *Extermination of Polish Jews*.

19. *Mémoire des camps*, op.cit, 3.

20. As emphasized by G. Didi-Huberman in *Images malgré tout* (Editions de Minuit, 2003), 77.

21. *Le Monde*, March 3, 1994.

22. To the question by the journalist ("Why would the Nazis have filmed the camps when they went out of their way to hide them?"), the filmmaker replied: "Because they recorded everything obsessively. The Germans are like a sick criminal who can't keep the proof of his crime to himself, who can't resist sending it to the police when he is in safe waters. . . . I have no proof to support my suggestions, but I believe that if I were to work alongside a good investigative reporter, after twenty years I would find images of the gas chamber. They would show the prisoners enter and the state in which they re-emerge. We shouldn't advocate banning things like Lanzmann or Adorno do. Their exaggerations only lead to infinite discussions over the issue of whether or not something is "unfilmable"—we shouldn't obstruct people from filming, and we shouldn't burn books either, because then we wouldn't be able to criticize them anymore . . ." (*Les Inrockuptibles* 170, October 21–27, 1998, 28).

23. Cf. Sylvie Lindeperg, *Clio de 5 à 7. Les actualités filmées de la Libération; archives du future* (Paris: CNRS Editions, 2000), 266–73.

24. The four shots, previously credited to David Szmulewski, were in fact taken by Alex, a Greek Jew whose surname is still unknown. Five members of the *Sonderkommando* who took part in this evidently risky operation have been identified: aside from David Szmulewski and Alex, they are Szlojme and Josel Dragon, and Alter Szmul Fajnzylberg. Cf. *Mémoire des camps*, op.cit, 86 and G. Didi-Huberman, op.cit.

25. *Mémoire des camps*, 217.

26. Godard's declaration was nonetheless based on the premise of images recorded by the Nazis.

27. Gérard Wajcman, "De la croyance photographique," in *Les Temps modernes* LVI, no. 163 (2001): 47–83; Elisabeth Pagnou, "Reporter photographe à Auschwitz," ibid.: 84–108; Georges Didi-Huberman, *Images malgré tout*, op.cit.

28. Since the negatives were lost, the Auschwitz Museum retains the four prints. Didi-Huberman suggests that these prints were struck from the inverted negatives (op.cit., 147–48). *Night and Fog* shows a cropped version that leaves out most of the mass of black around the scene of the incineration. For the effects and reasoning behind these different framings, see Didi-Huberman, 50 et al.

29. Probably a phonetic transcription of the name of David Szmulewski, of whom we know today that he did not take these photographs (cf. supra).

30. Which serve merely as markers at the end of the film.

31. See the inquiry by Frederick Alexander Riches (no. 9937/3) recorded on September 19, 1987, and kept at the Imperial War Museum. Quoted by Clément Chéroux in *Mémoire des camps. Photographies des camps de concentration et d'extermination nazis (1933–1999), dir. C. Chéroux* (Paris: Éd. Marval, 2001), 15, note 10.

32. Extracts from Resnais' film would be used regularly in magazines or news broadcasts in order to "clarify" certain memorial aspects of state collaboration or for an occurrence involving anti-Semitism. The first instance of such use appears to date from November 17, 1978: clips from *Night and Fog* were shown in Antenne 2's *Aujourd'hui Madame* program in the wake of Darquier de Pellepoix's comments in *L'Express* that only fleas were gassed in Auschwitz.

33. All the more paradoxical because the version of *Night and Fog* shown before 1997 still contained the doctored shot of Pithiviers camp.

34. At the same time, the images from Belsen were used by French television in a disconcerting aporia of proof through images, in reports dedicated to negationism (see S. Lindeperg, "Scénarisation du négationnisme par la télévision française : les temps et logiques d'un média," in *French Television*, ed. Lucy Mazdon, French Cultural Studies [October 2002], 259–80).

35. The first line in the American text is close to Cayrol's: "These shots were taken a moment before an extermination."

36. I would refer the reader to Judith Keilbach's well-documented essay "Des images nouvelles" in *Trafic* (2003).

The Work of the Filmmaker

AN INTERVIEW WITH CLAUDE LANZMANN

C LAUDE LANZMANN CREATED A film that played a decisive role in the construction of our contemporary rapport with the extermination of the Jews of Europe, the film to which we owe the term largely utilized to designate the event itself, the Shoah. This film, *Shoah*, the work of a man who is, among other things, a great artist of the cinema, also reveals some of the major issues of the cinema itself. Since its release in France in 1985 the film has circulated ceaselessly, and is being screened somewhere in the world, in theatres, on television, in classrooms, in universities, museums, associations, and so on, every day. Since 1985, it has also been the object of an immense amount of written work, reprised more and more closely, with varying approaches, at times contradictory, by innumerable people: historians, philosophers, teachers, and critics. Claude Lanzmann has also written a great deal regarding the film and what it represents, in addition to the innumerable public presentations, conferences, and debates that he has held.

The intent here was not to add one more text, but to offer Lanzmann a different approach, upon which he had not expressed himself a great deal, that of the work of a director of cinematography. This interview is therefore entirely focused on the technical and artistic choices of this filmmaker—the writing, the production, the filming, the relationships of sound and image, the editing—that were part of creating *Shoah*.

J-M.F.

How did you organize the filming of Shoah? *What material choices did you make?*

The choice in the means of production was fairly limited. First of all for financial reasons. But regardless, I wouldn't have wanted to make such a film with a huge crew, a huge amount of material, etc. The film was made with just one 16mm camera. We tried, once or twice, to use two cameras to deal with some particular filming constraints, but I don't like it, and it didn't work. Or you'd have to have a lot more people to work on the filming. A 16mm camera meant having to reload new film every eleven minutes. It's very important to do so. You also have to reload the Nagra reel for sound, but it's never at the same time.

Another thing is that I have an extreme dislike for what people call "continuity shots": generally, after filming, especially if it's an interview, the director makes a few extra shots of the interviewee or of "ambiance" details, etc. The reason given is that it can help in the editing. Of course this is all the more the case when you're forced to stop frequently to recharge the camera or the microphone, when you sometimes have sound with no image—and it is important sound!—sometimes image with no sound: these "continuity shots" are used to fill in the "blanks." That means that once you've finished the interview, you have to film some more. Each person takes the same pose, smiles or tries to look natural or serious, the Polish farmer scratches his chin, the ex-deportee stares blankly, the interviewer tries to look attentive and intelligent . . . I've done it but I hate doing it and I've never used it. In *Shoah*, there is not one filler shot. In *A Visitor from the Living* (1997), there are two, and I just hate them.

So what do you do when the eleven minutes are up and you have to reload the camera?

Well, you change the location, go outside, go somewhere else, or shoot a landscape shot, for example. We could also have switched to another person, but I don't like to edit one face after another, it's not what we needed in this film, it's not that type of film. I only did it once or twice. The film strives for some sort of harmony; it is born of extreme demands in form, in which time is an essential element. So this choice, which is both technical and ethical, determined the general construction of the film to a great extent—its symphonic construction: when I shoot away from someone it's hard to come back to that person immediately. But I may return later on, like the reprise of a musical theme. I have to move away *and* come back, but differently, at a different level of depth.

In addition, I absolutely refused to add sound that had not been recorded at the same time as the image, so as not to introduce any doubt regarding the rapport of image to sound. There are ethics to filming, and there are ethics in editing. Nowadays, there is absolute immorality, when you see how an interview or a debate is made for television. The use of video cameras is in itself potentially a bearer of great changes, but when you use four or five cameras, it is the temporality of the spoken word that you kill. There is no continuity, there is contiguity, a series of "appearances," coordinated through various tricks—among others, "continuity shots." To each his own circus . . . There is also a tendency to make fiction in this way, nowadays. This seems deeply immoral to me.

How is it immoral?

It is the killing of time that is immoral! It is the loss of the relationship to the real world, sacrificing it for spectacular complacent advantages. This is a misadventure that has happened to me often: to participate in a filmed debate and discover that after editing everything has changed. The beginning is at the end, everything is chopped up . . . a meeting between two people is transformed into a series of appearances. Time is dead! Reality is dead! That is the ethical crime. Television is the mistress of time, the mistress of truth: there is no more truth.

In finding a certain place in the relationship of what is being filmed to time, to real space, to the people in the image, one of the choices concerns the frame. In Shoah, *did you choose the frames?*

Yes. I didn't have preestablished rules for these decisions, but in each situation, for each shot, it was I who, looking through the viewfinder, chose the frame. After that, according to the intensity of the discussion, the emotions resulting from it, the reality of the dialogue that was really happening and was not foreseeable, I had a system of gesture codes, a manner of touching the technician to indicate, during filming, that he should change frames, enlarge the frame or come in closer. A technician is by definition deaf and blind while his camera is filming; blind because he only sees what is in his eyepiece and deaf because he removes himself from all other sources of information, all the more when the interview is in a language that he doesn't know, which was often the case for *Shoah.* In any case the technicians don't see the same things I see. So I had this system of tactile signs, notably to use the zoom—I've never been afraid of the zoom. I've always felt complete liberty in my directing choices. I've done a lot of tracking shots also; there was an internal need for that, the idea of making that last trip, physically. This is why we are at one point on the train to Auschwitz, or in Chelmno by car, the Citroën station wagon that I drove myself, on horrible potholed roads.

Do you try to remain the same at all times? To maintain the same attitude, no matter what is in front of the camera or in front of you?

No, no, not at all. I take a different approach in filming each subject. This is true with the different categories of characters: I can't see addressing Jewish, German, or Polish characters in the same way. But it's also true for each separate case, within those categories. Regarding the Jews, I realized as I went along—none of it was planned, I learned while working, little by little—how to address them, in what "posture" I should place myself. You see, there was also a time where I met these people without a camera, without even a microphone. I went to see them empty-handed, and I took notes afterward. It was while I was doing this work that I started realizing that I couldn't approach the different categories of people in the same way. I met a lot of people, of whom many were not included in *Shoah*. My "approach" when facing the Jewish protagonists was to find out as much as I could about them, through them, before filming, because I knew how hard it would be—and it was, with all of them. It was difficult to ask them questions, and so very difficult for them to respond, for words cannot possibly describe such experiences.

Did you have to do some sort of "casting," to choose the people you would include in the film?

The "casting" happened all by itself. With regard to the Jewish interviewees, casting was very compelling to me; I wanted only men from the special commandos. This choice had tremendous consequences, and still does: they were the only witnesses to the extermination of their people. They were present in the last stages, at the last station of the process of destruction, inside the gas chambers and the crematoria. *Shoah*, as I've said a thousand times, is not a film about survival; it is not, in particular, a film about their survival, their personal survival. And it is not of themselves that they speak in the film. They never say "I," they are never telling us their personal story, or how they escaped. There was a type of very profound tacit pact between us that we would not discuss this while we were filming: it was part of the form of the film, in the strict sense, the *Gestalt*, which irrevocably determines what has a place or does not in the film. The survivors do not use the "I," they say "we," they are literally the spokespersons of the dead. This is the deep meaning of the film, and it is why I've had so many problems, since the film was released, with the survivors. They don't see themselves in *Shoah*: the film does not speak of them.

So, then, how did you choose the other people in the film?

The Germans who are in the film (I met many more, and I filmed some who don't appear in the final edited version) are those from whom I obtained what I was looking for by deceiving them, or by paying them, or filming them without their knowing it. There were many others I was not able to approach, or whom I was not able to deceive. The filming is marked with little defeats, particularly the absence of members of the *Einsatzgruppen*. I was able to approach one of their leaders, Heinz Schubert, the organizer of the great Crimean massacres, convicted and sentenced to death and then pardoned by the American High Commissioner in Germany, John McCoy. I got beat up by Schubert's family, they stole the hidden camera I was using. It is a failure for me that there are none of the *Einsatzgruppen* killers (they assassinated 1.3 million people), nor any of their victims in the film. I found one in Tel Aviv, a magnificent woman called Rivka Iossilovska, seriously wounded in a mass execution in Ukraine, but she did not want to speak in front of the camera.

With the Germans, I tried to behave without any moral judgment, to have the attitude of a technician. With the Polish, it was different; I discovered that I was often the first person who had offered an opportunity to discuss this period; that they really wanted to tell their experience. I felt early on that I had to suspend the flood of words before filming. I didn't want to hear anything ahead of the filming. Otherwise I would lose the natural spontaneity, the virginity of this expression of feeling.

I went to Poland very late, I didn't want to go; I had a mental block about this country. Which proves that the act of creating obeys other logic than that of, say, a historian, a researcher, who would not have this type of concern. For me, there was nothing to see in Poland, so why film there? Where would we find any trace of what was called the Holocaust? Not there. It is in the conscience of those who came back and who are now elsewhere, all over the world. I had to struggle with myself to convince myself to go. While I had started working on *Shoah* in 1973, I went to Poland for the first time only at the end of 1978. Five years later! In the meantime, I had traveled all over the world. And when I arrived in Poland, laden with all the knowledge accumulated during my lectures and my investigations, I was like a bomb ready to explode. But I still needed a detonator. I didn't know it yet, but Poland was to become the detonator.

When I arrived, my first interpreter was a remarkable young woman . . . who looked noticeably Jewish. I didn't keep her; I chose to replace her with a Christian. If I had kept her, it would have been impossible to interview the Polish farmers. In Warsaw, I rented a car and left for Treblinka, where there is nothing left to see except for the symbolic raised stones. I stayed there for quite a while, not all that moved, waiting for something that didn't happen. Then I got back into the car and started filming the area around the camp. That's when I discovered villages that adjoined the site of the camp. I met people of all ages, who had children, teenagers, already adult in 1942. A kind of formidable contemporaneousness happened. And then I came to a road sign, "Treblinka." It was such a shock! It seemed impossible to me that there would still be a village with that name, that people in 1978 would be the inhabitants of Treblinka. It was a village like any other, and I came to the train station, and there were rails, freight cars lined up there, nothing commemorative, just a normal train station, with normal traffic. And once again, the shock of a sign: the sign to the Treblinka train station. This connection of the name and the place was decisive. The name was, for me, so charged with horror that it was practically legendary, that no reality named "Treblinka" seemed to be able to exist in the present time. Treblinka was a reality, of course, without any possible doubt, but a reality that was *in illo tempore*. And there I was, in a place bearing that name, today, in 1978. The shock between this quasi-mythical word and this banal place, peaceful and contemporary, produced a considerable effect on me. Everything I had accumulated for five years (and of course for far longer than that) exploded then. I went into a true hallucinatory state, inhabited by a formidable urgency. It was the winter of 1978–79, and I began filming the following summer.

But that day, in Treblinka, a farmer told me about a man who drove the trains during the war, and who lived in a neighboring village, Malkinia, ten kilometers from Treblinka. I immediately went to see him. It was late, almost midnight, when I arrived at their house. I woke the man and his wife up; they welcomed me, gave me food, and were adorable. The man began to speak, to tell me his story, and I thought, "I have to stop him, he must stop speaking! There's the film! Not yet!" I left at four a.m., telling him, "You'll see me again soon." If I made an ethical mistake, only one, in *Shoah*, it was that I made him repeat the things he told me that night. He told me that he didn't pull the train cars with his locomotive, that he pushed them. When I asked the question in the film, I knew the answer and made him repeat it. That's the only time, the only time I broke my own rules, but for me it was such an important thing to say. As much as I wanted to know as much as possible ahead of time with the Jews for personal reasons, with the Polish I didn't want to know anything before filming.

So this man, the train conductor, you knew how you would film him, how to frame him, how close to get?

Yes. It was very clear, it's the same thought that guides all choices, it comes in a flash. It's the logic of creativity.

The creation of cinematography. If you had chosen to make a book of Shoah, *it would also have been creative, but you would have made other choices . . .*

A book? What a crazy idea! *Shoah* is not a book, it is a film. It would be impossible for it to be a book.

Why?

Because . . . the faces. [Claude Lanzmann hesitates] The face is something that is totally incompatible in any other context. Faces, trees, nature. *Shoah* is an incarnation.

All these director's choices imply that, faced with the manipulative immorality that you have denounced regarding television earlier in this interview, you do not oppose neutrality in filming or editing, but you do for other choices, other interventions on your part.

Obviously. There is a way of "writing," there must be writing of certain choices, and not others. While filming and while editing. There is a morality in filming that must be used in the reality of what is happening between the different people, and a morality in filming that must espouse the flow of real time, even if it is not happening in real time. *Shoah* is certainly not the recording, in sound and image, of a preexisting reality. There was nothing. We had to create the reality, from beginning to end. That's where there is direction. It begins from the first image of the film. Simon Srebnik in his boat that's completely directed, he would never have gotten into that boat on his own, he had not been in it since his childhood. But when I heard Srebnik tell his story one day, long before that, the story of a singing child, I knew it would be the first shot in *Shoah*. I knew it. Long before I knew whether he would consent to come back, or whether I could film it, etc. I wanted it that way. And that's how all of it happened.

Shoah *is presented like a story. The first words we hear, "The action begins," are those of a storyteller beginning a story.*

Shoah is not a string of bits of information one after the other, it is a construction . . . including the use of the word *action*, which has many meanings. There is the Nazi meaning that is underlying but present: the Germans used the word *action* for the raids, the deportations, and the exterminations. There is also the Racinian meaning of the word, in all the prefaces of Racine plays, the word action in the sense of tragedy. The film is intended to be a long process of discovery, through the writing of cinematography. It is no doubt two successive writings, the filming and the editing. The two acts of writing must of course be coherent with each other.

When in the film I ask the fat farmer in Treblinka whether he remembers the arrival of the first convoy of prisoners, he says he remembers it well, but in fact he is incapable of speaking of it. He is immediately in the routine of the convoy. When I ask the same question, later on, of the Sobibor train station switchman, he remembers it well, but what he says is in a completely different tone. Since it was the same question, it could have been expected that I would edit these two sequences together, whereas for me it was impossible because of the radical difference in tone. The difference is what made it impossible to group the two together. This is the whole problem in the narration of *Shoah*. What is at stake in the narration is not to restore the flow of the filming, nor to follow a thematic logic, but to reveal the truth. In *Shoah*, the truth is revealed throughout the film, and more and more the art of storytelling consists in giving rise to revelation. In the example I gave, the second witness, the switchman, appears in the film two hours after the first man. What he says about the arrival of the first convoy has a completely different meaning.

There is no "objective flow of time"; I don't even know what that means. There are ways of laying out the shots that are part of the revelation of truth, and others that have the indignity of manipulation. It is always a matter of searching for what works. Of course, *Shoah* aims at what works best, but in the revealing of a truth that is not "already there." That is actually "extremely absent."

On occasion, I have compared the film to a drill going deeper and deeper. The film is organized according to a narrative structure that plunges like a drill. In the beginning of the second period, it can seem as though it is starting all over from the beginning. But the witnesses are not the same. In the first part, what did we learn? In a sense, we know everything already. But through whose voice? Whose point of view? The first period is conceived from the exterior of the gas chambers, the second is from the inside. What I just said is schematic; there are a great deal of more orderly lines that organize more subtle evolutions from within this process.

Did you write out the manner in which the film would be organized ahead of time?

No. I didn't write anything. Before filming of course there was a lot of historical research and a lot of preparation work, in order to be materially ready to do the recording, but there was nothing premeditated regarding the construction of the film. There was nothing remotely resembling a script: I didn't need it. I didn't know the film would be divided into two periods, I had no idea how long it would be. The structure of the film, in its detail as well as its outline, was imposed upon me. Not to talk of two parts but of two periods, like Alexandre Dumas, may seem a minor detail, but for me it was very important, and this was imposed upon me. The entire creation of the film, in particular the filming, was an adventure. That's a very important word for me. And each day had its share of dangers.

Did you start editing before you finished filming?

No. I didn't touch one thing before finishing the filming. Well . . . to be exact, one thing that did happen is that when I thought I had finished all the filming and had started editing, I went back to Poland and filmed a little more because I needed some more footage. It happened twice. In Treblinka there's nothing to film. The technician said there was no point in shooting more, but he was wrong. So I went back with William Lubtchansky and Caroline Champetier and it was kind of a freestyle hunt for shots in Poland. We would stop when I liked something I saw, snow banks along the road, things like that. During filming, you depend upon the production logistics; appointments are made, hotel rooms are booked, etc. It's a pain in the ass! You're not free. For a film of fiction I guess it can work but for this, not at all.

How do you deal with the enormous amount of footage? How do you begin the process of editing?

It's very complicated; to know everything that is at your disposal, image and sound, is impossible. At times I found shot descriptions and I thought: I didn't film that. So I began by editing little things, small shot assemblies that could make up a small film by themselves.

I made the part concerning Chelmno, what happened in Grabow, etc. I moved forward timidly in this superhuman mass of image and sound. Several times I felt completely blocked and didn't know how to continue. Just like a mountain climber on an unknown path who might come upon a crevasse or a sudden enormous cliff. You have to find your way. There is one, and only one way.

I remember being blocked for two weeks while editing one of the Auschwitz scenes. We discover suddenly that there is a town called Auschwitz. Madame Pietyra, a lady who lives there, tells about the past, and says that it was eighty percent Jewish before the war. Then I had to introduce the camp into the film and I didn't know how to do it. I had filmed the Jewish cemetery in Auschwitz, which she told me was closed—that "people aren't buried there any more." It is through these older dead, those who were buried there before the war, who had died of natural causes and who lie in this cemetery, that it became possible to introduce the sinister entrance to the extermination camp for the first time in the film.

Did you realize ahead of time that you would be in the film?

First of all, in the nine and a half hours of film, I am visible less than forty minutes total. And contrary to what some heinous and imbecilic commentators have said, I do not at all like to be on film. Besides, my position is that generally speaking, I do not need to appear on film. I appear on film only when it can't be helped. This is the case when it's necessary for me to show a location, for example to show the layout of the farm of Borowi, the fat Polish farmer, in relationship to the train tracks and the station. You see me a little in the Polish village because it's necessary to understand that it is my actual presence that triggers what is happening in the moment. And you see me interviewing the ex-Nazis with my hand holding the hidden camera, because it's unavoidable, you can't control the frame. You see me very little, contrary to what an Israeli pseudo-historian wrote.

That's true. And yet, in this film as in others you have made, you are extraordinarily present, which is different to what happens most often in the cinema, just as much for documentaries as for so-called fiction, which lean toward wanting to erase all presence of the person making the film, to make that person imperceptible.

I think that's the way it should be. I don't mind people saying I inhabit *Shoah*. It's true that I do. It would not have been possible to make such a film, and thus construct through the cinema a relationship to the Shoah that the film enables and that exists today, without inhabiting the film. This is why I have said on occasion that I "invented the Shoah." But I realize that that is a difficult thing to hear.

Very often in the film, you don't speak the language of the person you are interviewing. You chose to keep the questions and the answers and the trans-

lations of both in the film, instead of subtitling or dubbing over the original voices, which are the two solutions systematically used in television, but also in the cinema in this type of situation.

Impossible!

Technically, it's rather easy . . .

Perhaps, but it would distort the whole nature of the rapport that took place, for example between my question in French to a Polish person, the translation of my question into Polish by the interpreter, the answer of the guy in Polish and the translation of his answer into French. How to skip one of those four steps, filmed with just one camera? Cut the continuity? That would be horrible. It's impossible.

And yet this is what the great majority of filmmakers do, especially when filming interviews.

For me it's unacceptable. When I started making *Sobibor* (2001), I started with scenes I had filmed for *Shoah* and didn't use in the end, and tried to make them work together, with editor Sabine Mamou. We made a number of attempts and it was horrible. We couldn't glue the shots one after the other, we were forced to go back and film more footage. Which changed the film entirely.

The presence of interpreters is also part of the polyphony of the film, its tower of Babel aspect. And the choice of languages is engaging. For example, when I went to Chelmno with Simon Srebnik, it seemed impossible to me for us to be speaking German. I decided he should speak Hebrew, and we had to use an interpreter. And then it didn't work, it all seemed stiff, the shots seemed dead. So, we just spoke German. I preferred to speak the language of the enemy, the language spoken by those who were mortal enemies—but also the language of many of the victims.

During the filming of Shoah, *did it ever occur that you filmed some shots for aesthetic reasons—because a landscape was beautiful or because you liked the light?*

Yes. And yet I would also say that there is nothing gratuitous, and there aren't any shots that are intended to embellish the film, in *Shoah*. But a locomotive at sunset, with its lights on, that's magnificent.

Did it ever occur during filming that you said to yourself, I don't know how to shoot this?

Yes, it did. It happened in Chelmno. How to film this place, which was where two extermination periods happened? Twice, the gas trucks came, in 1942 and 1944. It is a place that has been completely destroyed. There is a very unremarkable village, along a Polish highway, with a church, a castle, a few houses here and there, seven kilometers into the forest with symbolic graves, near a river. How to film all that, to bring it together, convey the feeling of what happened here? The first scene, in the forest with Simon Srebnik, does not show Chelmno. When I come back with the Nazi teacher's wife (filmed in Germany), we go to the village; this time I had the idea of going through the village in a horse-drawn cart, and I was proud of my idea, the sound of the horse's hooves on the asphalt [Claude Lanzmann imitates the sound by tapping his desk in the rhythm of the sound] with the rear of the horse, the movement, and it was possible to enter the town.

How did you record the sound?

Most of the time with a boom, again with only one mike. I remember Bernard Aubouy, always elegant.

Did you know ahead of time how decisively important the voices would be, the power of invocation they'd have? That it would be through them that we would realize what had disappeared. The role of the voice is central, whereas the lazy consensus is that the cinema is always about image.

It seems that I knew a long time ago that voices are images. And that the images are voices. It is impossible to separate the two in *Shoah*. You have to add the numerous strategies of passage between the voices, from on to off and from off to on, between my voice, that of the interviewed people, the interpreters. All of this weaves a complex network that is never accidental. Often the offscreen voice has more impact than if it were synchronized with the face that expresses it. It gives a completely different result at times. It is no longer the expression of an individual, it is the earth that speaks.

Does the offscreen voice invoke what is definitively offscreen, the extermination itself?

[With reticence] You could say that.

Were there voices you could have used onscreen that you chose to edit as offscreen?

Yes. Simon Srebnik's monologue narrating the images of the Chelmno forest is more powerful than if you saw it being spoken onscreen. Also, the scene in the Ruhr where I read Nazi administrative documents about the improvements to be made to the gas trucks.

Did you ever say to an interviewee, "Let's do it again"?

Yes, of course. As rarely as possible, but there were times when a person felt blocked, or took off on a tangent that went nowhere. But I didn't do a number of takes like people do when filming fiction. You stay in the moment; there are no retakes or second chances. How could I ask Abraham Bomba to repeat the emotion he feels, evoking what he lived through in the gas chamber in Treblinka? It is neither theatre nor the work of actors. Interruptions due to the reloading of the camera allowed us not to repeat the same thing but to go in different directions, to reformulate a question, to change a point of view.

If you were making this film today, would you film Shoah *on video? The constraints you had with the 16 mm camera would not exist and it would make for a very different film.*

This is not a film you can make on video. Today, I would still want to work with film, with a 16 mm camera. I would refuse to use video, so perhaps as a result I couldn't do it at all. Perhaps making a film like *Shoah* has become impossible today. It required the traditional editing console, and the discipline that that implied. Video has destroyed one way of making movies. It has made everything spatial to the detriment of time. "Technical time," the interruptions and the down time due to technical constraints, at all the stages of creating a film, have perceivable effects, which you feel in a film. In *Shoah*, I believe you feel the power of these constraints. Baudelaire said, "When you are constrained by form, the idea emerges more intensely." Form, in *Shoah*, was extremely constraining.

While you were making Shoah, *did you think about images in the cinema, about other films?*

No. Of course, when you film a steam locomotive, *The Human Beast* (1938) by Jean Renoir may come to mind, but really the answer is "no," in the sense that such memories do not serve any purpose for me, do not interfere with what I do. I am not a cinephile, even though I've seen a lot of movies. I don't function in reference to existing images, whether they are from cinematography or not.

The preceding interview of Claude Lanzmann, comprised of numerous conversations as well as three work sessions on January 26, April 18, and October 14, 2006, was prepared by Jean-Michel Frodon.

Translated from the French by Anna Harrison

Conversations at the Mill

N SEPTEMBER 17 AND 18, 2005, Arnaud Desplechin (filmmaker), Jean-Michel Frodon (film critic), Sylvie Lindeperg (historian), Jacques Mandelbaum (film critic), Marie-José Mondzain (philosopher), and Annette Wieviorka (historian) met at the warm and welcoming setting (also filled with movie lovers' memories and memorabilia) of the Moulin d'Andé, in the Eure region in France, to watch and discuss four films. The participants were familiar with these films, even if their knowledge of them was very different. The differences were developed along with the particular configuration of a new vision of these films, during discussion that immediately following this shared viewing experience and that rendered the most fruitful common reflection. This was not a "film debate," as people do at film clubs, but an attempt to put into play, in relation to each film, the issue that is at the heart of this book, which is: How did the Shoah affect, and how does it continue to affect, the cinema? It was necessary to first ask this question in a formal way at the beginning of these two days of exchange.

The conversation that follows is a compilation of these conversations and debates.

The purpose of such a collective work, which was planned at the onset of the conceptualization of this book, is based on the conviction that on a subject that is as complex as the rapport between the cinema and the Shoah, an exchange of points of view, at times conflicting, should be included in an organization of personal contributions of varying origins. The approaches, the references, the aims are different for each participant, and the format for discussion for each participant was intended to allow the questions to unfold and to reveal what brings together (this is what is essential) and what distinguishes the work of each. The endeavor was fraught with a double risk: the heterogeneity of positions among participants, vis-à-vis the cinema; and the acceptance by all to "allow the films to take us where they will"—which would be at times far adrift from the "subject"—in order that we might explore the

107

echoing systems and suggestions which derive from the story each film tells and its methods of staging, and also from the manner in which each participant, with his own personal emotional baggage, receives it.

J-M.F.

JEAN-MICHEL FRODON: The program of four films that Jacques Mandelbaum and I selected echoes a vaster program that endeavors to nourish reflection upon the cinema and the Shoah.[1] It aims at helping us to reflect together on the manner in which the Shoah affected the cinema, the manner in which the Shoah created or reformulated a whole category of issues, in an explicit, implicit, conscious, or subconscious way in relation to the cinema. The four films are, in chronological order: *To Be or Not to Be* by Ernst Lubitsch (1942), *Night and Fog* by Alain Resnais (1955), *L'Avventura* by Michelangelo Antonioni (1960), and *Drancy Avenir* by Arnaud des Pallières (1997).[2] Three of them have a direct relationship with the historical events in which the Shoah is situated, and the other, *L'Avventura*,[3] is tied to those events in a more circuitous manner, but each film cultivates, in a more or less deliberate manner, a fairly problematic rapport with the Shoah in order to elicit commentary that is in turn more or less intrusive.

JACQUES MANDELBAUM: These four films have to do with a central point of the Shoah: disappearance, or absence. The question that results from this is: How does each one of these films deal with this challenge to an art of representation, how does each one give body to absence? Beyond their intrinsic importance, each film constitutes a form of response, by its very nature. *To Be or Not to Be* is classical fiction; *Night and Fog* is an edited documentary; *L'Avventura* is a fiction that is representative of modern cinema; *Drancy Avenir* asks the question to which genre it belongs: fiction, documentary, essay? These films are good examples of the diversity of ways in which the cinema can attest to, or react to, the event of the Shoah.

SYLVIE LINDEPERG: We should elaborate on what we mean by the "event." Are we really talking about the Shoah? The commentary in *Night and Fog* does not evoke the genocide of the Jews explicitly, and in the case of *To Be or Not to Be*, Lubitsch attaches himself more to the "strange game" of the Resistance within the framework of World War II.

JMF: It seems to me that *To Be or Not to Be* and *Night and Fog* are also in relation to something that is more limited than World War II; that we can see concentric circles within them. What Lanzmann said about the Shoah only designating the obscure center of the event, the interior of the gas chamber, the place where nothing can be seen, must be kept in mind as a horizon point, but that of course does not say everything that needs to be said about the subject, all the more at the moment when Lubitsch was making his film, or when Resnais was making his. I agree with the word *event*, for what it signifies that is troubling: that with this "particular event," what we mean when we use the word *Shoah*, the outlines are blurred and have the vocation to remain in fluctuation, in the form of a question.

ANNETTE WIEVIORKA: We must also reflect on the films in terms of what is called, in literature, their "intertextuality": we make films as simply a product of our time, out of the air of our time, and also based on the cinema, just as we write history based upon what other historians have written, or just as writers write within the framework of literature. In this sense, without saying that the event did not exist, which would be outrageous relativism, we cannot avoid reflection on the manner in which it appears as such in our conscience, how it penetrates, imposes itself, identifies itself and has evolved. In fact the Shoah is in movement, and what is perceived by Lubitsch and his contemporaries is not the same thing as what is perceived by Resnais, who situates himself directly in the representation of the event.

SL: We must no doubt take two temporalities into consideration. The first thing to consider is historical fact, which is the persecution and extermination of the Jews of Europe at work in many of the films contemporary to the war. The second is that of the Shoah's progressive constitution as the particular event working on the historiographical level, on the memory and on mental representations of social imagination and art, a constitution in which Lanzmann's *Shoah* (1985) played a major role. But the genocide of the Jews is already present in the choice of archival footage in *Night and Fog*, in the stages of its writing, even if its auteurs have not yet managed a collective thought process in their differences and in their points of contact including, in terms of images, the "final solution" and the concentration camp system.

JMF: We can elaborate this further: we had deliberately included a film that was made before the war, *The Great Dictator* (1940), in the programming for the sixtieth anniversary of the opening of the Auschwitz camp (see page 6) arranged by the Fondation de la Mémoire de la Shoah. With this film, we broach the question of anticipation: Chaplin's film works on the hypothesis of radical destruction, of identity crisis, and goes as far as extreme dehumanization. We must remain cautious with regard to the power of anticipation in art, but we can retrospectively establish the disturbing emergence of this approach, which would become so easy to spot later on, even if effectively it would take the film *Shoah* to clearly express its framework and demands.

SL: That raises the issue of prophecy in the cinema. Godard attributes this power to it.

JMF: He does so in the name of an idea of the cinema that has nothing to do with the prophetic capacity of a person or an artist but that may be inherent to the process of cinematography. The cinematic process may be capable of warning us that "something" is coming. It is this capacity for the rapport with reality and stories that should have been the bearer of these tidings. So we must understand this notion of "prophecy" as an idea of retrospective light, and not as prophecy per se. *The Great Dictator* is a film that is absolutely of its time, and which attests to how much we knew of what was going on, already then. Chaplin was not the most sophisticated thinker or theoretician of his time, but he was someone who dared to express a sensitivity to things which were evident at that moment in history.

ARNAUD DESPLECHIN: Very early on, the cinema was aware of the Shoah, even though the awareness may have been very awkward. To make the film *Shoah*, which played such a particular and decisive role in the construction of our rapport to the event itself, it took a great deal of time: first of all, the time between the extermination itself and the emergence of the desire to make this film, to be able to think of it as such; and then the time to effectively make the film. The perception of an attempt against the living and against leaving any trace of it, including in the future (when the Nazis, knowing full well they had lost the war, made absurd efforts to erase all trace and any future trace of what they'd done), is constituted in this double time lapse. We see it again much later with the Rwanda massacres, for which there were images. But nonetheless this event has remained invisible.

AW: We must come back to the issue of understanding how representational art faces the subject of disappearance, how invisibility is defined—a question which is posed also in museography. For example: how to represent and eventually monumentalize the extermination, the suppression of millions of human beings. The word *Shoah* allows us to elaborate a number of specific historical phenomena. For some, the Shoah is the persecution of the Jews and their destruction by the Nazis, from 1933 to 1945. Ghettoization is part of this historical period. But with regard to the cinema, the ghettos pose other questions. They were photographed or filmed, notably for the needs of Nazi propaganda. The cinema as representational art is faced with a great number of questions, including that of disappearance—for which Lanzmann's film is an example—but disappearance is not the only question. Does Lubitsch, for example, pose the question of disappearance? Personally, I doubt it.

JM: It is clear that when it came time to make his film in 1941, Lubitsch did not formulate the question in those terms. But we can imagine how, faced with the Nazi horror, an artist could have premonitions about something. And it just so happens that in the work of Lubitsch there are bodies that disappear, disappearances that are negated, and appearances that are trafficked in direct relation to death. The classicism of the film, because of its period and the framework of its production, imposed certain limits on it; for example, the executioners and the victims appear on the same terrain, as if they belonged to the same world, which would not be the case later on.

JMF: *Night and Fog* belongs to the same period as *To Be or Not to Be*, in the sense that Resnais made a film about an atrocious event which took place ten years before, using rules that came before this event and that don't seem to have been challenged at that point in time, with voiceovers, music, etc. The film is in a cinematic vocabulary that does not immediately take into consideration the formal ruptures which are called upon or questioned by such an event. In the same way, *To Be or Not to Be* is very disturbing because it is of classical form. When it was released, people did not understand it all, it was a complicated film, and all the more disturbing because it had recourse to comedy.

SL: In the case of *Night and Fog*, Alain Resnais situates himself on a narrow threshold. He does his best to sidestep the tall order, a very classical one, that he has taken on. By confronting the various objects of what is visible, he holds the commemorative logic of his commissioners at a distance. He particularly invents a form that is distinct from the historical documentary matrix, such as it was defined in the fifties. Far from the prevailing certitudes that were held over our heads then, far from the images brandished as proof, *Night and Fog* proposes a critical distancing of the image and the verb. The making of this film emerges as an attempt to outmaneuver the false evidence of the classically edited documentary.

JM: There is nonetheless a great divide between Lubitsch and Resnais, for the latter of whom the event had already taken place. Moreover, when it came time for him to make his film, Resnais was under a great deal of pressure, between the commission he had received and what he actually wanted to do. So he decided to divert this commission. The importance of the film consists to a large extent in overlapping the past location of the extermination and the current location, now become an ordinary, normal place, in order to reveal that what seems to be a "normal" landscape is actually haunted.

SL: Resnais was also very influenced by the work done by ex-deportee Jean Cayrol, who combined the refusal to provide testimony with the desire to demonstrate that modern art and literature are inhabited, innervated by what he calls the "concentrationate." This is the sense of his reflection on the "lazarean Romanesque" which does not explicitly evoke the concentration camp system but, according to Cayrol, bears the stigma of it: floating and elusive people, the theme of disappearance, deconstruction of classical storytelling, etc. The *Night and Fog* project extends this reflection. It is haunted by the conscience of a universe contaminated by evil. It attests to the concern of its auteurs regarding the advent of new executioners. With Resnais' film, we are witness to the maturation of a redefining of this event.[4]

MARIE-JOSÉ MONDZAIN: This issue brings us to another area: How did the cinema participate in the construction of a definition of this history, in its memorization, and then in the handling of this memory? Whereas the initial question was: How was the cinema affected from within by the Shoah? How is it inhabited, haunted, modified by this history including in the films where it doesn't seem to deal with this history? Now we are asking what the Shoah owes to the cinema for its very transmission. In what way is the cinema a machine that captures such symptoms? And how does it go from a symptom of the autopsy of history, to the grave of the bodies that it leaves in its wake, to critical and anticipatory vigilance?

In one manner or another, the cinema has always been a ghost-making machine. How is what happened with Nazism, and in particular with the Shoah, touched in detail by this art of ghosts? The rapport with ghosts has changed. For example, in the film *I Accuse* (1919) by Abel Gance, things are still pretty "heated" and the dead are still warm. It is a matter of raising the dead, to have them say something about history. In 1937, another version of the same film: this is no longer an autopsy; the ghosts have been summoned to warn us of what may happen. Then, the European and worldwide ordeal of the Shoah questions the cinema, rearranges the summoning of ghosts. The issue then becomes: How can we remake a film when the people are no longer alive, bearing in mind that the ghosts are no longer just dead but bodies that have been voluntarily erased—which was not the case for the dead of World War I, in spite of the horror of that war. The cinema found itself challenged by its industry no longer just to speak of ghosts but to represent disappearance resulting from an intent to erase. This would later be dealt with in a very direct and powerful manner by the Cambodian filmmaker Rithy Panh with his film *S-21* (2003).[5] It is about not just horror but also the enigma of the enormous gap that results from this intentional erasing.

JM: The specificity of the event is that this disappearance affects the dead who are not cadavers. This is the sense of the word *disappearance*; there is no more body. What do you do with disappearance when there is no body? That is the essence of this issue.

MJM: For both Lubitsch and Chaplin, for whom we can do a symptomatic reading, something has been announced, in a very particular manner, about the intention to make disappear, although the effective disappearance is not yet known in general.

AW: But couldn't we have the same discussion if we were talking about literature? Why just the cinema? Aren't literature, museography, and history faced with the issue of storytelling and with the fact that one can write a great deal about life in the ghetto, because there is life, a temporality, and therefore the possibility of telling about it? Whereas the putting to death by mobile killing groups or by gas chambers is something we don't know how to handle. There is certainly a period before the fact, but mass killing is not representable. What is different in treating this question for the cinema?

MJM: The rapport with the image is a determining factor. The cinema is a hallucinatory industry that makes us believe what it presents to us, which is not the case in literature. Because the cinema has hallucinatory power over us, it is responsible for the way it represents what has disappeared.

JMF: Yes. But first, the cinema has one thing in particular: it records real bodies that are present, and the entire industry and means of expression are based upon the idea that there is something real and present before the camera. From that basis, the question of disappearance, of the erased body, is posed in terms that are completely different—not only from what is played out in literature but also in other types of figurative art, particularly painting. It is not artistic privilege but something that is specific to the cinema.

MJM: Speaking of literature and the cinema, and in relation to her collaboration with Alain Resnais on one of the great modern films, *Hiroshima mon amour* (1959), which also had a basis in disappearance—the rapport with the event itself ("*You saw nothing . . .*"), the construction of memory, and the experience of the present—it is interesting to evoke the situation of Marguerite Duras. It is she who, throughout her body of work and in her literary writing, has brought together and worked separately on a voice emanating from both cinematography and the so-called literary. She has annoyed and enthused readers because she has always placed the voices of ghosts in her texts. In the cinema she has found the possibility of introducing the voices of the dead. She has managed to make use of the offscreen voice and, while she is not alone in doing so, has made the specificity of that voice seem very alive. Godard's use of the offscreen voice is more connected to the thought of what is invisible than to the scene of the disappearance. What do we mean by offscreen voices? How do we give voice to those who have disappeared? What voice do we use to make their disappearance heard? This question of offscreen voices constitutes part of the framework of the film *Drancy Avenir*.

JMF: The critical rapport with the voice is already very present in *The Great Dictator*, the film that was Chaplin's passage to the talkies (as if he could not make this type of film without the use of the voice).

JM: Insofar as reality itself acquires a ghostly character, can it include ghosts? What about fear in the cinema?

MJM: It is the mechanism of the cinema itself that is haunted.

JMF: Does this have to do with a guilty conscience? Historically, there is an initial stage in which people are assassinated. And then comes the next stage, in which there is the denial of having killed anyone at all. A specific rapport to the bodies, to the ghosts, is created, and the ghosts are different from the ones who come to greet the voyager who has crossed the bridge in the beginning of Murnau's film *Nosferatu* (1922).

MJM: The guilty conscience is part of what we could call "dread," just as the intent to erase is related to ghosts. And we are inhabited by the question of the invisible survival of this intent to erase, which is everywhere in society. It is a hypothesis than can be shocking, but I believe that the historical proof of Nazism and the Shoah has favored the removal of censorship regarding cruelty, a fantastic liberation of the desire to kill. There is a perverse climactic effect. From this intent to erase, the cinema (and literature as well) has recorded this climax. The cinema has become a cruel machine. Sadistic climax places a subject in the position of being the master of the desire and pleasure of another person. We understand Lanzmann's reaction to films that play upon this climax, and the idea that one can place oneself in a sadistic position when making a film is unacceptable to him. He has a very violent reaction in denouncing the idea that showing such things can be fulfilling.

JMF: This is also what Jacques Rivette reviled in his critique of *Kapò*'s tracking shot.

SL: The notion of disappearance without any trace was not perceived in France in 1945. On the contrary, as testimony to and proof of what took place in the Nazi camps, edited documentaries and the filmed press brandished (to saturation) the bodies of the dead and the survivors. And we are back to defining the cinema: the recording of real bodies. In these first edited scenes, the mass graves and the *danse macabre* do not enable us in any way to consider the disappearance of the bodies and the erasing of all trace of them, which today constitutes a certain definition of the Jewish genocide. Specifically, the 1945 French newsreels do not talk at all about the destruction of the Jews of Europe. They show us the images of the liberation of the concentration camps of the West, to denounce the crimes committed by the Germans in what was then known as the "death camps" or the "Nazi penal colonies." But the impact of these first revelations through imagery was such that it contributed later to producing a screening effect: at the end of the seventies, at the moment when the "Final Solution" began to impose itself and be prevalent in the social memory of the deportation, the scenes of the mass graves would serve to evoke the genocide of the Jews. The images of the emaciated bodies, taken out of context, would be substituted for the absent images, those of the Jewish victims who were gassed immediately upon arrival in the death camps and whose bodies immediately were turned to smoke and ashes. From that point of view, how can we not ask the question of what the cinema allows us to see in this glimpse of the singular nature of this event by offering us filmed answers?

JMF: The most important thing in this approach should be not so much the gas chamber as the crematorium, a second crime exponential to the first, inasmuch as it destroys any trace after having killed and destroys the idea that "*they*" even existed. The Final Solution program is double, it is an extermination program and it is the extermination of all trace. The cinema is particularly concerned since it is in fact the art of the trace.

JM: A crime without trace is something that wants to be the equivalent of a crime that never took place. We cannot help being struck by the film *To Be or Not to Be* which takes place before anyone knew about the gas chambers or the crematoria, but which shows Resistance members killing a Nazi spy and replacing him with an actor playing his role, who says, "No, the crime did not take place." And we can wonder whether, even before the event itself, people more "equipped" than others, more able to comprehend the things that are implied in a speech, were able to anticipate, to hear, to understand. Which brings us to the question of symptom: the cinema become symptom.

AW: The intent to erase is part of us, as individuals. When it becomes something that inhabits society as a whole, it brings about a different type of reflection, another concern. This process of denial goes through an organized triple erasure: the murder of the person, the disappearance of the material traces that are the body itself and the tools used for the crime, and then the erasing of the name. We've often seen state crimes on a grand scale drowned in the act of organized forgetting. The particularity of this event is based on the fact that a state would make a structural objective of this intention to forget, and that it is a question not of destroying one's enemies but of destroying an entire people as such, the Jews, a people that hold a founding place in Western culture, so often qualified as Judeo-Christian culture.

MJM: The cinema holds a place in a long history of images, in the history of the Western world and its relationship to images. The figuration of hatred, of death, of the enemy, in the cinema has been the object of fairly detailed reflection, including what Jean-Michel called mechanical redemption.[6] The cinema bears a "redemptive" function, so to speak (without giving this word a theological significance). The image has been connected to the recognition of the other as other; therefore it is inseparable from a history of the relationship to otherness. This is what the cinema displays fully: on a screen, the worst enemy is no longer deprived of his humanity. From the moment we have images, we enter into a relationship of otherness, of humanity, with that which has become images. This is what we can call the "redemptive function of the cinema." And precisely because we are speaking of image it is very important to say that we are talking about the Jews. In those years, the figuration of the Jew in the cinema very quickly became an issue. For the Jew to become the ghost twice erased is not accidental in a Christian history haunted by deicide. The Christian world has always been haunted by the Jews and now it has gotten rid of its ghost. The cinema also has to do with this history of the Jew as ghostly member of the Christian world. When it amputates itself of this ghost, it cannot avoid feeling the presence and the pain of it forever.

JMF: It is in the nature of the cinema to show "something other." In being situated historically and symbolically in a place that speaks of both sameness and otherness in the Western world, the Jews become automatically both the stakes and the markers of this issue. This dimension is very clearly described in the book by Michael Rogin, which reveals this construction: in relationship to the dominant social norm, Christian and white, the place of this "other" radical entity—who are the African Americans in the United States—is occupied by the Jews, the official and made-up players who represented African Americans in early (1900s to the 1940s) American cinema.[7]

After Having Watched *To Be or Not to Be*

SYLVIE LINDEPERG: We should remember that this film was not at all well received when it was released. The choice of making it a comedy was criticized harshly, especially since when it came out its star, Carole Lombard, had just been killed in a plane crash while she was on tour to promote American military involvement in the war. In addition to that, some critics couldn't wait to point out that Lubitsch was a German and criticized him sharply for making a mockery of Polish suffering.

ANNETTE WIEVIORKA: It is intriguing that the two major films that came out before the war, *The Great Dictator* and *To Be or Not to Be*, both have to do with a play between what is true and what is false, that goes as far as questioning the reality of Hitler's body. The possibility of showing it, of falsifying it.

MARIE-JOSÉ MONDZAIN: For Lubitsch, the circulation of the body of Hitler takes place between the dupers and the duped, while for Chaplin it is the same body that is used in two implacable instances: the instance of life and the instance of death. In the tension of the paradoxical identity, between the body of the executioner and the body of the victim, Chaplin goes further.

JEAN-MICHEL FRODON: This is true, and yet in *To Be or Not to Be*, the Nazi professor offers Carole Lombard's character the Shylock quote, "We Nazis are also made of flesh and bones, we too are capable of love." From that point of view, Chaplin and Lubitsch say the same thing: these are just human beings. No matter what.

MJM: This film helps us to understand why there was so much criticism against Roberto Benigni's *La Vita è bella* (*Life is Beautiful*) (1997), a film that seems to be inspired by the capacity to fool others in the midst of such suffering. It calls for reflection upon the legitimacy of the mask and the processes of substitution: "All just human beings," yes, but up to what point? Up to what point before falling into sophism: "All just human beings, therefore the victims can be executioners as well"? How far can we go, without offending the memory and without betraying history, and, since in the theatre as in the cinema one is play-acting, how far can we play upon this humanist basis? If the message is "all just humans," then one same body can take on equally the role of victim and of executioner. Are there not rules and limits, even if they are not expressed in the manner in which a film is made?

AW: *To Be or Not to Be* is not a film about the Shoah but a film about resistance, in spite of the scene in which the expression "concentration camps" is repeated. And it is about resistance being a strange game.

JMF: The difference between Lubitsch and Benigni bears to a great extent upon the place assigned to the spectator, who absolutely does not have the same historic references. The impulse of the game depends absolutely on what we know. For Benigni, there was no intention of revealing or teaching something, but a play upon a state of knowledge and collective fantasy.

MJM: The difference between the two films is situated also in the status of belief and trickery. In *La Vita è bella*, the person who is masked is fooling his child. What place is made for the belief of the spectator, in what he is being shown? Whereas in *To Be or Not to Be*, the person who is being fooled is the Nazi, and there is no doubt for the spectator about what place is given to his belief.

AW: But the "message" of the film is that the Polish resistance is alive and well. If we removed the "concentration camps" scene, would we be asking these questions?

JMF: Yes, without a doubt. What is at stake is neither factual transmission nor "message."

JACQUES MANDELBAUM: Lubitsch made a film, a comedy, of Walter Benjamin's thesis on the rivalry of art and politics as systems of representation. *To Be or Not to Be* is entirely composed of mirror effects between the actors and the Nazis. It is also a film about delusions of grandeur, in its trivial version and in its tragic version.

There is the capacity for both (actors and Nazis) to make a travesty of reality.

JMF: The film reveals a concern that brings us back to Benjamin's thought on the aestheticization of politics as catastrophe, a reflection which was inspired by "the setting of the Nazi stage."

AW: We should think of other films based on other systems of oppression: dictatorships, terror; because all of this is not just about the Shoah. Making a travesty of reality is about totalitarianism in general, not just the Shoah.

JM: Of course, but it is remarkable that this should appear in the cinema, with such force, and at that precise moment. And regarding setting the stage for the rivalry between art and politics, the film (like Chaplin's film) is exemplary. *To Be or Not to Be* pushes the versatility of appearances to a great extent, and precedes by very little the reality in which the Nazis would make extreme use of dissimulation.

AW: But the versatility of appearances was not originated by the Nazis in relation to other political regimes, and is characteristic neither of Nazism nor of the Shoah.

SL: We can think of this in terms of photographic and filmed images. Before the mass extermination took place in the death camps, the Nazis abundantly photographed and filmed the steps they took in the persecution of the Jews: the humiliations, the destruction of their belongings, the arrests, the sporadic executions, and the ghetto. In addition, the practice of photography was well developed in the concentration camps as early as 1933 and some photographs, notably of Dachau, were published by the Nazi press. These images, taken in great number, even if they were shown with parsimony, are a radical contrast to the secret politics, to the absolute proscription of photography in the death camps.

JMF: We are in agreement that all exertion of power, and in particular that of a dictatorial power, has recourse to the arms of dissimulation, of travesty, of erasure. The cinema was made aware of this in 1940, including what played out between actual news and fiction. Is it because we know what we know that the film takes on its power? What more does this film contain than a theatrical bedroom farce, with a mechanism drawn exactly from popular theatre? Instead of the cuckolded husband, we have Hitler. Lubitsch puts his filmmaker's virtuosity in the service of a game that suddenly implicates no longer just the lovers who can't connect or the married couple with things to hide but the assassins and the victims of a historical tragedy.

MJM: We should make the distinction between historical representation within the filmmaker's limits of operation, the politico-historical dimension, and the political operation of the cinema. For as a historical representation, many things are left unsaid here. Whereas if this film was a political operation, then it still remains one, it places us as spectators in a political situation, because there is the question of masks, of ruse, of the versatility of appearances.

AW: *To Be or Not to Be* explicitly mentions a date, that of December 17, 1941, which is exactly the moment when Lanzmann has *Shoah* beginning. Consciously or not, the Jewish issue is at work here, as shown by the triple repetition of the Shylock declamation. And yet, I don't see a tragic dimension to it. In the Nazism portrayed as taking place before the beginning of the Shoah, before the war (and before there was knowledge of the real facts of the extermination), the German Jews, Klemperer for example, display a feeling of absolute aporia, a feeling that there is no end in sight. Whereas this film takes us from one issue to another, and for this reason there is no tragedy in it, and not just because it is a comedy.

JM: It is in fact presented as a farce. The equivalence suggested between the two worlds, that of the actors and that of the Nazis, is constituted as the tragic point, because of the concern that it can provoke.

JMF: Lubitsch is extremely dark. *To Be or Not to Be* is an unsettling film, constantly moving. In this way, he breaks with the typical resistance film that develops the vision of a project that places one side against the other. Hence the rejection of the film when it came out. The film deviates from its essential reference points, those constructions of meaning that structure our relationship to the world around us—to the point of certain aporias in the script, which are difficult to consider as Lubitsch's mistakes, given that he's a master of his craft: Why do the husband and then the wife, having succeeded in escaping the *Kommandatur*, return? Why do they make a parachute jump over England instead of landing the plane? There are forces more complicated than the apparent dramatic mechanism at work here. He gives it an "absurd" dimension in the strongest sense of the word. It is not a question of reestablishing the eventual logic, but of noting the jolts that the film gives the viewers, the spaces that it produces of uncertainty of all kinds.

SL: Throughout the film, there is the question of what creates the "little" gap between the actor and Hitler, in terms of representation. What is the nature of this difference that seems so tiny and is nonetheless so essential? The little mustache, which he doesn't yet have, and that he will add as an accessory in the vestibule of the theatre? Or the strength of the image based on the effect of belief, as in the first scene in which the director tells the actor that he doesn't resemble Hitler by showing him a poster of the Führer? To which the actor answers that the person in that poster is none other than himself.

MJM: In that sense, Shakespeare is put to good use, not in the metaphysical sense that is most often attributed to Hamlet's monologue but in the sense of politics and burlesque: To be or not to be Hitler? To be or not to be Tura? On what stage do we exist, and how do we exist there?

AW: Which brings us back to the identity crisis, which I think comes from modern times and not the Shoah.

MJM: Talking about a film in which the theatre is the first impulse, we should avoid using the word *tragic* in an approximate manner. In the world of theatre, tragedy belongs to a system of storytelling that is very specific, that of the fable. If it is Shakespeare we choose here, and not Sophocles, it is because Shakespearean theatre is at work on the stage of history with the participation of the spectators, with the people, and therefore it constitutes the first form of deliberately political theatre. This theatre can say and depict "cruel" things, "ferocious" things, but they are not treated as tragedy because it is the human gesture that is at the center, in a world that is not governed by gods.

AW: And we are shown men who have a hand in destiny, whereas what is proper to Nazism is to deprive men of all capability of initiative.

JM: In this film, all the characters can aspire to be other than what they are (to be or not to be), except the Jewish character, who only aspires to become Shylock, in other words himself. And he will manage to do so. The Jew is therefore the one who cannot break character, who is the prisoner.

MJM: And there is one more character, both symmetrical and opposite to him: the female character. In *To Be or Not to Be*, the situation of the woman is very disturbing: she is the only one who wears no disguise, while always remaining within the game. And this woman's body is at play from beginning to end. She is always the object of seduction, and she uses that to fool everyone, all the time. While remaining what she is, she can be everywhere, without disguise, and very freely. The film is not at all misogynous, but it does say something about the power of seduction, of desire, and about what the body of the woman can be in society and in the cinema: women are naturally disguised.

After Having Watched *L'Avventura*

JEAN-MICHEL FRODON: Why Antonioni's film? *L'Avventura* is one of the great works of the modern era of cinema. And it is a film in which the disappearance of a body, its erasure, is at work. What is the world when someone around whom it was built is subtracted? The entire film is deprived of this young woman, Anna, for a reason that is never divulged to us. And this world is inhabited, in a manner that is not psychologized, not historicized, not dramatized, by someone who has disappeared. This is a work of symbolism, an artistic transcription of the event of a disappearance, accompanied by the disappearance of any trace—an event that is not referred to here as the period of war—in order to make us feel how much the absent person is missed forever. Through the means of cinematography, and not through discourse, we experience this disappearance. And the feeling it creates, its strangeness, its mystery, is not assignable to a chain of events or cause and effect. Beneath any explanation, it is the black hole of her absence that inhabits the world.

ARNAUD DESPLECHIN: The beauty, and at the same time for me the limit, is that we cannot cry for *L'Avventura*, we cannot identify with it. It differs from *Je t'aime je t'aime* (1968) by Alain Resnais, for example, in which the fragments of reminiscence of the camps are at work from within, in relation to emotion.

JACQUES MANDELBAUM: Still following this idea of the body that disappears, what is interesting with Antonioni is what is artificial. What does this event do, what does it provoke, or cause, in the economy of a film? If we compare it to *To Be or Not to Be*, we observe two opposite movements. For Lubitsch, the disappearance of the body produces more people, in other words the film is even more inhabited, more full, and the characters share the same world. For Antonioni, on the contrary, we experience fewer people. Once the body has disappeared, we have the impression that the survivors no longer live in the same world. There is no "collective": each person who searches for Anna searches alone. Even when there are several people in one shot, they are placed in such a manner that they do not share the same space; some are seen from behind, some frontally, but never together.

MARIE-JOSÉ MONDZAIN: One scene, when they are searching for Anna on the island, seems very significant: they find an antique relic, which falls from their hands, shatters, and the debris falls into a crevasse. This is a strong indication of an archeological, archaic apparition, of something that has to do with the vestiges of memory that shatter and, when they disappear, create an emotion, a violent sensation.

AD: The film was released in 1960, after the destruction of Europe's Jews, and at the moment of the reconstruction of this event. It is a period during which it is therefore logical for attempts at symbolization of the "event without witnesses" to emerge. Instead of something being transmitted, it is metaphorized, which is to say it fades in transmission. *L'Avventura* seems to me to be a metaphor for an absolute lack of conscience, for loss, for collapse, for absence. Antonioni films some of the same premises of Lanzmann's film, in particular the metaphor of the shattered amphora. And at the same time, Antonioni had not read the work of Primo Levi at that time, even though it was available in Italy.

MJM: But it isn't just a film about loss and collapse, since it ends with a very important moment, which we could consider "positive," that redefines the film itself. The device of the film is not only based upon collapse: the relationship between Sandro and Monica Vitti is nourished by the disappearance; the couple is nourished by

this death and cannot escape the eroticization of this disappearance. Besides, she says it herself: "One moment I was searching
for her, and now I would like her to be dead." Because of this
eroticization of the relationship to the disappearance of the other
person, which leans toward erasure, the relationship falls into an
impasse: what renders their desire possible is the disappearance of
the woman they want to have reappear. The man and woman find
themselves in solitude and suffering that are totally distinct: she
with identification and rivalry, he with repetition and guilt. Only
the final moment—when she places her hand on the man's head
and cries—puts something of an end to their desire as a desire for
death: she approaches him but it is not erotically.

AD: What is striking in *Shoah* is the desert, with all those who
are absent. It is the silence. From this point of view, consider the
impossibility of transference or acceptance even when knowledge
is there. We witnessed this during the Rwanda genocide. A historic
event happens, for which we have all the elements to know that it
is happening, and either people don't discuss it or they're lying to
each other or to themselves. What results is the impoverishment
of language, the impoverishment of the world, which *L'Avventura*
depicts very well—the fact that people can no longer speak to each
other, about anything. The entire film becomes an enigma, and the
characters themselves are captive.

JM: From the beginning of the film, we observe the disqualification
of politics characterized as the art of lying: the father, a diplomat,
says to his daughter, "I've been lying all my life, but today I'll tell
you the truth. He will never marry you."

JMF: And right after that she says, "It's unbearable to be apart;
it's unbearable to be together," and we are already in this situation
which keeps closing in upon itself. We are already in an unlivable
situation, even before Anna vanishes completely.

AD: For thirty years, we did not utter the name of those who
were missing in Europe: the Jews. We can also pose the question
differently: *How* was it said? Repression and absence were at work
in history. The stories . . . the media speaking of other things. And
we should also ask *for whom* this question was missed.

MJM: Anna is not the repressed person in the film. A ghost is not
repressed. On the contrary, she is always present. The characters

are haunted by the presence of this absent person, and they can't conceal it.

JMF: This film, which at the time was not considered an experimental or marginal film, and which was a relatively costly production, is entirely constructed upon the disappearance without reappearance, barely a third of the way through the film, of the main character, and this disappearance is never explained. In doing some artistic research we can find antecedents with Beckett or Ionesco, but this is an event without precedent in the dramatic art of the cinema. At a time when Jean-Luc Godard's editing style was introducing the radical use of jump cuts, in this film we see a major jump cut in that the heroine completely disappears in a splice.

MJM: What is eroticized here, and what is erotic, is the profound uncertainty about the nature of this disappearance: it is impossible to grieve because we don't know if she is alive or dead. The invisibility of what has disappeared awaits its mediation in the visible to enable us to live without the "missing person."

JM: What is terrifying is the necessity of this absence for the other characters. It's as if they needed this to happen.

AD: It is also disturbing in the beginning, when we get the feeling that Anna is sleeping with Sandro only because her girlfriend is waiting for her outside: via the playing of curtains, half open and half closed, from which it is impossible to know how much they dissimulate. And then in the boat, when the two girls are changing and Anna hands over her clothes—in other words transfers her costume, her role as an actress.

After Having Watched *Night and Fog*

JEAN-MICHEL FRODON: *Night and Fog* has a dual role. It is the principal film through which a problematic and powerful rapport was disseminated regarding the history of the "camps," while at the same time, seen retrospectively, it was the key marker of the unspoken, or a limit of what the cinema would do with this history until the time when, with *Shoah*, another way of recounting history would be constructed, and another way of making films in relation to the Shoah would take place. This film has not aged, but it is dated. Today there is another means of speaking of this, largely founded by Lanzmann: the constant questioning and revisiting through the use of words, sounds, and images. And we can really feel that *Night and Fog* is anterior to *Shoah*.

JACQUES MANDELBAUM: Pro-Lanzmann critics were concerned in particular by his utilization of archival footage, by the illusion the film might give that archives could say everything there is to say about what happened. This is an illusion that Resnais never used and his film attests to that fact. The second criticism often heard denounced a synthetic vision of the crime, a division that says nothing of the specificity of the extermination. The nature of the victims is lumped into a general discourse—meaning he doesn't speak of the Jews as such.

JMF: The film never stops telling us that it is not showing us everything: "We can only show you the outer crust and the color." And it underlines the specificity of the extermination (". . . in 1942 Himmler delegated the productivity problem to others . . .") within the concentration camp phenomenon. He therefore makes a distinction between extermination and concentration. On the other hand, one fact is obviously full of meaning: the enterprise of extermination is not connected, as such, to the Jews. He does not name the victims. To say there is extermination without naming the Jews is not maintaining the hidden and singular nature of this extermination, which was programmed and industrialized. Not directly naming the Jews is also saying, as a general statement: "States are capable of coming to this, and this threat weighs upon all of us."

ARNAUD DESPLECHIN: There is no clear statement, even though the fact that it concerns the Jews is very obvious. The first time I saw the film, I knew that the names were Jewish names, and everyone in the movie theatre knew it, too. When Resnais shows the falsification of accounts, we see the names on the registers and all the surnames are Jewish.

JMF: Yes, but there is a difference between saying it and not saying it. Moreover, there is what we might call a doubt, regarding what we hear, knowing what we know, formulating things the way we formulate them and have been doing so for twenty years. Whereas we could ask, How was this film heard, how was the film received at the time? Let's remember that this film was distributed everywhere and had an enormous effect.

ANNETTE WIEVIORKA: Naming is essential. There are many genocides, Rwanda no doubt being the most recent, although what is
happening in Darfur may put that into question. The Shoah is not
just a genocide among other genocides, not just because of the
uniqueness of the place of Jews in Western society and particularly
vis-à-vis the Germans. The location is very important: these Jews
who are missing are missed because they are our neighbors. And
it is also the question of proximity that makes us able to ask for
justification. Remember, thirty years ago, the question of genocide was asked regarding Biafra; who is asking questions nowadays
about what we did to prevent that? The Biafran people were not
our neighbors.

AD: When Resnais made *Night and Fog*, he had in mind a European
scope, a rebirth of Europe during the period in which the war in
Algeria was taking place. The universal warning contained in the
film is clearly addressing Europeans, and France, about what was
happening in Algeria. We understand, from this point of view, why
he doesn't name the victims.

MARIE-JOSÉ MONDZAIN: *Night and Fog* speaks only of the executioners, not the victims. The offscreen voice talks only about the
executioners, even if the images show us especially the victims. This
voice therefore does not designate what is shown. On the contrary,
it designates what we don't see. The film is constructed in a violent
and paradoxical manner regarding the executioner, without taking his
position. It gives speech not to those it shows, but to what we see
only rarely: a Kapo, an SS soldier. It shows us the face of the executioner, with the architectural, murderous, and ideological construction of his intent to exterminate. The archival footage is therefore
summoned not in order to "show" everything that took place but to
establish a shift in what is being said of the executioner.

AD: *Night and Fog* speaks of what can be transmitted. It is exactly
what we are told by the postscript, which places the film in the
present moment of the time it was filmed. The film is admirable
in saying what must absolutely be transmitted, and in this regard
the absence of nomination does not bother me. But *Shoah* is the
experience of what is not transmitted.

JM: With an intense and novel acuity inscribed in its very form,
Night and Fog deals with the rapport of the past to the present, how

we can be inhabited by the past, how it comes back to haunt us "underneath the grass growing back." It is an admirable lesson in vigilance. However, the lesson would perhaps be more pertinent if what was being said about this past was more detailed, for there is an incoherence between the two parts of the film. The first depicts the reality of the concentration camps and points out the identity of the victims in an indistinct manner: French, Jewish people, people in the Resistance, etc. Then it tells how, after a while, the extermination began, and the spectator, logically, can deduce that all the people in the concentration camps were the subject—or could be the subject—of the process of extermination.

SYLVIE LINDEPERG: This is a film that contains several voices and several projects. The genesis of the film can help us understand its hesitations, its repentance, which result notably from the diversity of personalities involved in the project, the state of history that was still in its infancy—that of the concentration camp system—while at the same moment the face of the resistant deportee was still largely dominant in the collective memory and in testimonies and the official discourse regarding deportation. The commission given to Resnais by the Comité d'Histoire de la Deuxième Guerre Mondiale (WWII Historical Committee) and the associations of ex-resistant deportees was for a film about the concentration camp system. In the initial stages of the film, the Nazi camps were depicted in a generic manner and were envisioned as interchangeable. This does not mean that Resnais and his two historical advisers, Henri Michel and Olga Wormser, disregarded the genocide, as was the case in the newsreels of the postwar period. They brought the "Final Solution" into the screenplay by evoking the turning point of 1942 designated by the visit of Himmler to Auschwitz-Monowitz. But they had a hard time putting the two events together, in articulating them historically and conceptually.

The contract signed by Resnais foresaw him having recourse to three elements: the editing of archival footage, a filmed segment on the location of the deportations, and finally the inclusion of relics, objects from the deportation of which some were collected for the exhibit entitled "Résistance-Libération-Déportation" organized in 1954 by Michel and Wormser. Resnais discovered and filmed others at the Auschwitz Museum and decided to record them in black and white, which led to incorporating them in the editing with the massive amount of archival documents, and assigning them to the stratum of the past. No doubt, for this filmmaker,

who created his own shots, this was a manner of holding the commemorative logic and the museum concept of his commissioners at
a distance. In this sense the filming in Poland appears as a moment
of clarification that blurs the initial logic of the interchangeability
of the camps. He displaced the center of gravity of the film to
Auschwitz-Birkenau, which gained a centrality not initially planned
in the project.

It is also in Poland, in the Warsaw ghetto and camp museums,
that Resnais pursued his research of iconography and innovated by
selecting archival images that had a rapport with the persecution
and extermination of the Jews: plans and photographs of arrests
and deportations, photographs of murders done by *The Einsatzgruppen*, a chosen portion of a selection of photographs known as the
Auschwitz Album, etc. But the filmmaker found it difficult to articulate all these elements, as we see by the wavering in the scene that
precedes the one in the gas chamber, and yet again at the stages
in the screenplay where there is an explicit reference made to the
"Final Solution," which is not in Cayrol's commentary.

JM: Why did they abandon the version in which the "Final Solution" was mentioned?

SL: It is very possible that it was Cayrol who chose not to use it,
no doubt both because this passage is fairly confusing—because the
poet recounted his own experience as a resistant deportee—and also,
I believe, because he wanted to give the film universal reach.

An "alert system" given to the film by Cayrol and Resnais,
who were both involved in the struggle against colonialism and the
war in Algeria, did not agree well with the consideration of the singular nature of this event. The universal reach of the commentary
allowed it to extend beyond the logic of monument-to-the-dead
and "never again" in order to alert contemporaries to what was
continuing, or beginning to happen again, in other latitudes. In
this sense, *Night and Fog* was a political film and a film of great
concern.

MJM: An important dimension to the film is the absence of silence:
the voice stops at times, but the music is ongoing. And this continuous taking over of the image by the music can be disconcerting.

SL: Resnais held to the principle of a continuous score, with which
he had experimented in previous short films. He liked Hanns Eisler's

concept of film music expressed through a refusal of illustrative clichés, hodgepodge, and redundancy, and preferred the effects of dissonance, space, and asymmetry. The result is disconcerting, in effect, because the music continues to speak even when Cayrol's voice is halted or interrupted.

AD: Throughout Resnais' film there is a narration. So we understand very well why there can be no music in *Shoah*. When the narrator can no longer transmit, nothing happens, or rather, nothing more comes through. Lanzmann shows us what cannot be transmitted, whereas music seeks to ensure that transmission continues. Music helps us to look at things together, to share.

JMF: Resnais has indeed created a work of transmission, and the film accomplished this task. But it is a particular modality of transmission, because there are both full areas and holes, and the film is not about communication. His aporias, his contradictions, his impotence as much as his accomplishments are what create his strength, including the lack of names, which we spoke of earlier.

AW: The historiographical question of articulation between concentration camp and genocide still remains a difficult thing to consider for historians today. In a sense we have two histories, which could have not intersected yet which do intersect. The extermination of the Jews takes place first in situ, with the *Einsatzgruppen*; and then in specific locations, like Belzec. Then the Nazis decide to utilize "ordinary" camps to exterminate them (Auschwitz, Birkenau). At the same time as well, for economic reasons, for reasons of war machinery, they abruptly decide to not exterminate all the Jews but to put some of them into concentration camps. Primo Levi and Robert Antelme do not attest to the genocide but to the "concentrationate."

Lanzmann was the only person to attempt to deal with the death machines from which no one returned. And this created problems, because it is death itself which he attests to—the place from which one cannot return. Suffice to say there are no witnesses to the gas chambers, and it is based on this fact that Lanzmann acknowledged the impossibility of transmission, which passes through a negation of time. In *Night and Fog*, time is very marked, the time that separates us from the event (by alternating between color and black and white), and he presents us with a time that opens upon the future. Lanzmann, like Klarsfeld, tells us that this event is not part of the past. When we watch *Shoah*, we never leave—we are prevented from leaving—this event. And at the Papon trials, we saw people brandishing portraits of children, who obviously would never age. This confirms that time has no bearing on this event, that there is no past, because *that* does not pass. The only transmission possible for Lanzmann is to lock us into *that*.

AD: As a spectator, this is what I am infinitely grateful to Lanzmann for. He transmitted this aporia to me. Because at the same time, this aporia, this doubt, is an encounter.

MJM: There are things that Lanzmann wants to accomplish, described by Annette. And in the body of his work there is what escapes completion, because we are talking about images. When dealing with a great filmmaker like Lanzmann, this implies that he accepts not being able to control everything, so that as spectators we remain absolutely free before *Shoah* to judge and ask ourselves about the future (as is the case with *Night and Fog*). What do we do with this now? Transmission serves the future, not the past.

AW: I am ready to recognize that historians—particularly myself— have a tendency to favor, no doubt excessively, what a film sets out to do, what it states as its intent. No doubt a film speaks more, including in contradiction, than this "objective" approach leads us to believe. I say this all the more willingly since I'm aware that I also write history while being affected by generational factors.

MJM: In spite of all that separates these two films, the same question is posed by both, and I am drawing from Laurie Laufer's book:[8] What do the dead want from me? Do they want me to live by separating myself from them, or do they want to keep me with them?

JM: We recognize, in the witnesses and artists who speak of the event, a relatively large proportion of negativity. We could almost compare Resnais to Primo Levi, and Lanzmann to Jean Améry. On one side, they seem to want to make this event something that is transmissible and oriented toward life, and on the other they see pure death, of which no one can make anything. This issue met with a number of important developments, such as the idea that in order to connect we can have recourse only to positivity: we end up with Spielberg and Benigni. In spite of everything, the paradoxical approach that Lanzmann's transmission was able to take is practically submerged by this requirement of positivity.

AW: In *Shoah*, there is at least one moment that opens a "third" space, in which the spectator finds his place, and that is Karsky's story.[9] It is the passage that I used for my students when I was teaching high school.

AD: The direction of the Karsky scenes is a very precise work, with one voyage in which we see him unable to take his assigned place on the couch and a second in which he is at a loss for words. It is clear that the failure of his mission, and the horrible weight that he carries afterward—in having been unable to prevent the murder of millions of people when he had the actual proof—erode his capability of staying in the film from within. And this horrible breakdown is also what affects the narrator of the film, its director. The film stages the acceptance of transmitting the fact that there is nothing to transmit. The breakdown of the narrator who puts himself in a position of failure (characteristic of Lanzmann's film) and who is "smoothed over" by the return to positivity in the films of Spielberg and Benigni which Jacques mentioned, also had an effect on the cinema. I'm thinking of two films that I would qualify as "Lanzmannian," not in the sense of influence but in the sharing of ethics. They are *Palombella rossa* (1989) by Nanni Moretti, in which the director invalidates himself through comic effects that ridicule him, and *Letter for L* (1994) by Romain Goupil, in which he takes a trip which he has already taken before, saying: I have to return, I didn't see enough the first time around.

And another reaction I had in seeing *Night and Fog* again: I was struck by the intact violence of the images, and at the same time the complete dignity of the way they were used. It is surprising to see how obscene the images in *La Vita è bella* are and how those of Resnais, nonetheless much more exposed to this risk, are not. One sees a comparable paradox in museums, where I often find the figurative approach obscene, in particular Boltanski, whom I consider unbearably kitsch.

SL: The comparison to museums is interesting because it was part of the *Night and Fog* project, in that commission Resnais did everything to get out of. His rejection of the reliquary dimension of the

Auschwitz Museum is not without emotion, as shown in the scene he filmed about the women's hair, which led him to create that heartbreaking caress, the displaced gesture.

MJM: The work of contemporary artists in museums is not comparable to the Auschwitz Museum and what is exhibited there.

AD: No, but in Resnais' film when, in the scene following the one about the women's hair, we see the big covers, we are reminded without reticence of the work of Joseph Beuys, and he is never obscene.

A Return to the Principal Theme

MARIE-JOSÉ MONDZAIN: We've discussed *Night and Fog* but we don't seem able to avoid mentioning *Shoah*. Is the question we asked at the beginning—the effects of the Shoah upon the cinema—not also encompassed, by definition, within the question of the effects of films that are fundamentally about this particular history? When we see contemporary films like *Tracks* (1999) by Emmanuel Finkiel or *S-21* by Rithy Panh, we are reminded of Resnais and Lanzmann. We clearly see, in Rithy Panh's work, that the heritage of the Shoah and the cinematic thought on the subject has affected his cinema. These effects are all the more interesting for us because he is not a Westerner, he is nourished by another culture, he has another type of relationship to image, death, and memory.

JACQUES MANDELBAUM: We find directorial techniques in his work that are indebted to both Resnais and Lanzmann. Rithy Panh operates in space whereas Resnais operates in time. On Cambodian soil we see the fusion of past and present play out, and it is the people themselves who are the vestiges of the places where the horror took place. The place becomes the body of executioners, the erased traces of the horror: erased but not nonexistent. He condenses in space the two strata that alternate in *Night and Fog*. And, as in *Shoah*, the gestures of horror must be replayed in order to express this.

JEAN-MICHEL FRODON: With Rithy Panh, the traces are the executioner's very body. The body of the executioner and his troubled, haunted spirit, evoked in the beginning of the film, are the place where the horror took place, as it is remembered in the present.

To replay it is like returning to that place to say: "This is the place." The place becomes the executioner's act, to which is added the supplementary device introduced by the paintings: images that are not recorded images, that are not traces but reconstructions which, in their turn, reconstruct something else as well. When photography is the instrument of oppression, painting becomes the instrument of truth, which sets in motion the capacity to designate the scene of the crime where it actually happened, in the gesture turned upon oneself.

JM: And yet, we find it hard to comprehend the taboo that they are trying to break by making these gestures. In Cambodia, the unsaid is so much more powerful on this subject; these gestures are endowed with a dimension that shatters silence, in a completely new way.

JMF: But this is about another dimension. If this film manages to affect us, the European spectators, it is not because we know something about Cambodia. The ordinary spectator knows nothing about the state of mind of today's Cambodians. In any case, the essential thing at stake in this question was not how to make films in relation to a genocide, but how to make cinema.

MJM: The question is that of the hallucinatory power of the cinema. In *S-21*, this question is embraced by the filmmaker, literally, since the body of the executioner creates a hallucination of the victim. It is the suffering of the executioner that brings back the hallucinated presence of the victim. Then there are the traces, the documents, the notebooks, and the photographs. But the main dimension comes from the Cambodian belief that those who die in chaotic and barbaric conditions, far from all ritual, social, or affective engagement, become "wandering souls" who haunt the bodies of all the living, and in particular the bodies of their executioners. The gesture of cinematography rewinds time in the direction of life. In *L'Avventura*, on the contrary, as long as nothing is said or done for time to be rewound, the dead body, or the missing body, also inhabits the bodies of the living in a time that has stood still. Antonioni films the stopping of time. The missing body has frozen the question of desire that we had for it and which must be taken over by the living. The absent Anna implicitly poses the question of the desire we have for her when our desire takes place in a void left by her disappearance. And Sandro transfers his desire from object to object, because the summoning of the dead person remains a failure.

S-21 reworks the rewinding of history through the staging of "ghosts" with particular force. How to live together, share the same earth, when the living—whether executioners or victims—have not worked this problem out?

JM: The films we have watched together here—and this would have been the case as well if we had watched *Drancy Avenir*—all bear this concern regarding the presence of the dead among us, even if in each case it is treated very differently. This relationship with the dead is also a manner of affirming, in the documentary, the need for fiction as a plea for truth.

AW: The question that keeps coming back now is that of living together, inhabiting the world together, in a nontraumatic manner, which is profoundly different from the question of transforming the world for this type of thing to never happen again, which was Alain Resnais' question as well as that of the forties, fifties, sixties, and even the seventies. To this we should add the fullness of the Shoah as a paradigm, which brings us to see other genocides only through its parameters. We have effected a reversal: we are no longer in a voluntary movement of comprehension and knowing but in a movement in which narrative forms come from a different event. And this creates a clouding, it creates something identical instead of creating a true historical and cultural comprehension of things that appear simultaneously "identical" and yet are incomparable—since there are invariables in the history of genocides.

AD: The Nazi extermination served as a model to the Hutus, both technically and organizationally. But not only films are paradigms, facts are as well. Furthermore, what constitutes a model is also written in History. No one has ever said that Europeans should have created a reconciliation commission at the end of World War II, in spite of the fact that everyone applauds the fact that Mandela did so in South Africa and that this model has been re-implemented, notably by Kagame in Rwanda.

SL: At this point, watching *S-21*, we could pose the question of whether the cinema can act as an altar.

MJM: If so, it is thanks to the act of being able to display living bodies in hallucinatory situations, in other words to summon the dead: and this is unique to the cinema and does not apply to any other form of art. For Resnais as well as for Lanzmann, this summoning is the object of prodigious reserve. The executioner, the system of murder, the vestiges of cruelty, the witnesses are all summoned here, but there is a certain reserve, like something unresolved, vis-à-vis the victims. This is why films of fiction, for example the "Holocaust" series or *Schindler's List* (1993), can have no bearing upon history or politics. The roles of executioners and victims are not distributed in the same manner. The question of sharing always hits back and remains decisive.

JMF: Once more, it is a matter of the possibility or impossibility of inhabiting the same world. We have seen that what was disturbing in *To Be or Not to Be* is the manner in which Lubitsch makes it possible for the actors and the Nazis to exist in the same world; in that case it is a critique of the Nazis to repute them as belonging onstage, to consider them as theatre, where they will be defeated by the means of theatre. When *Night and Fog* came along, executioners and victims, while they inhabited the same place, did not inhabit it in the same manner. The victims were dead, and any trace of them had been erased. At that point it is the status of fiction that is in place, as a "world" in which we can see victims and executioners cohabitate with impunity, and it will be the moral problem of filmed reconstitutions to pretend to show us a world that does not make the different place of the dead and the living a problem. There is a similar ignorance in the manner in which the Jewish question is not posed; and in the manner of unproblematically "representing" real beings played by actors playing roles. This question is common to all devices of performance. It is formulated by the cinema by the fact of recording real bodies, and pushed to paroxysm when these actors portray the dead of the Shoah, those dead who continue to haunt our history. What *Night and Fog* does is to recoil before this evidence, at the very location of the genocide, when Resnais arrives in Auschwitz. And of course this is also at the heart of Lanzmann's work.

SL: The relationship to the location was decisive in the making of *Night and Fog*. I think Resnais' discovery of Birkenau deeply modified his concept of the film at that point.

JMF: It is because they are artists that Resnais and Lanzmann placed something that creates a tremor and brings us back to what is invisible, between the blades of grass, the piles of gravel, and us, back to those who are there, even though they are dead and without body or grave. For this did not come about just like that. And even when one is aware of these questions—an awareness that neither Spielberg nor Benigni nor Polanski have—it's not enough to go with a camera to a place that is charged with history, where millions of people have been killed, and for their presence to come haunt the screen in a manner that halts us when confronted with this event. The circumstances of the event, the conditions of the process, must be recreated, as Resnais and Lanzmann have done, as Rithy Panh has done for the Cambodian genocide, and as no one, to my knowledge, has done for Rwanda.

AD: The essential thing is not the location itself, in the sense of filming a place that is charged with history, but filming a location in its own spirit, in the name of what makes it specific. This is also what we see very clearly in *West of the Tracks* by Wang Bing (2004),[10] in which the subject was not genocide but again a matter of letting us see what was kept secret when an act took place, what has disappeared as a result.

SL: But the question of time passing also plays a role here. Sometimes, after historical events, an initial story emerges, fairly well articulated, which then disappears before it is discovered. This original story does not manage to settle in, it is subject to an effect of dissolution, parasite additions are thrown in, and it becomes covered with other stories, often the stuff of legend. It takes time, forgetting, interference, for the work of a historian, a work of art, to finally offer a deeper understanding of the event, to make it more intelligible and to modify the way we look at it.

AW: We did not hear the testimony of survivors in the years just after the war. And while some of us read about them, we realized that most of them said the same redundant things and didn't offer much, and that—as hard as it is to admit—the accounts were hard to read because they were so poorly written. And then there was a witness who was capable, in telling exactly the same thing, of giving it form, and that was Primo Levi. Even if it is the view of a period that makes a work of art acceptable. It would be interesting to find out what effect Jean Hatzfeld's book, *Into the Quick of Life*,[11] had in Rwanda, or the effects of *S-21* in Cambodia.

JMF: At what point does the artistic event take form? Hatzfeld's book, a great achievement in writing, is only available to the French at present, and Cambodians haven't yet seen *S-21* (Rithy Panh is trying very hard to change that), nor has *West of the Tracks* been seen by the Chinese.

AD: In Rwanda, what is important is what the Rwandan people are doing themselves, in their country, regarding what is said about the genocide or what is remembered of it. They are making history more quickly because they have a state. Just as the construction of representations of the Shoah, as they exist today, are connected to the creation of the state of Israel, to the existence of a political presence, to an administration.

AW: It is rare for a state to create works of art. When commissions for truth and reconciliation were set up in South Africa, everything was documented on film, but to my knowledge there is no official move regarding the manner of filming. Also, when I took part in the recordings of a number of testimonials by Shoah survivors, the issue of "how to film" them was discussed only in terms of the respect due to the witnesses and the interest of recording these testimonials for the future; what was important was to be as neutral as possible, to preserve them as archives, to keep a trace of them.

JM: True, whereas *Night and Fog*, for example, through its clear choices, gives doubt to confidence, the innocent aspect of representation and recording what is visible. The act of creating art is appropriated and in part deflects from the institutional commission. The black and white parts are laden with emotional intensity, but we are aware that this is insufficient to articulate a thought. And the parts that are in color, that take place in the present, also are clearly limited and impotent. The film is held in the balance between the two. It is this distinct construction that constitutes its particular strength.

MJM: All through the film each spectator makes a journey, thanks to the cinematic choices, thanks to an act of articulation which has as much to do with color as with black and white, thanks to archival footage as well as filming in the present, thanks to the relationship of sound to image, the relationship of text to music, etc. The film was made with great difficulty and yet presents a unity as if worked from within, and through the modern techniques of editing. These techniques have to do with adjusting not the story but the thought process itself to the world and to the desire that it should be seen in order to be understood.

SL: It is because *Night and Fog* is a work made with all its frailties and all its gaps that it has withstood the test of time. And this is also the reason it is under attack today.

AW: Fragility is inherent in art. It makes the criticism of historians, who have an approach that is ultrareductive, strictly positivist, one which doesn't recognize the particular power of another approach of an artistic nature. On the contrary, our approaches, which are different, should speak to each other and support each other. Because it is this frailty that is, in *Night and Fog*, the strength of our resistance to the danger of which the film warns us. This alert calls upon our capacity to be fragile. Lanzmann also designates the place of the spectator as a place in which we are made fragile—through film—and in which we can resist.

MJM: We should distinguish between the words *fragility* and *uncertainty*. Uncertainty is displaced with time, as we accumulate the elements that will eventually construct a story involving form, consistency, and coherence. Fragility has to do with the image itself, and it is what makes it impossible for an image to equal reality, for on its own it is never in charge of the truth. The Shoah ordeal touched upon a point of fragility that concerns humanity itself. We are no longer certain of being human beings, or in any case, we know that our humanity can be undone. It is this fragility that the image takes on. And since it is fragile, the image gives us humanity but also makes us doubt it. And at the same time, it makes us doubt ourselves.

AW: This fragility does not have the same relationship to learning or knowledge with Resnais and with Lanzmann. *Night and Fog* creates knowledge, although the film is full of uncertainty. For at the time there was still no official story, no really constituted historical knowledge upon which Resnais could lean or to which he could be opposed. There was neither one story nor a number of stories. The essential part of this work was done by Raoul Hilberg,[12] when Lanzmann made *Shoah*, in which Hilberg also appears several times. In this film, Lanzmann is not trying to add another layer of knowledge. It is not about collecting more testimonials—besides, most of the escapees seen in *Shoah* have already testified, many during the Eichmann trials—but about making a movie, in other words creating images with a new meaning.

JMF: In *Shoah*, the voice of witnesses is not testimony per se. Their reason for being is not meant to provide information. When Lanzmann says to Abraham Bomba or Philip Mueller: "You must continue to speak, you know that," it is not to get them to reveal hidden information. It is because the work he is doing depends upon the utterance of speech, the fragility in the outpouring of feeling, the point of emotional collapse that this can bring on.

SL: But just as an image is not true in itself, it is also not fragile in itself. We can take away its fragility as soon as we strike it as proof. And one of Resnais' disruptions consists in avoiding the administration of proof. This allows him to change our way of looking at well-known images that were heretofore deprived of their fragility.

JMF: This relationship and access to proof are at the basis of the modern cinema as it was born at that point—and which Italian neorealism, its contemporary, explored with other premises, also rooted in World War II, with similar questions. Godard could not have made *Le Petit soldat* and *Les Carabiniers* (both 1963) if *Night and Fog* had not preceded them. It is not that the film was a model or that it created taboos. It set the horizon lines, in relation to which one could situate oneself in order to do other things.

JM: Whether about death's presence in the world or the rapport between documentary and fiction, the manner of directing one's eye upon the articulation of contradictions would become decisive for the modern cinema.

JMF: Before we interrupt this discussion, I would like to draw your attention to one point. We have been trying to ask ourselves, in general terms, questions regarding history, the cinema, ethics, and relationships to fiction, the imagination, and politics. But we must be conscious that these conversations we've been having for two days could not have taken place in any other country than France. The different approaches that we've been sharing, including those that distinguish us, have as their scope a rapport to the cinema for which there is no equivalent anywhere else.

AD: This is no doubt tied to France's history. We have a particular rapport with this event, to what was seen and shown in France regarding this historical turning point. I'm thinking in terms of the Collaboration in its entirety and in terms of the sending of the Jews to the extermination camps more precisely. To make a film is to bear witness. I believe I've done my job well as a filmmaker when, looking at the rushes, I can say, "Here, in this spot I witnessed something." A film is the construction of two views which can concur, that of the filmmaker on the world, that of spectators on the screen. The French cinema did it so poorly in relation to historical events in the beginning of the forties in particular, that it is only logical that people like Resnais, Bazin, Truffaut, Marker, Godard, or Rivette stepped up to say: This cannot be, we can't see it; we need to see and it is a moral catastrophe not to see it.

AW: Jean-Michel and Arnaud are right to point out the particular French approach with regard to the ethics of this question, which are at the heart of the history of criticism in this country. But we should also add the very particular place that the historical discourse holds in France, the role that has been assigned to historical recounting in the symbolic construction of the nation, and in a manner that we don't see elsewhere. Let's remember that in France, the history of World War II was not taught in schools before the sixties, whereas the history of World War I was taught immediately after that war. Instead of history courses, a number of educational processes were put in place, among which were projections of *Night and Fog* in schools, the Journée Nationale de la Résistance (National Resistance Day), organized for the same reason, and the Réseau du Souvenir (Memorial Network). All of these helped to make these subjects appear as belonging to lessons in ethics and civics, not history lessons. And this happened at a time when ethics was no longer taught as a subject in schools. To a certain extent, this is an ethics lesson. Later on, the events of this period would be dealt with in various ways, including testimonials by survivors and people who were in the Resistance, educational journeys to Auschwitz, and different films. But it was always about morality rather than a historical issue. This very particular rapport to events would leave its mark on several generations.

AD: We should also add the history of philosophy in France—both the decisive role of phenomenology and the political place assigned to morality.

MJM: Absolutely. Of course, Husserl, who comes from Germany, is a founder of phenomenology, so we cannot say this is strictly

French history, even if it was Merleau-Ponty who would bring about the newest developments regarding the relationships between visible and invisible, which is what concerns us here.

But we should also come back to the use of the word *morality*. Generally when this word is used, we are talking about ethics and not morality. What is the difference? To synthesize it to the extreme, I would say that morality covers Good and Evil, whereas ethics are about our relationship to the Other. Human fragility is not a moral question but one of ethics. Psychoanalysis modified the question of ethics because it modified the significance of the word *subject*. He who says "I" is neither a substance nor an instance laden with consistent and stable unity. There is no subject except where there is the other.

What is the subject of thought? Is it the subject of speech? The subject of perception, of sensibility, of relationship to the other? There is only subject if there is another. This marking of the subject of thought requires that it first be defined as the subject of perception, of sensibility. Being the subject of sensible perception, it is the subject of the relationship to the other, to that which is not oneself. In other words, there is no subject unless there is non-subject, and only when there is a world to designate it from another subject.

Philosophy could no longer live without working out what the world wanted it to see and what was constituent or discharged for the subject. It is on this point of discharging the subject through the operation of the visible that philosophy reconnects with ethics. The work of Lévinas is exemplary on this point, but his meditation is in dispute on the question of images and the works in the realm of the visible. Phenomenology found in the cinema, not an art to which it needed to pay attention but rather a manner of addressing the world with regard to subject, of constituting it, and of the community between subjects that view the images of the world. It found an act of men regarding men to send signs that were constituent or discharging on the world, in a manner in which it could produce or not produce a subject. Hence the fate of the cinema became fundamentally linked to the history of thought as of the beginning of the twentieth century.

And with the Shoah, history became painful to observe. No longer in an oedipal way. That which scratches our eyes out no longer has to do with libido; it is what shakes the very roots of the dignity of the subject, to the point where we wonder whether the world is even worth looking at and whether we are still worthy of being looked at by others in such a world. And then we wonder at the possibility of showing the face of our destitution and our downfall in a manner that might constitute something, that might once again give place to subjects, myself and others. The films that we have watched here have offered other answers still. Philosophy and the cinema henceforth find themselves embarking into a common question, through their history, but especially because the state of the world is facing them now, simultaneously. The "sharing of the sensible," to use Jacques Rancière's expression, becomes the political stakes surrounding what allows us to cohabitate in the visibly shown. And it just so happens that it is in France that this constant relay movement between the cinema and philosophy, in these terms, has specifically taken place.

This chapter of "Conversations at the Mill" ends here. It will surprise no one that there is no conclusion. Those who partook in these conversations continue elsewhere, in different settings, at times alone, at times reunited, often with other participants, to explore these paths.

Translated from the French by Anna Harrison

Notes

The transcript of this exchange was the work of Elsa Jonquet.

1. In view of the events celebrating the sixtieth anniversary of the liberation of the Auschwitz camp, the Fondation pour la Mémoire de la Shoah (Foundation for the Memory of the Shoah) asked Jacques Mandelbaum and Jean-Michel Frodon to put together a thirty-film program.

2. Even though it was programmed to be watched during this weekend gathering, *Drancy Avenir* by Arnaud Des Pallières was not screened for lack of time. We wished to mention that it was considered part of this project nonetheless.

3. For the first three films, see Filmography. *L'Avventura* tells the story of a young woman who disappears mysteriously in the first third of the film, and of the relationship between a man and a woman who are both united and separated by her absence.

4. Sylvie Lindeperg, *Nuit et brouillard. Un film dans l'histoire* (Odile Jacob, 2007).

5. This film deals with the Khmer Rouge genocide and the effects it had on the victims as well as the executioners.

6. Jean-Michel Frodon, *La Projection nationale* (*National Projection*) (Odile Jacob, 1998).

7. Michael Rogin, *Black Face, White Noise* (Berkeley: University of California Press, 1996).

8. Laurie Laufer, *L'Enigme du deuil* (*The Enigma of Grief*) (PUF, 2006).

9. Officer Jan Karsky, an eyewitness to the process of extermination, gave a description of it to Churchill and Roosevelt, without obtaining any modification in the Allies' strategy.

10. A documentary about survival in a large Chinese industrial city destroyed by the economic crisis.

11. *Dans le nu de la vie: récits des marais rwandais* (*Into the Quick of Life*) (Paris: Seuil, 2000).

12. The American historian who authored the authoritative work, *The Destruction of the Jews of Europe*, begun in 1955, of which the final version was published in French shortly before his death (Folio, Gallimard, 2006).

Cinematography Put to the Test

Hollywood and the Shoah, 1933–1945

BILL KROHN

I T HAS BECOME A COMMONPLACE that the Hollywood studios were silent about what was happening to European Jewry between 1933 and 1945, even though many of them were run by Jewish moguls. That is why Daniel Anker's documentary *Imaginary Witness: Hollywood and the Holocaust* (2004) builds its narrative around the idea of "the return of the repressed" during the postwar period and after.[1]

Hubert Damisch locates the beginning of the latter process in *The Stranger* (Orson Welles, 1946), in the stroboscopic lighting effects of the scene where Edward G. Robinson shows Loretta Young the first images of the death camps in a Hollywood film.[2] Welles's uncredited collaborator John Huston was in the midst of filming traumatized veterans recovering buried memories for his documentary *Let There Be Light* when he contributed to the screenplay for *The Stranger*, and his experience appears to have shaped this scene and later ones where Young, in denial about the fact that she has married a Nazi, comes unraveled: "Her unconscious is our best ally," says Robinson.

Historical memory is also the subject of the scene—it is as if Young were seeing these images of the camps for the first time, even though we know that millions of Americans saw newsreels and photos of them after the war. But the footage she's watching has been censored—images of the crematoria that were trimmed appear without commentary as illegible hieroglyphics. And why does Robinson never mention the Jews while he narrates the projection, identifying Franz Kindler, the Nazi played by Welles, as the architect of the camps? He says that Kindler's plan was

149

to exterminate the entire populations of conquered nations—a sweeping statement that obscures the identity of the race that the camps were built to destroy. The only reference comes in an earlier scene: Kindler gives himself away when he denies that Marx, a Jew, was a German.

To answer these questions, we need to understand the forces of truth and the forces arrayed against them between 1933 and 1945. Given that only six of the 24,000 stories that appeared during the same period on the front page of *The New York Times* (owned by a Jewish family that was under the same pressures as the Jewish moguls) referred to Hitler's war against the Jews, the moguls did rather well, although today many of their films strike us as timid and euphemistic. *The Stranger* is part of a *danse macabre* of repression and revelation that went on throughout this period and didn't end when the war ended.

The Demon

By 1942 the Shoah was not a secret. *The New York Times* announced in the back pages of their June 25, 1942, edition that a million Jews had already been massacred in Eastern Europe. On November 24 Rabbi Stephen Wise, a political ally of FDR, confirmed publicly that Hitler was proceeding with his plan to exterminate Europe's Jews. "Millions of people, most of them Jews, are being scooped up with ruthless efficiency and murdered," Edward R. Murrow reported in his December 15 broadcast from London. Two days later FDR made a speech vowing that the Nazis' crimes would be punished, but did not mention the Jews as the principal target of those policies.

What did the average moviegoer know about the Shoah in 1942? What image did the words *concentration camp* call up? Commenting on Leo McCarey's daring in putting Cary Grant and Ginger Rogers in a concentration camp in *Once upon a Honeymoon*, *The Hollywood Reporter* (November 2, 1942) noted that the audience would be aware that the characters could face "a firing squad." But in the B-movie *Hitler—Dead or Alive* (Nick Grinde), filmed a few months earlier, four crooks just out of Alcatraz who've come to Germany to kill Hitler are not impressed when they're put in Dachau. "I could sneeze my way out of this joint," says one, surveying their spacious accommodations.

A Hal Roach film also made in 1942, *The Devil with Hitler* (Gordon Douglas), paints a more familiar picture. Seeking to reform the Führer, a dangerous rival for his job as CEO of Hell, the Devil asks him if he's ever been in a concentration camp. Hitler: "No!" Devil: "Have you ever seen one?" Hitler: "Yah. Das newsreels. They are terrible places." Devil [voice serious]: "They're pretty bad." Hitler: "Each time I see those people they're getting thinner and thinner, and wobbling about on the feet weak [sic]. And their cheeks is all thin. It's too cruel!" According to his biographers, Hitler never visited a concentration camp, but how this bizarre fact, and an accurate description of a camp, found their way into a B-movie produced by Hal Roach in 1942 is something of a mystery.

Another gauge of what was known is the list of subjects treated in three independent documentaries made in New York and given such limited distribution that no prints of them have survived, *Victims of Persecution* (1933), *The Wandering Jew* (1933), and *Hitler's Reign of Terror* (1934): Nazi persecution of Jews, laws against intermarriage, Jewish concentration camps, conspiracy theories, burning of Jewish books, Jewish resistance groups, torture, and atrocities—all known and documented on film by 1934. Why was Hollywood so reluctant to depict these things?

The fact that Roosevelt did not mention the Jews in his denunciation of Nazi war crimes points to a powerful counterforce that was at work in the '30s and '40s: the upsurge in American anti-Semitism. More than one hundred organizations were publishing newspapers spewing the same brand of hatred that had taken over Germany. (In these circles FDR's administration was known as "the Jew Deal.") Anti-Semitism often went hand in hand with isolationism, as it later would with McCarthyism. Three weeks before Pearl Harbor, Jack Warner, a leader of the anti-Nazi movement in Hollywood, was being raked over the coals by a Senate committee for being part of a "Jewish monopoly" that was using film as a propaganda tool to drag America into the war.

Supporters of Hitler profited from this climate to intimidate Jewish producers. The American ambassador to England, Joseph Kennedy, came to Hollywood and called a meeting for that express purpose. "He apparently threw the fear of God into many of our producers and executives by telling them that the Jews were on the spot, and that they should stop making anti-Nazi pictures," Douglas Fairbanks Jr. wrote to FDR in November 1940. "He said that anti-Semitism was growing in Britain and that the Jews were being blamed for the war. . . . He continued to underline the fact that the film business was using its power to influence the public dangerously and that we all, and the Jews in particular, would be in jeopardy, if they continued to abuse that power."

"As a result of Kennedy's cry for silence," Ben Hecht wrote later, "all of Hollywood's top Jews went around with their grief hidden like a little Jewish fox under their gentile vests." Even after Pearl Harbor, using cinema to rally the nation meant suppressing references to Hitler's policy of systematically murdering Jews, so that the American Bund could not preach that Americans were being drafted to fight "a Jewish war." American anti-Semitism, according to the pollsters, actually *peaked* in 1944.

An especially ridiculous example of censorship occurred at RKO, which was drawing on polls conducted by George Gallup for marketing and production decisions during the war. After Jean Renoir's *This Land Is Mine* (1943) was finished, the film's tiny subplot about anti-Semitism was eliminated—a scene where a boy whose father is about to be taken off to prison has the letter J painted on his face by his schoolmates. The scene was eventually included in the French version of the film, and the American version was restored in 1990, but there is a telling continuity error in all three versions of the film: When the boy sees his father being taken away, his face is clean; in two subsequent shots the J suddenly appears—a goof that could only have happened if the farewell scene was shot two ways to permit the editing out of the anti-Semitic incident in the American release version. That ectoplasmic J speaks volumes about the era that conjured it up.

Actually, the Jews fared better than the French in *This Land Is Mine*—they still got two mentions ("He's a Jew," the Nazi colonel says to explain why the boy's father won't be released), whereas this film obviously set in a French village opens with the words "Somewhere in Europe" because Americans had told pollsters they hated the French for collaborating: the very attitude Renoir had made the film to change.

But films were not the only medium that audiences had access to. *Hitler's Children* (Edward Dmytryk, 1942), a sleeper hit based on a nonfiction best-seller about the education being given to the Hitler Youth, was also trimmed by RKO to remove references to anti-Semitism, an important part of the indoctrination described in the book. But the producer of *Hitler's Children*, who also wrote the book, was a master of tie-ins: *Education for Death*, which had already been turned into a short cartoon by Walt Disney, had been excerpted in *Reader's Digest* and in leaflets the Allies dropped from planes over occupied countries in Europe. It was also broadcast with some of the original actors on the radio, where some of the films we'll be looking at enjoyed a second life, and where restrictions on content were less than in films. Spectators who had read the book in one of its many forms, or who read newspapers and listened to the radio, could fill in the blanks, and for those who couldn't, town meetings were organized around screenings of the film.

Another reason for Hollywood to keep quiet was fear of reprisals. Before America entered the war the German consul in Los Angeles, George Gyssling, fought to prevent any anti-Nazi films from being made. His trump card was the threat that Hitler would inflict worse suffering on Jews if angered, and in particular on relatives of those making the films. When an independent producer announced plans to make *I Was a Captive of Nazi Germany* (1936), Gyssling called the German-born actors cast in the film to his office and threatened their relatives in Europe. Many émigrés used assumed names for this film and for Jack Warner's *Confessions of a Nazi Spy* (Anatole Litvak, 1939). Warner, who wanted an "entirely non-Aryan cast" led by fellow anti-Nazi activist Edward G. Robinson, was forced to cast his film on the East Coast.

Otto Preminger may be portraying Gyssling in *Margin for Error* (1943), which he produced and directed for Twentieth Century-Fox, based on a "satirical melodrama" in which he had starred on Broadway. Everyone has a motive to kill the German consul (Preminger): He is blackmailing his Czech wife, whose father is in a camp, and his male secretary, who had a Jewish grandmother, because the latter plans to denounce him for embezzlement. Shot, stabbed, and poisoned at the end of Act I, the consul turns out to have poisoned himself by mistake while trying to frame Moe Finkelstein, a Jewish cop assigned by New York City to guard him, for murdering the head of the American Bund.

Insinuating references to someone having "relatives in Germany" became a Hollywood cliché, but Hitler was blackmailing the whole American Jewish community when he announced the Nuremberg Laws on September 15, 1935, and warned that if "Jewish agitation both within Germany and in the international sphere" continued, he would be forced to find a "final solution."[3] This would presumably have been on the minds of the unnamed producers who begged Chaplin not to make *The Great Dictator*, as recalled by his assistant Dan James in Kevin Brownlow's documentary *The Tramp and the Dictator*.

Luigi Luraschi, the Paramount censor, voiced that concern in a letter to the head of the Production Code Association when Warner Bros. announced plans for *Confessions*, warning that the filmmakers were going to have "the blood of a great many Jews in Germany" on their hands. "They have not heeded the action taken by Charles Chaplin in dropping his burlesque of Hitler," Luraschi wrote. "Chaplin announced, and we think quite rightly, that in making a picture of this kind he would be devoting his money-making talents to a film which could have horrible repercussions on the Jews still in Germany." Dan James recalls in the Brownlow documentary that Chaplin did cancel *The Great Dictator* and only proceeded with the project when FDR sent the architect of the New Deal, Harry Hopkins, to tell him that the film had to be made. This sheds new light on FDR's role in Hollywood before the war, which was not always so encouraging.

Anti-Semitism in the audience continued to pose its own problems. Luigi Luraschi, who had feared Nazi reprisals before the war, found something new to worry about when his own studio released the most outrageous anti-Nazi film of all, *The Hitler Gang* (John Farrow), in 1944.

After a colleague in the Foreign Marketing department reported that some of his associates in New York "feel the picture is wholly incomplete without realistic sequences showing the pogroms against the Jews," Luraschi wrote: "Audiences [here] are split. On the Jewish question Jews themselves are the most split. Some would have liked to see more and others less. I am inclined to agree with the latter." Later he reported that there had been applause for Hitler's diatribe against the Jews in a theatre in Boston. Should the speech be cut from all prints?

The near-absence of the word *Jew* from films made during the period of the Shoah was not censorship of the usual kind—it was a taboo that, when broken, might have the power to summon a demon. A film that referred to German attitudes toward the Jews was also holding up a mirror to the divided audience in the theatre, and the films that did speak out took this into account.

Anatomy of a Legend

One more motive has been suggested for the reluctance of the moguls to make films about Hitler's war on the Jews: money. Jewish characters became rare in Hollywood films during the '30s. Noting this quasi-disappearance, the author of a study of Jews in American film points to the rise of American anti-Semitism, then adds: "It is apparent that American films also reacted to European exigencies in an effort to maximize revenues abroad. Beginning in 1934, Hollywood films with Jewish actors and actresses were banned in Germany." This claim, which conjures up images of cackling Shylocks knuckling under to Hitler by erasing their co-religionists from the screen, has been made by several writers, but no evidence is ever given for it.

Writer Budd Schulberg sums up the received wisdom about the moguls' motives in Brownlow's documentary, adding that Louis B. Mayer screened MGM films for George Gyssling and cut scenes he disliked in order to safeguard German revenues. Although Schulberg could have heard that from many sources, he probably read some of the published accounts of how the adaptation of Erich Maria Remarque's *Three Comrades* made for MGM by Frank Borzage in 1938 was stripped of contemporary political references at the behest of Joseph Breen, the head of the Production Code Association. It was through Breen that the German consul in Los Angeles applied pressure when he wanted to intimidate the people running the studios.

Breen had shown his teeth as a political watchdog in the early days of the PCA by forcing Paramount to withdraw from circulation Borzage's

1932 adaptation of *A Farewell to Arms* because of immoral content and an unflattering portrayal of Italy's performance on the battlefield during World War I, which had provoked boycotts and lobbying by Italian American organizations and Roman Catholic pressure groups. The film sat on the shelves for four years before Paramount secured permission from Breen to recut it and release it.

The moguls no doubt loathed Gyssling, so Breen became his ombudsman on *Three Comrades*, vigorously lobbying Mayer to cancel plans for the production. MGM went ahead anyway. After Breen received a script full of anti-Nazi references in January 1938, he asked to speak to Mayer: "I raise the question from the standpoint of the 'good and welfare' of the industry *as a whole*," he wrote, "as to whether the production of this picture by your company may not result in considerable difficulties in Europe for other American producing organizations."

This would have been understood as referring not only to banning of film imports by Germany, but to seizure of the studios' assets if they continued to have Jews as top executives—a threat Hitler hoped to use as leverage to control picture content in Hollywood. And of course no one would have forgotten what Breen had done to *A Farwell to Arms*, or—of no small importance to the paternalistic Mayer—what had happened to Warner Bros.' main representative in Germany, who had been beaten to death by Nazi goons in 1934 for being Jewish. The one thing Breen's rumblings didn't refer to were German revenues for *Three Comrades*. As he pointed out to Mayer in a letter written after he had been assured that his cuts would be implemented, no film based on a Remarque novel could ever be released in Germany, where Remarque was on the Nazis' list of proscribed authors: one of the cut scenes would have shown his books being burned.

The same day Breen spoke to Mayer on the phone, the film's producer, Joseph Mankiewicz, and three other MGM executives went to Breen's office and hammered out a plan for a compromise script that would permit the production to move forward: The story would be confined to the years between 1918 and 1920, and all references to anti-Semitism would be removed, along with any flags and other emblems indicating that the thugs who cause the protagonist's problems were followers of Hitler. At some point after the meeting with Mankiewicz the censor suggested identifying the thugs as communists, but this suggestion was refused.

Finally, after Breen saw and passed the film, it was screened for him and Gyssling. At Gyssling's request a shot of a drum bearing the emblem of a political club was removed and a riot scene was trimmed. (A scene of a fist fight that Breen promised would be "materially shortened" in his letter to Gyssling of May 16 shows no signs of tampering.) In the finished film, released in May 1938, nameless mobs appear from nowhere to cause trouble. The last line is the vaguest call to arms in any anti-Nazi film made before the war: "There's fighting in the city."

As the producer, Mankiewicz negotiated and made all the script changes, no doubt following Mayer's orders to accommodate Breen, but would later recall that he vetoed the suggestion about the communists. His account of how he threatened to resign from MGM rather than blacken the name of the German Communist Party is the only invariant in a story he kept revising, changing the chronology, setting, and cast of characters who were present when he made his stand, which must have taken considerable courage. The tale became one of his favorites because F. Scott Fitzgerald, whose script for the film was heavily rewritten for a variety of reasons, emerged from the experience hating Mankiewicz, and talked about it. Being denounced as a Philistine by Fitzgerald was particularly abhorrent to the producer, and noted Philistine L. B. Mayer made a convenient whipping boy. Mankiewicz's version of events eventually morphed into this passage in *Crazy Sundays*, Louis Latham's 1971 book about Fitzgerald in Hollywood, which Budd Schulberg, who had his own history with Fitzgerald, may have read:

> L. B. Mayer, Mankiewicz, and a Nazi sat together in a projection room in the basement of the Thalberg Building. . . . The Nazi was obviously uncomfortable, and Mayer, who watched the German the way a honeymooning wife watches her husband, was uncomfortable, too. . . . Mayer had invited the Nazi, a representative of the German consulate in Los Angeles, to this secret screening, to see if he had any objections to the film. He had, but Mankiewicz said he would not make any cuts.

Latham goes on to say that Breen "was brought into the fight" and suggested reshooting some scenes to make the Nazis into communists, which provoked Mankiewicz's threat to resign. "'The next day I went into the commissary,' the producer remembers, 'and Scott was there. He ran up, threw his arms around me and kissed me.'"

Everyone on the assembly line of the legend[4] seems to take it as an axiom that L. B. Mayer, the best-paid executive in America, would have dug up his own mother and sold her to Hitler if the price was right. They overlook the fact that while Chaplin was still filming *The Great Dictator* Mayer made *The Mortal Storm* (Frank Borzage, 1940), in which a family in an idyllic German village right out of the Andy Hardy movies is ripped apart by Nazism. The paterfamilias, a respected physiology professor, dies in a concentration camp for being "non-Aryan" and for maintaining that there is no scientific difference between Aryan and non-Aryan blood.[5]

This very tough film never uses the word *Jew*, although the father's concentration camp uniform has a J on the sleeve. Victor Saville reportedly produced the film with Borzage but took no screen credit because he feared American audiences would be distrustful of an anti-Nazi film made by an English producer. As recounted in the Brownlow documentary by the actor who played the youngest son, Saville also cut a scene where the scientist tells the boy why he's proud to be a Jew. It is unlikely that concern for the German market played any role in the decision. Three months after the film was released, the Reich banned all imports from the last companies whose films were still being shown there: MGM, Paramount, and Twentieth Century-Fox.

Warners and Fox

"Warner Bros. had guts," Mankiewicz told his biographer, adding somewhat unfairly: "They hated the Nazis more than they cared about German grosses. MGM did not. It kept on releasing films in Nazi Germany until Hitler finally threw them out. In fact, one producer was in charge of taking anyone's name off a picture if it sounded Jewish." The comparison of Mayer to Jack and Harry Warner betrays a certain political naivete, for Mayer, an intimate of Herbert Hoover, may have had a freer hand in these matters than Jack Warner, a Democrat.

The Warner brothers' hatred of Hitler stemmed from the murder of their employee Joe Kaufman. "Like many an outnumbered Jew, he was trapped in an alley," Jack Warner wrote in his autobiography. "They hit him with fists and clubs and then kicked the life out of him with their boots and left him dying there." Outraged, the Warners pulled their distribution offices out of Germany and banned the German language from the lot. But according to historian Colin Shindler, who has made it his business to unravel the political activities of Hollywood's fiercest anti-Nazi mogul, Warner's filmmaking activities were hobbled by his ties to FDR.

Confessions of a Nazi Spy (1939) was made at the height of Breen's blitz against "hate films" portraying Nazism in a bad light. A thriller about the espionage activities of the American Bund, it touches on anti-Semitism very lightly. In particular, Breen succeeded in eliminating references to anti-Semitic literature being brought into the United States on German ships. Before *Confessions*, Warner Bros. made *The Life of Emile Zola* (1937), directed by anti-Nazi activist William Dieterle, with the noted Jewish actor Joseph Shildkraut playing Captain Alfred Dreyfus. But despite the fact that the film was made because of the contemporary resonances of the Dreyfus Affair, the only actual mention of anti-Semitism is the words *Religion—Jewish* highlighted on Dreyfus's dossier.

Apart from that image, Warner Bros. pictures before and during the war shied away from explicit references to Jews. This restraint continued even after Pearl Harbor, when the studio started turning out rousing war pictures, each with a multicultural platoon that would not have been complete without its comic Jewish character. One of the last of these was Raoul Walsh's *Objective, Burma!* (1945), about the war in the Pacific. The script gave Errol Flynn a Jewish second-in-command, Sidney Jacob, who is like Flynn's son. At the film's darkest moment Jacob is found barely alive and begging for death after being tortured by the Japanese, provoking a cry from a reporter accompanying the commandos that people who would do such a thing "should be wiped off the face of the earth."

This savage outburst would have functioned as a displaced reference to the Shoah, but when the picture went into production in September 1944, Warner is reported to have told Walsh: "See that you get a nice clean-cut American type for Jacobs." Erased by casting, the writers' discreet allusion was flattened into a racist diatribe against the Japanese, which Walsh softened by cutting to a close-up of a member of the Chinese Army who has been fighting alongside the Americans.

The head of Twentieth Century-Fox, Darryl Zanuck, was a Republican, like most of the moguls, and he had the added advantage of being an Episcopalian, although his president, Jospeh Schenck, and his production head, Bill Goetz (who produced *The Stranger* after the war), were Jewish. In 1934 Zanuck and Goetz produced *The House of Rothschild* (Alfred Werker), which opens with a sign reading "Jew Street" and announcing a curfew in the ghetto. The film traces the rise of the Rothschild family to a position of power that enables them to bankroll the war with Napoleon, thereby saving the lives of their fellow Jews in Germany, where five thousand have already been killed in pogroms. The references to anti-Semitism were left in despite concerns expressed by Schenck.

In 1940 Zanuck and Goetz made their own *Confessions of a Nazi Spy*, which did not shy away from showing Nazi anti-Semitism. In *The Man I Married*, directed by Irving Pichel, Joan Bennett is a woman who marries a German (Francis Lederer) and goes home with him on their honeymoon. Reassured by her husband, she discounts what she's heard about Germany as propaganda, but while Lederer is succumbing to the ecstatic mood of the country she encounters a series of half-explained enigmas: a cattle car full of people under armed guard, a man who is reported to have died of appendicitis in a concentration camp even though he had no appendix, and well-dressed people being forced to pick up garbage in the street.

Wised up to the truth about the Nazis by an American reporter, she learns that her husband has joined the party and won't let her take their son back to America. He is forced to relent when his German father reveals to him that his mother was a Jew and threatens to tell the authorities. This delayed reference to anti-Semitism, like the end of a mystery story, gives meaning to those earlier scenes. *The Man I Married* could unfold allusively because cinema wasn't the only mass medium in 1940. It was simply the most powerful, and therefore the most censored.

Part of its power had to do with belief. People outside Europe were slow to understand the Shoah because they simply couldn't believe the stories they'd been reading in the press since 1933. When reports of mass murder began to make their way across the Atlantic, "believing the unbelievable" became even more of an issue. (The debunking of atrocity stories that the American press had published in the lead-up to World War I no doubt played a role in this.) The purpose of *The Man I Married* is to get Bennett over her fear of "believing in propaganda"—to help her believe what she already knows.

In 1942 Fox released *The Pied Piper*, also directed by Pichel, about an Englishman (Monte Woolley) who is saddled with a swarm of little refugees he has to get to England. Once again the deus ex machina that saves the refugees is anti-Semitism. This time Otto Preminger plays a Gestapo officer who suspects Woolley of spying and sarcastically dismisses his assertion that the children are being taken to America for safekeeping. Pointing out that a French orphan the little band has picked up is Jewish, Preminger asks incredulously: "Are you telling me that America would accept a Jewish child like that?" When Woolley assures him that America would, Preminger reveals that he has a niece who is part Jewish. Woolley and the children can go if they take her with them.

What makes this more than sheer contrivance is the fact that America, in the '20s, had imposed quotas for immigrants, who were still being blamed for unemployment by Right-wing politicians in the '40s. Preminger's incredulity has a basis in fact: during the period when Jews were still being allowed to leave Germany, many countries including the United States denied them a haven.

Preminger's conviction that Woolley is a spy is also not just a plot point. Americans feared that refugees might be fifth columnists, and this fear had serious consequences. It encouraged Breckenridge Long, FDR's assistant secretary of state, to fabricate obstacles to Jewish refugees in the '30s—Roosevelt himself was not immune to such fears. So the makers of *The Pied Piper* were being shrewder than Jack Warner, who had gone to such lengths to arouse fear of fifth columnists the year before. The Warners probably did more good with *Casablanca* (also made in 1942), where the plot is about letters of transit and the voice of Warner Bros. sets the stage during the opening images by describing refugees streaming across Europe in flight from the Nazis.

Three Comedies

The three films that broke Hollywood's silence about the Shoah were independent productions distributed by smaller studios: *The Great Dictator* (Charles Chaplin: UA, 1940), *To Be or Not to Be* (Ernst Lubitsch: UA, 1941) and *Once upon a Honeymoon* (Leo McCarey: RKO, 1942). They were all comedies. Because *The Great Dictator* had been a hit, the idea of using comedy to reach the widest possible audience no doubt looked viable to Chaplin's peers.[6]

Like *Meet John Doe*, released the same year, *The Great Dictator* ends with a speech, and other anti-Nazi films followed suit. A converted Hitler Youth subverts a radio broadcast at the end of *Hitler's Children*, and in *This Land Is Mine* Charles Laughton's character seizes the platform a Nazi show trial affords him to do the same thing. But the idea of speaking out is crucial to these three comedies, which are partly about the situation of the filmmakers, faced with the taboo on referring to the Shoah in a movie.

The Great Dictator was made to break that silence. We see daily persecution in the ghetto; the Jewish barber is hanged from a lamppost; Herr Garbidge murmurs his plan to cleanse Europe—"first kill all the Jews"—in Hynkel's ear; all Jewish property is confiscated after the invasion of Osterlich; Jews are stripped of their citizenship; and an unarmed Jew is shot for resisting the invaders. Even the words that galvanize the barber into speaking at the end concern the Shoah: "The rights of citizenship will be taken away from all Jews and non-Aryans," Garbidge proclaims when he introduces the man he believes to be Adenoid Hynkel to the radio audience. "They are inferior, and therefore enemies of the State."

But the barber's speech is not about the Shoah. It is a general plea for democracy and tolerance that ends with an angry call to arms. What the film shows but does not explicitly denounce is put into words in Hynkel's first speech, a masterpiece of Teutonic doubletalk that reaches its paroxysm with the dictator's rabid denunciations of "der Juden."

The two speeches—one where the word *Jew* is barely spoken, and one where it is the only word that is intelligible—are an astute solution. Hitler's message is burlesqued to avoid transmitting it to the divided audience in the theatre, and the barber's message is an appeal to all of humanity, especially Americans: equality of "Jews and gentiles" is mentioned only once at the beginning along with "blacks and whites," a bigger issue in the United States than in Germany. Chaplin's artful doubling of himself enabled him to elude the double bind in which film artists found themselves in 1940: the need to rally the democracies to fight the Nazis without letting the genie of indigenous anti-Semitism out of the bottle. Critics still complained that the film dwelt too much on the plight of European Jewry.

Lubitsch begins *To Be or Not to Be* by subverting the kind of realistic propaganda film that we fleetingly imagine we're watching—a play rehearsal that comes to a halt when Bronski, a bit player for whom playing Hitler is the chance of a lifetime, decides to get a laugh by saying "Heil myself." Bronski's buddy Greenberg, another bit player with a Jewish name and a Jewish nose, comes to his friend's defense when the rehearsal is halted, and when we next see them we learn that "Heil myself" was Greenberg's idea: "I knew it would get a laugh," he says when they enter costumed as soldiers for the first scene of *Hamlet*. By the end of the sequence they are already planning to drop the pompous Rawitch, playing Claudius, when they carry his body out at the end of the play.

But Greenberg's dream is to play Shylock, whose Rialto speech he performs so passionately for his admiring friend that he makes the curls in Bronski's wig flutter. In his rendition, "Hath not a Jew eyes?" becomes "Have I not eyes?" and Shylock's sense of racial victimization is elided by Greenberg's rancor over the professional slight that condemns him to be a spear carrier.

After the Nazis invade Poland, Greenberg and Bronski are obliged to trade in their spears for snow shovels, and during a break from their sordid labors Greenberg repeats the Rialto speech, this time just the lines where Shylock speaks for "us." "Us" is now the conquered Poles, and in particular two conquered Poles who are being used as slave labor.

Finally Greenberg gets a chance to play a Jewish assassin in a new production of the melodrama "Murder in the Opera House" that will be performed for an audience of SS men guarding Hitler's box at the opera. Instantly captured when he appears, he is confronted with Hitler—Bronski again—and his personal guards, played by members of the troupe, while inside the theatre the audience is singing "Deutschland über alles." To clinch his characterization, Greenberg performs the Rialto speech with growing rage, ending with a line that was omitted before: "If you injure us, shall we not revenge?" "We" now means the Polish resistance, and Greenberg rises to the grandeur of the occasion.

In no version of the speech is the word *Jew* uttered. It doesn't have to be—Greenberg's name, nose and Shylock obsession identify his cultural heritage. Lubitsch's solution to the taboo on references to the Shoah is not to use the taboo word at all—it is never spoken in *To Be or Not to Be*—while having Greenberg ring all the changes on the most famous denunciation of anti-Semitism ever written. Greenberg incarnates the spirit of carnival derision, and Greenberg's nose is the film's *punctum*, the visual detail that irradiates all the images with a meaning that is oblique to the official subject, like the grinning spectator glimpsed out of focus in the background of Goering's archery demonstration in a still from *Ordinary Fascism* (Mikhail Romm, 1965) that fascinated Roland Barthes.[7] But Greenberg remains a bit player: Even when his big moment comes, he is still delivering the Rialto speech to Bronski, his eternal audience of one.

Anti-Nazi films made before Pearl Harbor were designed to encourage America's entry into the war, and *Once upon a Honeymoon*—set in the prewar period but put into production six months after America was already at war—is perfectly aware of its place in that history. A comic version of *The Man I Married*, it posits a marriage between an ambitious burlesque queen, Katie O'Hara (Ginger Rogers), and a Nazi spy, Baron von Luber (Walter Slezak), who spends their honeymoon setting up European democracies for the Nazis to march in. She is wised up by an American reporter, Pat O'Toole (Cary Grant), who follows her honeymoon itinerary, becoming a famous radio broadcaster in the process and alerting America to the approaching danger.

But none of this really happens in the film. In a drawn-out series of wordless close-ups, O'Hara and O'Toole fall madly in love the instant they set eyes on each other. Their affinity is so strong that they spend the rest of the movie essentially performing for each other's amusement. Except as a melodramatic villain, Von Luber is never a threat to their relationship, although Katie goes through the motions of going on her honeymoon. The last scene of the film is a metaphor for its belatedness. On the boat to America Katie encounters the Baron again; they struggle and she throws him overboard. By the time she and O'Toole have alerted the captain to turn the ship around, von Luber, who can't swim, has already drowned.

Every scene in the first act of *Once upon a Honeymoon* is played as if whatever is supposed to be at stake in it is a foregone conclusion, and this mood carries through to the second act, when tragedy is barely averted. Katie gives her passport to Anna, the Jewish maid in her hotel, which eventually lands Katie and O'Toole in a concentration camp. ("He thinks we're Jewish," says O'Toole. "This could be serious.") At this point in the version of the film that was shown to critics, the Gestapo goons took a derby hanging on the wall and jammed it on O'Toole's head so that it came down over his ears, sending Katie into hysterical laughter—the scene was later cut.

In the concentration camp, silhouetted Jewish men sing a Hebrew dirge in the background while O'Hara and O'Toole discuss the situation in the foreground, like Jane Fonda and Yves Montand imagining themselves as factory workers in *Tout va bien* (1972). "We're really in a mess," says O'Hara, momentarily recalling McCarey's first couple, Laurel and Hardy. "Oh now, O'Hara," says O'Toole. "What about these people?" McCarey left the next scene blank in the script, to be supplied "at the time of shooting." O'Hara and O'Toole are summoned to the commandant's office, where a guard tells them to go through a door with a poster on it. O'Toole reads the poster and informs Katie that behind the door people are being selected for forced sterilization. When the guard has had his little joke, he shows them into the commandant's office, where the American consul is waiting. Fade out on their relieved babble.

Ultimately, the film doesn't even take its own role as a warning about the Nazi menace very seriously. The first time we see O'Toole broadcasting from an occupied city, the room he's in collapses before he can say much. (Headline: "Warsaw Falls.") And the big speech he makes at the end of the film evokes Nazi anti-Semitism for purely personal reasons. When von Luber, holding Katie hostage, forces O'Toole to make a radio broadcast telling Americans to accept the invasion of France, the Resistance urges him to seize the chance to denounce the Nazis. Instead he contents himself with making a feeble pun to warn America and then gets down to business: destroying von Luber by announcing that he's after Hitler's job, and that his wife is Jewish.

A film that constantly proclaims its own uselessness, *Once upon a Honeymoon* nonetheless shows things that were not shown in other films, including a stylized but fairly accurate portrayal of a concentration camp and the forced sterilization of its Jewish inmates, about which it was still urgent to sound the alarm. The contrast between the stars and the grim environments they pass through, as if in a fairytale, makes this possible by representing the audience's relationship to the unimaginable, imagined in a film.

Four Tragedies

The last group of films about the Shoah made in Hollywood during the war is very dark. Two of them look forward to the time after the end of the war, and three raise the problem of dealing with the Nazis afterward.

When Reinhard Heydrich, the Nazi military governor of Czecho-slovakia, was assassinated in May 1942, the village of Lidice was mas-sacred in retaliation. *Hitler's Madman* (Douglas Sirk, 1942) is one of three films that were made on the subject. Recalling *J'Accuse*, the film ends with images of the dead villagers rising up to warn other nations to avoid their fate in the words of the poem that inspired the film, Edna St. Vincent Millay's "The Murder of Lidice."

Taking as its point of departure FDR's 1942 declaration about war crimes, *None Shall Escape* (Andre De Toth, 1944) is framed by witnesses addressing an as-yet-imaginary tribunal of an as-yet-imaginary organiza-tion called the United Nations that is trying the case of one war crimi-nal, Wilhelm Grimm. Each witness tells part of the story of Grimm's life from the end of World War I to the massacre he orders of Jewish prisoners who refuse to board cattle cars bound for "labor camps." The script was vetted by the State Department to ensure that the atrocities depicted—including a scene where Grimm orders horses to be stabled in the synagogue—were factual.

The Hitler Gang, a film initiated by Y. Frank Freeman, the head of Paramount, was actually made at the behest of the State Department. The omnipresent Luigi Luraschi explained the film's ideological project to a colleague from the Foreign Marketing department in a memo dated October 29, 1943: "The danger of Nazism in Europe is not Hitler but German militarism. Our picture is to show how Hitler, an egocentric fanatic, and his gang were taken and used by the militarists. . . . When you read the script, therefore, and say that Hitler is the fall guy, I feel that the studio has succeeded in writing the story correctly."

Anticipating the dangers of a Nazi resurgence was the aim of two other films made just before the end of the war: *Tomorrow, the World!* (Leslie Fenton, UA 1944) about a Hitler Youth improbably adopted by an American family, and *The Master Race* (1945), made for RKO by Herbert J. Biberman, about the postwar activities of a German general hiding out in a Belgian village.

Anti-Semitism is certainly part of the problem posed by the trans-planted Hitler Youth in *Tomorrow, the World!*—his casual reference to sitting next to a "big fat Jew" on the plane is the first indication that the transplant may not take. But *The Master Race* was made for RKO, so only the British got to see Biberman's subplot about a Jew who returns from a concentration camp to his village after the war, learns that his family has been killed, and donates a candelabra with seven branches to the altar of the village's reconstructed church. When the altar is shown for the first time, the other inhabitants are singing, in English, a hymn for "the race of David." But a Latin hymn was substituted and the character was reduced to a passing reference that makes no mention of his race in the version prepared for American audiences.

In contrast to those films, the common ideological project of *Hitler's Madman*, *None Shall Escape*, and *The Hitler Gang* is complicated by their common artistic project, which Sirk explained in an interview about Hans-Jürgen Syberberg's Hitler film in 1983. What he said seems more appropriate to *Hitler's Madman* than to *Hitler, ein Film aus Deutschland*: "When I saw [Syberberg's] film, I thought of Shakespeare's *Königsdramen*. It's like *Richard III*, for example, because it's more than propaganda—you get inside a man. I think that in the future there will be many plays—tragedies—about Hitler, Goering and Goebbels. They are definitely great dramatic figures. Is the *Oresteia* anything else?"[8]

That description also fits Welles's postwar film about the danger of a Nazi resurgence and *Address Unknown* (William Cameron Menzies, 1944). All these films are tragedies in the sense meant by Sirk, who was probably thinking of German Baroque tragedies about tyrants when he referred to *Königsdramen*. In the last years of the war, when the Nazis' crimes were no longer in doubt, such stories helped spectators understand and believe what was happening.

Menzies had sets recalling *Citizen Kane* built as a frame for the rise and fall of his German-American protagonist, played by Paul Lukas. Set in 1938, the story of *Address Unknown* intertwines Lukas's destiny with letters passing between him and his Jewish partner in the States. "The Nazis' Jew-baiting," he assures his friend at the beginning, "is just for the rabble—nothing will come of it." Not an anti-Semite, he becomes an accomplice out of fear: He has brought with him his friend's daughter, who is engaged to his son but wants to be an actress in Berlin. When she offends the Nazis, Lukas, terrified of the Gestapo, refuses to hide her, and she is killed. A new series of letters from the States that are obviously written in code bring about his own destruction at the hands of the Gestapo—letters written by his son to avenge his fiancée's death.

For *The Hitler Gang*, John Farrow created his own paranoid version of the Wellesian Baroque. Frances Goodrich and Albert Hackett wrote the script using extensive research about the rise of Hitler. But the list of sources they consulted included only four works on anti-Semitism, and while the film certainly does not give the subject short shrift, it's

clear that when it came to this part of the story, they didn't have much
to go on.

Among those offering Goodrich and Hackett advice was film and
theater director Herman Shumlin, who wrote them a letter expressing
a familiar concern: "When Hitler begins pounding away on the Jews,
it would be better if he did not pound on this point alone. There is a
frightening positiveness about a repetition of a single statement. It begins
almost to take on the quality of truth. Did Hitler in those early days not
attack other groups?" This advice inspired the scene where Hitler and
his cohorts are trying to come up with a scapegoat. Someone suggests
the Catholics. "The Church is too large," says Hitler. "We must choose
an enemy we're sure we can defeat. Some small minority group . . ."
After he rejects the idea of the Bolsheviks as "premature," Himmler
suggests going after the Jews, an idea that everyone ignores until Hitler
seizes on it.

The Catholic paper *Tidings* was appalled at the absurdity of this
scene, although the writers were careful to work in the Freudian idea
of projection (used by Ben Hecht to explain anti-Semitism in his 1944
book *A Guide for the Bedevilled*), which had been suggested to them by
a propaganda expert who read the script. The scene ends with Hitler
saying that he will make the lie that "the Jew is responsible for all our
troubles" into the truth by repeating it in myriad forms. In the next
scene he gives his first big speech on the subject, which culminates in
the denunciation of "the Jew" as "the great master of the art of lying."

When Luraschi's friend in the Foreign Department pointed out
that the violence of the protagonist's anti-Semitic diatribes might have
the wrong effect on certain members of the audience, the censor assured
him that everything was being done to portray Hitler and his gang as
"the perverse turkeys they are." The screenwriters accordingly threw in
incest (Hitler), homosexuality (Röhm), drug addiction (Goering), and
anything else they could document, and all of it sailed past the PCA
because the State Department had given the project its blessing. In the
absence of a cogent theory, this generalized atmosphere of perversion
became the film's psychological explanation for anti-Semitism, a perversion like all the other crimes of the "gang."

After the Night of the Long Knives, Hitler sets out to conquer
Europe, "exterminating whole peoples, the Jews, the Poles [sic]," for
reasons that the movie has not fully explained. Yet Farrow's inspired
direction makes *The Hitler Gang* a good film, filled with the kind of
juicy character parts we associate with Paramount productions: a cross
between *The Damned* and *The Great McGinty*, which does not deserve
the oblivion into which it fell after the war.

Hitler's Madman was made independently by German émigrés. Shot in eight days and partly reshot when L. B. Mayer picked it up for distribution by MGM (a first for the studio), it has a surer sense of European realities than the two projects just described. In the same way, André De Toth, a Hungarian émigré who had filmed the invasion of Poland, was recalling his own experience when in *None Shall Escape* the inhabitants of a Polish village are fed so that a Nazi camerman can shoot a newsreel.

In the mediocre protagonist of *None Shall Escape*—made, like *Address Unknown*, under the benevolent eye of Harry Cohn at Columbia—De Toth and screenwriter Lester embodied the idea of the banality of evil while the man for whom the phrase would be coined was still earning his place in history. In collaboration with De Toth and Cole, Alexander Knox was able to create that "indivisible nucleus of a Nazi being,"[9] Wilhelm Grimm, using a theoretical framework that is never made explicit: according to Dr. Alfred Adler's theory of the inferiority complex, quite popular in America in the '40s, an individual who is unable to convert feelings of inferiority into feelings of superiority will try to fill the void he feels inside himself with power.

Accordingly, the film's first movement is an exercise in nonstop humiliation: Grimm, a German teacher in a Polish village, fought for Germany in the Great War. Returning to the village minus a leg, he is so crushed to find himself still a provincial schoolteacher that he alienates the fiancée who has waited for him, attributing to her feelings of contempt for his poverty and his wound, when what horrifies her is his contempt for the people of her village, whom he refers to as "the village idiots." When Grimm rapes an underage girl, his own fiancée exposes him, and he has to beg money from the priest and the rabbi to get out of town before he is lynched—but not before he has his eye put out with a hurled rock.

In Munich, where he joins the Nazi party, we meet his older brother Karl and see where Grimm's inferiority complex came from. Karl, who has a family and a good job as a journalist, is intelligent, handsome and a few inches taller than his little brother. (Adler's other name for the inferiority complex was the Napoleon Complex.) The Nazis buy Grimm a prosthetic leg and a glass eye, and make him Minister of Education. When Karl threatens to publish what he knows about the Reichstag Fire, Grimm has him sent to a concentration camp, and the stage is set for Grimm's return to the village where he was humiliated, now a Nazi party official. Irrespective of its scientific value, Adler's theory supplies the conceptual basis for a powerful tragedy with an evil protagonist, in which the Jews of the village become the principal victims of Grimm's egomania.

Made in 1942, *Hitler's Madman* is more discreet about Nazi anti-Semitism than *None Shall Escape*, except for one reference: After Heydrich is assassinated, a colleague in Prague suggests blaming his death on a Jew—"That's always good." Instead, Heydrich's mentor, Heinrich Himmler, decrees the destruction of Lidice. The symbolism accompanying this hecatomb is Christian, appropriately for the real Czech village that was razed on June 10, 1942. What links the film to the Shoah is its protagonist, Reinhard Heydrich, who was one of the architects of the Nazi genocide. Heydrich was in charge of the death squads that accompanied the Germany Army. After being named military governor of Czechoslovakia, he chaired the Wannsee Conference in January 1942, where the Final Solution was put into effect under Himmler's authority.

The émigrés who made *Hitler's Madman* knew about Heydrich's role overseeing the *Einsatzgruppen* and his close relationship with Himmler. The strongest scene in the movie portrays Heydrich's last moments, with his mentor at his bedside—the dying man's face filmed from a high angle, caught in a slash of light: "I want to live. . . . I don't want to die for the Führer or anyone else. You'll face death, too, one of these days, Himmler, you and your Führer. All of you will face death, all of you. . . . Every day I'd shoot thirty. It should've been three hundred, three thousand. I should've done away with them all, all of them. Kill them if you want to be safe, every day. All of them."

Whoever wrote that scene—and at least seven people had a hand in the script—it anticipates something Elias Canetti wrote years later. "The moment of survival is the moment of power. Horror at the sight of death turns into satisfaction that it is someone else who is dead. . . . In survival, each man is the enemy of every other, and all grief is insignificant measured against this elemental triumph. Whether the survivor is confronted by one dead man or by many, the essence of the situation is that he feels unique . . . and when we speak of the power which this moment gives him, we should never forget that it derives from his sense of uniqueness and from nothing else. All man's designs on immortality contain something of this desire for survival. He does not only want to exist for always, but to exist when others are no longer there."[10]

Canetti's analysis of the paranoid solitude at the heart of fascism certainly describes Himmler's reaction to his protégé's death: he smokes a cigarette, phones his boss with a lie designed to reassure both of them, smooths his hair and looks at himself in the mirror with great satisfaction. (In pointed contrast, just before Heydrich's death the assassin's sweetheart dies in his arms, and everything they say during her last minutes is about the ties that bind them to each other and to other people.) When Himmler orders the destruction of Lidice, he bolsters his own "survivor" complex, founded on the power to give death to others (when we first see Heydrich, he is signing execution orders)—to *all* the others. As he dies prophesying the defeat of the Reich, Heydrich is no longer talking just about the Czechs. The makers of *Hitler's Madman* are attempting to portray something like the primal scene of the Final Solution in this sequence: "Kill them if you want to be safe, every day. All of them."

Postscript

With the last example, we have crossed over into allegory. When the scene of the conference following the news of Heydrich's assassination was reshot at MGM, the remark about blaming it on a Jew may have been the first time an utterance containing the word *Jew* was ever filmed on an MGM soundstage. It is used again in *The Seventh Cross* (1944, Fred Zinnemann), where one of the seven men who escape from a concentration camp at the beginning of the film has a star on his uniform and is described by the narrator as "the little Jew." The film follows the escapee who eventually makes it while the others are being recaptured and crucified as a warning to others. Although the director would have preferred a more documentary style, MGM's scenic wizards enshrouded the camp and the swamp surrounding it in hellish fog and darkness that gave new meaning to the words "concentration camp."

The Seventh Cross follows the policy set forth by a group of producers in response to a query from the American Jewish Congress in February 1943: "It might be unwise from the standpoint of the Jews themselves to have a picture dealing solely with Hitler's treatment of their people, but interest has been indicated in the possibility of a picture covering various groups that have been subject to the Nazi treatment. This of course would take in the Jews." Portraying atrocities committed against other groups was one kind of Shoah allegory, and appropriating the forms of America's majority religion for films that touched on the Shoah supplied an interpretative framework for them that veiled their content, as when Grisella, the Jewish actress who is murdered in *Address Unknown*, appears onstage in white robes reciting the Sermon on the Mount before the Gestapo stops the performance.

Neal Gabler's *An Empire of Their Own* argues that Hollywood's image of America is an extended allegory of Jewish themes. L. B. Mayer was the master of the form—which may shed light on another anti-Nazi film from MGM, *Escape* (Mervyn Le Roy, 1940), in which Robert Taylor returns to Germany to smuggle his mother, drugged to make her appear dead and nailed in a coffin, out of a concentration camp. The characters aren't Jewish, but how could Mayer, whose reverence for mothers was famous, not have been drawn to the story as a dark Jewish fantasy?

The Hunchback of Notre Dame, which William Dieterle directed for RKO in 1939, with its persecuted gypsy girl (another race the Nazis tried to exterminate), has been read as an allegory of the Shoah, if only for these lines: "Praying cannot help you. You belong to an evil race." *Samson and Delilah* (Cecil B. De Mille, 1949), *The Ten Commandments* (DeMille, 1956) and *Ben-Hur* (William Wyler, 1959), three of the biggest blockbusters of the postwar era, are all allegories of the Shoah.[11] So is *Esther and the King* (Raoul Walsh, 1959), which ends with a shot of the Star of David. *Esther* is a companion piece to *The Yellow Ticket* (1931), a contemporary drama of anti-Semitism set in Russia and based on the story of Judith that Walsh produced and directed at the beginning of the period when anti-Semitism was winning so many converts in the United States.

After the war, Mayer's former production chief Dore Schary (who had commissioned Sinclair Lewis to write an anti-Nazi western for MGM) co-produced émigré director Robert Siodmak's *The Spiral Staircase*. Someone added to Ethel Lina White's story the idea that the serial killer stalking the mute housemaid believes he is practicing eugenics by eliminating the weak and unfit. It could have been Schary's co-producer, Joan Harrison. A protégée of Alfred Hitchcock, she had worked on *The Lady Vanishes*, which turned White's *The Wheel Spins* into an anti-Nazi allegory.

Perhaps the most poignant allegorical reading of a Hollywood film made during the period of the Shoah was supplied by the writer of the film. Robert Siodmak's brother Curt only realized near the end of his life that his script for *The Wolf Man* (1941) had been inspired by his experiences of Nazism in the '30s. "I am the Wolf Man," he told an interviewer in 2001. "I was forced into a fate I didn't want: to be a Jew in Germany. I would not have chosen that as my fate. The swastika represents [*sic*] the moon. When the moon comes up, the man doesn't want to murder, but he knows he cannot escape it, the Wolf Man destiny."

The fact that Lawrence Talbot, who becomes a hunted half-human creature when the moon is full, bears the mark of a five-pointed star on his chest certainly supports this interpretation, which finally came to Siodmak after years of trying to understand the reason for the huge success enjoyed by the myth he had created in 1941. Lawrence Talbot is cured of his unwanted destiny in *House of Dracula* (Earl Kenton, 1945), filmed during the euphoria following VE Day. This last roundup for the monsters that kept Universal in business during the Hitler years took shape in a treatment one Edward T. Lowe turned in on April 13, in the midst of the most wonderful and terrible spring in human history, as the death camps were being liberated one by one and the horrors they contained were being told to the world.

Notes

Research on Paramount and RKO films was done at the Margaret Herrick Library of the Academy of Motion Picture Arts and Sciences, which also has the files of the Production Code Administration; and at the Arts Special Collection of UCLA's Young Research Library. The American Film Institute catalogue of American films made during this period was an invaluable resource. My thanks for their help to Donovan Brandt, Joe McBride, Bernard Eisenschitz, Karl Thiede, Dan Sallitt, John Landis, Hadrian Belove, and the members of the Raymond Sapene Group, especially Matthew Clayfield, Richard Modiano, Brent Kite, and Joe Kaufman.

1. The claim is made in useful books by Patricia Erens, Judith Doneson, Annette Insdorf, and Lester Friedman, and in Kevin Brownlow's documentary about *The Great Dictator*. Anker's documentary and Neal Gabler's *An Empire of Their Own* take a more nuanced approach to the subject.

2. *Cahiers du Cinema* 599.

3. On blackmail as one of Hitler's "signature crimes," see the chapter on the contemporary exposés published by the *Munich Post* in Ron Rosenbaum's *Explaining Hitler*.

4. See also published accounts in *New Masses* (February 15), *Time* (June 6), *Variety* (June 8: Mankiewicz, told the paper the cuts were made "for length"), Mankiewicz's 1944 letter to Edmund Wilson, quoted by Latham, and Kenneth Geist's Mankiewicz biography.

5. Scott Eyman prints the legend in his recent Mayer biography, where he also reports that *The Mortal Storm* was "a creative failure that cruelly reveals the limitations of MGM's worldview. The script didn't specify that the events were happening in Germany, even though it is clear that's where the story was set." Eyman has obviously never seen the film, where Germany, Hitler, and the Nazis are all named.

6. The Three Stooges beat Chaplin to the punch with *Oh, You Nazty Spy* (Jules White, 1940), in which Moe plays Hitler and reference is made to "minorities" fleeing Hitler to neighboring countries. It was reportedly one of the Stooges' anti-Nazi shorts that provoked Joseph Kennedy's wrathful visit to the Jewish moguls.

7. "Le troisième sens," *Cahiers du Cinéma* 222. Murray Pomerance extends the idea of the punctum, elaborated in Barthes' *La Chambre claire*, to films in *Johnny Depp Starts Here* (New Brunswick: Rutgers University Press, 2005), 109–14.

8. *Cahiers du Cinema* hors-serie *Hans-Jürgen Syberberg*.

9. Sylvie Pierre, *Trafic* 35.

10. *Crowds and Power* (Noonday Press), 288.

11. Patricia Erens, *The Jew in American Cinema*, 225–28.

"The Past in the Present"

The Films of Producer Artur Brauner and the Dominant Narratives on the Genocide of European Jews in German Cinema

RONNY LOEWY

A T A 1999 CONFERENCE ENTITLED "The past in the present. Confronting the consequences of the Holocaust in post-war German cinema,"[1] film specialists and Holocaust researchers came together to look at the way West and East German films have portrayed the extermination of Europe's Jews by Nazi Germany. The focus was the presence of the Holocaust[2] and its aftereffects in the two German societies after the war. There have been numerous fiction films and even more documentaries that centered around, or at least clearly referred to, the National Socialist politics of extermination. However, the different ways the Federal Republic of Germany (FRG) and the German Democratic Republic (GDR) viewed Germany's past—plus a whole host of imponderables originating from the different social politics—have had their repercussions on film production in the two countries. As the conference assessed, rare have been the cases in which the Holocaust was treated in films—particularly in the films of the FRG, which form the focus of this essay—as an event that continued to affect postwar German societies, an event of the present time, which is to say a subject relevant to West German as well as East German society.

The Auschwitz trial that took place in Frankfurt during the mid-1960s and the Eichmann trial in Jerusalem before it, were the principal instigators for documentary film to start treating the subject. They also sparked a few initial fiction films, but the volume of these would remain restricted until the end of the 1980s.

The story of the Berlin-based film studio Central Cinema Comp. (CCC) owned by Artur Brauner could be considered a good indicator of the evolution and the particular status of fiction films about the Holocaust. Himself a survivor of the Lodz camp, Brauner made a constant, obstinate effort to impose mass-audience films dealing with the Holocaust onto the German film circuit—with, it should be said, middling results.

The question is hypothetical, but it nevertheless springs to mind: What would have happened if Artur Brauner, returning from the East to the American sector of Berlin in 1945 in the wake of the Liberation, had decided, even as late as 1946 or 1947, as a displaced person in a camp near Munich, to get himself a visa for the United States or to surreptitiously head for Palestine? Most likely he would have made a career for himself as an independent producer in America or Israel, similar to the one he had after founding CCC in Berlin. This remains pure speculation. What is of interest here is to ponder how different West German cinema would have been after 1945 and how that cinema would have approached the twelve years leading up to 1945, the Nazis, the war, the persecution of the Jews, and the Holocaust—without Artur Brauner.

Most likely, other West German producers would have green-lighted a good number of the more conventional projects that Brauner brought to the screens of a young FRG and with which he did good business. The success story of West German film is a phenomenon that runs perfectly parallel with the "economic miracle." Without him, however, the images and voices in these films, which allowed Brauner to tell the stories of the victims of the extermination of Europe's Jews and to denounce the Germans responsible for these crimes, would have had a much harder time finding their position in West German fiction cinema.

Let us also not forget that it was Brauner who gave some of the Jewish filmmakers forced into exile by the Nazis a chance to make films in Berlin again. Without him, Fritz Lang, Robert Siodmak, Gottfried Reinhard, Gerd Oswald, Max Nosseck, and several others would never have made their "homecoming" films.

Long Is the Road (*Lang ist der Weg*, Herbert Fredersdorf and Marek Goldstein), which tells the story of a group of Warsaw ghetto survivors who make their way to a camp for displaced persons in Landsberg, near Munich, to finally arrive in Israel—a film that premiered in June 1948—would not have been followed by *Morituri* (Eugen Yorck, 1948) in September of that same year. Giving no thought to market concerns, *Morituri* marked the start of Brauner's initially intermittent but gradually more frequent attempts to reopen the wounds of German history in the repressive euphoria of the conformist postwar German cinema.

On September 16, 1946, Brauner founded his company Central Cinema Comp.-Film and went looking for a project. He had neither the financial means nor the authorization to film, but he had an idea of which he was completely convinced: he wanted to build an autobiographically inspired monument to the victims of the Holocaust. The fact that UFA's former head of production Erich Pommer, who had returned to Berlin as the American officer in charge of film, sent back the screenplay of *Long Is the Road* without comment and that the Allies had refused the project did not deter Brauner in the slightest. With the support of the Soviets and the Red Army, the film was finally made in the winter of 1947–48, in the fields and inns of the Eastern zone and under harsh conditions—this film in which the young producer made a pathetic appeal to the "world's conscience."[3]

The film *Morituri*, which dealt with an escape from a concentration camp and life in a forest hideout, may have received a good critical reception but it was a failure upon release, even provoking scorn. Audiences booed the film and demanded their money back. Theater owners sent back their copies of the film and the distributor had no choice but to cancel the release plans.

Certainly, Brauner devoted himself almost entirely to commercial cinema and produced entertainment films—including pictures from his own studio from 1950 onward. There is no doubt that he became West Germany's wealthiest independent film producer. But he never relinquished his plans, be it in 1955, when he intended to have Victor Vicas direct an adaptation of the life of the leading female member of the Jewish resistance, Hannah Senesh, or in 1961, when he attempted to produce a film about the kidnapping of Adolf Eichmann by Israeli agents in Argentina. He was unable to get either project off the ground, or several others that had National Socialism and its consequences as their main topic.

In 1955 he did produce *The Plot to Assassinate Hitler* (*Der 20. Juli*, Falk Harnack), a spectacular production about resistance among German officers. He also tried in vain to adapt the story of the student resistance group "White Rose" and mounted two further antiwar films that same year: *Hotel Adlon* (Josef van Baky, 1955) and *The Captain and His Hero* (*Der Hauptmann und sein Held*, Max Nosseck, 1955). But he never produced a film whose main theme was the genocide of the Jews or which referenced it.[4]

Other producers, from both East and West, took different approaches to this theme. Earlier films such as *Murderers Among Us* (*Die Mörder sind unter uns*, GDR, Wolfgang Staudte, 1946) and *Between Yesterday and Tomorrow* (*Zwischen gestern und morgen*, FRG, Harald Braun, 1947) believed they could beg favor with audiences by trying to compensate for the suffering of the victims by focusing on that of the executioners. After the films about ruined Germany, West German cinema tended toward self-pity, as in *Love '47* (*Liebe 47*, Wolfgang Liebeneiner, 1949), *Stalingrad: Dogs, Do You Want to Live Forever?* (*Hunde wollt ihr ewig leben*, Frank Wisbar, 1949), or *Darkness Fell on Gotenhafen* (*Nacht fiel über Gotenhafen*, Frank Wisbar, 1959). With the exception of Kurt Maetzig's *Marriage in the Shadows* (*Ehe im Schatten*, 1947), East German fiction film systematically transformed Jewish victims into antifascist resistance fighters when not busy complacently denouncing the ex-Nazis who were able to make careers for themselves in the capitalist FRG, as in *Council of the Gods* (*Der Rat der Götter*, Kurt Maetzig, 1950), *Der Prozess wird vertragt* (Herbert Ballmann, 1958), or *Now and in the Hour of My Death* (*Jetzt und in der Stunde meines Todes*, Konrad Petzold, 1963). The GDR, too, had its fair share of films featuring Nazis and even more featuring antifascists, but no Jewish victims. In any case, the state-run East German film industry was less concerned with Germany's past than with condemning the careers of former Nazis west of the border.

It wasn't until 1963 that Brauner was at last in a position to produce another film on the subject, *Man and Beast* (*Mensch und Bestie*, Edwin Zbonek, 1963), the story of a family and a curse and the mortal conflict between two brothers, one an SS officer and the other an escaped convict from a concentration camp. But it would take the Auschwitz trial in Frankfurt (December 1963-August 1965) for Brauner to produce the exceptional *Witness Out of Hell* (*Zeugin aus der Hölle*, Zica Mitrovic, 1967). Even before judgment in the trial was handed down, shooting began on this film in which postwar German society holds judgment over itself. It is not exactly a film about the Auschwitz trial; the film asks the question whether a tribunal in the FRG is capable of handing down justice not only on the accused but also on the victims, in other words, on the witnesses summoned before the court. This exceptional film, which managed to penetrate into the very heart of the Nazi politics of extermination like no other German film of the period, adopts the point of view of a Holocaust survivor and follows the traces of a woman who actually testified at the Auschwitz trial. District Attorney Hoffman of the Zentrale Stelle, the bureau for Nazi crimes in Ludwigsburg, is in search of this woman, whom he wants to have testify against the accused. He goes to Belgrade to visit the author Bora Petrovic, who published a book just after the war on the crimes committed in the German death camps, a book largely based on the eyewitness accounts of survivor Lea

Weiss (Irene Papas). She now needs to repeat the same statement she gave Petrovic before the tribunal hearing evidence against a concentration camp doctor. Weiss refuses and claims that the words attributed to her were entirely invented. Hoffman asks Petrovic to accompany him to Germany to change her mind, but in vain. The victim's shame is too strong to face the perpetrators' clear conscience. In the camp, Lea Weiss had been forced to satisfy the camp commander's sexual demands and was subsequently subjected to medical experiments. Twenty years after the end of the war, the only desperate escape from her situation is suicide.

Although *Witness Out of Hell* was not a commercial success, Brauner continued to invest in films on the subject, such as Vittorio De Sica's *The Garden of the Finzi-Continis* (*Il Giardino dei Finzi Contini*, 1970), which deals with the persecution of Jews in Italy. He produced *The Martyr* (*Sie sind frei, Dr. Korczak*, Aleksander Ford, 1974), a paean to the Jewish doctor who accompanied his Jewish orphans from the Warsaw ghetto into death. In the 1980s, and often in collaboration with author Paul Hengge, he finally mounted a series of films in memory of the victims of the Nazis, Jewish and otherwise: *Charlotte* (Frans Weisz, 1980), a portrait of an exiled young Jewish painter; *After Your Decrees* (*Zu Freiwild verdammt*, Jerzy Hoffman, 1984), a prison-break story about a child pursued through Poland by the occupying German forces; *Angry Harvest* (*Bittere Ernte*, Agnieszka Holland, 1985), a cruel claustrophobic tale about an Austrian Jew and the Polish farmer in whose house she is hiding; followed by *Hanussen* (István Szabó, 1988), a film about a magus which shows how much he overestimated himself during the rise of fascism; *The Rosegarden* (*Der Rosengarten*, Fons Rademakers, 1990), which commemorates twenty Jewish children executed during the final days of the war; *Europa, Europa* (*Hitlerjunge Salomon*, Agnieszka Holland, 1991), about a boy's escape and change of identity; *Warsaw—Year 5703* (*Der Daunenträger*, Janusz Kijowski, 1992), about life in the Warsaw ghetto; *From Hell to Hell* (*Von Hölle zu Hölle*, Dimitri Astrachan, 1997), in which Holocaust survivors fall victim to a postwar pogrom in Poland; and finally, *Babiy Yar* (*Babij Jar*, Jeff Kanew, 2003).

Contrary to what was happening in film theatres, television showed a great number of productions on the subject, such as "Kaddish for the Living" ("Kaddisch nach einem Lebenden," Karl Fruchtmenn, 1965), *One Day—A Report from a German Concentration Camp 1939* ("Ein Tag— Bericht aus einem deutschen KZ 1939," Egon Monk, 1968), or "Murder in Frankfurt" ("Mord in Frankfurt," Rolf Hädrich, 1968). These TV features joined the increasingly intense confrontations with German history offered by numerous made-for-TV documentaries—a nuanced confrontation that despite the diverse quality of these productions has continued until recent years.

Many other films joined Brauner's exceptional big-screen productions, but not until much later, after the upheaval in West German cinema caused by the 1962 Oberhausen Manifesto:[5] *Yesterday Girl* (*Abschied von Gestern*, Alexander Kluge, 1966) and, much later still, *Death Is My Trade* (*Aus einem deutschen Leben*, Theodor Kotulla, 1977), *In a Year of 13 Moons* (*In einem Jahr mit 13 Monden*, Rainer Werner Fassbinder, 1978), *David* (Peter Lilienthal, 1978), *The Nasty Girl* (*Das Schreckliche Mädchen*, Michael Verhoeven, 1989), and *Abraham's Gold* (*Abrahams Gold*, Jörg Graser, 1989). As diverse as they were, these films had in common at least that they preserved the dignity of the victims and, more so, didn't confuse victims and perpetrators. This fact deserves to be underlined when we compare these films to a string of other productions in which the executioners and their passive helpers were presented as victims. The directors of what was at that time the young German cinema were turning their backs on their parents' generation and by extension on the generation of filmmakers whose career spanned both Nazi Germany and the postwar period.

Regarded in more detail, these films prove themselves very diverse, shot as they were at different points during the FRG's history when their makers succumbed to the Germans' stubborn desire to regard themselves as victims. Fassbinder's *Lili Marleen* (1980) depicts the acts of an entertainer working for the German troops like a tragedy. The same goes for "Heimat" (Edgar Reitz, 1984), which spread out its complacent portrayal of misery in the German countryside under the Nazi rule over several prime-time broadcasts. Or *Fathers and Sons* (*Väter und Söhne*, Bernhard Sinkel, 1985), which presents the rise and fall of the family that founded IG Farben as a story of victims, forced by the Nazis to produce toxic gas. *The Ogre* (*Der Unhold*, Volker Schlöndorff, 1986) even boasts about innocence and seduction over the backs of the victims—at the end of the film, a death convoy departs ghostlike from an extermination camp—even when all it shows is daily life at an elite Nazi school. This tendency to turn history on its head seems irresistible when the misfortunes of the German in his favorite role, that of the victim, are once more the subject in *Stalingrad* (Joseph Vilsmaier, 1992). There is no stopping the German "master narrative" when, in a film such as *After the Truth* (*Nichts als die Wahrheit*, Roland Suso Richter, 1999), the fictitious return of concentration camp doctor Mengele can pose serious judicial and moral problems to 1999 Germany when it comes to judging this Nazi physician's crimes.

The radicalism of *In a Year of 13 Moons*, in which Fassbinder recounts the life and death of transsexual Elvira Weisshaupt in Frankfurt and in the same breath presents the prejudice to which she was subjected as the consequence of her lot, that of a survivor of the Bergen-Belsen camp, is also an exception in West German cinema. This is a film that could not be corrupted or integrated into an existing discourse, a film that offered West German audiences no possibilities of identification that would free them from their burden and thus allow them to spurn the victims.

A more recent example would be Dani Levy's *The Giraffe* (*Meschugge*, 1998), which powerfully shows how the pasts of victims and executioners catch up in entirely different ways with their children. Since the film is constructed as a thriller, we voluntarily or otherwise create passages between the world of the criminals and that of the victims, and the film concludes in the heart of disaster—even if the final shot ends the romantic encounter on a note of happiness. *The Giraffe* shows that what should in theory be irreconcilable could in real life find itself united and even lead, against all odds, to happiness.

Or to death. The Brauner-produced *Witness Out of Hell* contributed to the motif of the victim's incapacity to shed his role. Even during a trial such as the one against the criminals of Auschwitz, we have seen that, no matter how righteous the judgment against the executioners, all parties behave shamefully toward a victim, witness, and survivor of the camps, whose history never truly interests them.

To the main current of popular cinema of the period, limited to presenting its audiences with plausible stories, recounting the crime of the Holocaust remained off limits, but not the art of communicating the memory of the reign of terror. If it remained impossible to create images that did justice to the reality of the extermination, one could at least, with some distortion, represent trauma in the form of images or narrate it in cinema. The producer Brauner transposed these stories to films for mass audiences.

In the end, Brauner's cinema is perhaps not so far removed from that of Steven Spielberg and his *Schindler's List* (1993). It is possible that this cinema devoted to the Holocaust, the past that will not pass, has a future that radically blurs the boundaries of documentary and fiction, and takes a form similar to that of Romuald Karmakar's *The Himmler Project* (*Das Himmler Projekt*, 2000), a fiction film in the shape of a documentary.

Fiction films, too, can become documents of recent history. Artur Brauner's films will become an episode in the history of German films on the Holocaust and its consequences. As time passes we can evaluate their capacity for reflection. Then we can measure the degree of ignorance that led producer Bernd Eichinger to present *Downfall* (*Der Untergang*, Oliver Hirschbiegel, 2004) as the first film that managed to talk about Hitler without mentioning the extermination of the Jews.

Translated from the German by Tom Mes

Notes

1. This meeting of the study group "Cinematography of the Holocaust" took place December 2–4, 1999, in Frankfurt-am-Main. The various contributions to the conference were published in the volume edited by Claudia Dillmann and Ronny Loewy, *Die Vergangenheit in der Gegenwart. Konfrontationen mit den Folgen des Holocaust im Deutschen Nachkreigsfilm*, (Frankfurt-am-Main: Deutsches Filminstitut [DIF], 2001).

2. Ronny Loewy requests that the word *Holocaust* and not *Shoah* be used in the English translation of his original German text. (Ed.)

3. Cf. Claudia Dillmann, "Der Filmproduczent Artur Brauner," in *Artur Brauner. Produzent* (Munich: Goethe Institut, 2003).

4. Ibid.

5. In February 1962 at the short film festival in Oberhausen, twenty-six young filmmakers signed a text inspired by the spirit of artistic freedom and political rebellion of the French Nouvelle Vague. This manifesto, signed by Kluge, Fassbinder, Fleishman, Schlöndorff, and others is seen today as the birth of young German cinema.

Forgetting, Instrumentalization, and Transgression

The Shoah in Israeli Cinema

ARIEL SCHWEITZER

I N THE FILM *KEDMA* BY AMOS GITAÏ (2002), we witness the arrival by boat of Shoah escapees in Israel. As soon as they disembark, they are sent to the battlefront, integrated with the Israeli army troops in the midst of the War of Independence. In one of the most moving scenes of the film, a group of Israeli soldiers asks one of the escapees, Menahem, a religious cantor who speaks Yiddish, to sing for them. He launches into song—"Thy will be done . . ."—but as soon as he does, the soldiers, mocking him, interrupt with "We're not in a synagogue here."

This scene is revealing of the trauma experienced by many of the Jewish escapees, from one day to the next forced to transform themselves into "Israeli soldiers." More generally speaking, it attests to the huge gap separating the Zionist-socialist value system and the cultural heritage of the Diaspora. As noted by Israeli historian Tom Segev in his book *The Seventh Million*, "The Yishuv leaders [a Jewish community in Palestine] wanted to build a new nation, liberated from the two thousand year oppression in the Diaspora." "The New Man" that Zionists wanted to engender was, from all points of view, opposed to the stereotypical "old Jew," who had been persecuted, was submissive, and was usually a merchant. The new Zionist society sought to be creative, socialist, and secular; it instilled in its children a sovereign pride and the capacity to defend itself and protect its honor. But the Zionist ideal was also hindered by reality: the "new man" was lacking in depth; he had neither past nor ties to Jewish history, nor the experiences of most Israelis.[1]

Thus, the integration in Israel of the survivors of the genocide was long and often painful: in the eyes of many Israelis, who did not realize the extent of the extermination at the time, they represented the living symbol of a miserable existence, of dependency and humiliation, of the Jews of the Diaspora. They were even accused of having allowed themselves to be led to their death "like sheep to the slaughterhouse" without even trying to rebel.

Largely influenced by Zionist propaganda, the Israeli cinema of the 1940s and 1950s did not distance itself from the negative views of the Jewish Diaspora in Israel. Whether in didactic documentary (called "Zionist realism"), or later on in the first fictional films (the so-called heroic-nationalist genre),[2] the cinema of the time promoted the idea that Israel was an alternative to the Diaspora and that the survivors of the Shoah should be wrenched from their original culture in order to be integrated into the unifying Israeli mold. Films such as *Tomorrow's a Wonderful Day* (Helmar Lerski, 1947), *My Father's House* (Meyer Levin, 1947), *Dream No More* (Joseph Krumgold, 1949), or *The Faithful City* (Joseph Leytes, 1952) describe the integration process of these survivors through a series of oppositions: the traumatized, the sick, and those who were too passive (or even considered effeminate) must learn to work the land and defend it in order to assimilate themselves into the virile and glorious Zionist order. The Diaspora is thus presented as a threat to Zionism, and the escapees of the genocide are at times described through stereotypes derived from anti-Semitic tradition (passivity, laziness, and idleness). It is striking to note that the very question of the genocide is rarely broached in these films; it is a "structured absence" which is explained by the desire to erase the past and place the accent on the process of transforming the Jew into an Israeli.

Many films show scenes of escapee children. In *My Father's House*, an adolescent orphan is sent to an internment camp upon arriving in Israel. Refusing to accept the death of his father, he escapes and takes off in search of him. He roams the country, encountering adults he mistakes for his father along the way. Toward the end of the film, the Jewish Agency informs him that his father died in the camps. He is distraught and taken in by adoptive parents who help him understand that in Israel, the entire nation is his new family. In his book, *Makhela Aheret (Another Heart)*,[3] Nurith Gertz analyzes this film and describes it as a family romance, in which the Freudian search for the father ends with a symbolic renouncing of the Diaspora and the adoption of Zion and Zionism as a new collective father.

Some of the works in the Zionist cinema do an ideological "instrumentalization" of the Shoah by integrating it into a story involving the "besieged syndrome."[4] This is a form of collective neurosis that would have Israelis believe that they are constantly threatened, that the entire world is hostile toward them, and that in case of danger they can count on no one but themselves. This tragic and paranoid view of the world, profoundly tied to the Shoah experience, emerged in a powerful way during the Israeli-Arab wars (notably the Six-Day War), fed by the threats by Arab leaders to destroy Israel and to "throw the Jews into the sea." Thus, themes associating the Arab threat to the Shoah were largely present in the cinema of the time, including international co-productions filmed in Israel.

In the Zionist epic *Exodus* (Otto Preminger, 1960), we see Arab rioters draw a swastika on the wall of an Israeli house whose inhabitants they have just massacred. In *Hill 24 Doesn't Answer* (Thorold Dickinson, 1955), an Israeli soldier takes hostage a wounded Egyptian officer who turns out to be German, an ex-SS. The hostage goes on to pronounce an anti-Semitic discourse, during which he is transformed (through editing) into an SS soldier threatening an orthodox Jew. His monologue ends with a "Heil Hitler," after which the Nazi collapses, dead. Based at times on actual fact (some Nazis did find refuge within Arab armies), these films nonetheless demonize the Arab enemy by suggesting notably that the conflict with Israel has no political basis, and is nothing more than racial hatred, a type of new Arab anti-Semitism.

The attitude of Israelis regarding the Shoah began to change during the Eichmann trial, which was held in Jerusalem in 1961. Widely covered by the media, the trial contributed to a collective realization of the extent of the genocide and the profound trauma experienced by its survivors. Several films made after the trial attest to this turnaround. Nathan Gross, a survivor of the Krakow ghetto, made his first fictional feature film, *The Cellar*, in 1963. The film's protagonist, an escapee of the Shoah, moves to Tel Aviv, remembers his departure from Dachau and his revenge on a neighbor, an ex-SS officer. The importance of this film resides in the description of the isolation in Israeli society of the survivor, haunted by memories on which he cannot turn his back, as Zionism advocates he should. In the early seventies, writer Haim Gouri and filmmaker Jaco Erlich began making their documentary trilogy on the Shoah: *The 81ˢᵗ Blow* (1974), *The Last Sea* (1979), and *Flames in the Ashes* (1985). These films were still marked by the Zionist master-theory, and the immigration to Israel, *The Last Sea*, is presented as the only answer to the ills of the Diaspora. The history of the genocide is still associated with stories of resistance, *Flames in the Ashes* thus reviving the official doctrine of the teaching of the Shoah in Israel, whose day of commemoration was named "The Day of the Genocide and of Heroism." Nonetheless, this trilogy manages courageously to render a more nuanced view of the subject. Comprised of survivors' stories (among which are those of the testimonies given at Eichmann's trial) mixed with archival footage (filmed in large part by the Nazis), these films give voice to the survivors for the first time, without omitting criticism of the manner in which they were received by Israeli society. The title of the first film in the trilogy, *The 81ˢᵗ Blow*, is revealing in this regard: it is drawn from the testimony of a survivor who was given eighty lashings with a whip by a Nazi officer, and then collapsed. Managing somehow to survive, he went to live in Israel after the war. When he tells his story, no one believes him. For him, this is "the 81ˢᵗ blow."

Israeli photographer and documentarist David Perlov made two films about the Shoah. In 1962, after the Eichmann trial, he made a short film, *In Jerusalem*, comprised of a series of photographs of anonymous faces demolished by the storms of history and threatened with being forgotten. Perlov pursues his reflection on photography as a tool for remembrance in 1979 with *Souvenirs du Procès d'Eichmann* (*Memories of the Eichmann Trial*). Almost two decades after the event, he discovered certain witnesses who spoke of their experience during the trial. The most poignant testimony is that of Henryk Roth, who was the Lodz ghetto photographer. Risking his life, he had filmed daily life in the ghetto, the misery, the famine, all the way to the deportation to the camps. Roth had managed to hide these photos, which remain to this day the strongest document about the process of annihilation of the Jews recorded by one of its victims.

Contrary to auteur cinema, it is interesting to point out that commercial Israeli cinema has practically never dealt with the theme of the Shoah. Aside from an indirect and vulgar allusion in *Entebbe: Operation Thunderbolt* (also known as *Raid on Entebbe*) by Menahem Golan (1978), in which German terrorists kidnap an airline passenger who is an escapee from the camps, we don't see in this cinema any of the spectacular reconstitutions of the ghetto or the sentimental intrigues done later by Roberto Benigni or Steven Spielberg (whose films were well received in Israel). This absence is due to the fact that, since its birth in the mid-sixties, commercial Israeli cinema has been dominated by social and ethnic themes. These issues have been treated, often in the manner of caricature, through popular comedies of the "Burekas," a genre centered on Sephardic folklore and therefore little concerned with the fate of European Jews.

In the 1980s, a radical turning point took place in the Israeli cinema: a movement that was highly critical of Zionist-socialist values emerged. In a climate marked by the war in Lebanon (1982), filmmakers influenced by the "post-Zionist" theses of new Israeli historians began to debate the dominant ideology in Israel through the face of the Other. The Palestinian, the Sephardic Jew, the homosexual—these stereotypical images, marginalized for so long by Zionism, were now displaced from the periphery of the story to its center.[5]

The survivor is one of the Others, and his character is constructed by opposition to his representation in the Zionist cinema. Hence, character traits that were negative in films of the forties and fifties take on another, more positive, dimension: selfishness becomes individualism, passivity and the lack of practicality are transformed into spiritual richness, and the effeminate character becomes sensitive. Films such as *The Wooden Gun* (Ilan Moshenson, 1979), *Transit* (Daniel Wachsmann, 1979), or *Tel Aviv-Berlin* (Tzipi Trope, 1987) reverse the narrative formula introduced by Zionist cinema. The survivor's immigration to Israel, this story of rebirth with biblical dimension (the climbing out of the hell of the camps into a Zionist paradise), is transformed into a story of failure and bitterness.

The immigrants at the heart of these films live in Israel as uprooted people, foreigners in the local culture, isolated in a society perceived at that point as violent, vulgar, and empty. They lock themselves up in a world raised on European culture and dream often of leaving Israel to return to live in their country of origin (the image of the immigrant roaming along the seashore and nostalgically looking out at the horizon is seen repeatedly in these films). In *The Wooden Gun*, a Shoah survivor locks herself up in a shack on the shore, which she transforms into a place to remember the family she lost. Her humanism and sensitivity are the very negation of the society that surrounds her: children who imitate the adult world by playing at war and who think she is insane. One of these children, who has just wounded his friend, is rescued by the survivor: he then learns to know her and realizes the vanity of his virility games.

In his work, Nurith Gertz demonstrates how the story of the search for the father in the Zionist cinema is transformed in *The Wooden Gun* into a search for the mother, there again with all the symbolic connotations.[6]

A variation of the search for the maternal figure is also offered in *Summer of Aviya* (Elie Cohen, 1988, based on a novel and play by Gila Almagor): a girl whose father died in the camps believes she recognizes him in another man, a neighbor. Grasping her mistake, she becomes closer to her mother, a psychologically damaged survivor, of whom she had always been ashamed. The originality of this film, which is based on Almagor's childhood memories, resides in an identification with the character of the mother, whom Almagor chose to play herself. In so doing, she created a metaphorical union between the child that she actually was and the mother she portrays in the film.

In 1988, during the first Intifada, Yehuda Elkana, an Auschwitz survivor, published the article entitled "In Favor of Forgetting," which raised a great deal of controversy. Shocked by the acts of violence committed by the Israeli army in the occupied territories, Elkana rises up against the instrumentalization of the Shoah to ideological ends: "I see no greater danger for the future of the State of Israel than the fact that the Shoah was systematically and strongly presented to the heart of the consciousness of Israeli society, even to the generation born and raised here. . . . What do we expect these children to do with these memories? For many, the images of horror have a risk of being interpreted as a call to blind hatred. It is perhaps important that the world remember, but this should not be our preoccupation. We, however, should forget."[7]

In his film *Izkor, Slaves of Memory* (1991), Eyal Sivan prolongs this bold reflection. His film deals with the manner in which Israeli education instrumentalizes the commemoration of the Shoah, like the War of Independence, by exacerbating nationalist sentiment among youth. Sivan integrated the virulent commentary of philosopher Yeshayahu Leibovitz in his film. And he devoted another work, *Itgaber: He Will Overcome* (1993) to him as well. Highly esteemed in Israel, Leibovitz shocked many by using the term "Judeo-Nazi" to criticize the repressive behavior of certain soldiers during the Intifada. His sense of provocation largely contributed to launching the debate on the subject, which had been previously taboo. Eyal Sivan pursued his work on this subject of memory in his film *The Specialist* (1999), about the Eichmann trial. Based on the Hannah Arendt thesis on the "banality of evil," Sivan's film presents Eichmann as "an ordinary man," "an office criminal," thus contradicting the official vision of Israeli justice that considers him a monster unique in the history of humanity. The filmmaker remains prudent this time by avoiding the intimation of an overly simplistic connection between the Nazi criminal and the Israeli-Palestinian conflict. But he does not hesitate in manipulating documentary images with digital effects to illustrate his point more effectively. He goes as far as to divert some survivor testimonies by having the speakers dialogue with people to whom they did not speak during the trial.[8]

The aftereffects of the Shoah felt by the children of survivors were another theme tackled at the time by Israeli documentaries. These films show to what extent trauma is profoundly anchored in Israeli society, transferred from one generation to the next, in spite of the Zionist claim of having turned the page on the past and eradicated the weight of these memories. *Because of That War* (Orna Ben-Dor, 1988) is devoted to two musicians who are sons of survivors, the singer Yehuda Poliker and the lyricist Yaacov Gilad. Together they made a deeply moving recording, "Cendre et poussière" ("Ashes and Dust"), marked by the identification of the experience of their parents, as well as their own childhood memories as young men raised in the shadow of the genocide. Here, art, and in this case musical creation, takes on a dimension of exorcism that allows them to face a past "that does not pass."

Other documentaries have been filmed by children of survivors, driven by a feeling of duty and urgency: the necessity of gathering the testimony of a generation that will soon disappear. In *Choice and Destiny* (1993), Tsipi Reibenbach chose to film her parents in their apartment in Lod. With meticulous care and great patience, the filmmaker captures their daily life through long sequence shots. Before their daughter's camera, the conversations in the living room and the ritual of meals in the kitchen are the basis of a return to what was repressed, bringing back painful memories of which they have rarely dared to speak. The film ends with a very beautiful scene of the Shabbat dinner, suggesting that the warmth of the family and the Jewish tradition can help, not to forget the past, but to be able to live with it.

Translated from the French by Anna Harrison

Notes

1. Tom Segev, *The Seventh Million*, trans. from the English and Hebrew by Eglal Errara (Paris: Editions Liana Levi, 1993), 589. The title, "The Seventh Million" refers to the survivors of the Shoah and the Jewish community that received them upon their arrival in Palestine, and later Israel.

2. Regarding these two movements, I would like to reference my book, *Le Cinéma Israélien de la Modernité* (*Modern Israeli Cinema*) (Paris: l'Harmattan), 50–69.

3. Nurith Gertz, *Makhela Aheret* (*Another Heart*) (Tel Aviv: Am-Oved, 2004), 25–28.

4. Regarding the "besieged syndrome" and its manifestations in the Israeli cinema, see Nitzan Ben-Shaul, *Mythical Expressions of Siege in Israeli Films* (Lewiston: Millen Press, 1997).

Tools for History

The Filmed Witness

ANNETTE WIEVIORKA

IN JANUARY 2005, THE COMMEMORATION of the sixtieth anniversary of the liberation of the Auschwitz camp was the subject of unprecedented media coverage in France as well as in most of the countries in the Western world. Television played a very large part in this coverage, multiplying subjects from the very beginning of the commemorative ceremony. Those in charge of these programs went in search of survivors of all sorts with veritable casting calls, trying to find the "best" deportees. The presenter on Channel TF1, Patrick Poivre d'Arvor, brought in two of the indisputable stars of these programs by private plane, Henri Borlant and Ida Grynspan.[1] Their visit to Birkenau opened the "8 O'Clock News" on January 27, 2005. Simone Veil, the ex-Minister of State and former president of the European Parliament, was presented in a number of television programs and on the radio. *Paris Match* devoted a report to her visit to Birkenau in the company of her children and grandchildren. For, as repeatedly stated by journalists, it was urgent to hear, to see the last survivors. Soon, there would be no more witnesses and the memory of the Shoah would be threatened by the death of these witnesses. And then the millions of published or recorded testimonies would be of no use. The witness—a term that has become a synonym for *victim* in today's language—would exist in the present tense only as one who is in the act of witnessing, preferably facing the lens of a camera.

In *L'Ère du témoin* (*The Era of the Witness*),[2] I noted the turning point that took several directions represented by the trial of Adolf Eichmann in Jerusalem in 1961. This trial was powerfully innovative and marked the advent of the witness. In Jerusalem, the prosecutor Gideon Hausner affirmed witnessing; it was not a question of judging a man but of giving a history lesson, to the Israelis as well as to the rest of the world. On the contrary, during the Nuremberg trials, prosecutor Robert H. Jackson intentionally based his accusations on documents, in spite of the opposition of his first deputy, William J. Donovan, a representative of the OSS (Office of Strategic Services, ancestor to the CIA) and an expert in propaganda, who pled in favor of a trial built upon eyewitness accounts. Such accounts were, in his eyes, much more humane and educational.[3] This was the option chosen by Hausner: to construct the staging of the trial upon the depositions by witnesses:

> The only way to actually touch upon the truth was to call witnesses to the stand in as large a number as the framework of the trial allowed and to ask each one for a small fragment of what he or she had seen and experienced. The story told of a certain sequence of events made by just one witness is tangible enough to be visualized. Given one after another, the successive testimonies of very different people, having lived very different experiences, would give a sufficiently eloquent visualization to be recorded. In this way I hoped to give another dimension to this ghostly past, that of a reality.[4]

The essence of the Eichmann trial was therefore the litany of 111 eyewitness accounts.

In Nuremberg, witnesses (sixty-one) were called to the stand by the defense, as well as by prosecuting lawyers (thirty-three). They were not there to "tell history," but to simply complete it, specify it, and document it. "Orders, status reports, official reports, projects, personal notes, and even typed transcriptions of phone conversations intercepted by the Gestapo. It appeared that all of the official, public, private or secret archives of the Third Reich were preserved by conscientious bureaucrats only so that they could later be used against the ex-leaders of Germany," noted the attentive witness Didier Lazard. These documents were read to those present, some of them several times. And these readings had a soporific effect. All those in attendance, including the accused, whose lives were at stake and who dozed behind their dark glasses, noted that Nuremberg was a trial that was very boring. "Straightaway the room seemed quiet and peaceful," noted one of the accused:

> We could hear someone speaking somewhere and had the impression of listening to a simple conversation. It appeared as though nothing was really happening: a play with no action, played by mutes. It was impossible to guess that the victors were evaluating

the responsibility of those who had started a war during which the world was almost destroyed. Only the earphones placed in front of each seat allowed one to assume that something was going on in the room, translating into four languages what the orator was quietly saying.[5]

Among the prosecution's witnesses, those chosen by assistant prosecutor Charles Dubost, in charge of presenting the Nazi atrocities perpetrated in the West, had the task of explaining what the concentration camps in fact were. A few minutes of their testimony was filmed, as were other excerpts of the trial.[6] We find the same slowness, the same murmuring discourse as in other parts of the trial. The first French witness was Maurice Lampe. A resistant arrested in November 1941, interned for two years in France, Lampe was then deported to Mauthausen. He described the infernal voyage in the livestock train wagons, his arrival in the camp on March 25, 1944, in a convoy of 1,200 French citizens, the work in the quarries and the ordeal that were the 186 steps that led to it. On Monday, January 28, Marie-Claude Vaillant-Couturier was called to the stand. Her testimony caused a sensation. Aside from being Foreign Minister Joachim Von Ribbentrop's secretary, she was the first woman to appear in this trial in which only men were present: public ministers, judges, the accused. She was indisputably a heroine of the Resistance. A communist deputy of the constituent assembly, she had just been appointed a chevalier of the Legion of Honor. But after the testimony given on April 15 by Rudolf Höss (commander of the camp), hers was also the only testimony of a deportee having survived Auschwitz. Vaillant-Couturier told her story: her arrest on February 9, 1942, by the Vichy police, who turned her over to the German authorities after holding her for six weeks; the five-month stay in the "health prison" and then at the Romainville fort; and finally, on January 23, 1943, the departure for an unknown destination in a convoy of 230 women, among whom were Maï Politzer and Danielle Casanova. She described her arrival in Auschwitz, how the train cars were detached and the women taken to the Birkenau camp—"It was a branch of the Auschwitz camp in an immense plain that, in January, was completely frozen." Then they were disinfected, their heads shaven, and the Auschwitz number was tattooed on their forearms: this happened only at Auschwitz/Birkenau. She described the unspeakable living conditions there, the roll calls, the labor, the pseudo-medical experiments—notably sterilizations—and the deaths. Charles Dubost questioned her on the fate of the Jews, and Vaillant-Couturier described the "selection," to which she was an eyewitness when she worked on the "cutting block," across from the ramp where the trains stopped:

When a convoy of Jews arrived, they made their selection: first the old men, the old women, the mothers and the children that they loaded into trucks, as well as the sick and those who seemed weak. They only kept the young women and men who were then sent to the men's work camp.

And this eyewitness explained: "Generally, for a convoy of one thousand to fifteen hundred people, rarely more than two hundred fifty—and this was the absolute maximum—actually entered into the camp. The rest were sent directly to the gas chambers."

As Vaillant-Couturier evoked her transfer to the Ravensbrück women's camp, the presiding judge seemed fed up, wanting the witness to get to the end of her testimony. He asked: "The conditions in the Ravensbrück camp seem to have been the same as those in Auschwitz; would it be possible, having heard all the details, to get to the question more generally, unless there was a substantial difference between Ravensbrück and Auschwitz?"

Dubost spoke up: "I believe there is a difference which was exposed by the witness and which is the following: in Auschwitz the interns were simply exterminated, so it was nothing more than an extermination camp, whereas in Ravensbrück they were interned to work. They were worked to death." Thus, the particular role of Auschwitz in the destruction of the Jews of Europe and that of the Jews of France had not been clearly perceived. Systematic death was the fate of all the deported. The only difference was in the modality of their death. For some it was gas chambers, for others they were worked until they died of complete exhaustion. It is significant that among the French prosecution's witnesses, there were no Jewish survivors from the deportation to illustrate the case of Auschwitz, so a resistant had to be found.

And yet, Vaillant-Couturier's testimony was not filmed in its entirety, far from it. But the excerpts that we have allow us to measure the assurance of this witness, her fluency in English and German, her accusatory posture, notably when she left the stand and threw a vengeful look at the accused. Marie-Claude Vaillant-Couturier is not a victim. She was and remains a combatant before and after her deportation. She is a heroine.

Other witnesses were also called to speak of the concentration camps, such as Jean-Frédéric Veith, deported to Mauthausen, Victor Dupont, who spoke of Buchenwald, where he spent twenty months, and François Boix, a Spanish refugee, a photojournalist who managed to take a number of pictures in Mauthausen, which he presented at the trial. And there was the evocation by Paul Roser from the Rawa Ruska camp, a reprisal camp for prisoners of war who had attempted to escape, often assimilated with the concentration camps but guarded by the Wehrmacht and not the SS. Finally it was the turn of Dr. Alfred Balachowsky, head of the laboratory at the Pasteur Institute, deported to Dora and then taken to Buchenwald. He began with a description of the Dora camp, which annoyed the presiding judge, Rt. Hon. Col. Sir Geoffrey Lawrence, who said impatiently:

> Mr. Dubost, you said you would call this witness to question him about his experiences. He is giving us all the details of life in the camps which we have already heard several times.
>
> • Mr. Dubost: Sir, no one has spoken yet of the Dora camp.
>
> • Presiding Judge: Yes, all the camps which we have heard about describe very much the same brutality according to the witnesses who have been called to the stand; I understood that you had called this witness to speak of his experience.
>
> • Mr. Dubost: If the Court is persuaded that all the camps used the same regime, my demonstration is done and the witness will move on to expose the camp experience at Buchenwald. But I wanted to demonstrate that all the German camps were the same. I believe the proof has been given.
>
> • Presiding Judge: If we needed this to be proven, we would have to call all the witnesses from all the camps, and that would be hundreds of people.

To hear all their testimonies, with the inevitable redundancies, interested no one at the time. Such accounts offered little interest in the writing of history. Moreover, the court could interrupt or stop a witness without giving the impression of committing an act of sacrilege.

The fictional reconstitution done by Yves Simoneau (*Nuremberg*, Canada/USA, 2000), filmed for television, shows through anachronism that it contains the migration of meaning given by testimony. In fact, prosecuting attorney Jackson (Alec Baldwin) shows concern about the boredom overtaking the trial participants and the casual attitude of the accused in the face of the crimes of which they are accused. A decision is therefore made to show the suffering by calling witnesses to the stand. Among those selected is Marie-Claude Vaillant-Couturier (Charlotte Gainsbourg). When she tells her story (the script is comprised of excerpts from Vaillant-Couturier's actual testimony), only sobs break the silence that has fallen over the courtroom. The presiding judge questions her gently, with great consideration and delicacy. This reconstruction shows what we now expect from witnesses: that they deeply move their listeners.

This sacralization of the witness came about during the Eichmann trial. What does it matter if one witness repeats what another has said, that the stories of atrocities pile up? The witness is not on the stand to "prove" anything. He is there for his word to be heard. His word is meant to be diffused, and to allow these things, according to Hausner, to be "visualized." In fact, Eichmann's trial was widely covered by the media. Israeli radio was in charge of recording the debates, which were diffused throughout the country, some on loudspeakers in the streets. This was an innovation. It was a matter of both providing images to the world, even though Israel did not have its own networks, and preserving the trial in its totality. As opposed to what happened at Nuremberg, the film of the Eichmann trial was intended to become archival footage.[7] These recordings are part of what Hannah Arendt denounced as "a show trial." Beyond what this designation carries in ambiguity (for the contemporaries of the Eichmann trial, it evokes the Nazi or Soviet trials, that of Dimitrov in Leipzig, those of Moscow or Prague), the complete recording of the trial enters well into this logic of spectacularization.

Our knowledge of the filming methods used is still minimal, and dependant upon the writings of Rony Brauman and Eyal Sivan,[8] who exhumed the images for their film *The Specialist* (1999). The historical decision to film the totality of the trial is responsible for its publicization. By accepting the filming, the court cited Bentham: "When there is no publicity, there is no justice. Publicity is the soul of the trial." Visualizing the trial is also part of the framework of the emergence of a new medium: in 1960, the American presidential election that brought John F. Kennedy to power was for the first time centered on television; in this case, it was to a private American company (CCBC) that the video recording of the Eichmann trial was granted. The thirty hours of the verdict were filmed by the Israelis in 35mm. Of some five hundred hours filmed, approximately 150 were lost.

The recording of the Jerusalem trial is the work of an authentic filmmaker, American Leo Hurwitz. While John Ford had been at the head of the crew hired to organize the filming of the Nuremberg trials, he was out of the picture quickly. His role was therefore tenuous, as opposed to that of Hurwitz. This son of immigrant Jews originally from Eastern Europe was one of the key people in the successive groups of documentary filmmakers from the American far Left—The Workers' Film (1930–35), Nykino (1935–37), and Frontier Film Group (1936–1942)—who notably affirmed his concern for the racism against black Americans, to which he had devoted his first postwar film (*Strange Victory*, 1948). In the footsteps of Alain Resnais, he made *The Museum and the Fury* in 1956, on and around the State Museum at Auschwitz. Therefore, Hurwitz already had a view of the genocide of the Jews and undertook his own portrayal of the event: choice of angles, use of continuity shots, variations of scale in shots, etc. At the end of each of the presentations that he made of his work, he offered a daily "synopsis" of the process that was sent to the American and European television stations. After the trial, a selection of seventy hours was preserved to be recycled. Here again, the archives that everyone had forgotten were rediscovered, digitized by Sivan and Brauman, who looked through them and used just a small part for *The Specialist*. As it happened, the images that circulated at the time of the trial were those of the most moving witnesses, chosen among the "One hundred ten emissaries who, one after the other, took the stand to guide us through the kingdom of desolation" (Haim Gouri). They were not testifying for the first time: they had written up their memories or participated in gatherings of testimony. But it was the first time that they were filmed. For some, it would not be the last time. Simon Srebnik or Mordechai Podklebnik would appear in Claude Lanzmann's film *Shoah* (1985); others would be recorded by video camera within the framework of large projects such as those undertaken by Yale University and by Steven Spielberg.

Each Nazi trial brought the emergence of a capital witness, who generally became the icon of that trial. For Nuremberg, it was indisputably Marie-Claude Vaillant-Couturier. Among the witnesses at the Eichmann trial, it was Ka-Tzetnik (which means "the concentration camp prisoner" in the slang of the camps) and his very brief testimony, which was among the most memorable and which is regularly repeated in films about the trial. His real name, Yehiel De-Nur, a Hebraization of Dinenberg, was revealed during the trial. In fact, this ex-member of "planet Auschwitz" was a writer whose two works, the first written in Yiddish immediately after his liberation and then his bestseller *House of Dolls*,[9] made him famous. To Gideon Hausner, who asked him his family name, he stated,

> It is not a pen name. I don't consider myself a writer in the literal sense of the word. I am just the historian of planet Auschwitz. I stayed there about two years. Time did not have the same measure as on earth. Each fraction of a second had a different measure. The inhabitants of this planet had no name, they had no family; they weren't born there and they did not bear children. They breathed according to laws that were not those of nature. They

did not live or die the way people do on earth. Their names were
number—Ka-Tzetnik.

Hausner then interrupted him, showed him the clothing worn by prisoners. "Yes," answered the witness, "here is the uniform worn on planet
Auschwitz. I believe with all my heart that I should continue to bear the
name Ka-Tzetnik as long as the world has not arisen after the crucifixion
of this nation to vanquish evil, the way it arose after the crucifixion of
just one person. I believe, with all my heart, that the stars influence our
destiny; this ashen planet of Auschwitz is in opposition to the planet
Earth and still influences it." A few more words by the witness who
designated himself as "historian"—and he fainted. This fainting became
the emblematic vision of the face-to-face encounter between victim and
executioner. Eichmann remained impassible in his glass cage (which
remains to this day part of the collection in the Museum of Ghetto
Combatants in Israel), whereas the simple mention of Auschwitz anni-
hilated the witness.

　　With the Eichmann trial, which instituted for the first time the
genocide of the Jews as a distinct event, with its own dynamic, pursuing
its own ends, and no longer just one aspect of the multiform criminality
of the Nazis, the witness acquired the social identity of survivor, because
society recognized this in him. Because technology allowed it, the witness
was now filmed. Before the Eichmann trial, the survivors—at least the
ones who wished to—maintained this identity by and in an associative
life, an associative life closed upon itself, that allowed one both to honor
the memory of the dead and to maintain a sociability among people who
had lived through the same events, a little like the gatherings between
fellow soldiers. Those—and they were many—who did not wish to be
considered as survivors built a family and a professional life and stayed
away from associations. The Eichmann trial changed the order of things.
At the heart of this newly attributed identity of survivors is that of messenger of history. But the messenger of history is also a victim, whose
story and face are revealed to everyone.

　　This change is in phase with those that affected Western society
more generally with the birth of mass media (television) and the society
of spectacle. It also reflects the surge of individualism. Psychological
difficulties are publicly exposed in many programs of what sociologist
Dominique Mehl calls *la television de l'intimité* (the television of intimacy).
The right to enter into the dignity of history is no longer reserved for
Great Men, as in the Pantheon; it is democratically the right of all.
All lives are equal and worth telling about. A psychoanalytical vulgate
also teaches us that finding words to tell a traumatic story has curative

value. And yet, in a period where, with and after the Eichmann trial, the genocide of the Jews acquired a centrality in the history of World War II and its aftermath, and where the Jewish victim is the victim par excellence, the search for the story of what he or she has lived becomes generalized, with new recording technologies, primarily video.

At the end of the seventies, following the controversies in the United States, as in France and Germany, pursuant to the broadcast of the American television series "Holocaust," the idea arose that we should gather video recordings of the testimonies of those the Americans decided to call the *Survivors*, defined as all the Jews who had lived under Nazi domination during the Third Reich or in the countries it occupied. The impulse came from the victims themselves, who did not recognize their history in the televised series and therefore wished to tell it themselves. On the initiative of a group of survivors in the city of New Haven, Connecticut, the recordings began. In 1982, Yale University offered them help through its representative, Geoffrey Hartmann. The Fortunoff Video Archives for Holocaust Testimonies were thus created.[10] Branches of it were formed in various cities in the United States and in a number of countries. In this way, some four thousand testimonies were gathered. At the heart of the project is the concern for the survivor as a person. Psychiatrist and psychoanalyst Dori Laub, who ensured a large part of the training of interviewers and was one of those who prepared the protocol for the interviews, explains:

> Lying is toxic and silence is suffocating. Each survivor has an intense need to tell his story in order to finally connect all the pieces, a need to face the ghosts of the past, a need to know his buried truth in order to recover the course of his life. It is a mistake to think that silence promotes peace. All it does is perpetuate the tyranny of past events, promote their distortion and allow them to contaminate daily life.

And he continues by insisting on the fact that speaking should only happen if one is listened to: "A story that is not listened to is as serious a trauma as the initial ordeal."[11] The testimonies are recorded with a method that reminds us of analysis, in a studio in order to allow self-reflection. The camera, practically immobile, films a close-up of the face, seeking to capture emotion. The interviewer intervenes as little as possible. He is simply there to allow for the process to happen: a story in which the witness is allowed to determine the length (at times several hours) and that happens in only one session according to the premise of unity in analysis.

Today, video archives have multiplied and some of them are available on the Internet. In 1994, having made *Schindler's List* (1993), and to respond to the wishes of "survivors" and create a factual counterpoint to his film, which certainly claimed historical accuracy but also belonged to fictional cinema, Steven Spielberg put together a Survivors of the Shoah Visual History Foundation, whose somewhat megalomaniac objective was to record the testimonies of all the survivors. To date, it has collected 52,000 testimonials.[12] Museums, memorials, and associations have also created their own archives. Hence, the same person may be interviewed several times. The multiplication of testimonials poses the problem that also calls to mind that of an archive in our present time, a problem Borges understood in creating his character Funes. After an accident, when he regained consciousness: "The present as well as the oldest and most banal memories had become unbearable from being so rich and clear. . . . His perception and memory had become infallible." Not only did he remember "each leaf on every tree in every forest, but each time that he had seen or imagined it. He therefore decided to limit the days spent to some seventy thousand, which he would then designate by numbers. He was dissuaded from this by two considerations: the awareness that the task was interminable, the realization that it was useless. He realized that at the hour of his death, he would not have finished classifying all his childhood memories." The narrator suspects Funes of not being "very capable of thought. Thinking is generalizing, making things abstract. In the overcrowded world of Funes, there was nothing but detail, almost immediately."[13] Hence, having too many memories kills memory, and above all thought, just as too many archives destroy archives and too many testimonies kill testimony.

The dual finality of these collections is the same everywhere: to create archives for the near future, when these men and women will no longer be with us; and based on these interviews, to create material for what we call "educating people about the Holocaust," which has become an international preoccupation. Education, not teaching. In fact, during the years when the question was being asked regarding the spoliation of Jewish belongings, first by Swiss banks and then in various countries, the "Holocaust," to coin the commonly used term in the United States, has become the object of international conferences. The one that took place in 1997 in Washington focused on the bank assets and the art having belonged to the assassinated Jews. Voices, notably that of Elie Wiesel, the witness par excellence in the United States, were raised expressing the fear that the question of material compensation for the victims and that of restitution of their assets masked what appeared to some to be the essential fact, that time was taking its toll and contemporaries were disappearing: for the generations born after the war, the memory of the extermination was getting ever farther from the event. Then a "Task Force for Holocaust Education" was created, whose membership extends to twenty-eight countries and which finances and runs educational programs primarily in Eastern European countries. Three years later, in January 2000, the heads of forty-six countries, among others Prime Minister Lionel Jospin and Chancellor Gerhardt Schroeder, met in Stockholm and adopted a declaration engaging the participants to promote education, memory, and research so that future generations would "learn their lesson" from this.

The ceremony organized on January 27, 2005, at Auschwitz-Birkenau for the sixtieth anniversary of the liberation of the camps by the Soviet armies attested to the political importance gained by the memory of the destructions of the Jews of Europe: about forty heads of state and governments took part in it, among them Vladimir Putin, Gerhardt Schroeder, and Jacques Chirac. Broadcast live on television the world over, it constituted to some extent the acme of an evocation—begun throughout the media in January and continuing through May 8—of the liberation of the Western camps (Buchenwald, Bergen-Belsen, Dachau, Mauthausen, etc.) by the Allies and the unconditional surrender of Nazi Germany. The following year, on January 27, the date of the liberation by the soldiers of the Soviet armies, the UN instituted an international day of commemoration.

"Educating" is not "teaching." The first imperative is about morality. It signifies that we will be handing over to young people the rules of society, what distinguishes good from evil. Teaching aims at transmitting knowledge.

Within this "education," the witness and the testimony, in flesh and bone when possible, filmed when it is not possible, occupy a principal place in a somewhat caricatured vision. On one side the executioner, who incarnates evil, but who no longer appears in the process of testimony, who is only present in the words of the witness-victim; on the other side the victim, on the side of good. The demonstration of this suffering, via the testimony, therefore has an "educative" quality. Certainly, the effects, notably on young people, cannot be the same. By his very physical presence, even before he utters the slightest word, the witness marks the contemporaneity of the events to which he attests. He says that several generations share the same world. No matter the proximity brought about through the methods of filming (the close-up on the face, or the total absence of the interviewer onscreen, which allows us to think that the witness is speaking directly to the viewer and only to him), the story is publicized. Even though those who came up with the

Yale project attempted to not make these interviews into films by using the camera only as an immobile eye that records, in which the survivor tells his story and the viewer watching and listening is supposed to forget that the camera is even there, nevertheless they are films.

The story the witness tells is, like any story, a construction. This construction/reconstruction is the very infrastructure, the backbone of the present life of the person telling it. The memory is constituent of the identity. But this memory is not history, which implies an operation of deconstruction and criticism, and above all distancing. In this sense, the invasion of the testimony, that of the French World War I soldiers, just as those drafted for the war in Algeria, illustrates a new rapport with the past, or rather the erasing of the past that Olivier Rolin in his novel *Paper Tiger* perceived. He opposed our era to that of the revolutionary youth:

> The world you had before you, in which you lived, was transformed by a power that connected each event, each individual, to a chain of events and to an older chain of events and individuals that were even more tragic. . . . Today there seems to be nothing but the present, of the very instant, the present has become a colossal mass, a prodigious innervation, a permanent big bang.[14]

The nonstop recording of the witnesses of the Shoah, today that of "hidden children," participates in this permanent "big bang."

With the fall of the Berlin Wall, the end of the great historical stories and the heroes who make history, the victim has become a great figure. In the "victims' Olympics" (Peter Novick), the survivors of the assassinated Jewish people have been alone for a long time, out of competition, so to speak. Today, the litany of those who have suffered in history, descendents of slaves, of the colonies, survivors of the Armenian and Cambodian genocides, the Tutsis who escaped the Hutu machetes but who bear the stigma, and so many others, also offer to the political scene the stories of their abject misfortunes, filmed when possible. And these sufferings, outside of the context in which they were inflicted, resemble one another. Hence the paradox of the Era of the Witness resides in the fact that in wanting to draw the individual from the masses, we end up, in this time of globalization, by unifying, by giving uniformity to individual destinies, making them into a whole in which sufferings are all mixed together. Hence the Shoah, this event without images—since no film shows what was at its heart, the mass assassination in gas chambers—will have finally produced the most vast corpus of images, probably a hundred million, of which we may ask ourselves to what, if any, use they will be put.

Translated from the French by Anna Harrison

Notes

1. Their testimony is available on a DVD, entitled *14 récits d'Auschwitz* (*14 Stories about Auschwitz*), MK2, 2005.
2. Plon, 1998.
3. Lawrence Douglas, *The Memory of Judgment. Making Law and History, Trials of the Holocaust* (New Haven and London: Yale University Press, 2001), 17. This remarkable work devotes its first part to the "film as witness," to the projection of *Nazi Concentration Camps* at the Nuremberg trials. The fact that it was not translated authorized all plagiarism.
4. Gideon Hausner, *Justice à Jerusalem. Eichmann devant ses juges* (*Justice in Jerusalem: Eichmann Faces His Judges*) (Paris: Flammarion, 1966), 384.
5. Didier Lazard, *Le Procès de Nuremberg. Récit d'un témoin* (*The Nuremberg Trials. The Testimony of One Witness*) (Paris: Editions de la Nouvelle Presse, 1947), 33.
6. The decision was made to film the trial, probably to provide footage for filmed newsreels and later to make a documentary. Contrary to what has sometimes been said, giving in to the sin of anachronism, the idea of making filmed archives was not part of the motivation for the promoters of the trial. Only a few dozen hours were recorded, following a logic that, without any serious research into the subject, remains unexplained.
7. This is a reiteration of a discussion I had with Sylvie Lindeperg.
8. Rony Brauman and Eyal Sivan, *Éloge de la désobéissance* (*In Praise of Disobedience*) (Le Pommier, 1999).
9. Published by Gallimard in France in 1958, in a translation based on the English version, which sold poorly in France.
10. Their site presents the archive contents. Excerpts from testimonies can be downloaded. www.library.yale.edu/testimonies.
11. Quoted in Annick Cojean's article, "Les voix de l'indicible" ("The Voices of the Unspeakable"), *Le Monde*, April 25, 1995.
12. It is now part of the University of Southern California. The site enables people to consult these testimonials: www.usc.edu/schools.colleges.
13. Jorge Luis Borges, "Funes the Memorious" (in French: "Funes ou la mémoire"), in *Fictions* (Paris: Gallimard, 1957).
14. Olivier Rolin, *Tigre en papier* (*Paper Tiger*) (Paris: Editions du Seuil [coll. "Fiction & Cie"], 2002).

Historiography/Holocaust Cinema

Challenges and Advances

STUART LIEBMAN

THE HISTORIOGRAPHY OF HOLOCAUST cinema has had to overcome several obstacles, both material and conceptual, in order to contribute more vitally to the broader field of Holocaust studies. For many decades, the most obvious problem was material: locating and gaining access to films, many long forgotten, that were often only transient visitors in the public spheres of different countries. Few were available for re-viewing after their initial public runs, sometimes in marginal exhibition venues. This problem has now been happily resolved, at least for some of the more prominent titles, with the advent of videotape and DVD distribution. But the vast majority of Holocaust films, especially of the more ephemeral sorts—newsreels, propaganda shorts, television programs, fundraising vehicles, etc.—have either been lost or are buried in archives around the world where only the most dedicated researchers will find them. Even more deeply buried or, alas, now lost, are various kinds of documentation that could help explain the genesis of such works, the vicissitudes of their production, and the nature of their marketing and reception in different countries at different times.[1] These materials are often as revealing as the finished films themselves. They provide crucial insights into how and why these films were conceived; what aims their makers or sponsors intended to serve; how the projects were amended to accommodate the at-times-conflicting demands of producers, exhibitors, and state authorities; where they were seen and by whom; and, finally, what audiences may have taken away to form the substrate of knowledge and feeling informing public discourse about the Holocaust that later films would have to renegotiate.[2] Locating such sources and understanding their *raisons d'être* necessarily constitute the ground of any adequate historiography of Holocaust cinema.

Two decades ago, Claude Lanzmann essentially declared such materials to be irrelevant. He quite correctly observed that the footage endlessly recycled in countless documentaries (and even in fiction films), and which has been widely identified as visual evidence of the Holocaust—namely, the thousands of feet recorded by the film and photographic units of the Allied armies during the liberation of Majdanek and Auschwitz in the East, or of Buchenwald, Bergen-Belsen, Nordhausen, and Ohrdruf, among many other Western camps—portrays precisely the awful aftermath of the war and not the core of the extermination operations against the Jews.[3] Many of the survivors we see in such films, moreover, were not Jews, and the fate of those we do see was *not* typical of their fellow Jews in the extermination camps in eastern Poland. He also proscribes simulacra of Holocaust scenes in fictional films.[4] Only oral testimonies by crucial eyewitnesses to the murder of the Jews provide an adequate foundation for any work purporting to be a Holocaust film.[5] Such strictures, although grounded in critical and moral principles I respect,[6] effectively consign to oblivion countless films about the Holocaust that do not depend on oral testimony, that have used archival footage, or that attempt to recreate or imagine stories about the experience of Jews during the most harrowing period of their existence in modern times. For better or worse, such films have constituted a significant dimension of public awareness of the Holocaust from the end of World War II. Examining them closely, explaining how and why they came into being, understanding their narrational, stylistic, and rhetorical strategies, and assessing what they have contributed to—or, how they have distorted—our understanding of the Holocaust must be, *pace* Lanzmann, the vital purpose of any historiographical account of Holocaust cinema.

Consider, for example, the corpus of films produced between 1944 and 1949. Dozens of such films in many different genres exist. These include newsreels produced by major companies such as Universal and Movie Tone; documentaries such as Aleksander Ford's *Vernichtungslager Majdanek, Cmentarzysko Europy* (1944), and the French compilation film *Les Camps de la mort* (1945); reeducation and propaganda films of which Hanuš Burger's *Todesmühlen* (1945–46) is perhaps the best-known example; fundraising shorts produced for Jewish relief agencies; films such as *Nazi Concentration Camps* (1945) and *Crimes of the German Fascist Invaders* (1945–46) used as evidence in the Nuremberg trials; and, last but not least, the wave of fiction films from Soviet-occupied Germany, Poland, Czechoslovakia, and Hungary, many of which were widely distributed internationally and won several prestigious festival awards. To occlude such early works from in-depth historical investigation on the grounds that they are not Holocaust films would be to ignore a formative moment in the history of Holocaust representation.[7] Overlooking them would also compromise our understanding of the way the crimes against the Jews percolated into public discourse and consciousness during this crucial period.

My point is not that these early films provide adequate accounts, let alone explanations, of the fate of the Jews at the hands of the Nazis. They do not. Most of the films made between 1944 and 1949 barely mention Jews except as one category of victims among many, that is, as an afterthought. The specificity and disproportionality of Jews as the principal targets of the Nazis' extermination plans are *never* acknowledged. Rather, most subsume Jewish fates in Christian, *resistancialiste*, antifascist, or universalist rhetoric that conceptually fogs the extent to which Jews were singled out for special treatment.[8] They hardly address, let alone measure up to, the enormity of the Jewish disaster. Nor are all of these films significant works of art. Exploring such films, however, should in no way be construed as an attempt to validate them at the expense of crucial later masterpieces such as *Shoah*. Rather, it is simply an effort to comprehend them as useful or deficient works of popular history that are more or less artful and linked at a particular moment in various important ways with larger public discourses about the Holocaust that do or should concern us.

Clearly, the filmmakers involved in these multifarious projects— and one should note that a high proportion of them were of Jewish origin[9]—were obliged to work within various kinds of ideological constraints and with differing degrees of knowledge of the full extent of what had happened to European Jewry. This is particularly the case for those working under the auspices of the new communist authorities in the East, but similar instructions to downplay the fate of the Jews were also operative in the West.[10] All the evidence I have seen, however, indicates that these men and women engaged the topic of the camps and mass murders with the utmost seriousness of intentions; to charge them with bad faith because of any inaccuracies or even the historical distortions they purveyed would be much too harsh. In any case, the films they made participated in discourses about the camp experience that were widespread at the time, to one or another of which many contemporary Jewish groups in both Europe and the United States willingly gave their consent. As such, they are essential moments in the history of coming to terms with what happened to the Jews. They can only be—indeed, must be—understood in the context of the evolution of notions of what we have subsequently come to call the Shoah or Holocaust.

The fact is that in nearly all these films the Jews *are* mentioned as victims (even if without the kind of priority they warrant). Gas chambers and crematoria *are* often shown and the process of mass murder is discussed—at times even illustrated.[11] The panoply of iconic figures (electrified barbed wire fences, tattooed bodies, etc.) that have come to serve as a visual shorthand for the victims of the Shoah *are* prominently displayed in these films for the first time. Several of the fictional narratives—certainly Jakubowska's *Ostatni Etap* (*The Last Stop: La dernière Étape*, 1948), Ford's *Ulica Graniczna* (*Border Street*, 1948), *Daleka cesta* (*Distant Journey*, Alfred Radok, 1948) and *Undzere Kinder* (*Our Children*, 1949)—specifically describe the singling out of Jews for persecution and murder.[12] To conclude that, because of their obvious failings with respect to Jewish victims, they should not count as Holocaust films would be unnecessarily to undermine the effort to understand how those inadequacies came about.

Such an effort would contribute much to our comprehension of how the Holocaust was first introduced into public discourse, and would also open to question certain claims some historians of the period have made. Peter Novick, for example, argues that, after the newsreels and journalistic accounts of late April and early May 1945 graphically portrayed the brutality and scale of German atrocities, the shock wore off as competing sources of concern (the ongoing war in Asia, the atom bombs dropped on Hiroshima and Nagasaki, and the emergence of cold war in Europe, etc.) quickly overshadowed the discovery of the camps. The emotional, social, economic, and political turmoil in the postwar period, moreover, distracted public attention from the issue of Jewish victims, which had just barely come into focus at Nuremberg.[13] Memories of the Holocaust, he argues, were only revived—or rather, the construction of a discourse about the Holocaust only emerged—decades later and for reasons having little to do with a quest for historical accuracy per se.[14]

Analyses of the ongoing production, distribution, and reception of many different kinds of Holocaust films from 1944 through 1949—when, in fact, productions of Holocaust-themed works *did* radically decline—throws Novick's account into question. It would be inaccurate, for example, to characterize this period in the United States as silent about the Jewish tragedy in Europe. Novick curiously slights or ignores films which were widely shown, advertised, and discussed in newspapers, at least in the major metropolitan centers in the United States.[15] Others were shown to significant numbers of occupation troops in Europe, or to select groups in the attempt to solicit relief funds for survivors.[16] I have not been able to obtain precise box-office or attendance figures for these works, but one must conservatively estimate many hundreds of thousands of spectators, and perhaps as many as a million or two. Many of these individuals, it should be noted, would have been among the best-informed opinion leaders of their day. If these numbers are correct, we must conclude that these films played a larger role than Novick—or anyone else, for that matter—has previously acknowledged in articulating awareness of the Holocaust during this formative moment.[17] Tracking the production and circulation of films would also correct Joan Wolf's similar claims about the alleged silence in postwar France where the Jewish tragedy was inserted in and, it is true, distorted by, several different memory frameworks.[18] In fact, the newsreel, documentary, and many fictional films seen in France have recently been explored in detail by Sylvie Lindeperg[19] and Christian Delage,[20] and their findings directly challenge the claim of silence. Despite some good initial research on England,[21] much work still remains to be done as well as on the United States, Germany, and particularly the new communist-dominated states of Eastern Europe. The cinema, the most important and influential mass medium of its time, cannot be so easily discounted as a dimension of postwar awareness of the Holocaust.

A better historical understanding of the purposes and social impact of such films would also help to correct several misleading theoretical conceptualizations of these early, as well as later, works. Fifteen years after the end of World War II, for example, the eminent German refugee film scholar Siegfried Kracauer refashioned the myth of Perseus slaying Medusa with the aid of Athena's polished shield to dramatically figure the meaning and impact of the horrible images of the Nazi camps the Allies had recorded.

> When Athena instigated Perseus to slay the monster, she . . . warned him never to look at the face itself but only at its mirror reflection in the polished shield she had given him. Following her advice, Perseus cut off Medusa's head. . . . The moral of the myth is, of course, that we do not, and cannot, see actual horrors because they paralyze us with blinding fear; and that we shall know what they look like only by watching images of them which reproduce their true appearance. . . . [They are] the reflection of happenings which would petrify us were we to encounter them in real life. The film screen is Athena's polished shield.[22]

By virtue of having been filmed, "the litter of tortured human bodies" were, Kracauer claimed, "redeemed" from their "invisibility behind the veils of panic and imagination." Therein lay both the "truth" of the cinematic index as well as its proper social function: to provide a unique, otherwise unavailable purchase on reality, leading to mastery over it.

Kracauer's conception of "realism" and his conviction of the truth rooted in photographic indexicality is hardly as naïve as the more literal-minded versions that dog commonplace conceptions of Holocaust representation to this day. Yet his famous and powerful metaphorical description of Holocaust representation is potentially misleading to the extent that it does not specify a number of necessary qualifications and explanations he himself would have very well understood and, indeed, routinely deployed in his writings about cinema. For example, in the early films using documentary footage of the camps made at the end of the war to which he alludes, each individual image they contain is an essentially unaltered reflection of an unmediated real fact.[23]

But every film in this corpus is, of course, a compilation of such images. Moreover, they are usually accompanied by distinctive voiceovers that insert the images into different rhetorical frameworks in order to direct audience attention toward a variety of purposes. The "truth" of any one image—whose veracity no one in their right mind should doubt—thus is not as univocal as Kracauer implies. Each image exists as a fragment of the larger audiovisual discourse in which it appears, and it is this complex context, more than the simple photographic reflection of an existing fact, that structures the shades of its meaning.

As one tries to comprehend the project of making films about such horrors, we might be better off trying to interrogate alternative implications inherent in his chosen metaphor of cinema as Perseus's shield. Were there not meaningful elongations, foreshortenings, or even distortions built into the curvature of Perseus's (i.e., the cameraman's) polished shield? Although he does not explore this notion as it affected Holocaust films, we might conclude that, *pace* Kracauer, his metaphor also validates certain deviations from literal truth; in other words, his rhetorical device authorizes expressive works of art that treat Holocaust themes, though he does not explore this notion in adequate depth.

How, furthermore, are we to understand the efforts of early—or subsequent—fiction filmmakers to fill obvious, unfilmed gaps in the visual record of camp life by creating simulacra of crucial moments or to develop searching narratives that, while typical, may correspond to no particular historical episode. How should we regard the "realistic" images of the endless roll calls and punishments administered on Birkenau's *Appellplatz* at the beginning of Jakubowska's *The Last Stop*? Recorded with the utmost attention to detail by the director, a former prisoner herself, and reenacted by camp survivors, these recreations can nevertheless still not be assigned the same ontological status as the brutal scenes registered by the Signal Corps, to which Kracauer referred in the passage I quoted. A theory legitimating expressive Holocaust representations would help fill a conceptual gap his brief metaphor leaves open.[24]

Annette Insdorf has argued precisely this point in her pioneering survey of Holocaust cinema, *Indelible Shadows*.[25] She focuses instead on an aesthetic and what she calls the "moral" evaluation of films about the Shoah, that is, how adequately respectful and innovative each film is in its address to this awful subject. In such a project, the investigation of important historical, political, ideological, and artistic factors that determined the production and shape of individual works plays only a negligible role. Unfortunately, by bracketing out such factors, she fails to recognize the importance of many works and removes crucial layers of complexity endemic to those of the early fiction films she has written about.

Jakubowska, for example, drew on the orthodox Socialist Realist aesthetics of her Communist Party milieu and she was emphatically committed to a communist-inspired insistence on the equality of suffering by all victims in the camps. Such political and aesthetic commitments could have led to moral opacity and an artistic stillbirth. Yet, despite pressure by the censors and rather against the grain of her own political instincts, Jakubowska nevertheless managed to pioneer a novel dramatized documentary form that included direct visual quotations from famous Soviet documentary footage,[26] as well as some surprisingly candid scenes leaving no doubt that the Jews were, in fact, the first targets of the SS. Recounting the plot in detail and throwing in an assessment of artistic quality hardly substitutes for the kind of analysis that would explain the most interesting and important aspects of this key film—as well as, I would add, of the many others made in Eastern Europe over the ensuing decades. Only an awareness of the broader discursive and historical frameworks in which films such as *The Last Stop* were conceived can help to illuminate their genuine contributions to the artistic embodiment of the Holocaust.

Finally, a careful historical analysis of the kind I have suggested would provide a useful corrective to a theorization of Holocaust cinema as "post-traumatic" that has emerged during the last decade in the United States. Some major writers have, indeed, advanced the concept of trauma as a useful way to approach a number of key facets, particularly the concept of memory, in Holocaust Studies.[27]

Several have, in fact, used a theory of trauma to develop critical readings and endorsements of some Holocaust films as "post-traumatic."[28] Such films are said to contest the "mastery over time, omniscience and flexibility of point of view and unself-conscious voice" identified with "realist narration," on display, for example, in well-known documentaries such as Erwin Leiser's *Mein Kampf* (1960). Instead, the forms of post-traumatic films are rooted in a failure of personal or public memory whose origin, in turn, lies in a failure to integrate fully the shock of an event experienced as traumatic. Thus, these films supposedly impose limits on intelligibility and narratability that ultimately derive from modernist artistic conceptions. They resist, for example, what the American psychoanalytic critic Eric Santner has termed "narrative fetishism," the recuperation of that which should remain traumatic through a smooth narration.[29] Indeed, they actively block such recuperation by collapsing linear chronology, thereby ensuring that "time is experienced as fragmented and uncontrollable."[30]

Such theoretical constructions are salutary to the extent that they are often exquisitely attentive to formal structures and narrative modes, primarily because, it is believed, the trauma the films seek to represent inheres—or fails to be inscribed—in the cinematic strategies themselves. Joshua Hirsch has even gone so far as to claim that such post-traumatic representations are essentially *more* historical because they are rooted in changing representational modes. It is here, however, that the theorization becomes noticeably more opaque. Attempting to explain the success of the post-traumatic narration allegedly employed by Alain Resnais' celebrated *Night and Fog* (1955), Hirsch claims that the French public after 1945 failed to register the trauma inherent in compilations of postliberation concentration camp footage such as the widely seen *Les Camps de la mort*. The "massive influx of data," he writes, "so overwhelmed the consciousness of the spectating public that the images failed to register in some sense; through its montage structure, *Night and Fog* staged the dialectic of forgetting and repetition engendered by this original failure."[31]

The equivocation built into the sentence just quoted highlights the need to ground this and similar claims about traumatic representation in precisely the kind of historical research I have been describing in this essay. In what sense, precisely, did the images fail to register? Who failed to register their shocks? What grounds does Hirsch have for making such a claim? Why, given the classical narration so familiar to audiences that informs *Les Camps de la mort*, could the images fail to have the impact we know from other sources that they had? The absence of more thoroughgoing historical contextualization, both for films and other media of information, unfortunately leads to empty or pseudo-historical abstractions about changing representations of the Holocaust. A textually mediated form of trauma *may*, indeed, inform the "dialectic of forgetting and repetition" that structures *Night and Fog*. But it remains at best murky how such a structure—the product of an impressive *collective* effort by a team of filmmakers, working on a particular commission with some degree of latitude—emerged from a hypothetical encounter with and contestation of the mode of earlier compilation films. Without a thorough investigation of the many sources for Resnais' work, a theory of traumatic representation alone is certainly insufficient.[32]

The historiography of Holocaust cinema has already begun to make significant contributions to the larger field of Holocaust Studies by enlarging our sense of the agencies conveying information—and, alas, disinformation—about the Jewish catastrophe in Europe, and by challenging the myth of silence in the early postwar period. Close historical study of films and their documentary sources has also revealed the limitations of several influential efforts to theorize and critically operationalize approaches to Holocaust representation. However, despite recent progress—perhaps most impressively demonstrated in the work of several younger French historians I cited above—this historiographical enterprise remains in its infancy. A great deal of work remains for the next generation of scholars.

Notes

The expression "Holocaust cinema," coined by Anglo-Saxon researchers, will often elicit reservations with regard to the use of the term *Holocaust*. Nonetheless it seemed legitimate to preserve the literal term in this book when referring to the work of people who make general use of it, among whom Stuart Liebman is an eminent representative. (J-M. Frodon)

1. Such documents would include scripts, relevant preparatory materials, and personal letters among the filmmakers and producers, censorship records (particularly for films made in Eastern Europe prior to 1989), marketing plans, and published interviews and reviews, among others, as well as variant versions of films distributed in different countries. Annette Wieviorka's detailed account of the French campaign for the French version of Wanda Jakubowska's *The Last Stop* is an excellent example of work that has benefited from such research. See *Déportation et génocide* (Paris: Plon, 1992), 307–12.

2. The most complete archives for any titles of Holocaust cinema I have yet seen are those for Leo Hurwitz's too little known *Strange Victory* (1948) and *The Museum and the Fury* (1956). Both are held by Eastman House, Rochester, NY. See as well the related materials held at the Film Study Center of the Museum of Modern Art in New York City, which distributed these films for many decades.

3. We know of only one short, unedited film, taken by the German naval officer Reinhard Wiener in 1941, that actually illustrates a murderous *Aktion* against Jews as it was taking place. A second film Lanzmann does not specifically mention, but surely knows, is an amateur 8mm. film (PS-3052) shown on

December 13, 1945, during the Nuremberg trial of major Nazi war criminals. It includes several shots taken anonymously of what appears to be a pogrom in process in a city tentatively identified as Lvov. See Christian Delage, *La Vérité par l'image* (Paris: Editions Denoel, 2006), 141–42. The latter can be viewed on Tape #402, File #2110 in the Steven Spielberg Archive at the United States Holocaust Memorial Museum in Washington, DC, as well as in other collections. Were footage showing the gas chambers in operation to come to light, Lanzmann has said he would destroy it as immoral. See his "Holocauste, la représentation impossible," *Le Monde* (3 March 1994), 1.

4. See his "Un cinéaste au-dessous de tout soupçon?" *Le Nouvel Observateur* (January 17–23, 1991), 70–73 (about Wajda's *Korczak*); and "Holocauste, la représentation impossible" (about Spielberg's *Schindler's List*).

5. Obviously, Lanzmann is well aware that films purporting to be about the Holocaust exist, but he dismisses them as grossly inadequate, misleading, or morally muddled. See "Le Lieu et la Parole. Entretien avec Claude Lanzmann." *Cahiers du Cinéma* 374 (July-August 1985), reprinted in Michel Deguy, ed., *Au Sujet de Shoah* (Paris: Éditions Belin, 1990), 296.

6. See the anthology I edited, *Claude Lanzmann's* Shoah*: Key Essays* (New York: Oxford University Press, 2007).

7. Obviously, the same claim could not be made for the countless television programs, documentaries, and fiction films produced in many countries over the six decades since the war's end. Nevertheless, a number of later popular theatrical and TV films—including the highly controversial "Holocaust" (1978)—also warrant close examination for their social impact.

8. One exception would be Natan Gross and Shaul Goskind's *Undzere Kinder* (1949), the last Yiddish film made in Poland, though it was never distributed because of government censorship. For more on this film, see Ira Konigsberg, "*Our Children* and the Limits of Cinema: Early Jewish Responses to the Holocaust," *Film Quarterly* 52, no. 1 (Fall 1998): 7–19.

9. Billy Wilder, Budd Schulberg, Aleksander Ford, Jerzy Bossak, Natan Gross, Shaul Goskind, Roman Karmen, Hanuš Bürger, and Sidney Bernstein were only the most prominent. Many of the cameramen, editors, and assistants were also Jewish.

10. See, for example, Peter Novick, *The Holocaust in American Life* (New York: Houghton Mifflin, 1999), 40–46, and 64 ff.

11. See, for example, Ford's *Vernichtungslager Majdanek* or Richard Brandt's *Todeslager Sachsenhausen* (1946).

12. See my article "Les Premières constellations sur l'Holocauste dans le cinéma polonais," in *De l'histoire au cinéma*, ed. Antoine de Baecque and Christian Delage (Brussels: Éditions Complexe, 1998), 193–216; and also "Les premières images des camps: l'Exemple de Maïdanek," *Les Cahiers du Judaïsme* 15 (Winter 2004): 49–60.

13. Novick, 66. On the role that photographic accounts played, see Barbie Zelizer, *Remembering to Forget* (Chicago: University of Chicago Press, 1998). Curiously, she hardly mentions any of the many films made at the end of and right after the war.

14. In the Soviet Union, as is well known, a different dynamic was at work. Stalin himself intervened to prevent the publication of Vassily Grossman and Ilya Ehrenburg's *Black Book of Soviet Jewry*, and to the best of my knowledge—although, further research in Russian archives is needed to establish the truth of this speculation—no films touching on the fate of the Jews circulated in the USSR after 1946. For the moment, the best, though rather meager, account of the immediate postwar period is Sergei Drobashenko, "Soviet Film Chronicles and the Fall of Nazi Germany," in *Hitler's Fall: The Newsreel Witness*, ed. K. R. M. Short and Stephen Doelzel (London: Croom Helm, 1988), 50–69.

15. See, for example, reviews of films such as *The Last Stop* or *Uliza graniczna* in major newspapers: *"The Last Stop," The New York Times* (January 12, 1949); and two different reviews of *"Border Street," The New York Times* (April 5 and 28, 1950).

16. See Ronny Loewy, "Die Welt neu zusammenfügen. Paul Falkenbergs Filme einer 'Displaced Society,'" in *Filmexil* (Berlin) 8 (November 1996). See also Bernard Genton, "A Sea of Shoes . . . La perception de la Shoah aux États Unis (1941–1945)," *Sources* 6 (Spring 1999), 99–136.

17. The American historian Samuel Moyn does not mention films per se, but notes aptly: "[H]istories of Holocaust consciousness that depict 'silence' and 'delay' in the emergence of attention to the Nazi genocide—Peter Novick's well-known work on the United States is an important example—often do so by slighting or ignoring local and often marginal subcultures whose texts and knowledge were . . . vulgarized to vast audiences as time went on." *A Holocaust Controversy: The Treblinka Affair in Postwar France* (Waltham: Brandeis University Press, 2005), xvii. See also Lawrence Barron's mapping of some of these popular treatments, "The Holocaust and American Public memory, 1945–1960," *Holocaust and Genocide Studies*, 17, no. 1 (Spring 2003), 62–88.

18. *Harnessing the Holocaust* (Palo Alto: Stanford University Press, 2004).

19. *Les Écrans de l'ombre* and *Clio de 5 à 7*, both published in Paris by CNRS Éditions in 1997 and 2000 respectively. See also Claudine Drame, "Représenter l'irreprésentable: les camps nazis dans les actualités françaises de 1945," *Cinémathèque* 10 (Autumn 1996), 12–27. These scholarly contributions about cinema complement Didier Epelbaum's recent account of the postwar press, *Pas un mot, pas une ligne?* (Paris: Éditions Stock, 2005).

20. *La Vérité par l'image*, op.cit., corrects a number of mistakes made by Lawrence Douglas in *The Memory of Judgment* (New Haven: Yale University Press, 2001).

21. Hannah Caven, "Horror in Our Time: Images of the Concentration Camps in the British Media, 1945," *Historical Journal of Film, Radio and Television* 21, no. 3 (August 2001), 205–53; and Toby Haggith, "Filming the Liberation of Bergen-Belsen," in *Holocaust and the Moving Image*, ed. Toby Haggith and Joanna Newman (London: Wallflower, 2005), 33–49.

22. Siegfried Kracauer, *Theory of Film: The Redemption of Physical Reality* (New York: Oxford University Press, 1960), 305.

23. This is attested to by the legal affidavits accompanying such images presented to the court trying major Nazi war criminals at Nuremberg in 1945.

See Delage, *La Vérité par l'image*, 91-177. It is also essential to point out, however, that some of the images were not specifically—or, at times, correctly—identified in films used for nonlegal purposes, say, in fundraising or propaganda films. No deception was intended, of course, but the aims of such films—to illustrate generally miserable, inhumane conditions in German concentration camps, for example—did not require precise identifications.

24. One might also mention in this regard Jakubowska's creation in *The Last Stop* of a composite, idealized heroine, Martha, from memories and legends about the Jewish resistance leader and escapee Mala Zimetbaum, who was later captured and publicly executed. On the historical Mala, see Anne Grynberg, "Mala Zimetbaum, un 'être lumineux' à Auschwitz," *Les Cahiers du judaïsme* 12 (2002), 115–28.

25. First published by Random House, New York, in 1983; the third expanded edition was released by Cambridge University Press in 2003.

26. See the comments of the great Hungarian screenwriter and film theorist Béla Balázs in "*The Last Stop*," whose catalogue number is MS 5014/198 in the Balázs Archives of the Magyar Tudomanyos Akadémia Könyvtára in Budapest, Hungary. English translation by Zsuzsa Berger and Stuart Liebman in *Slavic and East European Performance*, 16, no. 3 (Fall 1996), 66–67.

27. Cathy Carruth, ed., *Trauma: Explorations in Memory* (Baltimore: Johns Hopkins University Press, 1995) and Dominick LaCapra, *Representing the Holocaust: History, Theory, Trauma* (Ithaca: Cornell University Press, 1994).

28. Shoshana Felman and Dori Laub, *Testimony: Crises of Witnessing in Literature, Psychoanalysis, and History* (New York: Routledge, 1992); Joshua Hirsch, *Afterimage. Film, Trauma, and the Holocaust* (Philadelphia: Temple University Press, 2004); and Dominick LaCapra, *History and Memory after Auschwitz* (Ithaca: Cornell University Press, 1998).

29. "History Beyond the Pleasure Principle: Some Thoughts on the Representation of Trauma," in *Probing the Limits of Representation*, ed. Saul Friedlander (Cambridge: Harvard University Press, 1992), 143–54.

30. Hirsch, 21.

31. Hirsch, 55.

32. The correspondence among the participants and the versions of the script have been carefully examined by Christian Delage and Vincent Guigeno in their *L'historien et le film* (Paris: Gallimard, 2004), 29–45, 58–78, and 215–26. Sylvie Lindeperg has recently published an even more thorough, in-depth analysis of the film's production. See her *Nuit et Brouillard un film dans l'histoire* (Paris: Odile Jacob, 2007). The film's international reception has also ben importantly mapped by various authors in Ewout van der Knapp, ed., *Uncovering the Holocaust: The International Reception of* Night and Fog (London: Wallflower Press, 2006).

Resources

Referent Images

THE QUESTIONING AND CONCERN regarding the role and status of images is present throughout the pages of this book. We therefore felt it would be impossible for us to *illustrate* this concern, in the habitual use of the term.

However, it did seem useful to put at the disposal of readers the images that, in one context or another, have played a role in these reflections upon the rapport between the Shoah and the cinema. These images are very diverse in nature, some are archival documents, others come from fictional works, and many have been used in a number of different ways through the years. These movements and the changes in meaning that have accompanied them are often rich in educational value, as demonstrated by Sylvie Lindeperg in her study of "migratory flux," of representations, in her book *Clio de 5 à 7* (Editions du CNRS, 2000). Many of these images have been the object of debate, and at times of violent controversy. We will not reiterate all that here, but simply offer the origin of the images and, where appropriate, the reason for their presence. The objective of this iconographical overview, which is intended as a separate chapter of this book, is to give each reader the possibility to see for himself.

J-M.F.

Translated from the French by Anna Harrison

The four photographs taken by *Sonderkommando* member Alex near one of the crematoriums at Auschwitz, thanks to a camera smuggled into the camp by the Polish Resistance. Though known about since the Liberation, their inclusion in the exhibit "Memories of the Camps: Photographs of Nazi Concentration and Extermination Camps" sparked controversy. They are sometimes referred to as "the cursed film."

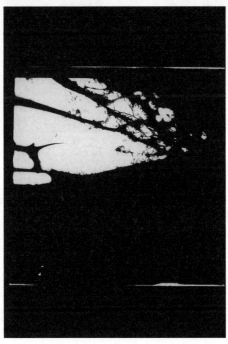

"The Auschwitz Album"
On April 11, 1945, 800 kilometers from the camp, Auschwitz survivor
Lily Jacob, a young Hungarian Jew, discovered an album containing 189
photographs taken by the SS on and near the train platform. This document
represents the most important collection of archival images produced inside an
extermination camp. Today it is kept at the Yad-Vashem museum in Jerusalem
as *The Auschwitz Album*.

Nach der Aussortierung

Noch einsatzfähige Männer

1

2

3

At the time a high level officer in charge of providing visual records of American Army operations as a member of the Signal Corps, a detachment specially assigned to this task (photos 1 and 2), George Stevens (who would later film *A Place in the Sun, Giant,* and *The Diary of Anne Frank*) was the first filmmaker to use color film for this purpose (3). He was part of a team filming the discovery of the camps upon their liberation by the Western Allies, and personally filmed Dachau just after it was opened (opposite page).

The American, British, and Soviet armed forces made widespread use of the cinema as a means of testifying to what they discovered when they liberated the concentration camps (in the West) and the extermination camps (in Poland).

226

The bulldozer of Bergen-Belsen

Without doubt the image most frequently used to "represent the camps," this bulldozer was used by the British troops that liberated Bergen-Belsen, in order to bury the corpses of typhoid victims as quickly as possible. Various extracts, often reframed, can be found in numerous documentaries. Already characteristic of the confusion between concentration camps (like Bergen-Belsen) and extermination camps, this sequence has also become known for the gap between what it shows (a sanitary operation by the liberators) and what it symbolizes (mass murder perpetrated by the Nazis, human bodies crushed by the industrialized extermination machine).

When they liberated the camps, Allied troops frequently forced Germans, former guards, or civilians from neighboring towns (1, 2, 3) to witness the results of Nazi terror, and often to dress, carry, and bury the corpses of the victims. These scenes were regularly filmed, thus creating a record of the ties, through gaze and touch, between the victims and the perpetrators or their accomplices. Allied high commanders (4 and 5) came to verify on the spot the true extent of the nightmarish reports they were receiving.

The screen at Nuremberg (above): used in this manner for the first time, the cinema played an important role in the trial of the principal Nazi dignitaries (November 20, 1945–October 1, 1946), in the shape of a montage of footage recorded during the opening of the concentration camps. This was also the first time a trial was captured on film, by a crew supervised by John Ford.

Next page: left, the scale model of the courtroom, with the screen given a prominent position; right, the filming of the trial.

THIS IS AN OFFICIAL DOCUMENTARY REPORT COMPILED
FROM FILMS MADE BY MILITARY PHOTOGRAPHERS
SERVING WITH THE ALLIED ARMIES AS THEY ADVANCED
INTO GERMANY. THE FILMS WERE MADE PURSUANT
TO AN ORDER ISSUED BY GENERAL
DWIGHT D. EISENHOWER, SUPREME COMMANDER,
ALLIED EXPEDITIONARY FORCES.

ROBERT H. JACKSON
UNITED STATES

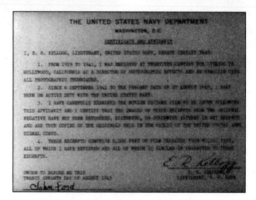

Documents testifying to the veracity of the images form the start of the montage film *Nazi Concentration Camps*, shown during the trial against Nazi war criminals in Nuremberg. The letters are signed by the officers that contributed to the film, including George Stevens and John Ford.

The inhabitants of a small German town attend a compulsory screening, May 10, 1945. A series of montage films was made with the distinct purpose of confronting the German population with the crimes that had been committed. Among these films was *Die Todesmühlen*, directed by Billy Wilder and Hanuš Burger, which was not allowed to be shown outside Germany.

Archive footage used in a fiction film, Orson Welles's *The Stranger* (1946).
A young woman who refuses to believe that her husband is a Nazi criminal
watches extracts from *Nazi Concentration Camps*. Projecting the images onto
the body of actor Edward G. Robinson expresses the interaction between the
documents and the work of fiction.

Scenes from Wanda Jakubowska's *The Last Stop* (1946) used in Alain Resnais'
Night and Fog (1955): here it is fictional images that become archival
documents through their use in a documentary.

Though re-used, this image has become "iconic" of the deportation of the Jews. This close-up of a teenage girl in a wagon departing the Dutch camp Westerbork for Auschwitz was the subject of an investigation in 1992, which revealed that the girl, Anna Maria Settela Steinbach, was not Jewish but a Sinti Gypsy. She was assassinated at Auschwitz on August 1, 1944.

Often used in film, this photograph was assumed to depict Jews rounded up in Paris and brought to Vel d'hiv' in July of 1942. In 1983, Serge Klarsfeld discovered that the picture was in fact taken after the Liberation and shows people suspected of collaborating with the Germans.

An image from Alain Resnais' *Night and Fog* (1955) showing the internment camp at Pithiviers, to which the censor objected. Below: the compromise that was the result of lengthy deliberation between the director and the authorities, a "masked" version that assured that this piece of evidence of collaboration by the French police didn't disappear from the film entirely. Above: the original image, restored for the video release of the film in 1997.

Night and Fog: the color sequences with which Alain Resnais wanted to underline the presence of the camps in the present day. Shot in 1955, they were transformed to black-and-white and presented as archive footage in a re-edited version of the film shown on U.S. television in July 1960 as part of a program titled "Remember Us."

Gillo Pontecorvo's *Kapò* (1961): frames from the death scene of the character played by Emmanuelle Riva, referenced in Jacques Rivette's review of the film, entitled "De l'abjection," which in turn inspired Serge Daney's essay, "Kapò's Tracking Shot."

241

The television series "Holocaust," first broadcast in the U.S. in 1978
and subsequently in many countries around the world, led to both an
unprecedented surge in interest in the Shoah among the general public and
to questions about how to portray the event onscreen. When it was shown in
Germany in 1979, the Marvin Chomsky-directed series provoked
a controversy that led to a debate in the Bundestag, where a new law was
voted that restricted the use of Nazi symbols and terminology.

242

An aerial photograph of Auschwitz taken by the U.S. Air Force, which was kept out of the Allied plans for aerial bombardments. This image is used in Harun Farocki's *Images of the World and the Inscription of War* (1988).

For *Shoah* (1985), Claude Lanzmann interviewed former SS *Unterscharführer* Franz Suchomel, who held an important position at Treblinka. The interview was shot with a hidden camera, the only way to obtain such precise testimony, including an extensive description of the workings of the extermination camp.

In *Shoah*, Claude Lanzmann asked Abraham Bomba to re-enact his former profession as a barber while recounting the conditions under which he had to work within the very confines of the gas chamber at Treblinka, on women and children about to be executed. Overcome by his emotions, Bomba interrupts his account. Lanzmann tries to convince him of the necessity of his testimony.

"War and Remembrance," a television series directed by Dan Curtis and Tommy Groszman for ABC in 1988, contains spectacular reconstructions of mass murder in the gas chambers.

Steven Spielberg's decision to reconstruct the Auschwitz camps in Poland for the production of *Schindler's List* (1993) sparked questions and criticism.

The shower scene from Steven Spielberg's *Schindler's List* (1993), which builds suspense around the wait for the showerheads to emit toxic gas, until they release a cleansing stream of water. The scene was often cited as an objectionable form of spectacular dramatization.

The scene of the intentionally botched translation is often mentioned as an example of the biased and cynical representation of the Shoah in Roberto Benigni's *Life Is Beautiful* (1997).

On ordonnait à ces gens de se déshabiller.

The trial of Adolf Eichmann, which played a major role in international understanding of the singularity of the Shoah, was filmed under the direction of Leo Hurwitz. Israeli filmmaker Eyal Sivan found the images and used them in his film *The Specialist* (1999), incorporating digital retouches and changes—including the reflections in the glass panes of the former Nazi official's cubicle.

The use of the photograph of the boy from the Warsaw ghetto in advertising for the rock group Trust provoked debate about the use of historical images, particularly those of the Shoah.

Three witnesses speak. James Moll's *The Last Days* (1998) was one of the films produced by the Spielberg Survivors of the Shoah Visual History Foundation. The idea and the procedure of the systematic recording of eyewitness accounts led to debate among historians.

Two snapshots from the album of 166 photographs that belonged to SS officer Karl Höckler, assistant to the commander of Auschwitz between May 1944 and January 1945. These peaceful scenes of the executioners relaxing inside or near the camp were found by an American officer who donated them to Washington's Holocaust Memorial Museum. Their appearance in the media around the world in September 2007 is an indication of the seemingly unquenchable thirst for images on the subject.

Filmography

Thematic Dictionary

Note: This filmography is intended to offer anyone, and more specifically researchers, educators, and programmers, a collection containing the most important films that have a direct relation to the Shoah. This filmography therefore does not include the totality of the much vaster corpus this book is concerned with: the modern cinema that has been influenced and questioned by the Shoah.

But we have included the most important titles that have an explicit rapport with the deportation, and that, accurately or not, were part of the construction of people's imagination of the camps. This filmography therefore calls for a critical approach, for which the other parts of this book will have hopefully provided the tools. With a range as yet unequalled in previous publications, it combines titles that seemed pertinent to us, including those upon which the authors of this book expressed their greatest reserves.

This list does not pretend in any way to be exhaustive (which would be impossible), and some subjectivity is inevitably required. We intentionally limited ourselves, so that it would remain manageable. The Fritz Bauer Institute's online site, www.cine-holocaust.de, accessible in German and English, provides a much more considerable database.

The classification of titles is also the result of a preconception proper to this filmography: whereas one of the recurring themes of this book bears upon the manner in which the Shoah radically questioned the status of images, shots, and films, as well as their methods of classification, we made the choice here to have recourse to a classical division by genre: fiction, documentary, and essays, reserving a place apart for programs specifically created for television. Within these genres, the

films are classified in chronological order. There again, a concern for
more practical utilization is what guided us. It seemed indispensable to
include certain Nazi propaganda films, designating them as such, as well
as a certain number of contemporary Nazi documents in which significant scenes were shown.

The following filmography was established thanks to considerable
work done by Ronny Loewy and Sarah Dellmann, based on the data
bank at the Fritz Bauer Institute. The translation into French was done
by Eve Münch and into English by Anna Harrison and Tom Mes. The
final compilation was directed by Jean-Michel Frodon.

Documentaries and Montage Films

Hitler's Reign of Terror
Director: Michael Mindlin. Screenplay: Edward C. Hill. Production:
Eureka Productions Inc./Special Pictures Company/Jewel Productions
Inc. Year: 1934. Country: USA. Run time: 55 min. Documentary.

Anti-Fascist American celebrities such as Rabbi Wise, Fannie Hurst,
and Samuel Seabury gather together to protest the rise to power of the
new German Chancellor Adolf Hitler.

Inside Nazi Germany
Director: Julien Bryan. Production: Julien Bryan. Year: 1938. Country:
USA. Run time: 100 min. Documentary.

Daily life in the towns and countryside of Nazi Germany. The
scenes describing the situation for German Jews show anti-Semitic propaganda methods used at the time: a day in a Jewish school, a synagogue,
a yellow bench on which "only for Jews" has been written, and anti-Semitic signs and periodicals. We also see Hitler welcoming Mussolini to
Berlin and the Party Congress in Nuremberg with a million people in
attendance. This film was part of an illustrated reading program. Julien
Bryan did the pre-screening presentation and commented on the images
as the film was projected.

Bound For Nowhere. The St. Louis Episode
Production: American Jewish Joint Distribution Committee, Inc. Year:
1939 Country: USA. Run time: 9 min. Documentary.

This film documents one of the Jewish community's efforts to save
Jews fleeing Nazi Germany. The JDC produced this film to record what
it thought would be a successful effort to save more than nine hundred
Jews, including two hundred children, by sailing them from Nazi Germany to Cuba on the ship St. Louis. When Cuba refused to allow the

passengers to land, the ship sailed to the Miami area where the U.S. government also barred the refugees' entrance. Finally, some European countries accepted them. Tragically, most of these refugees ended up in countries subsequently occupied by Germany.

Swastyka/Szubienica

Director: Kazimierz Czynski. Production: Wytwornia Filmowej Wojska Polskiego (Polish Army Film Studio). Year: 1944. Country: Poland, Soviet Union. Run time: 26 min. Documentary.

The first Majdanek trial in Lubin, which took place from November 27 to December 2, 1944. A considerable section is devoted to the testimony by Kapo Heinz Stalp and shows the execution on December 4 of six SS officers who were convicted. Some scenes from *Majdanek— Cmentarzysko Europy* were included in this documentary.

Majdanek—Cmentarzysko Europy
(Majdanek Death Camp—The Cemetery of Europe)

Director: Aleksander Ford, Irina Setkina. Production: Wytwornia Film-owej Wojska Polskiego (Polish Army Film Studio), Central Studio for documentaries, Moscow. Year: 1944 or 1945. Country: Poland, Soviet Union. Run time: 21 min. Documentary.

This documentary produced in two versions (a Polish and a Soviet version) is about the liberation of the Majdanek extermination camp on July 23, 1944, by the Red Army. The film includes a great deal of very explicit images, interviews with survivors and with the Germans who perpetrated these crimes. The filmmakers almost entirely suppressed the fact that Jews were in majority the victims of the extermination.

Auschwitz
Oswiecim

Production: Soviet Army Film Unit, Zentrales Studio für Doku-mentarfilme. Year: 1945. Country: Soviet Union. Run time: 21 min. Documentary.

A compilation film containing film footage of Dachau, Auschwitz, and Auschwitz-Birkenau taken in the camps a couple of weeks following Germany's surrender after the liberation by the Red Army. It is comprised of material made by a Soviet film unit of the Red Army. The film shows scenes from "Stammlager Auschwitz" (Auschwitz I), Birkenau (Auschwitz II), and the IG Farben factory of Buna-Monowitz. Soviet doctors treat the survivors. All the film footage of Auschwitz that was shot between February and May 1945 in Auschwitz and Auschwitz-Birkenau is used here, among which is footage from May 1945 of a staged liberation of the death camp. Material from this film was used for many documentaries on Auschwitz.

Les Camps de la Mort
The Death Camps
Production: Actualités Françaises. Year: 1945. Country: France. Run time: 19 min. Documentary.

A compilation of documentation regarding the conditions in the camps as found by Allied soldiers. The film shows the Allies trying to rescue the camp prisoners and care for them, as well as bury the massive quantity of dead. We also see General Dwight D. Eisenhower visiting Camp Ohrdruf, and journalists interviewing the prisoners and the SS talking about the "souvenirs" they kept (heads, lampshades made of human skin). Contains shots of the following camps: Colditz, Langenstein, Ohrdruf, Buchenwald, Dachau, Leipzig-Thekla, Bergen-Belsen, and Mittelgladsbach.

Todesmühlen
Death Mills
Director: Hanus Urger. Production: Information Control Division, Office of Military Government for Germany, United States. Year: 1945. Country: Germany, USA. Run time: 23 min. Documentary.

Intended for the "re-education" of the German people, this montage film shows the atrocities that the Allies found in the concentration camps upon their arrival. The montage and the narration are intended to imbue guilt and repentance in the Germans. The short version was made under the supervision of Billy Wilder. Some scenes were also used in the film *Cmentarzysko Europy* as well as in *Oswiecim*.

Memory of the Camps
Director: Steward McAllister. Production: Sidney Berstein, British Army. Year: 1945. Country: UK. Run time: 60 min. Documentary.

A montage film comprised of a large quantity of filmed footage made during the liberation of the camps, notably that of Bergen-Belsen, and intended to prove the guilt of the Germans. Alfred Hitchcock was an adviser for the editing of the film. The documentary remained unfinished and was not released at the time, but was rediscovered in 1985 (see the chapter on this film by Jean-Louis Comolli).

Nazi Concentration Camps
Director: George Stevens. Production: US Army Signal Corps, US Counsel for Prosecution of Axis Criminality. Year: 1945. Country: USA. Run time: 59 min. Documentary.

This Film was made to document the findings of Allied armies as they entered Nazi concentration camps. Footage of camps includes Leipzig, Penig, Ohrdruf, Hadamar, Breendonck, Nordhausen, Hannover, Arnstadt, Mauthausen, Buchenwald, Dachau, and Bergen-Belsen. Scenes showing bodies and survivors demonstrate the extent of Nazi crimes. This is one of the films shown at the Nuremberg Trials.

The Nazi Plan:
Part 1: The Rise of the NSDAP, 1921 to 1933
Part 2: Acquiring Totalitarian Control of Germany, 1933 to 1935
Part 3: Preparation For Wars of Aggression, 1935 to 1939
Part 4: Wars of Aggression, 1939 to 1944
Director: E. Ray Kellogg. Production: US Counsel for Prosecution of Axis Criminality Year: 1945. Country: USA. Run time: 194 min. Documentary.

A compilation of official German newsreels and other German films, made from 1919–1945. This film was shown at the Nuremberg trial.

Le Retour
Director: Henri Cartier-Bresson. Production: American Information Services. Years: 1944–46. Country: France, USA. Run time: 32 min. Documentary.

A compilation of documentary scenes filmed at the time surrounding the unconditional surrender of Germany and the work of the Allies to help former prisoners return to their homes. It shows the liberation of the concentration camps, the transport home of freed French prisoners of war and Displaced Persons in France, and scenes of the Americans arresting German soldiers. It also contains scenes of the freeing of prisoners from the Dachau concentration camp. The film ends with the joyous arrival of French former prisoners in Paris.

Nous Continuons!
We Continue!
Mir Lebn Do!
Direction: Moshe Bahelfer, O. Fessler, A. Hamza, I. Holodenko, J. Weinfeld. Production: Union des Juifs pour la Résistance et l'entraide en France (U.J.R.E.) (Union of Jews for Resistance and Aid in France). Year: 1946. Country: France. Run time: 53 min. Documentary.

This film shows the care and medical attention given to orphans in France after the end of World War II. The children were also given lessons in French and Yiddish.

Sud Narodov
Direction: Roman Karmen, Jelisaweta Swilowa. Production: Zentrales Studio fur Dokumentarfilme. Year: 1946. Country: Soviet Union. Run time: 62 min. Documentary.

Filmed by the Soviets, this is a recording of the trials of Nazi war criminals at Nuremberg from 1945 to 1946.

Assignment: Tel Aviv
Director: Lasar Dunner. Production: Educational Documentary Films for Keren Hayessod, United Palestine Appeal. Year: 1946–47. Country: USA, British Mandate Palestine. Run time: 20 min. Documentary.

A travelogue accompanying a young family (Kurt Pepperman from Frankfurt, Leah Pepperman from Prague, and their young son Daniel) and showing life and work in the city of Tel Aviv for former displaced persons. Normalcy and modernity are the principal theme; the film shows scenes of beaches, boulevards, dancers on a rooftop, and a visit to the zoo, and ends with aerial shots of Tel Aviv.

Sachsenhausen Death Camp
Todeslager Sachsenhausen
Director: Richard Brandt. Production: Deutsche Film-AG (DEFA). Year: 1946. Country: German Democratic Republic (GDR) (East Germany). Run time: 35 min. Documentary.

A detailed account of the mistreatment of concentration camp prisoners, using documentary footage and reconstructed scenes, filmed by Russian soldiers. The Russian secret services forced their prisoners to portray the roles of concentration camp victims. The film only mentions Soviet prisoners of war and German communists as concentration camp victims, but never the Jews.

The Last Parteitag (Party Congress) in Nuremberg
Ostatni Parteitag w Norymberdze
Director: Antoni Bohdziewics, WacBar Kazmierczak. Production: Wytwórnia Filmowej Wojska Polskiego (Polish Army Film Studio). Year: 1946. Country: Poland. Run time: 21 min. Documentary.

An account of the Nazi war crime trials in Nuremberg.

We Must Not Forget
Production: United Jewish Appeal. Year: 1947. Country: USA. Run time: 5 min. Documentary.

A fundraiser to gather funds to help the United Jewish Appeal (UJA) to rehabilitate refugees from Europe in Mandate Palestine.

Mir Lebn Geblibene (am Yisrael Chai)
Director: Nathan Gross. Production: Kinor-Film-Kooperative. Year: 1947–48. Country: Poland. Run time: 80 min. Documentary.

Jewish Survivors of Warsaw after World War II and their attempts to start living and working again. The film also shows what was left of the Jewish Ghetto, the discovery of hidden belongings there, and newly opened craft shops.

Nuremberg and its Lesson
Nurnberg und Seine Lehre
Director: Stuart Schulberg. Production: Information Services Division, Dokumentarfilm-Abteilung / Zeit im Film, in cooperation with Film-studio Tempelhof for the Office of Military Government for Germany, United States (OMGUS). Year: 1947–48. Country: USA. Run time: 78 min. Documentary.

The trials led by the International Military Court of Justice in Nuremberg from November 14, 1945, to October 1, 1946. The film combines archival footage of the trials, from the prosecutor's opening to the verdict, and retraces the different stages in the advance of Nazi Germany.

Berlinskij Prozess
Direction: Zentrales Studio fur Dokumentarfilme. Year: 1948. Country: Soviet Union. Run time: 26 min. Documentary.

The trial against the Nazi murderers of the Sachsenhausen death camp. The trial took place in Berlin-Pankow.

Schones Bielefeld
Director: Gustav Wittler. Years: 1938–1953. Country: Germany. Run time: 20 min. Documentary.

Amateur documentary with shots of a burning synagogue in the town of Bielefeld. The film was compiled over a long period of time and also shows bombings in Bielefeld and then the reconstruction of the town. The filming continued until 1953. Newsreel clips were also inserted into part of the film.

Nuit et Brouillard
Night and Fog
Director: Alain Resnais. Narrator: Jean Cayrol. Production: Argos Films, Como Films, Cocinor. Year: 1955–56. Country: France. Run time: 22 min. Documentary.

This compilation film was commissioned by deportee organizations and is one of the first French films dealing with the concentration and extermination camps. The montage of archival footage and present-day scenes constructs a back and forth sequence between what is history and what remains in the present. The visual composition and the commentary by Jean Cayrol connect the past to the present. The commentary for the German version of the film was translated by Paul Celan for the Federal Republic of Germany (Western Germany) and by Henrik Keisch for the German Democratic Republic (Eastern Germany). The music, composed by Hanns Eisler, offers yet another level of commentary. Historian Sylvie Lindeperg later demonstrated how the aspect of the Jewish genocide, which was absent from the original commission, took on much greater importance for the film's creators during the making of this film, notably in the work on location in Poland.

Prozess in Ulm
Production: DEFA-Studio fur Wochenschau und Dokumentarfilme. Year: 1958. Country: GDR. Run time: 2 min. Documentary.
A brief moment in the trials of the SS expeditionary corps who were in charge of the mass annihilation of victims in Lithuania during the first three months of the German invasion of the Baltic States. These forces were also guilty of mass or individual executions of many thousands of Jews and communists in the Memelland region, which bordered Prussia and Lithuania. On August 29, 1958, the jury pronounced its verdict in Ulm. Hans Joachim Behme and Bernard Fisher Schweder received the heaviest sentences: respectively fifteen and ten years of imprisonment.

Wieder Aufgerollt: Der Nurnberger Prozess
Director: Felix von Podmanitzky. Production: Continent Film GmbH. Year: 1958. Country: Federal Republic of Germany (FRG) (West Germany). Run time: 90 min. Documentary.
An account of the Nuremberg Trials, with a description of the rise of Nazism, including footage taken in the concentration camps.

Mord in Lwow. Archive Sagen Aus
Director: Walter Heynowski. Production: Deutscher Fernsehfunk. Year: 1959–1960. Country: GDR. Run time: 55 min. Documentary.
The agricultural economist Oberländer was a member of the National Socialist Party from 1933 on, and temporary head of the East European economy in Königsberg. Oberländer was involved in a number of Nazi activities: for example, he took part in the attack on Russia with his battalion, made up of three hundred Ukrainians and three hundred Germans, which reached Lwow (Lemberg) on June 30, 1941. The film

emphasizes Oberländer's responsibility for the murder of a great number of Jews, focusing on the important role Oberländer played later on in West German politics under Konrad Adenauer.

Mein Kampf
Den Blodiga Tiden

Director: Erwin Leiser. Production: Minerva International Films. Year: 1960. Country: Sweden. Run time: 122 min. Documentary.

Leiser compiled this film from more than twenty thousand meters (65,000 feet) of documentary footage and newsreels from French, Soviet, English, Polish, and Austrian archives as well as from archives of the former Propaganda Ministry. It was the first film to show a part of the extensive archives preserved in East Germany on the subject and notably on the Warsaw Ghetto. Maurice Croizat wrote the French commentary.

Eichmann und das Dritte Reich
Eichmann, the Man of the Third Reich

Director: Erwin Leiser. Production: Praesens-Film AG in Cooperation with CCC. Year: 1961. Country: Switzerland. Run time: 90 min. Documentary.

On the occasion of the Eichmann trial, this film examines the Nazi persecution of Jews beginning with the elaboration of racial theories that engendered various forms of discrimination and the construction of the first concentration camp, all the way to the politics of total extermination.

Le Temps du Ghetto

Director: Frederic Rossif. Screenplay: Madeleine Chapsal, Frédéric Rossif. Production: Les films de la Pléiade. Year: 1961. Country: France. Run time: 82 min. Documentary.

In this story of the Warsaw Ghetto, from its creation to its brutal destruction in 1943, Frederic Rossif assembled archival footage and interviews with survivors. He tells of the building of the ghetto, the horrendous daily life of its inhabitants, their uprising, and their desperate struggle. The film was strongly criticized for its indiscriminate use of footage filmed by the Nazis.

Verdict For Tomorrow

Director: Leo Hurwitz. Production: Capital Cities Broadcasting Corporation. Year: 1961. Country: USA. Run time: 28 min. Documentary.

A montage intended as a summary of the events of the Eichmann trial held from April to December 1961 in Jerusalem. The film contains clips from eyewitness testimonies given at the time. Leo Hurwitz, the director, filmed the entire process of this trial and this footage was also used, with different editings, in television coverage of the Eichmann trial in America, the United Kingdom, and West Germany.

Edith Stein. Breslau 1891–1942

Director: Dominique Delouche. Production: Les Films du Prieuré. Year: 1962. Country: France. Run time: 13 min. Documentary.

A study of the life and beliefs of Edith Stein, a young Jewish woman who converted and became a Catholic nun. She was deported and killed in Auschwitz.

Krigsfurbrytare
The Victors and the Vanquished

Director: Tore Sjöberg. Screenplay: Erik Holm. Production: Minerva International Films. Year: 1962. Country: Sweden. Run time: 84 min. Documentary.

An account of the rise of Hitler and the Third Reich, comprised of British, German, and Russian archival footage. Among other material, scenes of the concentration camps at Bergen-Belsen, Buchenwald, and Dachau are shown, as well as footage of the Nuremberg Trials.

Gericht Über Auschwitz. Der Prozess in Frankfurt

Director: Emil Gregor Walter. Production: Hessischer Rundfunk. Year: 1965. Country: FRG. Run time: 49 min. Documentary.

The Auschwitz trial opening in Frankfurt. Survivors of the camp give interviews and tell of their experiences. The accused are shown on the way to the trial. The film shows scenes of the beginning of the trial, as well as Fritz Bauer talking with Soviet journalists.

Warsaw Ghetto

Director: Alexander Bernfes. Production: BBC. Year: 1966. Country: UK. Run time: 51 min. Documentary.

A compilation of shots filmed by Gestapo and SS cameramen, as well as photographs taken from Himmler's personal collection. It gives a detailed view of the daily struggle to survive, the horrendous sanitation conditions, the illegal smuggling of food from outside sources, the deportation, resistance for some and collaboration by others. The final images show the ghetto after it was completely destroyed as the narrator enumerates what the Germans took with them after having destroyed it.

Frauen in Ravensbrück

Director: Renate Drescher, Joop Huisken. Production: DEFA-Studio fur Wochenschau und Dokumentarfilme for the Committee of Antifascist

Resistance Fighters in the German Democratic Republic. Year: 1967–68. Country: GDR. Run time: 38 min. Documentary.

A survivor of the women's camp in Ravensbruck tells the visitors about the cruelties she experienced. The film shows photos of the women who resisted the SS and who were killed for it. The president of the Ravensbruck International Committee gives a speech and a wreath of flowers is placed on the monument to the dead. A few ex-victims gather on the occasion of the conference of the Ravensbruck International Committee.

Le Chagrin et la Pitie. Chronique D'une Ville Francaise Sous L'occupation
The Sorrow and the Pity
L'effondrement [Part 1] (The Collapse)
Le Choix [Part 2] (The Choice)
Director: Marcel Ophuls. Production: Télévision Recontre, Société Suisse de Radiodiffusion, Norddeutscher Rundfunk. Year: 1969. Country: Switzerland, Germany. Run time: 270 min. Documentary.

This film chronicles what happened during the occupation in Clermont-Ferrand during World War II. Located near Vichy, this town was both receptive to the collaborationists under Pétain and a central location for the Resistance. Ophuls combined archival footage with newsreels and witness testimonies to offer this complex portrait of a collective environment that differs greatly from the simplistic impressions that were prevalent in France at the time of the making of this film.

Why Didn't They Bomb Auschwitz?
Director: Daniel Shalit, Hananya Amotz. Production: Israel Broadcasting Authority. Year: 1972. Country: Israel. Run time: 53 min. Documentary.

A careful reconstruction of the debate that took place during the second half of 1944 among the Allies, about whether or not Auschwitz should be bombed. Bezalel Moldovitch was able to inform diplomatic circles of it. The film retraces the diplomatic and strategic debates among the Allies and the Vatican, as well as the many attempts by escapees and Jewish organizations to convince them to bomb this camp. The Allies ended up refusing to do so, giving various reasons: that they wanted to "limit any further damage," that the "plans were imprecise," that they feared endangering the people incarcerated there and also needed to concentrate all their forces on the Western front. This documentary shows the conflict between the Jewish organizations and the American and British armies, who preferred to put "their" people first.

The 81st Blow
Ha-Makah Hashmonim V'echad
Le 81ème Coup
Director: Haim Gouri. Screenplay: Haim Gouri, David Bergman, Jacques Ehrlich, Miriam. Novitch, Zvi Shner. Production: Beit Lohamei Haghetaot. Year: 1974. Countries: Israel, France. Run time: 115 min. Documentary.

This documentary was produced by Shoah survivors now living in Israel, and retraces the rise of Nazism and the escalating persecution of Jews, culminating in their deportation to the extermination camps. Scenes show the Jewish partisan and resistant groups. The title makes reference to Michael who managed to survive eighty blows with a whip inflicted upon him by a German soldier: for him, the disbelief of his liberators is "the 81st blow." The film contains a number of photographs and archival footage filmed by the Germans, the Polish, and the Allies. The soundtrack consists primarily of witness testimonies given at the Eichmann trial.

Erscheinungsform Mensch: Adolf Eichmann
Director: Rolf Defrank. Production: Aurora Television Produktions GmbH & Co. Year: 1978–79. Country: FRG. Run time: 107 min. Documentary.

The preparation and sequence of events of the Eichmann trial (1961–62) in Jerusalem. The people who arrested Eichmann in Argentina and who brought him to Israel are interviewed, as well as chief of police Avner Less, who interrogated him in prison, the doctors and psychiatrists who looked after and cared for him, and a number of Auschwitz escapees. These statements are compared to the recorded statements Eichmann made.

The Last Sea
Ha-yam Ha'aharon
Director: Haim Gouri, Jacques Ehrlich, David Bergman. Screenplay: Haim Gouri, David Bergman. Production: Te'udah Films, Beit Lohamei Ha'Ghettaot. Year: 1979. Country: Israel. Run time: 100 min. Documentary.

After World War II, many Jewish refugees immigrated to Israel. In this film, Jewish survivors remember their perilous flight to Palestine, by train or by truck, crossing the Alps on foot, or sailing on boats that were dangerously overloaded with people. It is a testament of their will to live.

Kitty: Return to Auschwitz
Director: Peter Morley. Production: Yorkshire Television. Year: 1979. Country: UK. Run time: 65 min. Documentary.

Kitty Felix Hart visits Auschwitz with her son, telling him of her ordeal and how she and her mother survived their eighteen-month internment there.

Lagerstrasse Auschwitz
Rue Auschwitz
Auschwitz Street
Director: Ebbo Demant. Production: Sudwestfunk. Year: 1979. Country: FRG. Run time: 60 min. Documentary.

Interviews with Josef Erber (SS-Oberschaarführer), Josef Klehr (SS-Sanitatsgrad), and Oswald Kaduk (Raportführer and Blockführer), who are serving life sentences in German prisons for Nazi crimes. They openly admit to the murders and gassing in Auschwitz, as two ex-prisoners of the camp give their testimonies.

Memories of the Eichmann Trial
Zichronot Mishpat Eichmann
Director: David Perlov. Production: Israel Broadcasting Authority. Year: 1979. Country: Israel. Run time: 60 min. Documentary.

A collection of interviews of survivors who were present at the trial, other people to whom some parts of the trial were shown, and a few native-born Israelis who were aged fifteen at the time of the trial in 1961–62.

Der Gelbe Stern
The Yellow Star
Director: Dieter Hildebrandt. Production: Chronos-Film GmbH. Year: 1980. Country: FRG. Run time: 89 min. Documentary.

A review of Nazi crimes during the 1930s and 1940s including footage not previously seen about the persecution of Jews during the Third Reich.

Und Sie Waren Gleich Tot
Director: Ebbo Demant. Production: Sudwestfunk. Year: 1980. Country: FRG. Run time: 51 min. Documentary.

Ebbo Demant interviewed three Auschwitz criminals: Oswald Kaduk (Rapportführer, Blockführer), Josef Klehr (SS-Sanitätsgrad), and Josef Erber (SS-Oberschaarführer). All of them received a life sentence at the Auschwitz trial in Frankfurt but were released from prison in the 1980s.

Zeugen. Aussagen Zum Mord an einem Volk

Director: Karl Fruchtmann. Production: Radio Bremen. Year: 1980–81. Country: FRG. Run time: 223 min. (in 2 parts). Documentary.

Sixty survivors were interviewed in this film: fifty-two in Israel and eight in Poland. They wanted to give their testimony regarding the extermination, to find an expressive way to testify to the living, on behalf of the dead.

It Went on Day and Night, Dear Child: Gypsies in Auschwitz
Es Ging Tag und Nacht, Liebes Kind: Zigeuner (Sinti) in Auschwitz

Directors: Katrin Seybold, Melanie Spitta. Screenplay: Melanie Spitta. Production: Katrin Seybold, ZDF. Year: 1981–82. Country: FRG. Run time: 75 min. Documentary.

Hundreds of thousands of Gypsies were deported to the concentration camps. In this documentary, a few of the survivors talk about the terror they felt, the murders, the medical experiments carried out by Josef Mengele, and the quantities of people stuffed into the gas chambers. The survivors brought their children to Auschwitz to transmit their memories and mourn over those who were lost.

Genocide

Director: Arnold Schwartzman. Screenplay: Martin Gilbert, Rabbi Marvin Hier, Arnold Schwartzman. Production: Arnold Schwartzman Productions, Simon Wiesenthal Center. Year: 1981. Country: USA. Run time: 90 min. Documentary.

A portrait of more than a thousand years of history of the Jewish people in Europe. Schwartzman introduces us to the various European Jewish communities, those of the rural areas in Eastern Europe (the Shtetls), and those that were integrated into modern life in the cities. In this way, we discover what was destroyed during just one twelve-year period. In 1945, the Ashkenazi civilization had become nothing more than a memory; it had literally gone up in smoke and ashes in the extermination camps.

Who Shall Live and Who Shall Die?

Director: Laurence Jarvik. Production: Blue Light Film Company. Year: 1981. Country: USA. Run time: 90 min. Documentary.

Laurence Jarvik talks to people who headed support groups for

Jewish people seeking asylum before and after World War II. He asks them if they couldn't have done more to save the future victims of the Shoah. In fourteen interviews, he shows that there were indeed ways to do more for these people.

Auschwitz and the Allies
Director: Rex Bloomstein. Production: BBC. Year: 1982. Country: UK. Run time: 110 min. Documentary.

This film analyses the passivity demonstrated by the Allies when faced with the monumental proportions of the extermination of Jews between 1942 and 1944. To do so, the director used interviews, archival footage, scenes from the Eichmann trial, photographs, and official documents and letters.

The Story of Chaim Rumkowski and the Jews of Lodz
Directors: Peter Cohen, Bo Kuritzen. Production: POJ Filmproduction AB, STV1. Year: 1982. Country: Sweden. Run time: 53 min. Documentary.

Chaim Rumkowski was head of the "council" overseeing the life of the Jews in the Lodz Ghetto. He organized the work force to attempt to make it indispensable to the industrial needs of the Nazis. In this way, he managed to delay the deportations, but he was not able to prevent the Nazis from carrying out their extermination plans. Three hundred thousand Jews were deported from Lodz and exterminated, and Rumkowski was considered an accomplice to these atrocities, even though he also died at Auschwitz. Archival documents and photographs taken by the inhabitants of the Lodz Ghetto were added to the telling of this story.

Life after Survival
Leben nach dem Überleben
Director: Erwin Leiser. Production: Erwin Leiser Productions. Year: 1982. Country: Switzerland. Run time: 60 min. Documentary.

Portraits of survivors of the Shoah and their children in Israel, Holland, Sweden, and America.

Schindler
Director: Jon Blair. Screenplay: Jon Blair. Production: Thames Television. Year: 1983. Country: UK. Run time: 78 min. Documentary.

This portrait of Oskar Schindler was a research source used by Steven Spielberg for his film *Schindler's List*. Survivors saved by Schindler, his wife, and his mistress were interviewed. Also included are other images, among them heretofore unseen archival footage of Oskar

Schindler.

Raoul Wallenberg: Buried Alive
Director: David Harel. Screenplay: David Harel, Peter Lauterman. Production: Rubicon Films. Year: 1983. Country: Canada. Run time: 79 min. Documentary.

This Canadian film contains a wealth of archival material that graphically shows the rise of the "Arrow Cross Nazis" in Hungary. Astounding footage of ghetto pogroms and the enforced death marches are interwoven with interviews of survivors who owe their lives to Mr. Wallenberg, as well as with people who have reported seeing him alive.

Auschwitz, the Album, the Memory
Auschwitz, l'album, la Mémoire
Director: Alain Jaubert. Production: CNRS-Audiovisuel, Hexagram, INCA. Year: 1984. Country: France. Run time: 41 min. Documentary.

This is an album of photos taken by an SS officer at the arrival of a convoy of deported Hungarian Jews at the Auschwitz station, which was discovered by a survivor, Lily Jacob. Since then, it is the property of Yad Vashem and it is known as the *Auschwitz Album*. It represents the largest corpus of images of this type (189 photographs) made inside the extermination camps. The camera looks at each photo in detail, searching for elements of meaning, and the film is narrated and commented upon by four survivors.

The Trial
Der Prozess
Director: Eberhard Fechner. Production: Norddeutscher Rundfunk. Years: 1975–1984. Country: FRG. Run time: 270 min. Documentary.

A documentary about the Majdanek concentration camp in eastern Poland and the trial forty years later (May 30, 1975-July 30, 1981) of camp guards accused of being involved in the murder of some 250,000 people. The director interviewed seventy major witnesses in Austria, Germany, Israel, and Poland.

Babi Yar: Lessons of History
Director: Clarissa Henry, Marc Hillel. Production: Ukranian Studio of TV Films, Maljack Productions. Year: 1985. Country: Soviet Union. Run time: 50 min. Documentary.

Survivors of the Shoah are interviewed about the Nazi invasion of the Ukraine and the Babi Yar massacre there, in which two hundred thousand Ukrainians, Jews, and Gypsies were killed.

Deckname Schlier

Director: Dieter Matzka and Wilma Kiener. Screenplay: Dieter Matzka and Wilma Kiener. Production: Hochschule fur Fernsehen und Film Munchen. Year: 1985. Country: FRG. Run time: 90 min. Documentary.

A hidden bunker was accidentally discovered in Zipf, Upper Austria. It was a secret Nazi rocket factory. Between 1943 and 1945, concentration camp prisoners from Mauthausen worked there, in the V2 rocket testing station called "Schlier." Now, fifty years later, survivors of the slave labor force, as well as staff and engineers who built and tested the V2 rockets, are asked to confront their memories of that time.

Dark Lullabies

Director: Irene Lilienheim Angelico, Abbey Jack Neidik. Screenplay: Gloria Demers, Irene Lilienheim Angelico. Production: National Film Board of Canada. Year: 1985. Country: Canada. Run time: 81 min. Documentary.

The impact of the Shoah on a generation of Jews and Germans born after World War II. Angelico, herself the child of concentration camp survivors, looks at how children of survivors have been affected by their parents' ordeal. The film also addresses the issue of how contemporary Germans cope with the guilt surrounding their parents' crimes.

Painful Reminder—Evidence for All Mankind

Director: Brian Blake. Screenplay: Richard Crossman, Colin Wills. Production: Granada Television International. Year: 1985. Country: UK. Run time: 75 min. Documentary.

In 1945, British forces liberated the Bergen-Belsen concentration camp. Sidney Bernstein was working in the Psychological Warfare Division and decided that what had been found must be exposed in such a way that no denial of the atrocities could ever take place. He produced the film *Memory of the Camps*. For various political reasons the film was never screened until 1985. Blake's film asks why *Memory of the Camps* was never shown and tells of its making. His film includes interviews with the people involved in the liberation and with survivors of the camp. The film also contains some original footage.

Partisans of Vilna

Director: Josh Waletzky. Screenplay: Josh Waletzky, Aviva Kempner. Production: Ciesla Foundation Inc. Year: 1985. Country: USA. Run time: 133 min. Documentary.

A chronicle of Jewish resistance fighters in Vilna. It blends songs, newsreels, and archival footage with interviews of more than forty

Holocaust survivors to produce a portrait of the Jewish resistance in Vilna, Lithuania, recounting how a commando unit was formed under tremendous risk to conduct sabotage missions against the Nazis.

Raoul Wallenberg: Between the Lines
Director: Karin Altmann. Production: Jethro Films Pty. Ltd., Simon Wiesenthal Center. Year: 1985. Country: USA. Run time: 90 min. Documentary.

The story of Swedish diplomat Raoul Wallenberg, who saved thousands of Jews from Budapest. This documentary is comprised of interviews with some of his colleagues and Shoah survivors, as well as archival footage filmed by Nazis.

Shoah
Director: Claude Lanzmann. Production: Les Films Aleph, Historia Films, Westdeutscher Rundfunk. Year: 1985. Country: France, FRG. Run time: 566 min. (2 parts). Documentary.

Shoah became the film of reference on the subject of this event. Its title became generally accepted to name the process of extermination, this last circle of hell. Claude Lanzmann made his film without the use of period archives, and instead solicited the testimony of escapees, the executioners, the witnesses, and researchers. Their words are heard against the images of the locations as they look now. The viewer is free to develop his own image of what has disappeared, of those who were erased, based on these voices and these images.

Pnei Hamered
Flames in the Ashes
Director: Haim Gouri et Jacques Ehrlich Production: Beit Lohamei Ha'Ghettaot, Te'udah Films. Year: 1985. Country: Israel. Run time: 96 min. Documentary.

The myth that Jews were led to their slaughter like sheep is dispelled by this documentary on Jewish resistance. The film retraces the history of the Shoah in Europe through the testimony of survivors who provide their stories and rare archival documents. One of the most appalling scenes shows Ukrainian farmers torturing a Jewish deportee. The film shows the many methods used by the resistance fighters.

Ein Einfacher Mensch
Director: Karl Fruchtmann. Production: Norddeutscher Rundfunk. Year: 1986. Country: FRG. Run time: 103 min. Documentary.

A portrait of the life of Jakow Silberberg, deported to Auschwitz and forced to work in the crematories as part of the Death Commandos

(*Sonderkommandos*), in charge of emptying the gas chambers and burning the bodies. After the liberation, he immigrated to Israel. When Karl Fruchtmann met him there, Silberberg was living with his family in Holon near Tel Aviv, working as a baker.

Elie Wiesel—Im Zeichen des Feuers

Director: Erwin Leiser. Production: Erwin Leiser Filmproduktion. Year: 1986. Country: Switzerland. Run time: 60 min. Documentary.

A portrait of writer Elie Wiesel, who became friends with Erwin Leiser in the sixties. Leiser describes the life journey of Wiesel. Born in Sighet, Romania (then part of Hungary), he was sent to Auschwitz, then Buchenwald, went after the war to Paris and finally to New York and Boston. Now Elie Wiesel is a professor in Boston, where he writes. He became well known as a spokesperson for the survivors of the Shoah and was awarded the Nobel Peace Prize in 1986. Wiesel writes about biblical figures, about the Jewish religion in a world that has completely changed since the Shoah. The author comments on his story and affirms, "Everything must be looked at through the shadow of these flames."

Transport 222

Director: Naomi Ben Natan-Schory. Production: Israel Film Service, NCRV, Belbo Film Productions BV. Year: 1986. Country: Israel, Holland. Run time: 20 min. Documentary.

German prisoners were secretly exchanged by the United Kingdom for Dutch Jewish concentration camp prisoners. The film retraces the journey of two groups: Germans returning to a collapsing Third Reich, and dazed Jews making their way to Palestine.

Biglal Ha'milchama Ha'hi
Because of that War
À Cause de Cette Guerre

Director: Orna Ben-Dor. Production: Manor Productions Ltd., Israel Film Service. Year: 1988. Country: Israel. Run time: 93 min. Documentary.

The effects of the Shoah on the so-called second generation. Yehuda Poliker, soloist of the group Benzin, created a new wave of Israeli rock. Yaakov Gilad discovered Poliker, and both worked together even after Benzin broke up—writing, composing, producing records, and performing. Poliker is of Greek origin, from a small town. Gilad, from the big city, grew up hearing about the culture of his mother, the writer and poet Helina. The parents of both experienced the horror of the concentration camps. Yehuda and Yaakov grew up with their parents' memories, and channeled the terror into their art.

Les Camps du Silence
The Camps of Silence
Director: Bernard Mangiante. Production: Les Films d'Ici, Films 13.
Year: 1988. Country: France. Run time: 104 min. Documentary.

This film is about the camps in Southern France: in February 1939,
five hundred thousand civilian and military prisoners as well as volunteers from international brigades that fled Spain were crowded onto the
beaches of Roussillon. Beginning in Summer 1942 and until Spring 1943,
these camps became a center for prisoner preselection, the antecham-
ber for Nazi extermination camps. In the meantime they were used in
all sorts of ways and interned various categories of French and foreign
"undesirables," political prisoners, and Jews. These camps, which were
initially improvised tent camps, became requisitioned factories and finally
veritable organized concentrationary projects.

Falkenau, Vision de L'impossible
Director: Emil Weiss. Screenplay: Emil Weiss, Samuel Fuller. Production: Michkan World Productions. Year: 1988. Country: France. Run
time: 52 min. Documentary.

This documentary is about the work of Samuel Fuller, who helped
liberate the Falkenau concentration camp in 1945 when he was a member
of the U.S. Army. Fuller shot footage of his commanding officers leaving the town to view the horrors of the camp, of which Czech locals
denied all knowledge.

Feuerprobe—Novemberpogrom 1938
Director: Erwin Leiser. Production: Erwin Leiser Filmproduktion. Year:
1988. Country: FRG. Run time: 90 min. Documentary.

Very few documentaries exist about the November pogrom perpetrated by the Nazis, because they forbade any filming or photography.
Leiser, who was living in Berlin in 1938, found people who witnessed
these events. His efforts to film policemen and Nazis who were involved
were unsuccessful, however. In this film, he shows that the persecution
of Jews began as early as Autumn 1938.

Hôtel Terminus. The Life and Times of Klaus Barbie
Director: Marcel Ophuls. Production: The Memory Pictures Co. Year:
1985–88. Country: USA. Run time: 267 min (cinema), 256 min. (TV).
Documentary.

Klaus Barbie was head of the Gestapo in Lyons, France, from 1942
to 1944. During the Nazi occupation of France, the Gestapo set up its

main headquarters in the Hôtel Terminus in Lyon and converted hotel rooms into interrogation and torture rooms. Marcel Ophuls used a number of elements and techniques to depict the man and the atrocities he committed. Former Gestapo officers, neighbors, employees, sympathizers, and victims reconstruct a terrifying and complex portrait of this man and of that time.

State of Israel vs. John Ivan Demjanjuk: A Courtroom Drama
Director: Naomi Ben Natan-Schory. Production: Belfilms, Capital Studios, NOS. Year: 1988. Country: Israel. Run time: 50 min. Documentary.

The film follows the trial and conviction of car mechanic John Demjanjuk, a Ukrainian immigrant living in the United States, accused of being a Nazi war criminal nicknamed Ivan the Terrible.

Temoins
Director: Marcel Lozinski. Production: La Sept, Gamma, Obsession. Year: 1988. Countries: France, Poland. Run time: 27 min. Documentary.

Residents of a town called Kielce in Poland murdered forty-two Jewish survivors of the Shoah in 1946. Forty years later, participants and witnesses of this pogrom were interviewed for this film. The film is also illustrated by archives from the Polish Film Chronicles.

Voices from the Attic
Director: Debbie Goodstein. Production: Siren Pictures Corp. Year: 1988. Country: USA. Run time: 60 min. Documentary.

The director does research on the experience of her parents, who remained hidden in the attic of a Polish farm from 1942 to 1945. She returned to the place with them, found the woman who saved her family, and encountered other survivors.

Betrifft Fabrikation
Director: Rosa Berger-Fiedler. Production: DEFA-Studio für Dokumentarfilme for Fernsehen der DDR. Year: 1989. Country: GDR. Run time: 32 min. Documentary.

The story of women who demonstrated around the "Große Hamburger Straße" (Great Hamburg Street) in Berlin against a Nazi raid that took place in February 1943. By means of a six-day demonstration at the windows of the assembled camp on the Rosenstrasse, these non-Jewish wives of Jewish men succeeded in forcing the release of their husbands.

Herr Schmidt von der Gestapo—Filmische Dokumentation
Einer Beamtenkarriere
Director: Rosa Berger-Fiedler. Production: DEFA-Studio für Doku-
mentarfilme. Year: 1989. Country: GDR. Run time: 107 min.
Documentary.

This film is about the trial, from September 15–29, 1987, of Henry Schmidt (SS-Obersturmführer), the Gestapo division leader who was
responsible for the deportation of Jews from Dresden and its surrounding area. After the war, Schmidt lived anonymously in Eastern Germany
as an inconspicuous and dutiful citizen. After the trial, East Germany
wondered whether Schmidt used his experience from the past during
his service in the postwar society of Eastern Germany. They questioned
whether he allowed ex-Nazis to remain in high-level positions, as was
the case in West Germany.

Yizkor: Slaves of Memory
Director: Eyal Sivan. Screenplay: Eyal Sivan. Production: IMA Pro-
ductions/Rhea Films/Zweites Deutsches Fernsehen (ZDF). Year: 1991.
Country: Germany. Run time: 98 min. Documentary.

A critique of the use of the Shoah as an ideological tool by the
Israeli government.

Premier Convoi
Directors: Jacky Assoun, Suzanne Bloch. Production: Ex Nihilo, La Sept,
Paradiso Productions. Year: 1991. Country: France. Run time: 116 min.
Documentary.

Twelve survivors of the first convoy of deportees from Paris to
Auschwitz that left on March 27, 1942, were interviewed fifty years later
at the site of their arrests. They attest to the meticulous organization
of the persecution and the atrocities they endured at the hands of the
Nazis and Vichy regime sympathizers.

Primo Levi: The Memory of the Offence
Director: Denys Blakeway. Screenplay: Denys Blakeway. Production:
Fine Arts Production for BBC. Year: 1992. Country: UK Run time: 50
min. Documentary.

The tragic life story of Primo Levi, told by using literary quotations
from his work and memories from his closest friends. Blakeway shows
how the experience in Auschwitz turned a chemist into an author many
regard as the greatest writer of the Shoah.

Choice and Destiny
Ha-behirah V'hagoral
Director: Tsipi Reibenbach. Production: Israel Broadcasting Authority.
Year: 1993. Country: Israel. Run time: 118 min. Documentary.

In her film, Tsipi Reibenbach says: "I want to introduce Yitzhak, eighty years old, and his wife Fruma, seventy-two years old. These are my parents. They are Shoah survivors. They live in Israel. This moving story is told through the routine of everyday life for a retired couple: preparing their food, their meals, eating with their grandchildren. Leaving their daughter a memoir."

Chronicle of the Warsaw Ghetto Uprising According to
Marek Edelmann
Kronika Powstania w Getcie Warszawskim
Director: Jolanta Dylewska. Production: Scarabeus. Year: 1993. Country: Poland. Run time: 72 min. Documentary.

The story of Marek Edelman, leader of the Warsaw Ghetto underground, using archival footage from that time as well as Nazi films made when the Ghetto was torn down. The film puts emphasis on Edelman's struggle during the Ghetto uprising from April 19 to May 10, 1943.

L'oeil de Vichy
Director: Claude Chabrol. Screenplay: Jean-Pierre Azéma, Robert O. Paxton. Production: Canal+, Centre National de la Cinématographie, Délégation à la Mémoire et à l'Information Historique, FIT Productions, INA, La Sofica Bymages, Ministre de la Culture et de l'Éducation Nationale, Secrétariat d'État aux Anciens Combattants et Victimes de Guerre, Sylicone, TF1 Films Productions. Year: 1993. Country: France. Run time: 110 min. Documentary.

This film was made using archival footage, official newsreels that were broadcast on French movie screens during the occupation. The Vichy government, which collaborated with the Nazis, controlled these newsreels; therefore most of the footage is propaganda. The purpose of the film is to show how much disinformation was spread, and to question the power of mass media. It reminds us that Vichy lost no time in applying German anti-Semitic laws, and in some cases made them worse. Historians protested that the film attributed some of the propaganda to Vichy, while it was actually German propaganda.

Strafsache 4 Ks 2/63. Auschwitz Vor Dem Frankfurter
Schwurgericht
Die Ermittlung [Teil 1]
Der Prozess [Teil 2]
Das Urteil [Teil 3]
Directors: Dietrich Wagner, Rolf Bickel. Production: Hessischer Rundfunk. Year: 1993. Country: Germany. Run time: 172 min. (3 parts). Documentary.

On December 20, 1963, a trial began to judge twenty-two members of the Waffen-SS, all of whom were employed at the Auschwitz concentration camp. After 183 days of trial and the testimonies of 409 witnesses, the verdict was given on August 20, 1965. This film was made to commemorate the thirtieth anniversary of the beginning of the Auschwitz trial, and contains audio recordings of the trial made public for the first time. Interviews with former prisoners, trial witnesses, and participants supplement the film, along with extensive archive materials.

Balagan
Director: Andres Veierl. Production: Zweites Deutsches Fernsehen. Year: 1994. Country: Germany. Run time: 95 min. Documentary.

"Balagan"—a Hebrew word (with origins in Russian and Turkish) meaning chaos—is a film about a Palestinian actor and a Jewish actress of the Akko Theatre Center (Israel). Through his work with Jewish actors, Khaled sees himself as a mediator, but to his friends in the occupied areas he is a traitor. Madi is the daughter of a Czech Jew who almost died in the Sobibor concentration camp. From their experiences, the actors developed a five-hour theatre play, *Arbeit macht frei*. The film weaves scene clips with biographical fragments of both actors and, in so doing, sheds new light on the situation in the Middle East.

Choosing One's Way: Resistance in Auschwitz/Birkenau
Director: Ted Kay, Allen Secher. Production: Ergo Media. Year: 1994. Country: USA. Run time: 30 min. Documentary.

The story of the resistance of prisoners working in the Death Commando, which resulted in the destruction of crematorium no. 4 in Auschwitz. But there were other acts of resistance, and survivors tell what steps people took to preserve their humanity and resist the Nazis.

Diamonds in the Snow
Director: Mira Reym Binford. Production: Mira Reym Binford in cooperation with Norddeutscher Rundfunk, Westdeutscher Rundfunk. Year: 1994. Country: USA. Run time: 59 min. Documentary.

Only a few Jewish children from the Polish city of Bendzin survived the Shoah. This documentary tells the story of three of these children—one of them the film's creator, Mira Reym Binford. The film gives a portrait of the remarkable individuals whose courage helped three little girls survive: other Polish Jews, Polish Christians, and even a German businessman.

Eichmann: The Nazi Fugitive
L'hidato Shel Adolf Eichmann
Director: Dan Setton. Production: SET Productions. Year: 1994. Country: Israel. Run time: 88 min. Documentary.

On May 11, 1960, at 8:05 p.m., Adolf Eichmann stepped off a bus in suburban Buenos Aires, was grabbed by the neck, and bundled into a waiting car that took off. Twelve days later, he resurfaced—thousands of miles away as a prisoner in Israel—and made headlines that stunned the world. His capture by Israeli intelligence agents marked the end of an exhaustive, fifteen-year manhunt. Nearly thirty-five years later, new top-secret details of the hunt, the kidnapping, and the trial of Eichmann are revealed in this documentary.

Les Justes
Tzedek
Director: Marek Halter. Production: Kurtz Production, Sara Films, Vega Films, France 2 Cinéma, Radio-Télévision Suisse Romande, Palmyre Productions, Centre Européen Cinématographique Rhône-Alpes. Year: 1994. Countries: France, Switzerland. Run time: 170 min. (2 parts). Documentary.

Marek Halter made this documentary searching out thirty-six people who saved the lives of Jews. Why this number? In the Talmud, Rabbi Abaye says that "the world is based upon thirty-six righteous people." The film consists of more than two hundred interviews, gathered from all over Europe.

Anne Frank Remembered
Director: Jon Blair. Production: Jon Blair Film Company in cooperation with Anne Frank Stichting, BBC. Year: 1995. Country: USA. Run time: 117 min. Documentary.

The life of Anne Frank and her family. Unlike previous documentaries it does not end with the death of Anne Frank at Bergen-Belsen concentration camp but covers the postwar period and focuses on Otto Frank's search for his daughters and family. It talks about all the family members: their life in Frankfurt, their flight to Amsterdam, the betrayal, and their arrest. Throughout the film, friends and people who helped Anne and her family give testimony about their fate.

Dire L'indicible: La Quête d'élie Wiesel
Saying the Unsayable: Elie Wiesel's Quest
Mondani a mondhatatlant: Elie Wiesel üzenete
Director: Judit Elek. Production: France 3 Cinéma, Hunnia Filmstúdió, Neuropa, Taxila. Year: 1996. Countries: Hungary, France. Run time: 105 min. Documentary.

In a remote corner of what used to be Hungary, in the shadow of the Carpathian Mountains, the life of Elie Wiesel was changed forever. He was fifteen when fascism took power. This documentary chronicles the adolescent years of Elie Wiesel and his long journey, the story of his many sufferings. Fifty years later, he returns to the town where he was born to walk the painful road of remembrance—but is it possible to speak of the unspeakable? Or does Auschwitz lie beyond the capacity of any human language—a place where words and stories are lost?

Jenseits des Krieges
East of the War
Director: Ruth Beckermann. Production: Ruth Beckermann. Year: 1996. Country: Austria. Run time: 117 min. Documentary.

During an itinerant exhibit on the crimes of the Wehrmacht during World War II presented in various German and Austrian towns, Ruth Beckermann gathered testimony from ex-soldiers from both countries.

My Knees Were Jumping—Remembering the Kindertransports
Director: Melissa Hacker. Production: Melissa Hacker. Year: 1996. Country: USA. Run time: 76 min. Documentary.

In the nine months prior to World War II, nearly ten thousand children were sent to Great Britain from Nazi Germany, Austria, Czechoslovakia, and Poland. The Kindertransport movement rescued these children. Most of the children never saw their parents again. The parents who had the strength to send their children off to an unknown fate soon boarded transports taking them to concentration camps. The children who lived the trauma and terror of being uprooted from secure homes tell amazing stories. Melissa Hacker's mother was one of the children rescued from Vienna by the Kindertransport movement in January 1939.

Reisen ins Leben. Weiterleben nach einer Kindheit in
Auschwitz
Director: Thomas Mitscherlich. Production: Bremer Institut Film Fern-
sehen. Year: 1996. Country: Germany. Run time: 130 min. Documentary.

The film is structured around three survivors from Auschwitz concentration camp who talk about their lives following their incarcera-
tion, the legal and illegal migration to Palestine/Israel, and the restrictive
immigration policies at the time in Western Europe. These three are:
Gerhard Durlacher, a sociologist researching the problems of survival;
Jehuda Bacon, professor of painting in Jerusalem and a witness at the
Eichmann and Auschwitz trials; and Ruth Klüger, professor of German
literature in the United States, who was deported with her mother and
father to the Theresienstadt camp. Archival footage is also included in
this documentary.

Shtetl
Director: Marian Marzynski. Production: David Fanning for Frontline
(PBS). Year: 1996. Country: USA. Run time: 180 min. Documentary.

On November 8, 1942, the Nazis took all the Jews from the
Shtetl of Bransk in Poland, by requisitioning horses from farmers for
the transport to the closest train station. In less than twenty-four hours,
the twenty-five hundred Jews from Bransk had died in the gas chambers
in Treblinka. The director interviewed people in present-day Poland and
researched living conditions in the Shtetl before the war and inquired
about how the village was destroyed.

Survivors of the Holocaust
Director: Alan Holzman. Production: Spielberg Survivors of the Shoah
foundation, Turner Original Productions. Year: 1996. Country: USA.
Run time: 70 min. Documentary.

Survivor testimonies, archival footage, newsreels, original music,
survivors' personal photographs, and artifacts. The film talks about the
richness of life before the war from the survivors' point of view, the
rise and fall of Nazi power, the liberation of the camps, and life fifty
years later.

The Hell
Transnistria
Director: Zolton Terner. Production: Israel Educational Television. Year:
1996. Country: Israel. Run time: 40 min. Documentary.

In Transnistria, in southern Ukraine near the Romanian border, three hundred thousand Jews were murdered by Romanian officials. Unlike the industrialized killings in Auschwitz, Romanian death camps used the old methods: burnings, shootings, typhus, and starvation. Aharon Appelfeld, one of Israel's foremost writers, is one of the survivors. This film was created to honor those who died in Transnistria, a place forgotten by almost everyone. Survivors give testimony with their memories and with paintings, letters, and photographs.

Ghetto Theresienstadt—Täuschung und Wirklichkeit
Director: Irmgard von zur Mühlen. Production: Chronos-Film GmbH. Year: 1997. Country: Germany. Run time: 90 min. Documentary.

The film shows the methods used by the Nazis in their campaign to deceive the public about the concentration and extermination camps. As a setting, they chose Theresienstadt, a transit camp for prisoners headed for Auschwitz, which, in order to impress the International Red Cross, was rearranged to look like a residential area for Jews. The Nazis made a propaganda film here and gave it the title, *Theresienstadt. Ein dokumentarfilm aus dem jüdischen siedlungsgebiet.* Historian Karel Margry explains how the public was manipulated into believing this fabrication. Conversations with survivors, drawings by prisoners, photographs, and documents describe living conditions in this ghetto. Aerial photographs are also shown in this documentary.

In the Shadow of the Reich: Nazi Medicine
Director: John Michalczyk. Production: First Run, Icarus Films. Year: 1997. Country: USA. Run time: 60 min. Documentary.

The collaboration of doctors in the Nazi regime, including their participation in the Final Solution program. The film describes how Nazi doctors went from racial theory, to sterilization of the "unfit," to euthanasia, and eventually to genocide and the most unbelievably monstrous experimentations. Filmed at the Auschwitz and Majdanek concentration camps, this documentary features a number of interviews with scholars and survivors of the Shoah, along with a 1995 interview at Auschwitz with a former S.S. doctor, Hans Munch.

Love Story—Berlin 1942
Director: Catrine Clay. Production: Timewatch. Year: 1997. Country: UK. Run time: 48 min. Documentary.

Lilly Wust, a German and an "Aryan" housewife is romantically involved with Felice Schragenheim, a Jewish woman living in the Underground. This documentary retraces their love affair, and is composed of interviews with Lilly, who lives in Berlin today, and various people who knew Felice.

The Last Transfer
Shanim Trufot
Director: Ilana Tsur. Production: Zavit Productions. Year: 1997. Country: Israel. Run time: 55 min. Documentary.

This film is about Shoah survivors who spent between fifteen and twenty-five years at the Abrabanel, which has now become a psychiatric-geriatric center. Staff members, families, patients, and volunteers were interviewed for this film. It asks why these people became mentally damaged whereas other survivors did not. Did Israeli society play a role in this by rejecting them as immigrants?

Theresienstadt Sieht aus wie ein Curort
Director: Nadja Seelich. Production: Extrafilm Arbeitsgemeinschaft Film & Video GmbH. Year: 1997. Country: Austria. Run time: 51 min. Documentary.

In 1948, just before her seventy-fifth birthday, Josefa Stibitzova recalled her memories of her stay in the Theresienstadt concentration camp with a tape recorder. This recording is the only commentary in the film. Nadja Seelich, Josefa Stibitzofa's granddaughter, links the words to private photographs from 1942–48, archive photographs from 1943–45, film footage from Theresienstadt, and correspondence written by Josefa Stibitzova. These pictures are expanded through the inclusion of associative shots and clips from an educational film about silkworm breeding.

Diese Tage in Terezín
Director: Sibylle Schönemann. Screenplay: Sibylle Schönemann. Production: Film-u. Fernsehproduktion "Der Ochsenkopf," MA.JA.DE. Filmproduktion. Years: 1995–98. Countries: Germany, Czech Republic. Run time: 82 min. Documentary.

Karel Svenk, a poet from Prague, was nicknamed the "Chaplin of Theresienstadt." He created and managed the cabaret at the last stop before hell. Three women attempt a reconstruction of his biography to draw him from the anonymity of the dead. With a photo and some documents, they uncover the remembrance of a few survivors.

News from the Underground
Nachrichten aus dem Untergrund
Director: Andreas Hoessli. Production: NZZ Format. Year: 1997–98. Country: Switzerland. Run time: 60 min. Documentary.

A portrait of three men—Karsky, Vrba, Riegner—who attempted, in vain, to put a stop to the extermination by alerting the Allies. Gerhart Riegner sent the first message from Geneva to the United States. Jan Karsky, a courier in the Polish resistance, gave a personal testimony to political leaders of the Allied Forces. Rudolf Vrba, an escapee from Auschwitz, gave an account to Jewish leaders in Slovakia. These three men talk about their attempt to inform the free world about the facts of the "Final Solution," to put a halt to a seemingly inevitable course of events. It is the third year of the war—in London, in Washington, in Geneva. And in Poland the machinery of death has been established.

Grüningers Fall
L'affaire Grüninger
Directors: Georg Hafner, Esther Schapira. Production: Lea Produktion, Television Suisse. Year: 1998. Country: Switzerland. Run time: 98 min. Documentary.

In August 1938, Switzerland closed its borders to Jewish immigrants attempting to escape the Nazi regime. Paul Grüninger, a police captain in the Saint-Gall canton on the Austrian border, did not obey his administration's injunction and because of this he saved hundreds and possibly thousands of lives. Reported to the authorities and convicted by the Swiss government, he died in disgrace in the seventies. Richard Dindo organized a rehabilitation trial in the very courtroom where he was convicted, involving some of the people he saved.

Akte B.—Alois Brunner. Die Geschichte eines Massenmörders
Directors: Georg Hafner, Esther Schapira. Production: Hessischer Rundfunk. Year: 1998. Country: Germany. Run time: 115 min. Documentary.

Alois Brunner, known as Eichmann's "best man," was responsible for the death of 120,000 people deported from Drancy and Vienna (and in particular a convoy of children shortly before the end of the war). Today, he still claims to be proud of making Vienna "judenrein" (free of Jews). The documentary retraces the life of Alois Brunner and how he escaped being tried and convicted for his crimes. Although attorneys knew where he lived, Brunner was never tried and lives retired and free, and was able to support his family, give interviews, and sign contracts with German companies. After three years of research, the directors were able to uncover the network of helpers, former comrades, and new friends all over the world who have helped Brunner.

The Last Days
Directors: James Moll, June Beallor, Ken Lipper. Production: James Moll, June Beallor, Ken Lipper, and the Spielberg Survivors of the Shoah. Year: 1998. Country: USA. Run time: 90 min. Documentary.

This is the third documentary produced by the Spielberg Survivors of the Shoah Visual History Foundation, after *Survivors of the Holocaust* and *The Lost Children of Berlin*. It focuses on five Hungarian Jews, now U.S. citizens, who are survivors of the Shoah: Bill Basch, a businessman with several children, U.S. Congressman Tom Lantos, who was placed in a labor camp by the Nazis; Irene Zisblatt, a grandmother; Renee Firestone, a teacher; and Alice Lok Cahana, who paints to express her experiences. As they return to their birthplace, some of them are overcome with emotion.

Drei Deutsche Mörder
Director: Ebbo Demant. Production: Südwestrundfunk. Year: 1998. Country: Germany. Run time: 45 min. Documentary.

This is a reworked version of Ebbo Demant's film *Lagerstrasse Auschwitz*, which he shot in 1980. Ebbo Demant interviewed three of the Auschwitz murderers, Oswald Kaduk (Rapportführer, Blockführer), Josef Klehr (SS-Sanitätsgrad), and Josef Erber (SS-Oberschaarführer). All of them were sentenced to life imprisonment in the Auschwitz trial at Frankfurt but were released from prison in the 1980s.

Der Fotograf
Directors: Dariusz Jablonski, Wolfgang Katzke. Production: Apple Film Production; in cooperation with Broadcast AV, ARTE G.E.I.E., TVP S.A., Canal+ Polska, APF for Mitteldeutscher Rundfunk. Year: 1998. Countries: Poland, Germany. Run time: 80 min. Documentary.

The main part of this film is made up of original color slides taken in the Lodz (Litzmannstadt) ghetto. They tie in with recordings and statements made by survivor Arnold Mostowicz who also appears in black and white pictures made more recently. The attempt to maintain the ghetto as a labor camp until it was finally destroyed is particularly well described by Chaim Rumkowski, the president of the Jewish Council.

Pola's March
Directors: Jonathan Gruber, Amy Cairns, Chris Harrison. Production: Black Eye Productions. Year: 1998. Country: USA. Run time: 65 min. Documentary.

An inspirational documentary chronicling the emotional journey of survivor Pola Susswein. Pola travels from Israel to Poland accompanied by two hundred teenage students in the "March of the Living" program, recounting the most intense experience of her life for the first time in fifty years. As the group visits Warsaw, Lublin, and Krakow, as well as several notorious death camps, Pola struggles to relate and examine her past with extraordinary honesty, optimism, and humility.

Remembering Anne Frank

Director: Wouter van der Sluis. Production: Anne Frank Haus in cooperation with Jon Blair Film Company. Year: 1998. Country: Holland. Run time: 50 min. Documentary.

Fifty years after Anne Frank's arrest, Miep Gies, one of the four helpers of Anne Frank's family, once again visits the building where she worked. Wandering through the place, her memories of Anne Frank come to life. Miep Gies recounts how she helped Anne Frank and her family hide from the Nazis.

La Chaconne D'auschwitz

Director: Michel Daeron. Production: Les Films d'Ici. Year: 1999. Country: France. Run time: 100 min. Documentary.

Twelve survivors from the Birkenau camp, part of a group of deportees who were passionate about music, formed an orchestra in the camp under the direction of Alma Rosé, who was Gustav Mahler's niece.

Children of Chabannes

Directors: Lisa Gossels, Dean Wetherell. Production: Wetherell & Associates. Year: 1999. Country: USA. Run time: 82 min. Documentary.

During World War II in Chabannes, a small village in unoccupied France, people chose action over indifference and saved the lives of four hundred Jewish children. The filmmaker Lisa Gossels returned to Chabannes with her father and uncle, two of the children who were saved, to recreate daily life in the village. Interviews with the teachers show the remarkable efforts made by the citizens of Chabannes, who risked their lives to protect these children.

Closed Country

Director: Kaspar Kasics. Screenplay: Kaspar Kasics, Stefan Mächler. Production: Schweizer Fernsehen DRS, Teleclub AG, eXtra Film. Year: 1999. Country: Switzerland. Run time: 85 min. Documentary.

Two Jewish families confront Swiss officers who controlled the border. The Sonabend family attempted to cross the border illegally in 1942 but were arrested by Fritz Staub, locked up in a cloister, and then turned over to French police. The Popowski family managed to cross the border in 1942 and were arrested by Heinrich Rothmund, who did not turn them over to authorities but the next day ordered all borders completely shut down. Newsreel material and interviews with people involved create a poignant documentary.

I Was a Slave Labourer
Director: Luke Holland. Production: Minotaur International Ltd. Year: 1999. Country: UK. Run time: 75 min. Documentary.

More than ten million people from occupied Europe, Jews and non-Jews, were forced to work for the Third Reich. Many died of exhaustion and starvation, or were murdered when they could work no more. Filmed over four years, *I Was a Slave Labourer* follows Jewish Auschwitz survivor Rudy Kennedy, who is campaigning against the companies who collaborated with the Nazis' "Extermination through Work" program. During his journey through postwar Europe, he evolved from a man fighting his own personal war to the leader of an international campaign for memory and compensation.

Kapo
Directors: Dan Setton, Tor Ben Mayor. Production: SET Productions. Year: 1999. Country: Israel. Run time: 55 min. Documentary.

During the fifties and sixties, violent stories of murder and theft were presented before the Israeli judicial system. A number of Shoah survivors were convicted for having aided the Nazi death machine, in exchange for their lives. Excerpts from newspapers, photos, testimonies, rare interviews, and legal documents gathered for this film allow us to see inside these tragic dilemmas of humanity and the difficulty in judging such circumstances.

Lager Westerbork 1939–1945
Directors: Karel Margry, Wolfgang Bauer. Production: Chronos-Film GmbH. Year: 1999. Country: Germany. Run time: 60 min. Documentary.

The documentary tells the history of Westerbork concentration camp, from the early days when it served as a Dutch camp for Jewish refugees, through the takeover by the Nazi authorities during the occupation, and finally at the liberation of the camp by Canadian forces in 1945. Two survivors describe their experiences in the camp. Scenes from an archival film *Westerbork* are included, as well as an interview with the former SS camp commander of Westerbork, Alfred Konrad Gemmeker.

Liebe Perla
Director: Shahar Rozen. Production: Eden Productions Ltd., in cooperation with Norddeutscher Rundfunk, Keshet Broadcasting, New Israeli
Foundation for Film and Television. Year: 1999. Countries: Israel, Germany. Run time: 63 min. Documentary.

A story of a friendship between two very short women. Perla, an
actress, is the last living member of a Jewish family of dwarves that
survived Mengele's experiments in Auschwitz. Hannelore is a German
Protestant born in postwar Germany. Hannelore began a quest to fulfill
Perla's wish—to search for a lost Nazi film featuring Perla's family, standing naked on stage before a group of high-ranking SS officers. In her
investigation, she believes she has uncovered similarities between Nazi
attempts to create a master race and today's abortions meant to prevent
the birth of abnormal children.

Mr. Death: The Rise and Fall of Fred A. Leuchter, Jr.
Director: Errol Morris. Production: Channel Four. Year: 1999. Country:
USA. Run time: 91 min. Documentary.

A portrait of an inventor of machines used in capital punishment,
Fred A. Leuchter, who became an inflammatory propagandist of negationism in the United States.

Paragraph 175
Directors: Rob Epstein, Jeffrey Friedmann. Production: Filmboard
Berlin-Brandenburg. Year: 1999. Country: USA. Run time: 81 min.
Documentary.

During the Third Reich, about one hundred thousand homosexuals
were tortured or deported to concentration camps. Originally, penal persecution of homosexuals came from paragraph 175 of a law dating back to
1794, which forbade all sexual contact between men. This paragraph was
integrated into the penal code in 1871 and, in 1935, the Nazis decided
to enforce it. Five men and one homosexual woman, all over the age of
ninety, agreed to give their testimony regarding their persecution and
imprisonment in the concentration camps. Photos and films from that
time are also included with these interviews.

Reise Nach Genf
Director: Irene Loebell. Production: Schweizer Fernsehen, 3SAT. Year:
1999. Country: Switzerland. Run time: 61 min. Documentary.

When Vichy France began extraditing Jews to Nazi Germany in
the summer of 1942, the Austrian writer Fred Wander fled to Geneva,
Switzerland, just after the Swiss government had decided to return refugees "on purely racial grounds." Fred Wander was arrested along with six

other refugees and turned over to the French police. He was deported to Auschwitz. He survived. Decades later, when Switzerland started looking seriously at the history of World War II, Fred Wander's photograph turned up in police files.

Auschwitz: The Final Witness
Director: Sheldon Lazarus. Production: British Sky Broadcasting. Year: 2000. Country: UK. Run time: 53 min. Documentary.
This documentary on *Sonderkommandos*, the prisoners forced to clean out the gas chambers in the concentration camp of Auschwitz, is seen through the eyes of three men from Saloniki who were taken to Auschwitz in April 1944. The film tells the story of Morris, his youngest brother Shlomo, and his cousin Dario. Upon their arrival at the camp, they were assigned to work in the gas chambers, cremating the cadavers. They return to Auschwitz for the first time since they left the camp in 1945, and tell of their experiences in this place.

Eyes of the Holocaust
A Holocaust Szemei
Director: Jánosz Szász. Screenplay: Jánosz Szász. Production: InterCom, Survivors of the Shoah Visual History Foundation. Year: 2000. Countries: USA, Hungary. Run time: 56 min. Documentary.
   A Holocaust szemei is part of Steven Spielberg's ambitious plan for a series of documentaries in which filmmakers track down and interview every living survivor of the Shoah. This film was compiled from a number of these interviews, which record the memories of survivors of the Nazi death camps in Hungary. The film also incorporates newsreels from the period, as well as archival photographs to illustrate the stories of the witnesses. The documentary was directed by Jánosz Szász, whose parents were both survivors of the Shoah.

Into the Arms of Strangers: Stories of the
Kindertransport
Director: Mark Jonathan Harris. Production: Sabine Films, Skywalker, United States Holocaust Memorial Museum. Year: 2000. Countries: USA, UK. Run time: 122 min. Documentary.
   In 1938 and 1939, parents sent about ten thousand children from Germany, Austria, and Czechoslovakia, most of them Jewish, to England where foster families took them in for the duration of the war. Years later, eleven saved children, one child's mother, a foster mother, a survivor of Auschwitz who didn't go to England, and two of the Kindertransport organizers remember the time and the Kindertransport.

Fall Adolf Eichmann
Director: Sabine Keutner. Production: Zweites Deutsches Fern-sehen, 3SAT. Year: 2000. Country: Germany. Run time: 75 min. Documentary.

Adolf Eichmann's abduction on May 11, 1960, his arrest, the crimi-nal proceedings against him in Jerusalem from April 10, 1961, until May 29, 1962, and his execution in the night of June 1, 1962, are shown from the perspective of three contemporary witnesses who then take part in a debate. This is accompanied by film material, mostly from recordings of the trial in Jerusalem.

Interview from the Underground: Eyewitness Accounts of Russia's Jewish Partisan Resistance During WWII
Director: Phillip Alloy. Production: Todd Productions. Year: 2000. Coun-tries: Belorussia, Russia. Run time: 20 min. Documentary.

This film is comprised primarily of interviews with Jewish men and women who fought against the Nazis during World War II in Russia. A survivor of the Shoah guides the director through Minsk and other settings of these events.

The Optimists (The Story of the Rescue of the Jews of Bulgaria)
Director: Jacky Comforty. Production: Comforty Media Concepts in cooperation with Chambon Foundation. Year: 2000. Country: USA. Run time: 83 min. Documentary.

On March 9, 1943, police arrived at the home of Jacky Comforty's family in Bulgaria. Jacky Comforty's father had already been interned in a nearby forced labor camp and then sent to Treblinka. The whole family was sent to a deportation center along with 8,500 Bulgarian Jews targeted for extermination. They waited all day and then, at the end of the day, were simply sent home. Fifty thousand Jews lived in Bulgaria, but none were murdered because Bulgarian Christians and Moslems found ways to protect them from their would-be murderers even in defiance of their own Nazi-allied government.

Gypsy Holocaust
Porrajmos
Director: Ágota Varga. Production: konnte ich nicht herausfinden. Year: 2000. Country: Hungary. Run time: 94 min. Documentary.

The fate of Gypsy victims during the Nazi period and the Shoah. This film claims to be the first documentary that tries to give an overall picture of the Gypsies deported from Hungary. The Hungarian Red

Cross helped find the survivors, who tell about their memories in the film. These survivors were also involved in the aid program launched by the Swiss government in 1988. Before making the film, the director met almost a hundred survivors.

Petite Conversation Familiale
Director: Helene Lapiower. Production: Margofilm, Arte. Year: 2000. Country: Belgium. Run time: 67 min. Documentary.

For seven years, actress Helene Lapiower, the daughter of Jewish-Polish immigrants, regularly met with members of her extended family scattered in France, Belgium, and the United States. Uncles, aunts, cousins, parents, and grandparents took part in this, answering questions she asked about their personal history marked by the memories of the Shoah: Why and how did they rebuild their lives in this manner or that? What has become of their family today?

Casting
Director: Emmanuel Finkiel. Screenplay: Emmanuel Finkiel. Production: Les films du poisson. Year: 2001. Country: France. Run time: 116 min. Documentary.

Between 1994 and 1998, Emmanuel Finkiel cast nonprofessional actors and actresses for his films *Madame Jacques Sur La Croisette* and *Voyages*. He looked for people aged sixty-five to ninety who spoke Yiddish. The film documents the potential actors/actresses in Finkiel's office, telling stories of their lives, presenting photographs, and rehearsing texts. This collage of faces, people, and stories shows the humor and energy of these elderly people.

Bearing Witness: American Soldiers and the Holocaust
Director: Jonathan L. Barkan. Screenplay: Glenn Litton. Production: Communications for Learning. Year: 2001. Country: USA. Run time: 30 min. Documentary.

In a compilation of contemporaneous interviews and rare archival footage, the story of the liberation of the Nazi camps is told through the eyes of American soldiers who were in the units that liberated the concentration camp prisoners.

Zygielbojm's Death
Mier Zygielbojma
Director: Damila Ankiewicz. Production: Bon & Axe Entertainement Ltd. Year: 2001. Country: Poland. Run time: 52 min. Documentary.

In 1942, S. A. Zygielbojm, head of the Bund, the Jewish Social--Democratic party, illegally fled Poland. He was sent abroad as a representative of the Bund to connect with the representative of the Polish government in exile. He attempted to divulge the atrocities perpetrated by the Nazis in Poland. Believing all his efforts had been futile, he committed suicide after the insurrection of the Warsaw ghetto, in the hope that the world would finally end its indifference.

Sobibor, 14 Octobre 1943, 16 Heures
Director: Claude Lanzmann. Production: Why Not Productions, Les Films Aleph, France 2 Cinéma; Canal+, Télévision Images. Year: 2001. Country: France. Run time: 95 min. Documentary.

During the filming of *Shoah*, Claude Lanzmann had interviewed Yehuda Lerner in Jerusalem, but did not include this interview of one of the principal protagonists in the sole successful revolt of the prisoners in a Nazi extermination camp in his final edit. When he was deported to Sobibor, Yehuda Lerner accomplished the first act of revolt. Beyond homage, in memory of this heroic uprising Lanzmann turned the date and place of this act into the birth certificate of the Jewish people taking their destiny into their own hands through armed revolt.

Struma
Directors: Radu Gabrea, Andrei Gruzsnicky. Screenplay: Stelian Tanase. Production: Romanie. Year: 2001. Country: Romania. Run time: 90 min. Documentary.

In an attempt to escape the Nazis and the persecution of the Antonescu regime, 769 Romanian Jews boarded the *Struma* in December 1941. Upon the ship's arrival at Istanbul, the Turks, under Nazi pressure, denied the refugees entry. The British refused to issue visas for Palestine, and Romania would not allow the ship to return. The *Struma* was towed to the center of the Black Sea and sunk on February 24, 1942, by a torpedo apparently fired by a Russian submarine. This Romanian documentary utilizes documents and testimonies including that of David Stoliar, the sole survivor. Shown at the Jerusalem Film Festival in 2001.

Porraimos: Europe's Gypsies in the Holocaust
Director: Alexandra Isles. Production: Chalice Well Productions. Year: 2002. Country: USA. Run time: 56 min. Documentary.

This film exposes how the pseudo-science of eugenics was used to persecute not only Jews, but also Gypsies. To the Nazis, Gypsies' dark skin and nomadic ways made them "not worthy of living." Using interviews with Austrian, Czech, and German Gypsy survivors, including a Jewish artist who was ordered by Josef Mengele to paint portraits of Gypsy prisoners at Auschwitz, as well as photographs and films from the Third Reich's Department of Racial Hygiene, this video reveals the oppression of the Gypsies—their registration and segregation, their sterilization, the medical experiments, and their eventual mass murder.

Against the Odds

Director: Jedrzej Jonasz. Screenplay: Maciej Jonasz. Production: Capital j. Films. Year: 2004. Country: Canada. Run time: 44 min. Documentary.

Against The Odds describes different forms of resistance that existed in the German concentration camps, such as: smuggling of medicines, sabotage in the weapons factories (especially the large effect it had on the German secret weapons programs), preparations for rebellions and escapes, elimination of Gestapo informers within the camps, and the mission of Captain Pilecki, a Polish officer who purposefully got himself sent to Auschwitz in order to set up an underground organization in that camp.

Imaginary Witness: Hollywood and the Holocaust

Director: Daniel Anker. Production: Anker Productions. Year: 2004. Country: USA. Run time: 92 min. Documentary.

A collection of excerpts of Hollywood films and commentary by film historians, directors, and producers who discuss the ways in which, over the decades, Hollywood has evoked and at times sidestepped or distorted the theme of the Shoah.

Belzec

Director: Guillaume Moscovitz. Screenplay: Guillaume Moscovitz. Production: V.L.R. Productions Jean Bigot. Year: 2005. Country: France. Run time: 100 min. Documentary.

Belzec was the first concentration camp to exterminate the Jews in German-occupied Poland according to the "Aktion Reinhard" (the Nazi plan to exterminate the Jews in the occupied Polish territories). In 1943, it was completely destroyed, according to the decision of the Nazis to erase not only lives but also all trace of their extermination industry. Besides Rudolf Reder, who died in the 1960s and Chaim Hirszmann, who was murdered in Lublin shortly after the war, no one is known to have survived the Belzec camp. The film questions if and how pure destruction can be portrayed, thanks in part to the testimony of one woman (a little girl at the time) who remained hidden for several months near the camp.

I'm Still Here: Real Diaries of Young People Who Lived During the Holocaust
Director: Lauren Lazin. Screenplay: Alexandra Zapruder. Production: MTV Networks. Year: 2005. Country: USA. Run time: 47 min. Documentary.

The director used the diaries of young people who witnessed first-hand the horrors of the Shoah. The film pays homage to these young courageous writers who refused to disappear in silence, through a montage of archival footage, personal photographs, and text from the diaries themselves. The diaries of these young people were collected for the first time in the award-winning book *Salvaged Pages: Young Writers' Diaries of the Holocaust*.

Der Unbekannte Soldat
The Unknown Soldier
Director: Michael Verhoeven. Screenplay: Michael Verhoeven. Production: Sentana. Filmproduktion GmbH. Year: 2006. Country: Germany. Run time: 97 min. Documentary.

Michel Verhoeven shot this film during the "Wehrmachtsausstellung," an exhibit that showed the crimes of the German army during the war. The exhibit was shown in several German towns between 1999 and 2004 and provoked a debate on the image of the German soldiers who said they were involved in none of these crimes. Verhoeven focuses on the extermination war in Eastern Europe (1941–44) and traces the path of German troops en route to Belorussia. Contemporary and historical footage is included. The interviewed witnesses bring to evidence that the image of the "clean Wehrmacht" and the "innocence of the average soldier" are historical lies.

Fiction Films

The Wandering Jew
Director: George Roland. Screenplay: Jacob Mestel. Production: Jewish Americans Film Arts, Inc. Year: 1933. Country: USA. Run time: 68 min.

A Jewish artist is faced with German anti-Semitism when his work is rejected by the Berlin Academy for the Arts. The character in his painting comes to life and narrates the history of the persecution of the Jews. The film ends with images of an anti-Hitler protest rally in New York. With Jacob Ben-Ami.

Victims of Persecution
Director: Bud Pollard. Screenplay: David Leonard. Production: Bud Pollard Productions. Year: 1933. Country: USA. Run time: 62 min.

A Jewish judge in 1930s Germany struggles to assure a fair trial for the accused, a black man. He becomes the target of anti-Semitic action. With Mitchell Harris and Betty Hamilton.

The Great Dictator
Director: Charles Chaplin. Screenplay: Charles Chaplin. Production: United Artists, Charles Chaplin Corporation. Year: 1940. Country: USA. Run time: 126 min.

Chaplin plays an unnamed Jewish barber in the "Tomanian" ghetto who wakes up from amnesia, finding himself living under the thumb of dictator Adenoid Hynkel, also played by Chaplin. He is beaten up by uniformed thugs but escapes to Austria with Hannah (Paulette Goddard), a downtrodden Jewish laundress who is in love with him. There, he is mistaken for Hynkel, who has recently "liberated" the country. This was Chaplin's first talkie. The film ends with him as Hynkel/Hitler addressing a message of peace and brotherhood to the world, while warning of the terror to come.

Escape
Director: Mervyn LeRoy. Screenplay: Archer Oboler, Marguerite Roberts from a novel by Ethel Vance. Production: MGM. Year: 1940. Country: USA. Run time: 104 min.

Preysing (Robert Taylor) comes from America to Germany to visit his mother Emmy Ritter (Alla Nazimova). He befriends the Countess von Treck (Norma Shearer), who is having an affair with a German general. Preysing learns that his mother is in a concentration camp for smuggling money out of the country. The countess falls in love with Preysing and helps him, introducing him to Dr. Ditten, who has the mother declared dead and gets her out of the camp. After several obstacles, such as a snowstorm and a jealous general, Preysing and his mother escape by plane. This film shows camps, but does not mention the persecution of Jews.

The Man I Married
Director: Irving Pichel. Screenplay: Oscar Schisgall and Oliver H. P. Garrett. Production: Twentieth Century-Fox Film Corporation. Year: 1940. Country: USA. Run time: 77 min.

A young American woman who is married to a German gradually discovers the dark side of the Nazi regime: she sees a cattle car filled with men and women, learns about a man who officially died of appendicitis in a camp even though he had already undergone surgery, etc. She tries to flee to the United States with her son. With Joan Bennett, Francis Lederer, Lloyd Nolan, and Otto Kruger.

The Mortal Storm
Director: Frank Borzage. Screenplay: George Froeschel, Hans Rameau, Claudine West from a novel by Phyllis Bottome. Production: MGM. Year: 1940. Country: USA. Run time: 101 min.

Viktor Roth (Frank Morgan), a Jewish Professor, lives in a small German university town in 1933. Roth, his daughter Freya (Margaret Sullavan), and family friend Martin (James Stewart) are apprehensive about Hitler's rise, but other family members are enthusiastic and join Nazi organizations. Martin returns to Austria, opposing Hitler's regime. Roth ridicules the master race notion and is deported to a concentration camp where he dies. Freya tries to join Martin in Austria by crossing the border illegally through the mountains. A patrol led by the Nazi family members fires at her and Freya is mortally wounded. This U.S. anti-Nazi film was one of the first to mention the persecution of Jews.

Hitler—Dead or Alive
Director: Nick Grinde. Screenplay: Karl Bow and Sam Neuman. Production: Ben Judell. Year: 1942. Country: USA. Run time: 70 min.

Four escaped convicts from Alcatraz find themselves recruited to assassinate Hitler. They travel to Germany but are deported to Dachau where they discover the truth about the situation in the camps. This was one of the first films to explicitly mention the concentration camps. With Ward Bond and Dorothy Tree.

To Be or Not to Be
Director: Ernst Lubitsch. Screenplay: Edwin Justus Mayer from a story by Melchior Lengyel. Production: Romaine Film Cooperation. Year: 1942. Country: USA. Run time: 99 min.

This satirical comedy is set in Warsaw in the late summer of 1939. A theatre group rehearses a political satire called "Gestapo." When Germany invades Poland, the troupe is forced to shut down their production. The Nazi agent Siletzky has gathered information about the Polish resistance, and to prevent him from passing it to the Gestapo and endangering the lives of some of their members, the troupe sets up a complicated plot full of impersonations and disguise. Made during the war, the film voluntarily employs black comedy (often misunderstood at the time) to portray a complex vision of the games of true and false and good and evil. Directed with great virtuosity by Lubitsch. With Carole Lombard, Jack Benny, Robert Stack, and Felix Bressart.

Once Upon a Honeymoon
Director: Leo McCarey. Production: RKO Radio Pictures. Year: 1942. Country: USA. Run time: 117 min.

In the early days of World War II, an ambitious young American (Ginger Rogers) marries an Austrian nobleman, Baron Von Luber (Walter Slezak). American radio reporter Pat O'Toole (Cary Grant) sees this as the ideal way to find out more about this man, whom he suspects of having ties with the Nazis. O'Toole falls in love with the young bride, who agrees to become a secret agent for the Allies after discovering the truth about her husband. One of the first films to feature scenes set in a concentration camp.

The Pied Piper
Director: Irving Pichel. Screenplay: Nunnally Johnson from a novel by Nevil Shute. Production: Twentieth Century-Fox Film Corporation. Year: 1942. Country: USA. Run time: 87 min.

An Englishman tries to save a group of Jewish children by bringing them to the United States. With Monty Woolley, Roddy McDowall, Anne Baxter, and Otto Preminger.

I Escaped from the Gestapo
No Escape
Director: Harold Young. Screenplay: Henry Blankfort. Production: King Brothers. Year: 1943. Country: USA. Run time: 75 min.

Lane, a counterfeiter, escapes from prison with the help of a group of Nazis, led by a certain Martin. When Lane discovers that they want him to forge securities of the United States and other countries to help the Axis war effort, he goes to the Allied authorities to put a stop to the Nazi spies. With Dean Jagger and John Carradine.

Address Unknown
Director: William Cameron Menzies. Screenplay: Herbert Dalmas, Kressmann Taylor. Production: Columbia Pictures Corporation. Year: 1944. Country: USA. Run time: 75 min.

A German-born American art dealer returns to his native country and becomes fascinated with Nazi propaganda. With Paul Lukas, Carl Esmond, and Peter van Eyck.

The Hitler Gang
Director: John Farrow. Screenplay: Frances Goodrich, Albert Hackett. Production: Paramount Pictures. Year: 1944. Country: USA. Run time: 101 min.

A well-researched (even if the extermination policy is largely swept under the carpet) portrait of the rise of Adolf Hitler from marginal political figure to absolute dictator. With Bobby Watson and Roman Bohnen.

None Shall Escape
Director: Andre de Toth. Screenplay: Lester Cole from a story by Alfred Neumann and Joseph Than. Production: Columbia. Year: 1944. Country: USA. Run time: 85 min.

German soldier Wilhelm Grimm is crippled during World War I. He returns to his home along the German-Polish border and resumes his job as a teacher. He gradually grows embittered with life and as his ideas become increasingly extreme, his fiancée Marja Pacierkowski leaves him. After sexually assaulting one of his female students, Grimm is banished from the village. He joins the Nazi party and soon rises to power. He returns home once more, this time as a Nazi commandant, and creates a wave of terror in the village. With Marsha Hunt and Alexander Knox.

The Seventh Cross
Director: Fred Zinnemann. Screenplay: Helen Deutsch from a novel by Anna Seghers. Production: MGM. Year: 1944. Country: USA. Run time: 112 min.

In 1937, seven prisoners escape from the Westhofen concentration camp in the Rheinland. The camp commander has seven crosses mounted on which the refugees should die. Six are caught but the seventh—resistance fighter Georg Heisler (Spencer Tracy)—returns to his hometown of Mainz. A former girlfriend who married a Nazi turns him away, a Jewish doctor treats his injuries, and a friend puts himself and his family in danger to help him. Heisler manages to escape abroad. The seventh cross remains vacant. With Jessica Tandy, Hume Cronyn, and Agnes Moorehead.

The Stranger
Director: Orson Welles. Screenplay: Victor Trivas. Production: Haig Corporation, International Pictures Inc. Year: 1946. Country: USA. Run time: 95 min.

Prosecuting attorney Wilson (Edward G. Robinson) is on the hunt for Nazi dignitary Franz Kindler (Orson Welles), who lives in the United States under a new identity. He finds him posing as a small-town watchmaker who is about to marry into a respectable family. Wilson convinces Kindler's fiancée (Loretta Young) by showing her footage shot by the Allies at the liberation of the camps.

Ehe im Schatten
Marriage in the Shadows
Director: Kurt Maetzig. Screenplay: Kurt Maetzig. Production: DEFA-Studio für Spielfilme. Year: 1947. Country: GDR. Run time: 105 min.

Actor Hans Wieland marries Elisabeth Maurer, who is Jewish, after it became too dangerous for her to live alone in Germany. Life gets harder as years pass: Hans loses his job and is sent off to war. When he returns, he is not allowed to return to the stage and his wife is threatened with deportation. They both decide to commit suicide. With Paul Klinger and Ilse Steppat.

Bet Avi
My Father's House
Directors: Herbert Kline, Joseph Lejtes, Ben Oyserman. Screenplay: Meyer Levin. Production: World View Films for Keren Kayemeth Le-Israel. Year: 1947. Countries: USA, British Mandatory Palestine. Run time: 85 min.

David Halevi, a ten-year-old concentration camp survivor, is brought illegally to Palestine by the Haganah. When they were separated in the Krakow ghetto, his father told him they would meet again in Palestine. David believes his family is still alive and immediately asks for his father when he arrives at the beach. He is sent to a boarding school where children therapeutically tell stories about their wartime experiences. David runs away and obsessively searches for his father, finally succeeding in discovering a family to whom he might be related. With Y. Adaki and Irene Broza.

We Lived through Buchenwald
Director: E.G. De Myest. Production: Belnapro. Year: 1947. Country: Belgium. Run time: 76 min.

In the style of documentary fiction, the film focuses on Belgian Underground workers who become prisoners in Buchenwald concentration camp.

Adamah
Tomorrow's a Wonderful Day
Director: Helmar Lerski. Screenplay: Mina Brownstone, Ziegfried Lehmann. Production: Forum Film Ltd., Hadassah, The Women's

International Zionist Organisation of America Inc. Year: 1948, Countries: Israel, British Mandatory Palestine, USA. Run time: 75 min. (American version: 48 min.).

The story is about the arrival of young Benjamin in the British mandated territory in Palestine. A survivor of the Shoah, he is sent to the children's village Ben Shemen. The burden of his memories and experiences hinders his integration into the new communal way of life. The boy remains a prisoner of his traumatic past, until he realizes how precious his new surroundings are. He proves himself to be an active member of this Jewish pioneer society, the Yishuv. With Sam Balter and Benjamin Hildesheimer.

Ostatni Etap
The Last Stop
Director: Wanda Jakubowska. Screenplay: Wanda Jakubowska, Gerda Schneider Production: Film Polski. Year: 1948. Country: Poland. Run time: 111 min.

Shot on the actual locations and featuring women who had for the most part been deported there, this film depicts the Auschwitz women's camp in an almost documentary manner, while at the same time serving as communist propaganda. Martha Weiss, a Jew, is sent to Auschwitz with her family. On the day of their arrival, Martha is chosen to be an interpreter, but her entire family is killed. Martha tries to escape but she is captured and tortured, and she dies as Soviet planes fly overhead. The two Polish women who wrote and directed this film were themselves prisoners in the Birkenau women's camp at Auschwitz. With Tatjana Gorecka and Antonina Gordon-Górecka.

Morituri
Director: Eugen York. Screenplay: Gustav Kampendonk. Production: CCC-Film. Year: 1948. Country: FRG. Run time: 88 min.

The film shows an escape from a concentration camp in Poland. The fugitives spend months in an underground hideout. Living in constant fear of being discovered by the Wehrmacht, they are threatened with starvation. The German-Russian Front passes by without noticing them. With a passionate appeal for international understanding, the film pleads against retaliatory measures. With Lotte Koch and Hilde Körber.

Lang is der Weg
Long is the Road
Director: Herbert B. Fredersdorf, Marek Goldstein. Screenplay: Karel Georg Külb, Israel Beker. Production: Internationale-Filmorganisation

(Jidische Film Organisazie / Jewish Film Organisation) GmbH. Year: 1948. Country: FRG. Run time: 78 min.

The story of the Jelin family, from the moment they are driven out of their home in Warsaw and into the ghetto, up until their evacuation to a camp for displaced persons. After the war, David, the son, leaves Poland with his beloved Dora. They travel to the American-occupied zone of Germany where David hopes to find his mother. The story ends with the couple being married and the mother being located in a German hospital, as they hope to soon leave Germany. With Israel Becker and Bettina Moissi.

Lo Tafhidenu
The Illegals
Director: Meyer Levin. Screenplay: Meyer Levin. Production: Film Documents Inc., Americans For Haganah, Inc. Year: 1948. Countries: USA, British Mandatory Palestine, Israel. Run time: 77 min.

A survivor of the Shoah travels across Europe to Palestine along the Haganah's clandestine route. In 1945, Sara and Mika, a young couple from Warsaw, cross the Czech border and Austria. Mika is caught and jailed, but pregnant Sara decides to continue her journey with a group of displaced persons, so that her baby will be born in Palestine. Using voiceover narration, the film documents the illegal journey on foot and the last stage by boat. Aboard a cargo vessel, Mika and Sara are reunited. Sara's friend is also pregnant and about to give birth. After she is caught by the British, the friend's baby is born on the ship as they approach Haifa harbor. With Yankel Mikalovitch and Tereska Torres.

Daleká Cesta
Distant Journey
Director: Alfred Radok. Screenplay: Mojmior Drvota, Alfred Radok from a story by Erik Kolár. Production: Ceskoslovensky Státni Film. Year: 1949. Country: Czechoslovakia. Run time: 108 min.

A story of Czech Jews who try to retain their honor in the face of humiliation and terror. A mixture of fictional sequences and documents, the film is set in the Terezin ghetto and revolves around the character of Hannah, a young doctor whose family was deported while she stayed behind in Terezin. With Blanka Waleská.

Retour à la Vie—Épisode: Le Retour de Tante Emma
Director: André Cayatte. Screenplay: Charles Spaak. Production: Kleber Film. Year: 1949. Country: France. Run time: 120 min. (all episodes).

This film consists of five episodes, each of which tells the story of one person returning to France from camps for prisoners of war or political prisoners, or from concentration camps. In May 1945, the Allies liberated about two million French. The episode directed by André Cayatte—the only entry to allude, albeit vaguely, to the horror of the camps—revolves around the return of Aunty Emma from Dachau. Her relatives are too preoccupied with their daily activities to take any notice of her physical and mental condition. With Bernard Blier and Nane Germon.

Ulica Graniczna
Border Street
Director: Aleksander Ford. Screenplay: Jan Fethke, Aleksander Ford. Production: PP Filmpolski. Year: 1949. Country: Poland. Run time: 115 min.

The construction of the ghettos separates the Jews from the rest of the population. The film shows the survival, the solidarity, and the resistance, culminating in the riots of 1943. With Mieczyslawa Cwiklinska.

Mi Klalah L'brahah
Out of Evil
Director: Joseph Krumgold. Screenplay: Joseph Krumgold from a novel by Yehuda Yaar. Production: Urim Israeli Film Company, Ltd. for Keren Hayessod. Year: 1950. Country: Israel. Run time: 87 min.

In the 1920s, a young couple give up their life on a pioneer kibbutz to move back to Germany. Their son returns to Israel after his parents are killed by the Nazis. The film shows the general development of Palestine and the kibbutzim in particular over two decades. Interwoven with the story is a puppet opera dramatization of the biblical tale of *Bilam and the Ass*. With Mordecai Ben-Ze'ev and Roberta Hodes.

Kirya Ne'emana
Faithful City
Director: Joseph Lejtes. Screenplay: Ben Barzman, Joseph Lejtes. Production: Moledet Films for RKO Radio Pictures, Inc. Year: 1952. Country: Israel. Run time: 88 min.

A story of an American social worker trying to rehabilitate a group of emotionally disturbed orphans that survived the Shoah. They live in Goldstein Youth Village in Israel during the War of Independence. With Jamie Smith and Ben Josef.

Singing in the Dark
Director: Max Nosseck. Screenplay: Ben Kandel, Ann Hood, Stephen Kandel. Production: A.N.O. Productions Inc. Year: 1956. Country: USA. Run time: 86 min.

After World War II, Leo, a concentration camp refugee, arrives in America. Suffering from amnesia, he gets a job as a hotel clerk and is then discovered by Broadway showman Joey Napoleon. He takes Leo on as a partner and the two become a successful burlesque-style song and comedy act. But Leo tires of showbiz and eventually becomes a cantor. With Moyshe Oysher and Joey Adams.

The Young Lions
Director: Edward Dmytryk. Screenplay: Edward Anhalt from a novel by Irwin Shaw. Production: Twentieth Century-Fox Film Corp. Year: 1958. Country: USA. Run time: 167 min.

1937. Margaret Freemantle spends the final days of her vacation in Bavaria with ski instructor Christian Deistl (Marlon Brando), who later becomes a Nazi lieutenant. Some years later, Margaret's fiancé Michael Whiteacre (Dean Martin) and his friend Noah Ackerman (Montgomery Clift) are called up for military service. Ackerman learns the bitter truth that his enemies are not just the Germans, but also some members of his own unit. Sergeant Rickett (Lee Van Cleef) is a violent anti-Semite and four of his comrades engage Ackerman in a brutal fight. In the meantime, Deistl and his friend Hardenberg (Maximilian Schell) are fighting for the Germans. U.S. troops storm Germany. In a forest, Deistl meets Ackerman and Whiteacre. He wants to surrender but is shot dead by Whiteacre. Ackerman returns home where his wife and children await him.

Kapò
Director: Gillo Pontecorvo. Screenplay: Franco Solinas. Production: Vides, Zebra-Francinex. Year: 1959. Country: Italy. Run time: 115 min.

Out of fear, a young French Jew (Susan Strasberg) becomes a "kapo," a prisoner in charge of a group of inmates in a Nazi concentration camp. The position gives her various privileges. Later she falls in love with a handsome communist officer (Laurent Terzieff) and tries to atone for her actions by heroically helping others. Upon its release in France, the film was heavily criticized in *Cahiers du Cinéma* by Jacques Rivette, in a review that would become a touchstone for a philosophy of the ethics of mise-en-scène.

Verboten!
Director: Samuel Fuller. Screenplay: Ryszard Golc. Production: Globe Enterprises, RKO Radio Pictures. Year: 1959. Country: USA. Run time: 87 min.

David, a young American soldier stationed in occupied Germany, breaks the no-fraternization rule and falls in love with a German woman named Helga. But her brother joins the Nazi guerrilla movement, the Werewolves, who also have plans for Helga. After seeing footage of wartime atrocities at the Nuremberg trial, the couple decides to join the struggle against the ex-Nazis. With James Best and Susan Cummings.

Zvezdi / Swesdi
Sterne
Stars
Director: Konrad Wolf. Screenplay: Sngel Vagenshtain. Production: DEFA Studio für Spielfilme, Studio for Feature Films (Sofia). Year: 1959. Countries: GDR, Bulgaria. Run time: 92 min.

In 1943, a train full of Greek Jews on the way to Auschwitz makes a halt at a Bulgarian village. To his own surprise, the Nazi officer Walter falls in love with the Jewish girl Ruth. His feelings make him ponder what is happening around him and confront him with fascism's inhumanity. He is wracked with guilt over his own role, and with the help of a Bulgarian resistance fighter, he plans Ruth's escape. When the moment is upon him, he realizes he hasn't been given the train's correct departure time. With Sasha Krusharska and Jürgen Frohriep.

The Diary of Anne Frank
Director: George Stevens. Screenplay: Frances Goodrich and Albert Hackett from the diary of Anne Frank. Production: Twentieth Century-Fox Film Corp. Year: 1959. Country: USA. Run time: 171 min.

The story of two Jewish Families hiding from the Nazis in Amsterdam. Based on the diary of Anne Frank and the play by Frances Goodrich and Albert Hackett. With Millie Perkins, Joseph Schildkraut, and Shelley Winters.

Exodus
Director: Otto Preminger. Screenplay: Dalton Trumbo from a novel by Leon Uris. Production: Carlyle Productions. Year: 1960. Country: USA. Run time: 208 min.

The shadow of the genocide looms large over this reconstruction of the Zionist expedition into Palestine that would contribute to the founding of the state of Israel. With Paul Newman, Eva Marie Saint, Lee J. Cobb, and Sal Mineo.

Spotkania w Mroku
Begegnung im Zwielicht
Encounters in the Dark
Director: Wanda Jakubowska. Screenplay: Hans Julius Wille, Wanda Jakubowska from a novel by Stanislawa Muskat-Fleszarowa. Production:

Film Polski, DEFA-Studio für Spielfilme. Year: 1960. Countries: Poland, GDR. Run time: 107 min.

Magdalena Novak, a famous Polish pianist, returns to a city in West Gemany where she was forced to work in the shoe factory of Ernst Steinlieb. Steinlieb and Mr. Wenk helped her and other concentration camp prisoners by smuggling food and medicine. Novak decides to look for those who helped and finds them on trial: Wenk is accused of being an "opponent to atomic war" and of theft, because he stole boots during the war and gave them to anti-fascists so they would be able to flee. Novak leaves the courtroom deeply disappointed. With Zofia Slaboszowska and Erich Franz.

Ambulans
Ambulance
Director: Janusz Morgenstern. Production: Studio Malych Form Film-owych. Year: 1961. Country: Poland. Run time: 10 min.

This short film refers to Janusz Korczak in detailing the gassing of a group of Jewish children and their teacher in a truck disguised as an ambulance.

Judgment at Nuremberg
Director: Stanley Kramer. Screenplay: Abby Mann. Production: Rox-lom Films for United Artists. Year: 1961. Country: USA. Run time: 190 min.

A dramatization of the 1947 trial of Nazi leaders for crimes against humanity. Dan Haywood (Spencer Tracy), an American judge, arrives in Nuremberg to preside over the trial of several German judges accused of destroying law and justice to support Hitler's infamous mandates, which took the lives of six million people. Colonel Tad Lawson (Richard Widmark) is determined to obtain maximum sentences for the judges, whose most eminent member is Dr. Janning (Burt Lancaster). Defense lawyer Hans Rolfe (Maximilian Schell) counters by charging that if these men are guilty because they upheld the laws of their country, then all of Germany must be tried. The film includes newsreel footage of concentration camp atrocities.

Operation Eichmann
Director: Robert G. Springsteen. Screenplay: Lester Cole. Production: Bischoff Diamond Corporation for Allied Artists Pictures Corporation. Year: 1961. Country: USA. Run time: 92 min.

Two Israeli agents, David and Jacob, both survivors of the Shoah, are assigned to arrest Adolf Eichmann. While they quarrel over whether to kill or capture him, Eichmann escapes and the agents pursue him all the way to Argentina. Meanwhile, the Nazi underground has decided that Eichmann is to be eliminated for disobeying orders. Before they can succeed, however, David and Jacob capture Eichmann and fly him to Israel to stand trial for his crimes against humanity. This film was padded with World War II newsreel footage and was released while Eichmann was awaiting trial in Israel. With Werner Klemperer and Ruta Lee.

L'enclos
Enclosure
Director: Armand Gatti. Screenplay: Armand Gatti, Pierre Joffroy. Production: Clavis Film, Triglav Film. Year: 1962. Countries: France, Yugoslavia. Run time: 105 min.

A French Jew and a German political prisoner are locked up together in an enclosure. A kapo and an officer order them to fight and tell them that the winner's life will be spared. The two officers call it an experiment and make a bet: they are sure that the German "Aryan" is bound to kill the "inferior" Jew. The conclusion is as bitter as it is unexpected, but nevertheless leaves a glimmer of hope. Only fifteen years after World War II, this film refuses to use stereotypical characters and introduces a German victim of the Nazis. With Slavko Belak and Hans Christian Blech.

Lisa
Director: Philip Dunne. Screenplay: Nelson Gidding from a novel by Jan de Hartog. Production: Red Lion. Year: 1962. Country: UK. Run time: 112 min.

In 1946, Lisa Held, a survivor of the concentration camp at Auschwitz, falls into the hands of ex-Nazi Thorens. He promises to smuggle her into Palestine, but in actual fact he is a white-slave trader who plans to ship her to South America. She is saved when Dutch policeman Peter Jongman accidentally kills Thorens. Jongman is plagued by his failure to save his fiancée from death at the hands of the Nazis, and decides to atone for the past by seeing that Lisa reaches Palestine. Overcoming various obstacles, he accomplishes his mission and Lisa is delivered into the hands of the Haganah. Peter turns himself in for the shooting of Thorens. With Stephen Boyd, Dolores Hart, Leo McKern, and Marius Goring.

Nackt unter Wölfen
Naked among Wolves
Director: Frank Beyer. Screenplay: Frank Beyer, Alfred Hirschmeier from a novel by Bruno Apitz. Production: DEFA-Studio für Spielfilme. Year: 1962. Country: GDR. Run time: 120 min.

In 1945, only a few weeks before the end of World War II, a prison transport arrives at the concentration camp Buchenwald. Among the new arrivals is Jankowski, a Pole who hides a little boy in his suitcase. Jankowski has so far managed to save the child from the Nazis in this way. Two camp inmates hide the child at the risk of their own lives, endangering the work of the resistance movement within the camp. The boy becomes not only a risk factor, but also a sign of hope and rebellion. The film is based on a true story written by Apitz, himself a prisoner at Buchenwald. With Erwin Geschonneck and Armin Mueller-Stahl.

Transport z Ráje
Transport from Paradise
Director: Zbynûk Brynych. Screenplay: Zbynûk Brynych, Arnost Lustig. Production: Ceskoslovensky Státní Film, Filmové Studio Barrandov. Year: 1962. Country: Czechoslovakia. Run time: 94 min.

In the Terezin ghetto, a group of inmates are to be sent on a transport to an extermination camp but the chairman of the Council of Jewish Elders refuses to sign the order. The Germans get rid of him and find a more compliant replacement. Not realizing where they are headed, the prisoners save places on the train for loved ones to join them on the convoy to death. With Zdenek Stepánek and Ilja Prachar.

Ha-martef
The Cellar
Director: Natan Gross. Screenplay: Ya'akov Malhin from a story by Shimon Yisraeli. Production: Shay Films Ltd. Year: 1963. Country: Israel. Run time: 90 min.

Emmanuel, a young survivor of the Shoah, returns to his native town in Germany. He finds Hans, a rival from his school days, living in his house. Hans persecuted Emmanuel and killed his father. The reason for his hatred was Lotte, a German girl, who did not respond to his love but chose Emmanuel instead. Emmanuel hides in the cellar at night, imprisoned with remnants of his past: his love, his parents, his childhood. With the rising sun he returns to reality, hesitating briefly because he realizes that vengeance is inevitable. With Zaharira Harifai, David Smadar, and Shimon Yisraeli.

Pasazerka
The Passenger
Directors: Andrzej Munk, Witold Lesiewicz. Screenplay: Andrzej Munk, Zofia Posmysz-Piasecka. Production: Altura films international, Film Polski. Year: 1963 (1970 in the USA). Country: Poland. Run time: 60 min.

When Liza and her husband Walter arrive at Southampton on an ocean liner, she is shocked to see a woman whom she believes to be Marta, a former prisoner at the concentration camp at Auschwitz. Liza never told her husband the truth about her activities in the camp and in the SS in Berlin. The reappearance of this woman whom she believed had been executed forms a threat to Liza's new existence. The film was never completed as a result of the director passing away. His collaborators "finished" the film, intentionally leaving gaps in the narrative. With Aleksandra Slaska and Anna Ciepielewska.

The Pawnbroker
Director: Sidney Lumet. Screenplay: David Friedkin, Morton Fine from a novel by Edward Lewis Wallant. Production: The Landau Company, Unger Co., Pawnbroker Co. Year: 1964. Country: USA. Run time: 115 min.
    The German Jewish professor Sol Nazerman (Rod Steiger) and his family were sent by force to a concentration camp, where he saw his two children sent to death and his wife raped by Nazi officers. Years after the war, he runs a pawnshop in New York City. Numbed by the horrors of his past, he considers himself conditioned against any emotion. When his shop assistant Ortiz tries to convince Nazerman that there is more to life than ugliness, Nazerman responds cruelly. Ortiz sets up a plan to wake his boss from his cynicism, but it backfires and he dies in the old man's arms. With Geraldine Fitzgerald, Brock Peters, and Jaime Sánchez.

Heure de la Vérité
Sha'at Emet
The Hour of Truth
Director: Henri Calef. Screenplay: Henri Calef, Edgar Morin. Production: Noy Films Ltd., Jad Films. Year: 1965. Countries: France, Israel. Run time: 90 min.
    An ex-Nazi officer disguises himself as a Jew and moves to Israel under an assumed name. A young sociologist who came to Israel to interview survivors of Nazi concentration camps discovers his secret. With Corinne Marchand and Karlheinz Böhm.

La Cage de Verre
Ha-kluv Hazehuhit
The Glass Cage
Directors: Philippe Arthuys, Jean-Louis Levi-Alvares. Screenplay: Philippe Arthuys, Production: A. D. Matalon, Telecinex, Noy Films. Year: 1965. Countries: France, Israel. Run time: 87 min.

Deported to a concentration camp as a child in 1942, Pierre has been married for fifteen years to Hélène, a non-Jewish French woman. In 1961, they are living prosperously in Tel Aviv, but the impending trial of Adolf Eichmann disrupts their calm routine. Pierre is tortured by reawakened memories of the camp and by his undisclosed guilt at having survived by letting another man die in his place. What's more, he is anguished by the arrival of Hélène's former lover Claude, a journalist sent to cover the trial. Only when Hélène reassures him of her love is Pierre able to confess what happened in the camp, to her and in the courtroom. With Françoise Prévost, Jean Négroni, and Georges Rivière.

Obchod na Korze
The Shop on Main Street
Directors: Ján Kadár and Elmar Klos. Screenplay: Ján Kadár, Elmar Klos from a story by Ladislav Grosman. Production: Filmové Studio Barrandov. Year: 1965. Country: Czechoslovakia. Run time: 128 min.

In Slovakia, the authorities expropriate Jewish businesses. The shop for sewing material owned by the old Jewish widow Lautman undergoes the same fate. Tono is supposed to take over the shop but the elderly lady does not understand what is going on and thinks that Tono is seeking employment. She hires him. With time, the two begin to like each other, but then the authorities decide that all Jews must leave the city. Tono starts looking for a way to save the old lady. With Ida Kaminska and Jozef Króner.

Ein Tag—Bericht aus einem Deutschen Kz 1939
One Day—A Report from a German Concentration
Camp 1939
Director: Egon Monk. Screenplay: Claus Hubalek, Gunther R. Lys, Egon Monk. Production: Norddeutscher Rundfunk. Year: 1965. Country: FRG. Run time: 90 min.

Concentration camp Altendorf holds mainly political prisoners and only a few Jews. The day starts with the Appell. The new arrivals are divided into different working commandos. One commando must dig a hole, while three prisoners die. The Jews are ordered to close the hole and level the ground by jumping onto it while singing "Death to the Jews." The film shows other crimes and forms of mistreatment. At the end of the day, the *Lagerkommandant* leaves the camp to spend a nice evening. Historical material is included, such as the New Years reception of the diplomatic corps in the *Reichskanzlerei* (Reich's Chancellery). With Achim Dünnwald and Harald Eggers.

Lebende Ware

Director: Wolfgang Luderer. Screenplay: Walter Jupé, Friedrich Karl Kaul, Wolfgang Luderer. Production: DEFA-Studio für Spielfilme. Year: 1966. Country: GDR. Run time: 97 min.

Budapest 1944. Kurt Becher, *Obersturmbannführer* of the SS and deputy of Heinrich Himmler in Hungary, proposes to a wealthy Jewish businessman that he will rescue his life and the lives of his family, if he signs the company away to Becher. Becher starts "trading" other objects of value against human lives and forces the Zionist movement to help him transfer the money to a Swiss bank. After the war, Becher becomes a successful businessman in the FRG. It is not until 1961 that his past is revealed, when the Attorney General of Israel announces that Becher will be arrested and tried if he should ever set foot on Israeli soil. With Horst Schulze and Marion Van de Kamp.

Zeugin aus der Hölle
Gorke Trave
Witness Out of Hell

Director: Zica Mitrovic. Screenplay: Frieda Filipovic, Michael Mansfeld. Production: CCC-Filmkunst, Avala Film. Year: 1967. Country: FRG, Yugoslavia. Run time: 83 min.

The prosecuting attorney Hoffmann visits the writer Bora Petrovic in Belgrade. In one of his books, Petrovic reported on crimes committed in German extermination camps, based on statements made by one Lea Weiss. Hoffmann wants Weiss to repeat the same statements in court, as a witness against a concentration camp doctor. She refuses. The victim's sense of shame is too strong, in contrast to the notoriously good conscience of the perpetrator. In the camp, Weiss was raped and abused during medical examinations. Twenty years after the end of the war, suicide becomes the only solution to her desperation. With Irene Papas and Daniel Gélin.

La 25ème Heure
The 25th Hour

Director: Henri Verneuil. Screenplay: Henri Verneuil, Wolf Mankowitz, François Boyer. Production: Carlo Ponti, Les Films Concordia, Avala Film, CC Champion. Year: 1967. Countries: France, Yugoslavia, Italy. Run time: 119 min.

During the German invasion of Romania in 1939, Johann Moritz (Anthony Quinn) is falsely branded as a Jew and sent to a German labor camp. His wife Suzanna is forced to divorce Johann in order to save their home from being confiscated as Jewish property. Johann escapes from the camp but is captured and selected by a Nazi colonel as the perfect example of "the pure German race." He is forced to pose for covers of Nazi magazines. After the war, he is brought to trial at Nuremberg, where a letter from Suzanna so deeply moves the court that Johann is freed. After eight years of separation, Johann is reunited with his family. With Virna Lisi, Grégoire Aslan, Michael Redgrave, and Marcel Dalio.

The Producers—Springtime for Hitler
Director: Mel Brooks. Screenplay: Mel Brooks. Production: Springtime Productions and Crossbow Productions for MGM. Year: 1968. Country: USA. Run time: 88 min.

Max Bialystock (Zero Mostel) and Leo Bloom (Gene Wilder) want to mount a Broadway play that is guaranteed to fail in order to keep the money of the investors. While looking for the worst script, they opt for *Springtime for Hitler*, written by Nazi fanatic Franz Liebkind (Kenneth Mars). They manage to convince the investors and cast the most untalented actors they can find. But the play becomes an unexpected hit. Bialystock and Bloom first conspire to kill the entire cast, but then opt to blow up the theatre. They are sent to prison, where they immediately stage a show.

Spalovac Mrtvol
The Cremator
Director: Juraj Herz. Screenplay: Juraj Herz, Ladislav Fuks. Production: Filmové Studio Barrandov. Year: 1968. Country: Czechoslovakia. Run time: 102 min.

Mr. Kopfkringl enjoys his job in a crematorium and leads a pleasant life with a caring family. Just before German troops invade Czechoslovakia, he discovers that he has German origins and is thus a member of the new master race. He becomes director of the crematorium, but when he finds out that his wife is of Jewish descent, he must choose between his job and her. For him the choice is an easy one: he kills his wife and then his son for befriending a Jewish boy. His daughter flees but is caught by Germans. New tasks await Kopfkringl, who already sees himself as the chief cremator of the German Reich. With Rudolf Hrusínsky.

Kaddisch nach einem Lebenden
Kaddish for the Living
Director: Karl Fruchtmann. Screenplay: Karl Fruchtmann. Production: Radio Bremen in cooperation with Isra-Film. Year: 1969. Country: FRG. Run time: 65 min.

Peri, an office clerk in Tel Aviv, recalls his time in a Nazi concentration camp and a fellow prisoner named Bach. Flashbacks reveal their suffering. He meets another fellow prisoner Gurfinkel and together they search for Bach. When they finally spot him on a street corner in Tel Aviv, he just stands there in apathy, oiling the prams of mothers passing by. He does not recognize Peri. With Günter Mack, Zalman Lebiush, and Rudolf Wessely.

Il Giardino dei Finzi-Contini
The Garden of the Finzi-Continis
Director: Vittorio De Sica. Screenplay: Vittorio Bonicelli from a novel by Giorgio Bassani. Production: Documento Film, CCC Film. Year: 1970. Country: Italy, FRG. Run time: 94 min.

In prewar Ferrara, a rich Jewish family lives isolated from the world in their house and garden. In this idyll, the son and daughter live a dreamy life, unperturbed by the rise of fascism in the rest of the country. Beautiful Micòl Finzi-Contini (Dominique Sanda) is in love with a young man from a middle-class Jewish family. Their romance becomes a tug-of-war that will eventually destroy this little world that believed itself at bay from the tides of history. With Helmut Berger and Lino Capolicchio.

The Day the Clown Cried
Director: Jerry Lewis. Screenplay: Jerry Lewis from a story by Joan O'Brien and Charles Denton. Production: Nat Wachsberger. Year: 1972. Country: USA. Run time: unknown.

Helmut Doork (Jerry Lewis), a once great and famous clown, is fired from the circus. Getting drunk at a local bar, he pokes fun at Hitler in front of some Gestapo agents, who arrest him and send him to a prison camp. Helmut angers his fellow prisoners by refusing to perform for them, wanting to preserve his legend. When Jews are brought to the camp, the Nazis soon come up with a use for Helmut: they order him to keep the children quiet as they are loaded into a boxcar to be sent to another camp. Helmut complies, but is accidentally locked in with the children and arrives the next day at Auschwitz. He stays by the children's side even as they enter the gas chamber. This feature film was never released. With Harriet Andersson.

Les Guichets du Louvre
Black Thursday
Director: Michel Mitrani. Screenplay: Albert Cossery, Michel Mitrani from a novel by Roger Boussinot. Production: Les Films du Parnasse, Les Films du Limon, O.R.T.F., Saga Cinéma. Year: 1974. Country: France. Run time: 100 min.

In July 1942, French Jews are rounded up in Paris. Paul, a student (Christian Rist), offers his help to families in walking across the barriers.

Because he is not Jewish, he is not afraid of the police or of being arrested himself. He feels that anyone accompanying him may get through the barriers and escape. Paul accidentally prevents a young woman named Jeanne (Christine Pascal) from getting rounded up. They manage to elude danger with the help of other Parisians, and that afternoon they talk about love, life, and the future. But when they arrive at the Louvre, Jeanne decides to join her family and be deported with them.

Jakob der Lügner
Jacob the Liar
Director: Frank Beyer. Screenplay: Frank Beyer. Production: DEFA-Studio für Spielfilme, Fernsehen der DDR in cooperation with Filmové Studio Barrandov (Prague). Year: 1974. Country: GDR. Run time: 104 min.

It's 1944 in an East European ghetto. Jakob wants to give his neighbors hope after he has overheard the Gestapo talking about the advancing Red Army. He then lies, telling them he possesses a radio which he listens to in secret, and invents good news. The suicides in the ghetto stop and everyone awaits the liberation. To keep up hope, Jakob continues to lie. One day, a little girl finds out that he doesn't have a radio and that everything was a lie. The inhabitants of the ghetto are about to be deported, but they continue to believe Jakob's lies. With Vlastimil Brodsky.

Il Portiere di Notte
The Night Porter
Director: Liliana Cavani. Screenplay: Liliana Cavani from a story by Barbara Alberti, Italo Moscati, and Amedeo Pagani. Production: Italonegglio Cinematografico, Lotar Film Productions. Year: 1974. Country: Italy. Run time: 115 min.

Vienna 1957. Former SS officer Max (Dirk Bogarde) works as a night porter in a hotel. He runs into Lucia (Charlotte Rampling), who is staying at the hotel with her husband. Lucia had been deported at age fifteen, after which Max complimented her for her beauty. She gave herself over quietly to his sexual desires and degradation. Today, she could easily denounce Max, but she says nothing. She even stays in Vienna after her husband's departure and resumes the sadomasochistic relationship. Max is part of an illegal organization of former Nazis who protect each other, and they push Max to kill Lucia.

Sie Sind Frei, Doktor Korczak
Korczak V'hayeladim
The Martyr
Director: Aleksander Ford. Screenplay: Ben Barzman, Alexander Ramati. Production: CCC-Filmkunst, Bar Kochba Film. Year: 1975 (1976 in the USA). Country: Israel, FRG. Run time: 99 min.

1942. Janusz Korczak is a doctor in the Warsaw ghetto who takes care of children orphaned by the war and manages to keep a children's hospital running inside the ghetto. When the Nazis clear out the area, he opts to remain with the children he loves and is sent with them to a concentration camp. With Leo Genn.

The Man in the Glass Booth

Director: Arthur Hiller. Screenplay: Edward Anhalt from a play by Robert Shaw. Production: American Film Theatre Picture Corporation, Ely Landau Organization in cooperation with Cinevision. Year: 1975. Country: USA. Run time: 117 min.

A man (Maximilian Schell) is brought to trial for committing Nazi atrocities during the war. He claims that he is Arthur Goldman, a wealthy Jewish businessman living in New York City. The story is based on the trial of Adolf Eichmann, who was put in a glass booth during his trial. This story was originally a stage play by Robert Shaw. With Lois Nettleton, Lawrence Pressman, and Luther Adler.

Monsieur Klein
Mr. Klein

Director: Joseph Losey. Screenplay: Costa-Gavras, Fernando Moranti, and Franco Solinas. Production: Adel Productions, Lira Films, Mondial Televisione Film, Nova Films. Year: 1976. Country: France. Run time: 123 min.

Paris, 1942. Robert Klein (Alain Delon), an established art trader, has no problems with the Germans occupying France: he is living a wealthy life, his business is flourishing, and he even profits from the laws discriminating against Jews. He can easily obtain valuable art works at bargain prices. His cosy life is disrupted when he realizes that there is another Robert Klein in Paris—a Jew with rather mysterious behavior. The case of confused identities attracts the attention of the police and begins to cloud Mr. Klein's mind. With Jeanne Moreau and Juliet Berto.

Aus einem Deutschen Leben
Death is My Trade

Director: Theodor Kotulla. Screenplay: Theodor Kotulla from a novel by Robert Merle. Production: Iduna-Film for Westdeutscher Rundfunk. Year: 1977. Country: FRG. Run time: 145 min.

The fictional biography of Franz Lang, a soldier who obeyed orders during World War I. Back in civilian life, he never questioned the orders he received from his superiors. After the Nazis come to power, they see in the obedient Lang the perfect man to execute their plans. His rises to the position of *Lagerkommandant* at Auschwitz. Based on the biography of Auschwitz commander Rudolf Höss. With Götz George and Elisabeth Schwarz.

Julia

Director: Fred Zinnemann. Screenplay: Alvin Sargent from the novel *Pentimento* by Lillian Hellman. Production: 20th Century Fox. Year: 1977. Country: USA. Run time: 117 min.

Julia (Vanessa Redgrave) is a childhood friend of Lillian Hellman (Jane Fonda). In the 1930s, while the adult Hellman struggles to establish herself as a playwright, Julia is involved in the struggle against the Nazis. Visiting Julia in Germany, Lillian realizes how much her friend's idealism has cost her, both physically and financially. Julia's friend Johann asks Lillian to smuggle a large sum of money from Paris to Germany, to help combat the Nazis from within. The film's success led to speculations about the identity of the real "Julia." Hellman refused to reveal it. With Jason Robards.

Reinhard Heydrich—Manager des Terrors

Director: Heinz Schirk. Screenplay: Paul Mommertz. Production: Sator Film GmbH, Studio Hamburg Filmproduktion GmbH. Year: 1977. Country: FRG. Run time: 96 min.

The film tells the story of Reinhard Heydrich, SS member and ruler of Bohemia and Moravia. Heydrich was one of the main organizers of the Shoah during the first years of World War II—he chaired the Wannsee conference at which plans for the extermination of the Jews were set up. On May 27, 1942, he was attacked by a team of British-trained agents of the Czech government. His death on June 4 at the age of thirty-eight led to mass retaliation by the Germans. With Dietrich Mattausch.

In einem Jahr mit 13 Monden
In a Year of 13 Moons

Director: Rainer Werner Fassbinder. Screenplay: Rainer Werner Fassbinder, Volker Spengler. Production: Tango, Pro-Ject Produktion. Year: 1978. Country: FRG. Run time: 124 min.

A tragedy that questions identity and the possibility of living according to one's own desires. Central roles are played by two figures whom Fassbinder believes to be typical for Germany: a Jewish brothel owner and a real estate agent. Their sufferings in the concentration camps are essential keys to understanding the historical background of the creation of contemporary German society, according to the filmmaker. With Volker Spengler, Ingrid Caven, and Gottfried John.

David

Director: Peter Lilienthal. Screenplay: Peter Lilienthal, Jurek Becker, Ulla Ziemann from the story by Joel König. Production: Von Vietinghoff Filmproduktion GmbH, Pro-Ject Produktion, Filmverlag der Autoren GmbH & Co. Vertriebs KG, Zweites Deutsches Fernsehen, Dedra Pictures Production. Year: 1979. Country: FRG. Run time: 125 min.

Even though Nazi Youth members turn up every now and then, Rabbi Singer is convinced that Germany is a safe place for his family and his fold. Some years later, his son David is not allowed to attend school because he is a Jew and Singer and his wife are deported. David now fears for his life and tries to flee from Germany with his sister. He manages to escape to Palestine with forged papers and the help of an anti-Nazi German. Based on the autobiography of Joel König. With Mario Fischel.

Roveh Huliot
The Wooden Gun

Director: Ilan Moshenson. Screenplay: Ilan Moshenson. Production: Makor Films, Hardy & Sanders Motion Pictures. Year: 1979. Country: Israel. Run time: 95 min.

Set in strife-torn Tel Aviv in the mid-1950s, this incisive Israeli drama depicts the gap that separates two groups of young people living there: the native-born Israelis, or "Sabras," and the European immigrants who sought refuge from persecution and extermination. With Nadav Brenner and Nissim Eliaz.

The House on Garibaldi Street

Director: Peter Collinson. Screenplay: Steve Shagan from a book by Isser Harel. Production: Mort Abrahams, Charles Fries Productions, ITC. Year: 1979. Country: USA. Run time: 102 min.

A dramatized account of how Adolf Eichmann was brought to trial in Israel, judged guilty of crimes against humanity, and executed in 1962. With Topol, Nick Mancuso, Janet Suzman, and Leo McKern.

Transit

Director: Daniel Wachsmann. Screenplay: Daniel Wachsmann, Daniel Horowitz. Production: Transit. Year: 1979. Country: Israel. Run time: 87 min.

Before the horrors of World War II, German Jew Erich Nussbaum fled from Germany to Palestine. Although he has lived in Israel for many years, he can't adjust to life in his new homeland. He considers returning to Germany as though nothing has happened. With Itzhak Ben-Zur.

Deutschland Bleiche Mutter
Germany Pale Mother

Director: Helma Sanders-Brahms. Screenplay: Helma Sanders-Brahms. Production: Helma Sanders-Brahms Filmproduktion, Westdeutscher Rundfunk. Year: 1980. Country: FRG. Run time: 123 min.

In the late 1930s, a young German woman (Eva Mattes) marries a man who is soon sent to fight in Poland. After the defeat of the Nazis, she is forced to leave her ruined house with her daughter and is raped by American soldiers. Her husband finds her and wants them to lead a "normal" life. Her experiences and the new Germany drive her to despair and she attempts to commit suicide.

Playing for Time

Director: Daniel Mann. Screenplay: Arthur Miller from the autobiography of Fania Fénelon. Production: Szygzy Productions. Year: 1980. Country: USA. Run time: 148 min.

Jewish cabaret singer Fania Fénelon (Vanessa Redgrave) works in Paris at the time of the Nazi invasion. She is deported to Auschwitz in 1944. The SS camp matron orders Fénelon to form a prisoner's orchestra with several other female inmates who have musical ability. They are to perform for those who are herded into the gas chambers. Fénelon and her fellow musicians continue to play, lest they too be exterminated. Based on the autobiography written by Fénelon (who died in 1988), the film raises questions about courage, guilt, and survival at any price. With Jane Alexander.

Charlotte

Director: Frans Weisz. Screenplay: Anke Taverne. Production: CCC-Filmkunst, Cineteam Features, Concorde Film Produktion in cooperation with Sender Freies Berlin, BBC, RAI, Filmalpha. Year: 1981 (1984 in West Germany). Country: FRG, The Netherlands. Run time: 95 min.

The film is based on the story of the life of Charlotte Salomon, who in January 1939 fled from Berlin to join her grandparents in the south of France. After the war breaks out in September 1939, the young woman learns that her mother has committed suicide and that her grandmother suffers fits of suicidal depression. To combat the feelings of despair, Charlotte begins to paint. As an artist, she manages to find herself. In 1943 she is deported to Auschwitz. With Birgit Doll.

Die Bleierne Zeit
The German Sisters
Director: Margarethe von Trotta. Screenplay: Margarethe von Trotta. Production: Bioskop Films / Sender Freies Berlin (SFB). Year: 1981. Country: FRG. Run time: 106 min.

Germany 1968. Two sisters vow to change German society, but they choose different paths to achieve their aim. Their decision to shake up the established order is largely influenced by learning about the Nazi past and the atrocities their country committed. With Jutta Lampe and Barbara Sukowa.

Das Boot ist Voll
The Boat is Full
Director: Markus Imhoof. Screenplay: Markus Imhoof. Production: Limbo Film AG, DRS Radio-und Fernsehgesellschaft der deutschen und der rätoromanischen Schweiz, Zweites Deutsches Fernsehen. Year: 1981. Country: FRG, Switzerland, Austria. Run time: 100 min.

After Switzerland has closed its border, a group of refugees (a Jewish sister and brother, a German deserter, a French orphan, and an Austrian grandfather with his grandchild) enters the country illegally in 1942. Anna shelters the motley group at her guesthouse, but the other villagers are distant or hostile toward the immigrants. The Swiss visa laws do not account for their situation and their demand for asylum is refused. The group is escorted to the German border, where they are rounded up and sent to Treblinka extermination camp. With Tina Engel and Hans Diehl.

Lili Marleen
Director: Rainer Werner Fassbinder. Screenplay: Renate Leiffer. Production: Roxy-Film, CIP, Rialto Film, Bayerischer Rundfunk. Year: 1981. Country: FRG. Run time: 120 min.

German singer Willie (Hanna Schygulla) is in love with Robert (Giancarlo Giannini), a Swiss musician involved in helping Jews. Her song "Lili Marleen" makes Willie a star and a favorite of the Nazis. Robert continues his resistance effort, is captured and then released, but Willie is suspected by the Nazi officers who know about their relationship. She continues to help him by collecting secret data and refuses to betray him. Willie and Robert both survive World War II, only for Willie to find out that Robert is married to another woman. With Mel Ferrer.

Sophie's Choice
Director: Alan J. Pakula. Screenplay: Alan J. Pakula from a novel by William Styron. Production: Incorporated Television Company. Year: 1982. Country: USA. Run time: 157 min.

This film portrays the relationship between Sophie (Meryl Streep), a survivor of the Shoah, and Nathan (Kevin Klein), a Jewish American intellectual. They befriend Stingo, the movie's narrator, a young American writer new to New York City. The couple's happiness is threatened by Nathan's obsessions and Sophie's trauma: in order to survive, she had to choose which of her children would be murdered and which would survive.

Eine Liebe in Deutschland
A Love in Germany
Director: Andrzej Wajda. Screenplay: Agnieszka Holland, Boleslaw Michalek, Andrzej Wajda from a novel by Rolf Hochhuth. Production: CCC-Filmkunst, Gaumont International, Stand'Art Productions in cooperation with Zweites Deutsches Fernsehen, TF1. Year: 1983. Country: FRG, France. Run time: 132 min.

A stranger and his son arrive in Brombach, a small German town near the Swiss border. His arrival unearths a story that the villagers would rather forget: the love of Pauline Kropp for a Polish slave laborer during World War II and its fatal outcome. All of them have taken on the burden of guilt, but no one really feels guilty. With Hanna Schygulla, Piotr Lysak, and Armin Mueller-Stahl.

Die Wannseekonferenz
The Wannsee Conference
Director: Heinz Schirk. Screenplay: Paul Mommertz. Production: Infafilm GmbH, Österreichischer Rundfunk. Year: 1984. Countries: FRG, Austria. Run time: 85 min.

A reconstruction of the meeting of Nazi dignitaries on January 20, 1942. It took fourteen Nazi officers eighty-five minutes to decide on the implementation of the Final Solution. The film includes an interview with professors Shlomo Aharonson and Robert M. Kempner. With Dietrich Mattausch and Harald Dietl.

Wedle Wyroków Twoich
Zu Freiwild Verdammt
After Your Decrees
Director: Jerzy Hoffman. Screenplay: Paul Hengge, Jan Purzycki, Bogdan Wojdowski from a story by Artur Brauner. Production: CCC-Filmkunst, Zespól "Zodiak," PRF Zespóly Filmowe, Sender Freies Berlin. Year: 1984. Countries: Poland, FRG. Run time: 101 min.

When the Germans invade Poland, Ruth is twelve years old. The persecution of the Jews begins immediately, but she manages to escape. Having to fend for herself, she struggles her way through the country. She finds help, experiences betrayal, and suffers from the constant danger of death, the ever-present fear of being discovered, and starvation. Nevertheless, Ruth survives. With Sharon Brauner.

Wundkanal. Hinrichtung für Vier Stimmen
Wundkanal
Director: Thomas Harlan. Production: Quasar Film, Reass Films, Cannon International. Year: 1984. Countries: France, USA. Run time: 107 min.

For this film, Thomas Harlan (son of Veit Harlan, director of *Jud Süss*) obtained the cooperation of former SS officer Albert Filbert, who was responsible for making murders of political prisoners look like suicides. After the war, a former colleague continued working for the German state, designing the high-security cells of Stammheim Prison, where members of the terrorist group Red Army Faction were held and officially committed suicide. The film speculates on the continuity of murder in the name of the state. This militant and experimental film fictionalizes a scenario in which the Nazi is kidnapped and put on trial by a terrorist organization. Robert Kramer shot his film *Unser Nazi* during the making of *Wundkanal*, and photographer Roland Allard made a third film, *Tout sera comme d'habitude*, about the production of both Harlan's and Kramer's films.

Bittere ernte
Angry harvest
Director: Agnieszka Holland. Screenplay: Katarzyna Röck-Skowrow. Production: CCC-Filmkunst, Admiral Film GmbH in cooperation with Zweites Deutsches Fernsehen. Year: 1985. Country: FRG. Run time: 105 min.

Poland, 1943. The rich Polish farmer Leon finds the Jewish fugitive Rosa collapsed in the middle of the woods. Leon hides Rosa and nurses her back to health. However, this situation of living together, which is forced upon the middle-class woman and the simple farmer, results in catastrophe. With Armin Mueller-Stahl and Elisabeth Trissenaar.

Zaproszenie
The Invitation
Director: Wanda Jakubowska. Screenplay: Wanda Jakubowska. Production: Film Polski. Year: 1986. Country: Poland. Run time: 96 min.

A woman in her early sixties who works for a pediatrician is confronted with her past by the appearance of her husband, who had been officially declared deceased. She remembers their brief period of happiness, the war, and her time in Auschwitz. Although they still love each other, she refuses the invitation to visit him in the United States. Her daughter takes her place and makes the journey. With Antonina Gordon-Górecka.

Escape from Sobibor

Director: Jack Gold. Screenplay: Reginald Rose, Thomas Blatt, Richard Rashke from a book by Stanislaw Szmajzner. Production: Zenith Productions Ltd. Year: 1987. Country: Yugoslavia, UK. Run time: 149 min.

In October 1943, six hundred Jews and some Red Army prisoners of war decide to escape from Sobibor extermination camp in Poland. This was the largest prisoner revolt and escape of World War II. The leader of the group is a rabbi's son who makes it to freedom with half of the group. With Alan Arkin, Joanna Pacula, and Rutger Hauer.

Tel Aviv-Berlin

Director: Tzipi Trope. Screenplay: Tzipi Trope. Production: Tel Aviv-Berlin Ltd., Admor International Pictures. Year: 1987. Country: Israel. Run time: 96 min.

Benjamin has just escaped the Shoah and has a hard time adjusting to his new life in Palestine. He gradually slips away from his family, back to his haunted past where he confronts a former kapo. With Zohar Aloni and Yosef Carmon.

Au Revoir les Enfants

Director: Louis Malle. Screenplay: Louis Malle. Production: NEF Filmproduktion, Stella Film, Nouvelles Editions de Films SA, MK2. Year: 1987. Country: France. Run time: 100 min.

In January 1944, eleven-year-old Julien returns to a Catholic boarding school. He befriends quiet newcomer Jean Bonnet and discovers that the boy is Jewish. Only occasionally does the German occupation affect country life. In a restaurant, a French collaborator threatens a Jewish guest. As revenge for having been treated unfairly, a young employee tells the Gestapo that the school is hiding Jews. Bonnet, two other Jewish pupils, and the principal are taken away and deported. Julien's stare may have betrayed them. The film is based on events from Louis Malle's own life. With Gaspard Manesse.

Ha-kayitz Shel Aviya
Aviya's Summer
Directors: Eli Cohen, Gila Almagor, Eitan Evan. Screenplay: Gila Almagor.
Production: HSA Ltd. Year: 1988. Country: Israel. Run time: 95 min.

One summer in the life of a young girl in the years following the
creation of Israel. Aviya is the daughter of a father who survived the
Shoah and a mother who was a resistance fighter. Her mother has a blue
number tattooed on her arm and walks a thin line between madness and
sanity. Aviya is ten years old and has a shaved head, because her mother
thought she saw "fleas." The mother falls deeper into mental illness, and
Aviya must grow up quickly. With Gila Almagor and Kaipo Cohen.

Küldetés Evianba
Mission to Evian
Directors: Erika Szántó, Akos Ravasz. Screenplay: Erika Szántó from
a novel by Hans Habe. Production: Daniel Film München, Magyar
Televízió Mûvelõdési Fõszerkesztõség. Year: 1988. Country: Hungary.
Run time: 92 min.

In July 1938, representatives from thirty-two countries gathered in
Evian-les-Bains prior to the war. The Nazis offered to sell their Jews for
US$250 each. Unless a deal was struck, forty thousand would be sent
to death camps. The story focuses on the efforts of Professor Heinrich
von Benda to close a deal. With Klaus Abramowsky.

I Skrzypce Przestaly Grac
And the Violins Stopped Playing
Director: Alexander Ramati. Screenplay: Alexander Ramati. Produc-
tion: Cinecitt rzym, Davis-Films, Film Polski Film Agency, WFF Lodz,
Zespol Filmowy "Tor." Year: 1988. Countries: Poland, USA. Run time:
119 min.

Dymitri is a Gypsy violinist living in Warsaw. After the Jews have
been rounded up, he learns that the Gypsies will be next. With his
wife and son, he seeks out a Gypsy camp outside of town, and becomes
involved in an attempt to flee from the Nazis. They are rounded up just
as they reach what they believe will be a safe haven in Hungary. They
are sent to Auschwitz, where most of them die. With Horst Buchholz
and Didi Ramati.

Berlin-Yerushalaim
Berlin-Jerusalem
Director: Amos Gitai. Screenplay: Amos Gitai, Gudie Lawaetz. Pro-
duction: Agav Films, Capital Studios, Nederlandse Omroepstichting,

Nova Films, Orthel Films, Rai Due Radiotelevisione Italiana, Transfax Film Productions. Year: 1989. Countries: Israel, The Netherlands, Italy, France, UK. Run time: 89 min.

During the 1930s, two women, friends from the Berlin intelligentsia, the German Else Lasker-Schüler (Lisa Kreuzer) and the Russian Tania Shohat (Rivka Neuman), travel separately to Jerusalem, looking for a new life. Their paths cross in the city. Based on the biographies of these two women, one of the first Russian Zionists and a German Expressionist poetess, the film moves back and forth between the dim cafés of Berlin in the 1930s and the hills of Jerusalem—the mythical place of their dreams but also a very real city whose reality they must confront.

Enemies: A Love Story
Director: Paul Mazursky. Screenplay: Roger L. Simon, Paul Mazursky. Production: Morgan Creek Productions, 20th Century Fox. Year: 1989. Country: USA. Run time: 120 min.

In 1949, a Jewish survivor of the Shoah finds out that his wife, whom he thought was dead, is still alive. He can't continue their relationship because he already has two other women in New York. One is a Polish woman who hid him in her attic and whom he married out of gratitude. The other is more passionate, but also linked with remembrances of the past that influence the present. The film deals with the difficulties of living on, using a mildly comic tone. With Ron Silver, Anjelica Huston, and Lena Olin.

Kornblumenblau
Director: Leszek Worcziwicz. Screenplay: Leszek Wosiewicz, Jarostaw Sander from a novel by Kazimierz Tyminski. Production: Karol Irzykowski Film Studio. Year: 1989. Country: Poland. Run time: 89 min.

Based on the true story of a Polish musician who survived a concentration camp. Tadzik is an accordion player who has been sent to a camp for his part in the resistance. There, he survives the brutal and dehumanizing conditions by any means possible, largely because he can play the song "Kornblumenblau" on the accordion. With Adam Kamien.

Music Box
Director: Costa-Gavras. Screenplay: Joe Eszterhas, Costa-Gavras. Production: Carolco Pictures. Year: 1989. Country: USA. Run time: 124 min.

The Hungarian immigrant Mike Laszlo (Armin Mueller-Stahl) has done well for himself since arriving in the United States fifty years earlier. He is particularly proud of his daughter, Ann Talbot (Jessica Lange), a successful lawyer in Chicago. Following the release of secret World War II documents by the Russians, Mike finds himself accused of being a notorious war criminal. He's convinced that it is a communist plot to discredit him and insists that Ann defend him in court. Ann discovers troubling facts about her father.

Triumph of the Spirit
Director: Robert M. Young. Screenplay: Andrzej Krakowski, Laurence Heath from a story by Shimon Arama and Zion Haen. Production: Arnold Kopelson, Shimon Arama Productions, Nova International Films, Indie Production. Year: 1989. Country: USA. Run time: 120 min.

This fact-based story portrays Greek Olympic boxer Salamo Arouch, who was deported to Auschwitz where the Nazis spared his life as long as he fought for their amusement. His father and brother were also held to make sure he would continue the show. With Willem Dafoe and Edward James Olmos.

Der Rosengarten
The Rosegarden
Director: Fons Rademakers. Screenplay: Andrea Buttenstedt from a book by Paul Hengge. Production: CCC-Filmkunst GmbH, Cannon Films NV in cooperation with Cannon Films, Inc., Globus-Pearce Productions, Zweites Deutsches Fernsehen, Österreichischer Rundfunk. Year: 1989 (in the USA; 1990 in the Netherlands). Countries: FRG, USA. Run time: 113 min.

The aged Aaron Reichenbach knocks down a man whom he recognizes as a concentration camp doctor, the tormentor and murderer of his sister. Aaron is put on trial and convicted of assault, while the child murderer remains unpunished. The screenplay was inspired by historical fact: the hanging, a few days before the end of the war in a school in Hamburg, of twenty Jewish children who were subjected to medical experiments. With Liv Ullmann, Maximilian Schell, and Peter Fonda.

Hitlerjunge Salomon
Europa Europa
Director: Agnieszka Holland. Screenplay: Agnieszka Holland, Paul Hengge. Production: CCC-Filmkunst, Les Films du Losange, SOFIMA, Telmar Film International, Studio Filmowe "Perspektywa" in cooperation with Bayerischer Rundfunk. Year: 1990. Countries: Germany, France, Poland. Run time: 114 min.

The Perel family has fled from Nazi Germany to Poland, but their pursuers also manage to catch up with them there. The fourteen-year-old

Salomon continues fleeing to the east and is educated in the Soviet Union as a member of the *Komsomol*. When the Germans invade Russia, he passes himself off as an ethnic German. He has to fight on the side of the Germans and is sent to attend a Nazi school. The film is based on the authentic story of Salomon Perel, who later emigrated to Palestine. With Marco Hofschneider and Julie Delpy.

Korczak
Director: Andrzej Wajda. Screenplay: Agnieszka Holland. Production: Perspektywa Film Studio, Regina Ziegler Filmproduktion, Zweites Deutsches Fernsehen, Erato Films, Telmar Film International, BBC. Year: 1990. Countries: Poland, FRG, UK. Run time: 118 min.

This film tells the story of Dr. Janusz Korczak, the Polish doctor, writer, and educational pioneer, and his Jewish orphanage in the Warsaw ghetto. The film traces the last months before the two hundred children and their doctor were deported to Treblinka in August 1942. The dream-like ending, in which the children are saved, sparked controversy at the film's première in Cannes. With Wojciech Pszoniak.

Abrahams Gold
Director: Jörg Graser. Screenplay: Jörg Graser. Production: Avistag Film in Kooperation with Project Filmproduktion im Filmverlag der Autoren, Adanos Film GmbH, Zweites Deutsches Fernsehen. Year: 1990. Country: FRG. Run time: 95 min.

Alois Hunzinger and his friend Karl Lechner travel from their Bavarian village to Auschwitz with the intent of digging up a box full of gold teeth that Hunzinger buried when he worked there as a camp guard. But the plan ends in disaster: Lechner finds out that he is the son of victims of the Shoah and Hunzinger's granddaughter commits suicide when she discovers her grandfather's past. With Hanna Schygulla.

God Afton, Herr Wallenberg—En Passionshistoria Från Verkligheten
Good Evening, Mr. Wallenberg
Director: Kjell Grede. Screenplay: Kjell Grede. Production: Sandrew Film & teater AB, Scansat, TV 3, Svenska Filminsitutet, Film Teknik, Hunnia Film Studios in cooperation with Svenska Filminsitutet, Swedish TV. Year: 1990. Countries: Sweden, Hungary, Norway. Run time: 115 min.

Raoul Wallenberg is thirty-two years old when he arrives in Budapest in July 1944. He manages to save the lives of hundreds of thousands of Jews in an unconventional manner. His was the largest and most successful rescue operation of World War II. Wallenberg was arrested by the Red Army in January 1945 and has been missing ever since. With Stellan Skarsgård.

Der Daunenträger
Warszawa. Année 5703
Warsaw—Year 5703
Director: Janusz Kijowski. Screenplay: Jerzy Janicki, Janusz Kijowski. Production: CCC-Filmkunst, Molécule, Zodiak. Year: 1992. Countries: Germany, Poland. Run time: 110 min.

During the closing of the Warsaw ghetto, a young Jewish couple (Lambert Wilson and Julie Delpy) escape and are given shelter by a Polish woman (Hannah Schygulla). Conflicts arise when a romance develops between the Jewish man and the Polish woman.

Genghis Cohn
Directors: Elijah Moshinsky, Ruth Galeb. Screenplay: Stanley Price from a novel by Romain Gary. Production: A&E Television Networks, BBC. Year: 1993. Country: UK. Run time: 79 min.

Cohn is a Jewish nightclub comedian and ventriloquist playing the European cabaret circuit in the 1930s until Otto Schatz, a Nazi officer, murders him. Sixteen years later, Cohn returns to haunt Schatz—now living a successful and peaceful life as police commissioner in small-town Bavaria. Cohn takes his twisted, ironic revenge against Schatz. Unexplained, unmotivated murders start to occur, while Schatz transforms into a Yiddish-speaking, chopped liver loving Jew. With Antony Sher, Robert Lindsay, and Diana Rigg.

Schindler's List
Director: Steven Spielberg. Screenplay: Steven Zaillian from a novel by Thomas Keneally. Production: Amblin Entertainment Inc., Universal City Studios. Year: 1993. Country: USA. Run time: 195 min.

In September 1939, Oskar Schindler (Liam Neeson) takes charge of a confiscated factory in Krakow. A businessman with connections to military officers and member of the NSDAP, Schindler obtains the right to employ Jewish workers through corruption. His accountant Stern (Ben Kingsley) draws up a list of all the people working for Schindler, who thereby are saved from persecution. After witnessing the brutal closure of the Krakow ghetto, Schindler decides to save as many people as possible by demanding more workers and transferring the factory to a safer place. In the epilogue of this film, 128 people who worked for Schindler stand together around his grave in Israel.

Leni Muss Fort
Leni
Director: Leo Hiemer. Screenplay: Leo Hiemer. Production: DAZU Film, SDR, arte, Westdeutscher Rundfunk. Year: 1994. Country: Germany. Run time: 80 min.

Just after her birth in 1937, Leni is adopted by a couple living on a farm in Bavaria. The Aibeles are childless and love Leni, but the mayor finds out that the child's origins are not "pure." Although Leni is baptised, she is not "pure of race" according to Nazi law. On Christmas Eve, a letter from the mayor is delivered; she is to be sent to Auschwitz. The machinery of the Nazis works perfectly, even in the more isolated regions of Germany: citizens, administrators, priests, and nuns all serve the system. The Aibeles and the village teacher cannot prevent Leni's deportation. With Johanna Thanheiser.

Le Jour du Bain
Bannii Djen
Director: Dominique de Rivaz. Screenplay: Dominique de Rivaz. Production: Dominique de Rivaz. Year: 1994. Countries: Switzerland, Ukraine. Run time: 20 min.

In September 1941, during the final days of the harvest, the Nazis killed 33,771 people, mostly women and children. The events leading up to this massacre are rendered in an impressionistic manner in de Rivaz's stark and mournful black and white film. The film focuses on the strong bonds among women as they battle for survival in their final days.

Drei Tage im April
Director: Oliver Storz. Screenplay: Oliver Storz. Production: Österreichischer Rundfunk. Year: 1995. Country: Austria, Germany. Run time: 105 min.

In April 1945, a train full of concentration camp prisoners is left stranded in a small German village. But none of the fearful inhabitants does anything to save them. Only a young girl, member of the Nazi girls' organization *Bund Deutscher Mädel,* refuses to watch the prisoners die. The film is inspired by a true story. With Karoline Eichhorn.

Anne No Nikki
The Diary of Anne Frank
Director: Akinori Nagaoka. Screenplay: Hachiro Konno, Roger Pulvers from *The Diary of Anne Frank.* Production: AF Production Committee. Year: 1995. Country: Japan. Run time: 120 min.

Adaptation of *The Diary of Anne Frank* as an animation film.

Mutter's Courage
My Mother's Courage
Director: Michael Verhoeven. Screenplay: Michael Verhoeven from a story by George Tabori. Production: Sentana Filmproduktion, Little Bird Ltd., Wega Film, Bavaria Film, Hessischer Rundfunk, Sender Freies Berlin, Westdeutscher Rundfunk, European Co-production Fund, BBS Films. Year: 1995. Country: Germany. Run time: 92 min.

In July 1944, four thousand Jews are deported from Budapest to Auschwitz. Elsa Tabori is arrested on her way to a friend. She is rounded up and in her despair she addresses the highest-ranking officer to demand a *Schutzpass*, a letter of safe passage. The soldiers want to shoot her immediately, but the officer, who wants to demonstrate his power, allows Tabori to go home. She survived the Shoah. With George Tabori as himself, and Pauline Collins.

Wielki Tydzień
Holy Week
Director: Andrzej Wajda. Screenplay: Andrzej Wajda from a novel by Jerzy Andrzejewskis. Production: Les Films du Losange. Year: 1995. Countries: Poland, Germany. Run time: 94 minutes.

As the Germans close the Warsaw ghetto, a young Jewish woman manages to escape deportation. She is taken in by a Catholic couple who hide her in their house near Warsaw. The film aims to reconcile Poland's Jews and Catholics. With Beata Fudalej.

Von Hölle zu Hölle
From Hell to Hell
Director: Dmitri Astrakhan. Screenplay: Artur Brauner, Oleg Danilov. Production: CCC Filmkunst GmbH, Belarus Film. Year: 1996. Countries: Germany, Russia, Belarus. Run time: 102 min.

Helene is about to be deported and gives her child away to her Polish neighbour Anna. Helene survives but Anna, who lost her own child directly after birth, refuses to hand Helene back her daughter. A battle for the seven-year-old girl is set against the background of growing anger of the Polish population against their former Jewish neighbors who have come to reclaim their houses. The situation leads to a gruesome massacre, in which forty-two people die. With Ya'ackov Bodo and Anja Kling.

Madame Jacques sur la Croisette
Madame Jacques on the Croisette
Director: Emmanuel Finkiel. Screenplay: Emmanuel Finkiel. Production: Les Films du Poisson, La Sept Cinéma. Year: 1997. Country: France. Run time: 40 min.

Every spring in Cannes, a group of elderly French Jewish women and men reflect on aging, love, and their underlying bond of Yiddish culture. Breaking away from the group and its monotonous rhythm, Maurice searches for love with Mme. Jacques, a widow who just returned from Israel. Despite gossip among their friends, Maurice and Mme. Jacques decide to share their lives. With Natan Cogan and Shulamit Adar.

Bent

Director: Sean Mathias. Screenplay: Martin Sherman. Production: Arts Council of England, Ask Kodansha Company, Channel Four Films, NDF. Year: 1997. Country: UK. Run time: 108 min.

Intentionally stylized, this film tells the story of Max (Clive Owen), who is deported to Dachau for being homosexual. He falls in love with Horst (Lothaire Bluteau), who carries the pink triangle with pride. *Bent* spotlights the tragic fate of homosexuals under the Nazis, as well as homosexual tendencies among Nazi officers. With Ian McKellen and Mick Jagger.

La Tregua
The Truce

Directors: Franceso Rosi, Leo Pescarolo, Guido De Laurentiis. Screenplay: Franceso Rosi, Sandro Petraglia, Stefano Rulli. Production: 3 Emme Cinematografica, Warner Brothers, Stéphan Films, UGC Images, T&C Films, Daniel Zuta Filmprodutkion, RAI Uno, Westdeutscher Rundfunk in cooperation with Capitol Films Ltd., Istituto Luce. Year: 1997. Countries: Italy, France, Germany, Switzerland. Run time: 123 min.

Following the liberation of Auschwitz, Primo Levi (John Turturro) returns to Turin. In 1962 he writes *The Truce*, a chronicle of his nine-month journey home from the camp. The film begins shortly after the Germans leave, as four Russian horsemen tear down the gates of Auschwitz and Levi boards one of the first outbound trucks. Over the next few months, he passes through many different countries, and the acquaintances he makes along the way slowly reawaken his appreciation for life and freedom. But with it also comes a deep rage and an abiding sense of guilt at having survived.

La Vita è Bella
Life is Beautiful

Director: Roberto Benigni. Screenplay: Vincenzo Cerami, Roberto Benigni. Production: Cecchi Gori Group, Melampo Cinematografica. Year: 1997. Country: Italy. Run time: 116 min.

This tragicomedy portrays the life of Jewish romantic Guido (Roberto Benigni) in Mussolini's Italy. He wins the heart of his beloved and manages to live with anti-Semitic laws through his humor and his naivety. Their son Giosùe is born. Four years later, they are deported. Guido tries to protect his son from the cruel reality by telling him it is all a game. If they follow the "rules," they will win a tank. He tries to do everything to retain the façade and not lose his son's trust.

Left Luggage
Director: Jeroen Krabbé. Screenplay: Edwin de Vries from a novel by Carl Friedman. Production: Shooting Star Film Company, Favorite Film, Flying Dutchman Productions. Year: 1998. Countries: The Netherlands, Belgium, USA. Run time: 100 min.

The identity problems of Chaya, a young woman of the "second generation." A student, Chaya finds employment as a part-time nanny with the Chassidic Kalman family. She has trouble fitting into their life-style, but she accepts the rules and is taken in by the family. She is attached to the five-year-old boy Simcha and finds an escape from her own family. Chaya's parents both survived the Holocaust. While her mother no longer wants to know about the past, her father endlessly turns over the soil to find two suitcases full of things dear to his heart, which he hid from the Nazis. With Laura Fraser, Adam Monty, Isabella Rossellini, and Jeroen Krabbé.

Meschugge
The Giraffe
Director: Dani Levy. Screenplay: Dani Levy, Maria Schrader. Production: X-Filme Creative Pool. Year: 1998. Country: Germany, Switzerland, USA. Run time: 103 min.

After the family chocolate shop burns down in what seems a racist attack, Ruth, a German Jew, goes to visit her daughter Lena in New York. One evening, at the hotel where they regularly meet up, they discover a woman badly wounded, who succumbs to her injuries soon after. At the hospital, Lena meets David Fish, the woman's son, and the two fall in love. With Maria Schrader, Dani Levy, and David Strathairn.

Train de Vie
Train of Life
Director: Radu Mihaileanu. Screenplay: Radu Mihaileanu, Moni Ovaia. Production: Belfilms, Canal+. Year: 1998. Countries: France, Belgium, The Netherlands, Italy, Rumania. Run time: 103 min.

One evening in 1941, the village fool of a small Jewish *shtetl* warns the townsfolk that the Nazis are deporting the inhabitants of neighboring villages. The Council of Elders decides to build a fake deportation train to escape the Nazis. Fiction becomes a weapon of resistance. With Lionel Abelanski.

The Devil's Arithmetic
Director: Donna Deitch. Screenplay: Robert J. Avrech from a novel by Jane Yolen. Production: Lietuvos Kinostudija, Millbrook Farm Productions, Punch Productions Inc., Showtime Networks Inc. Year: 1999. Country: USA. Run time: 95 min.

Thirteen-year-old Hannah Stern (Kirsten Dunst) is neglectful of her Jewish heritage and tired of "remembering." As she goes to open the door to the prophet Elijah during the Seder, she finds herself in 1940s Poland. After being sent to a Nazi concentration camp she must use her knowledge of the future to survive the past, and learns something about the importance of remembering. With Paul Freeman.

Gloomy Sunday—Ein Lied von Liebe und Tod
Gloomy Sunday
Director: Rolf Schübel. Screenplay: Ruth Toma, Rolf Schübel. Production: Studio Hamburg Produktion für Film und Fernsehen GmbH; Dom Film GmbH; Focusfilm Kft. in cooperation with Westdeutscher Rundfunk, Arte G.E.I.E., Premiere Medien GmbH. Year: 1999. Countries: Germany, Hungary. Run time: 144 min.

Budapest in the 1930s. Laszlo hires the pianist András to play in his restaurant. Both men fall in love with the beautiful waitress Ilona who inspires András in his compositions. His song "Gloomy Sunday" is first loved and then feared, for it triggers off a chain of suicides. The ménage à trois is destroyed when German officer Hans falls in love with Ilona as well. Hans makes a fortune out of the desperate situation of the Jews by delaying their deportation in exchange for jewelry and money. András commits suicide. Fifty years later, Hans—now a rich businessman—dines at the restaurant. Ilona still works there. With Erika Marozsán.

Jacob the Liar
Jakob le Menteur
Director: Peter Kassovitz. Screenplay: Peter Kassovitz, Didier Decoin from a novel by Jurek Becker. Production: Blue Wolf Productions, Global Entertainment Productions GmbH & Company Medien KG, FiKasso Inc. Productions, TriStar Pictures. Year: 1999. Countries: France, USA, Hungary. Run time: 120 min.

A remake of the 1975 film by Frank Beyer. Jakob (Robin Williams) lives in a ghetto and wants to give hope to his followers after hearing about the advancing Red Army. Lying, he invents good news, telling people he possesses a radio to which he listens in secret. The suicides in the ghetto stop and everybody awaits the liberation. These lies keep hope and humor alive among the ghetto inhabitants. The Germans learn of the mythical radio, however, and begin a search for the resistance hero who dares to operate it. With Hannah Taylor-Gordon.

Voyages
Directors: Emmanuel Finkiel, Yael Fogiel. Screenplay: Emmanuel Finkiel. Production: Les Films du Poisson, Studio Canal+, Arte France cinéma, Héritages Films, Paradise Films. Year: 1999. Countries: France, Belgium, Poland. Run time: 115 min.

In 1999, three elderly women, one from Paris, one from Warsaw, and one from Tel Aviv, make a journey into their past, marked by the extermination and the memory of Yiddish culture. With Shulamit Adar, Liliane Rovère, and Esther Gorintin.

Nuremberg
Director: Yves Simoneau. Screenplay: David W. Rintels. Production: Alliance Atlantis Communications, Inc., Productions La Fête; in cooperation with TNT, Leahy Ross Conners, British American Entertainment, Cypress Films. Year: 2000. Country: Canada, USA. Run time: 180 min.

The preparations for the Nuremberg trial, the proceedings, and its aftermath are shown through the eyes of Chief Prosecutor Robert Jackson and of Reichsmarschall Hermann Goering. The twenty-one Nazi defendants, led by Hitler's second-in-command Goering, try in vain to impose their own view of the events. Some of the film's dialogue is taken directly from court transcripts. With Alec Baldwin, Brian Cox, Charlotte Gainsbourg, and Christopher Plummer.

Anne Frank: The Whole Story
Director: Robert Dornhelm. Screenplay: Kirk Ellis. Production: American Broadcasting Company. Year: 2001. Countries: USA, Czech Republic. Run time: 189 min.

This film is about Anne Frank's life, beginning with her childhood in Frankfurt before the harsh war years in Amsterdam (covered in her diary), and continues ultimately to her death in Bergen-Belsen. With Ben Kingsley, Brenda Blethyn, and Hannah Taylor-Gordon.

Conspiracy
Director: Frank Pierson. Screenplay: Loring Mandel. Production: BBC, Home Box Office. Year: 2001. Countries: UK, USA. Run time: 96 min.

A drama about the 1942 Wannsee Conference, in which Nazi and SS leaders gathered in a Berlin suburb to discuss the "Final Solution to the Jewish Question." With Kenneth Branagh and Stanley Tucci.

Amen

Director: Costa-Gavras. Screenplay: Costa-Gavras, Jean-Claude Grumberg from the play *Der Stellvertreter* by Rolf Hochhuth. Production: Katharina, TF1, KC Medien, Canal +, KG Productions, Mediapro Pictures, Renn Productions. Year: 2002. Countries: USA, France, Germany, Rumania. Run time: 132 min.

Kurt Gerstein (Ulrich Tukur) is a German scientist and SS officer. He is asked to develop a "vermin killer" and creates Zyklon B gas, but soon realizes that his invention will be used to kill people instead of animals. On the basis of his Christian values, he decides to denounce the crimes by alerting the Allies, the Pope, and the German churches. He encounters Ricardo Fontana (Mathieu Kassovitz), a young Jesuit, one of the priests who struggled against savagery, going against hierarchy and often paying for their courage with their lives.

The Grey Zone

Director: Tim Blake Nelson. Screenplay: Tim Blake Nelson from a book by Miklos Nyiszli. Production: Killer Productions. Year: 2002. Country: USA. Run time: 108 min.

The only armed act of resistance at Auschwitz-Birkenau took place on October 7, 1944: 451 members of an isolated Jewish *Sonderkommando* died or were executed afterward. Prisoners in the *Sonderkommandos* worked at the crematoriums and gas chambers. In parallel, the film tells the story of a Jewish child who survives the gas chamber and is hidden by the commando, and that of the female prisoners working at the arms factory, who manage to smuggle the gunpowder that was used to blast the crematorium no. 4. Five diaries of *Sonderkommando* members that were found in Birkenau after the war served as the basis for the script. With David Arquette, Steve Buscemi, and Harvey Keitel.

Kedma

Director: Amos Gitai. Screenplay: Amos Gitai, Mordechai Goldhecht. Production: Agav Hafakot, BIM, MK2 Productions, R&C Produzioni, Arte France Cinéma. Year: 2002. Countries: Italy, Israel, France. Run time: 100 min.

Reconstruction of the battles fought by survivors of the Shoah enrolled in the Palmach, the clandestine Jewish fighting force in Palestine, against the British army and the Arab resistance along the road from the coast to Jerusalem. With Andrei Kashkar.

The Pianist

Director: Roman Polanski. Screenplay: Ronald Harwood from the book by Wladyslaw Szpilman. Production: RP Productions, Heritage Films, Studio Babelsberg, Runteam Ltd., Agencja Produkcji Filmowej, Beverly Detroit, Canal+ Polska, Canal+. Year: 2002. Countries: France, Germany, UK, Poland. Run time: 148 min.

In 1939, Wladyslaw Szpilman (Adrien Brody) is performing classical pieces on the radio as bombs begin to fall on Warsaw. As the months roll by, Szpilman witnesses the restrictions the Nazis place on Polish Jews and their enclosure in the Warsaw ghetto. While his family is deported to concentration camps, Szpilman manages to escape and moves from one bombed-out house to the next until the Red Army finally liberates him. One day, he saves himself by performing for a Nazi officer against the backdrop of a world in ruins.

A Rózsa Énekei
Rose's Songs

Director: Andor Szilágyi. Screenplay: Andor Szilágyi. Production: Grantfilm Ltd. Year: 2003. Countries: Hungary, Italy. Run time: 98 min.

During the fall of 1944, the Jewish inhabitants of Budapest await their deportation. The only solace is the voice that resounds over the city once a week, the voice of Imre Rose, the world-famous opera singer and a Jew himself. Caretaker Géza Halász believes no Jew has reason to fear as long as Imre Rose is there, since the singer could easily flee Budapest thanks to his connections. Halász visits the singer every Friday to dine with him. After the meal, the hope-inspiring concert begins. Rose is known for his eccentricity and so no one is surprised that he never leaves the house or meets anyone. With Franco Castellano.

La Petite Prairie aux Bouleaux
The Birch-Tree Meadow

Director: Marceline Loridan Ivens. Screenplay: Marceline Loridan Ivens, Jeanne Moreau. Production: Capi Films, Ciné Valse, Hertigae Films, Mascaret Films P'Artisan Filmproduktion GmbH. Year: 2003. Countries: France, Germany, Poland. Run time: 91 min.

At an Auschwitz Survivor's Association meeting, the people gather, joke, and reminisce. Underneath, however, pain and sadness remain. One woman (Anouk Aimée) returns to Auschwitz sixty years later. She unexpectedly meets a young German man who is photographing the place to make an archaeological record. He decides to follow her on her voyage into memory.

Posledniy Poezd (Polednij Poezd)
The Last Train
Director: Aleksei German Jnr. Screenplay: Aleksei German Jnr. Production: Non-Stop Productions, PIEF Film Studio. Year: 2003. Country: Russia. Run time: 80 min.

A German army medic works at the Russian front during World War II. The countless deaths and the erasure of human life without trace expresses the absurdity of life. With Aleksei Devotchenko.

Sortalanság
Fateless
Director: Lajos Koltai. Screenplay: Imre Kertész. Production: EuroArts Entertainment, H2O Motion Pictures, Hungarian Motion Picture Ltd., Magic Media Inc., Renegade Films. Year: 2005. Countries: Hungary, Germany, UK. Run time: 140 min.

Based on the novel by Nobel Prize winner Imre Kertész, this film shows a Hungarian youth coming of age at Buchenwald during World War II. György Köves, the son of a merchant, is fourteen when he is arrested on a bus and deported. In the camp, György finds camaraderie, suffering, cruelty, illness, and death. He discovers hatred, is unkind to his fellows, and is not presented as a character the spectator wishes to identify with. He returns to Budapest without knowing what awaits him. With Marcell Nagy.

Zug um Zug—Budapest 1944
Jews for Sale—Payment on Delivery
Directors: Axel Brandt, Elias Perrig, Bertram von Boxberg. Screenplay: Axel Brandt, Peter Jakob Kelting, Josef Rölz. Production: Axel Brandt Filmproduktion. Year: 2005. Country: Germany. Run time: 90 min.

This film addresses negotiations for the release of Hungarian Jews conducted between the Jewish Rescue and Relief Committee (Vaadah) and Adolf Eichmann. When the German army invaded Hungary in March 1944, a million Hungarian Jews were in danger. In this hopeless situation, Hungarian lawyer Rudolf Kasztner dared to stand up to the man behind the deportations, Eichmann. Taking advantage of tensions within the SS, Kasztner managed to sabotage Eichmann's deportation machinery, thereby saving the lives of countless people—among them 1,683 Hungarian Jews who arrived by train in Switzerland, in December 1944.

Der Letzte Zug
Poslédni Vlak
The Last Train
Director: Dana Vávrová, Joseph Vilsmaier. Screenplay: Stephen Glantz. Production: CCC, Diamant Film, Perathon Film- und Fernsehproduktions GmbH. Year: 2006. Countries: Germany, Czech Republic. Run time: 123 min.

Berlin 1943. The Nazis plan to turn Berlin into a "Jewless" city. More than seventy thousand Jews have already been deported. In April, a train with 688 Jews leaves the station of Berlin Grünewald for Auschwitz. Young and old, intellectuals, boxers, and artists are squashed together in the wagon. The journey into death lasts six days. The battle against hunger and thirst begins. In their desperate situation, some deportees attempt to flee the transport. Among them the couple Henry and Lea Neumann and the young woman Ruth Zilberman. With Sibel Kekilli.

Zwartboek
Black Book
Director: Paul Verhoeven. Screenplay: Gerard Soeteman, Paul Verhoeven. Production: Fu Works, Hector BV, Motel Films, Clockwork Pictures, Egoli Tossell Film AG, Motion Investment Group, Studio Babelsberg Motion Pictures GmbH, Studio Babelsberg, VIP 4 Medienfonds. Year: 2006. Country: The Netherlands. Run time: 145 min.

When her hiding place is destroyed, Rachel Stein decides to cross the Biesbosch river delta with a group of other Jews and escape to the already liberated south of the Netherlands. Their boat is intercepted by a German patrol and all the refugees except Rachel are killed. She joins the resistance, and manages to get close to German SS officer Müntze. Meanwhile, the resistance plans to free some of their members with Rachel's help. The plan is betrayed and fails. Both the Resistance and the Germans blame her and she is again forced to hide. Liberation does not bring Rachel freedom, even after she has managed to expose the real traitor. With Carice van Houten.

La Question Humaine
Heartbeat Detector
Director: Nicolas Klotz. Screenplay: Elisabeth Perceval, Nicolas Klotz. Production: Sophie Dulac Production. Year: 2007. Country: France. Run time: 143 min.

A young human resource manager (Mathieu Amalric) devotes himself to making the company for which he works more profitable. As he begins to uncover evidence that the company was involved in the Shoah

sixty years earlier, he starts to notice the similarities between its procedures then and now. With Michael Lonsdale.

The Nazi Officer's Wife

Director: Mike Figgis. Screenplay: Craig Shermann from the biography of Edith Hahn Beer. Production: TBA (in production). Year: 2008.
Country: UK. Run time: TBA.

The film is based on the true story of Edith Hahn Beer. In the
1940s a young Jewish woman is living in Vienna. She is sent to a labor
camp but manages to escape. When she returns home, she finds that
her mother has been deported. Her search for her mother leads her
to Munich, where a Nazi officer falls in love with her and marries her,
despite knowing of her origins. A documentary with the same title was
made for American television in 2003, directed by Liz Garbus.

The Fence

Director: Philip Saville. Screenplay: Harris Salomon, Matt Salzberg. Production: Atlantic Overseas Pictures, Angel Baby Entertainment, Dalka
GmbH. Year: 2009. Country: UK. Run time: TBA

This is the fact-based story of Herman Rosenblat, a survivor of the
Shoah. In the midst of persecution, Rosenblat's faith is restored by the
magical love of a young woman—a love even the greatest war in human
history could not silence.

Essays

Do You Hear Me?

Screenplay: Mina Brownstone. Production: Hadassah, The Women's
International Zionist Organization of America Inc. Year: 1947. Country:
USA. Run time: 15 min. Essay.

The offscreen voice of an anonymous woman describes one of the
six million victims of the Shoah and tells her life story, accompanied
by war and postwar scenes in Europe. She calls upon the Jews who are
survivors of the Shoah to go to Palestine to find peace and happiness.
This propaganda film was one of the first to deal with the subject of
the Shoah and its trauma.

Our Children / It Will Never Happen Again
Unzere Kinder

Director: Nathan Gross. Production: Kinor-Film-Kooperative. Year:
1947–48. Country: Poland. Run time: 75 min. Documentary.

This semi-documentary film features the comedy duo Szymon Dzigan and Israel Shumacher who had recently returned from the Soviet

Union, and some Jewish children who survived the Shoah. This film was shot on location at the JDC-supported Helenowek Colony, an orphanage near Lodz. Dzigan and Schumacher portray all the characters in Sholem Aleichem's "Kasrilevke is Burning," and then there is an exchange of roles where the children go onstage and they become the children's audience. Reversals continue during the performers' visit to the children's residence, as the children teach adults about the healing possibilities of music, dance, and storytelling.

Strange Victory

Director: Leo Hurwitz. Production: Target Film Productions. Country: USA. Year: 1948. Run time: 75 min. Documentary.

The film provocatively questions whether the World War II triumph of the Allies was indeed a victory for everyone. Hurwitz discloses a discrepancy between ideals and reality in America and points out the racism and anti-Semitism in this country. A victory over fascism, according to Hurwitz, can be achieved only if the American ideals of freedom and equality are applied in America. Documentary footage of the last days of war in Berlin are compiled with scenes in New York and footage the Allies shot when liberating the concentration camps. The film culminates with statistics, interviews, and testimony regarding racial segregation in the United States.

The Museum and the Fury

Director: Leo Hurwitz. Production: Film Frontiers. Year: 1956. Country: USA. Run time: 60 min. Documentary.

This documentary is intended to reveal the principles that were the basis for creating the Auschwitz-Birkenau Museum. Excerpts of films about the liberation of the camp and the Nuremberg trials were edited with images of museum visitors, in order to compose an essay on memory and its representation, questioning what connects and separates an art museum from a historical museum.

Tagebuch für Anne Frank

Director: Joachim Hellwig. Production: DEFA-Studio für Wochenschau und Dokumentarfilme. Year: 1957–58. Country: GDR. Run time: 20 min. Documentary.

This documentary talks about the rise of former Nazis to leading economic and military positions in West Germany. It reveals the connections between I.G. Farben and the SS, notably in the politics of extermination. These documents are inserted into the framework of the story of a young actress who obtains the role of Anne Frank for a theatre production.

Memo to Eichmann

Director: Bernard Euslin. Production: United Jewish Appeal. Year: 1961. Country: USA. Run time: 15 min. Documentary.

The birth and growth of the nation of Israel immediately following the end of the Shoah is presented in the form of a memo to Adolf Eichmann fifteen years after the war.

In Thy Blood Live
B'damayich Chay

Director: David Perlov. Screenplay: Adam Greenberg. Production: The Israeli Film Service, World Zionist Organization. Year: 1962. Country: Israel. Run time: 17 min. Documentary.

David Perlov's camera travels over photographs and focuses on faces that are no more: candles, tears of crying women, and memories are the images of the beginning of the film. The history of the Shoah is revealed in a condensed, intensive way: first the memorials for the victims throughout Israel, and then the beginning of it all—the rise of the Nazi regime, the ghetto with its hunger and death, but also its music and theatre, the uprisings, and the death camps. The film concludes with the Eichmann trial, in which Zivia Lubetkin and Yitzchak Zuckerman were among the witnesses.

Requiem dla 500,000 Tysiecy

Director: Jerzy Bossak, Waclav Kazmierczak. Production: Wytwornia Filmow Dokumentalnych. Year: 1963. Country: Poland. Run time: 28 min. Documentary.

This is a collage of photographs of the Warsaw ghetto, shot by Nazis. Several pictures in this film had already been exposed at the time and were used in training the SS and Gestapo. Ironically, some images were considered "too horrible" and were classified in the archives of the Third Reich. The film shows the cynicism of the Nazis in filming the suffering of the Jews. According to the filmmaker, the baroque music accompanying the images is a manner of mourning for the dead.

L'authentique Procès de Carl Emmanuel Jung

Director: Marcel Hanoun. Production: Marcel Hanoun. Year: 1966. Country: France. Run time: 66 min. Documentary.

The "reconstruction" of the trial of an imaginary Nazi criminal for crimes that are very real, through a purely verbal evocation, in defiance of the images shown.

Mord in Frankfurt
Director: Rolf Hädrich. Screenplay: Rolf Hädrich. Production: Westdeutscher Rundfunk. Year: 1968. Country: FRG. Run time: 77 min. Fiction.

The murder of a taxi driver triggers a call for the death penalty. A Polish man is accused, perhaps mistakenly, and meanwhile in a parallel story, rehearsals for the stage play *Die Ermittlung* by Peter Weiss are taking place.

Memory of Justice
Director: Marcel Ophuls. Screenplay: Marcel Ophuls, Frank Hilton. Production: Stuyvesant Films, Polytel International, Visual Programme Systems, BBC. Years. 1973–76. Countries: USA, FRG, UK. Run time: 278 min. (2 parts).

A philosophical reflection on the setting of the Nuremberg trials, their unfolding, and the principles upon which they were established. The film is an enquiry into the relations between the history of modern societies and their notions of justice, of individual destinies, and of collective destinies, allowing reflections on the present and the future.

Hitler, ein Film aus Deutschland
Our Hitler
Director: Hans-Jürgen Syberberg. Screenplay: Hans-Jürgen Syberberg from a script by Helga Beyer and Lydia Pieger. Production: INA, BBC, TMS Film, Westdeutscher Rundfunk. Year: 1977. Country: FRG. Run time: 429 min. (4 parts). Fiction.

In seven hours, Hans-Jürgen Syberberg approaches the character of Hitler and the fantasies and images linked to him. The working title of the film was *Hitler in Us*. The film analyzes the desires, the secret feelings, and the drives of the German people, which all lead to an understanding of the figure of Hitler.

Protokoll
Director: Dieter Wedel. Production: Televersal Hamburg. Year: 1983. Country: FRG. Run time: 120 min. Fiction/ Documentary.

A "live" recording of the performance of a play based on the records of Eichmann's initial interrogation by Avner Less prior to the real trial in Israel, staged by the theatre of the city of Bonn.

Unser Nazi
Notre Nazi
Our Nazi
Director: Robert Kramer. Screenplay: Robert Kramer, Thomas Harlan. Production: B. P. I. Centre Georges Pompidou, Quasar Film, Reass Films. Year: 1984. Countries: FRG, France. Run time: 116 min. Documentary.

During the rehearsals and filming of *Wundkanal*, Robert Kramer filmed the crew, and all children of victims or with a personal link to the period of the film. Kramer documented the ambivalent feelings toward the old man, who inspired kindness and respect even though everyone knew that he did not regret anything and was a mass murderer. It shows the reactions of the crew and the process of making this film, as well as the ethical questions of those who were involved.

Bilder der Welt und Inschrift des Krieges
Director: Harun Farocki. Screenplay: Harun Farocki. Production: Harun Farocki. Year: 1988. Country: FRG. Run time: 75 min. Documentary.

Harun Farocki poses the question of the various uses of photography. What does the photograph of a woman, deported to Auschwitz and shot by an SS officer, convey? What about photographs of Algerian women that show not only the women but also their fear of being identified in photographs? This film raises questions about how war, the production of images, and the industry are linked, and how these images are used; and also returns to aerial photographs of Auschwitz taken by the Allies that were never used to put an end to the Shoah since they were never taken into consideration by the Allies.

A Day in the Warsaw Ghetto: A Birthday Trip in Hell
Director: Jack Kuper. Screenplay: From diaries by Mary Berg, Adam Czerniakow, Chaim A. Kaplan, Michael Lewin, and Emmanuel Ringelblum. Production: Kuper Productions Ltd. Year: 1991. Country: Canada. Run time: 30 min. Documentary.

Heinz Joest, a German soldier, decides to spend his birthday in the Warsaw ghetto taking photographs of the people who live there, although it is forbidden to do so. Jack Kuper, a filmmaker who survived the Shoah himself, has woven a documentary from these horrific images, adding Yiddish music and writings found in diaries of ghetto residents. In the schools and places of worship, the Jewish spirit endures in the face of impossible odds. In spite of their miserable lives, the starving residents manage to find some humor and a sense of community in this horrible existence.

In Memory
Director: Abraham Ravett. Screenplay: Abraham Ravett. Year: 1993. Country: USA. Run time: 13 min. Essay.

This archival montage film about the Lodz ghetto and documentary scenes is accompanied by a funeral hymn. It became an homage to the filmmaker's family and all the victims of Nazism.

Don't Touch My Holocaust
Al Tigu Li B'shoah
Director: Asher Tlalim. Production: SET Productions. Year: 1994. Country: Israel. Run time: 140 min. Documentary.

A film adaptation of the prize-winning play *Arbeit Macht Frei*, produced in Israel. The play was also staged in Berlin and the film shows the reactions of German spectators to this provocative thesis on the Shoah. The question raised is: What significance does the mass murder of Jews have for the second generation living in Israel?

Auschwitz. Fünf Tage im November
Directors: Cilly Kugelmann, Hanno Loewy, Ronny Loewy. Production: Tele Potsdam Fernsehproduktion for 3SAT. Year: 1994–95. Country: Germany. Run time: 37 min. Documentary.

The creators of the film describe five days in November 1994 at the concentration camp at Auschwitz, which is now a museum. Auschwitz was both a forced labor camp and an extermination camp. But what is Auschwitz today? Auschwitz is a cemetery, a didactic exhibit, a memorial, and a place of pilgrimage. The complexity of this place elicits historical debate and questions the manner in which to consider and remember it.

Die Grube
Director: Karl Fruchtmann. Screenplay: Karl Fruchtmann. Production: Radio Bremen. Year: 1995. Country: Germany. Run time: 90 min. Documentary/Fiction.

This drama focuses on the fate of ninety Jewish children, whose parents were shot during the massacre of nine hundred Jews in Bjelaja Zerkow (near Kiev) in 1941. The children are imprisoned because the Nazis were occupied with other assassinations. Helmut Großcurt (Generalstabsoffizier) tries to prevent the murder of these children—in vain. The order had been given. These events were reconstructed from files, the statements of the officers responsible, and witness accounts.

La Mémoire Est-elle Soluble Dans L'eau . . . ?
Does Memory Dissolve in Water?
Director: Charles Najman. Production: SEM. Year: 1996. Country: France. Run time: 95 min.

The director films his mother, who, along with other Shoah survivors, is experiencing a spa treatment in Evian offered to the deportees as compensation by the German government. The individual and collective rapport with past experiences in this unusual context is the occasion for a light and tender reflection for this filmmaker.

Drancy Avenir
Director: Arnaud des Pallières. Screenplay: Arnaud des Pallières. Production: Les films du Requin. Year: 1997. Country: France. Run time: 84 min. Essay.

Drancy Avenir combines three stories that can be considered documentary, fiction, and poetic essay. The last survivor among the deportees in Drancy wonders about the nature of the legacy of memory he is capable of leaving. A young historian inquires about what came of the location of this camp and the manner in which the past haunts it at present. The captain of a ship outlines a meditation on the conquering civilization. Obsessive train traffic carries images of the past and current visions in a suggestive manner that allows each viewer his own present reflection.

Vivant Qui Passe. Auschwitz 1943-Theresienstadt 1944 ˉ
Director: Claude Lanzmann. Production: La Sept, Les Films Aleph, MTM Cineteve. Year: 1997. Country: France. Run time: 66 min. Documentary.

The film is based on an interview Claude Lanzmann had with Maurice Rossel, a Swiss army officer, while he was making *Shoah* in 1979. During World War II, Rossel was sent to Berlin as delegate of the International Red Cross, and was the only foreigner allowed to visit Auschwitz concentration camp in 1943. There he was given a warm welcome by the camp commander but did not find anything serious to add to his official report based on what he had seen "with his own eyes." In 1944, Rossel visited the Theresienstadt concentration camp. Beyond complicity and complacency, the film reveals the unreliable nature of witness observations.

Mendel Lebt
Director: Heinz-Dieter Grabe. Production: Zweites Deutsches Fernsehen. Year: 1999. Country: Germany. Run time: 98 min. Documentary.

In 1971, Heinz-Dieter Grabe shot his first film, *Mendel Schain-felds Zweite Reise Nach Deutschland* with Mendel Szajnfeld. Szajnfeld, a Jew from Poland, was unable to work because he was handicapped. He almost died because of poor health resulting from his imprisonment at the Plaszow and Tschenstochau camps. Twenty-seven years later, Grabe and Szajnfeld met again in Oslo. Grabe accompanied Szajnfeld on a journey to Auschwitz where Szajnfeld told visitors about his experience.

Un Specialiste, Portrait d'un Criminel Moderne
The Specialist: Portrait of a Modern Criminal
Director: Eyal Sivan. Screenplay: Rony Brauman, Eyal Sivan. Production: Momento, Bremer Institut Film Fernsehen, Westdeutscher Rundfunk, Lotus Film. Year: 1999. Countries: France, Israel. Run time: 123 min. Fiction.

Sivan uses footage of the Eichmann trial to portray a man with no regrets and no remorse, who never doubted his actions, in spite of the fact that survivors testified to the suffering he inflicted upon them. Sivan intervened upon the way events transpired in the real trial through montage, and he modified some images with computer manipulations.

Das Himmler Projekt
The Himmler Project
Director: Romuald Karmakar. Screenplay: Romuald Karmakar. Production: Pantera Film GmbH. Year: 1999–2000. Country: Germany. Run time: 185 min. Fiction.

Actor Manfred Zapatka reads a speech given by Heinrich Himmler, Reichsführer of the SS, to SS generals before the camera, without any attempt to imitate or "give the tone" of the original speech. This "flat" delivery of the speech allows us to hear in greater depth the monstrosity of what is being said, while at the same time questioning the conditions in which these ideas were received at the time. Himmler's speeches were recorded on gramophone machines, typed up by his staff, and presented for correction. The corrected versions were then filed away in the SS archives. They were subsequently used as evidence at the Nuremberg Trials and presumably as a source for many quotes in history books. The film uses one recording, the Posen speech of October 4, 1943. All the mistakes in sentence structure, omitted verbs, and the changes in rhythm were kept.

La Dernière Lettre
The Last Letter
Director: Frederick Wiseman. Screenplay: A text drawn from "Vie et Destin" by Vassili Grossman, translated by Veronique Aubouy. Produc-

tion: Ideale Audience, Arte, Comédie Française. Year: 2002. Country: France. Run time: 62 min.

On a theatre stage, actress Catherine Samie speaks the words from the letter of a Jewish woman writing for the last time to her son. She is experiencing the Nazi terror and will soon be deported. The actual text from this letter filled with love, compassion, and terror can be found in chapter 17 of *Life and Fate*, the great novel written by Vassili Grossman.

Eichmann—The Secet Memoirs
Director: Nissim Mossek, Alan Rosenthal. Production: Biblical Productions, Blue Rose Productions in cooperation with EO Television, DRT, MTV, Budapest. Year: 2002. Countries: Israel, Holland. Run time: 112 min. Documentary.

Forty years after his trial and execution, this documentary takes the point of view of Adolf Eichmann to attempt to understand how this ordinary civil servant was able to attain the responsibility of implementing the Final Solution, what motivated his actions, and how this limited mind was able to accomplish crimes of such magnitude.

Imaginary Witness: Hollywood and the Holocaust
Director: Daniel Anker. Production: Anker Productions. Year: 2004. Country: USA. Run time: 92 min. Documentary.

This film analyzes filmmakers' reactions in the United States to Germany's persecution of Jews before, during, and after the war. It explores how films have shaped our perception of the Shoah in examining Hollywood's responses to the horrors of Nazi Germany. Beginning with American ambivalence and denial during the height of Nazism, the film goes on to explore the silence of the postwar years and the impact of television. Rarely seen footage, firsthand accounts by directors, actors, writers, and producers, as well as clips from such films as *The Great Dictator*, *The Pawnbroker*, *Sophie's Choice*, and *Schindler's List* are also included.

La Langue Ne Ment Pas
Language Does Not Lie
Director: Stan Neuman. Screenplay: Stan Neuman, based on the notebooks of Viktor Klemperer. Production: Les Films d'Ici (Richard Copans). Year: 2004. Country: France. Run time: 79 min. Essay.

This film revives the extraordinary work on language transformed by totalitarian regimes, voluntarily and involuntarily, in order to achieve their ends of oppression and destruction. This work was accomplished, during the reign of Nazism, by writer and philologist Viktor Klemperer.

Land der Vernichtung
Director: Romuald Karmakar. Screenplay: Romuald Karmakar. Production: Pantera Films. Year: 2003–04. Country: Germany. Run time: 127 min.

Romuald Karmakar did research for a fiction film on the involvement of Hamburg's police battalion 101 in the extermination of the 1.7 million Polish Jews between 1942 and 1943. From this research, filmed with a simple mini DV-camera, the documentary film project evolved: it shows the location of the massacre and shots of the Belzec, Sobibor, Treblinka, and Majdanek extermination camps. Karmakar spoke with witnesses and survivors and attempts to describe how the past influences present life in the area. In the most memorable scene, he walks along the former wall of an extermination camp, counting each step.

Respite
Director: Harun Farocki. Production: Jeonju International Film Festival. Year: 2007. Country: Korea. Run time: 40 min. Essay.

Farocki presents a montage of scenes filmed at the Westerbork camp, and then, through his commentary and other montage effects, reveals the various manners in which one should read these images and questions their various meanings.

Television Programs

This is Your Life: Hanna Bloch Kohner
Director: Axel Gruenberg. Production: Ralph Edwards Productions for NBC. Year: 1953. Country: USA. Run time: 30 min.

Commissioned by the United Jewish Appeal, this is the story of Hanna Bloch Kohner, a survivor of the Shoah who lived in Los Angeles after World War II.

Judgment at Nuremberg
Director: George Roy Hill. Production: CBS. Year: 1959. Country: USA. Run time: 90 min. Fiction.

This is a courtroom drama about the trial of German judges in Nuremberg in 1947. Excerpts from films made of the liberation of the camps are included in this docudrama. Telford Taylor (the key American prosecuting attorney at the Nuremberg trials) presents the prologue of the film.

Engineer of Death: The Eichmann Story
Director: Paul Bogart. Production: Robert E. Costello, Talent Associates, CBS. Year: 1960. Country: USA. Run time: 60 min. TV Series, Documentary.

This is the story of the life, career, and capture of Adolf Eichmann. A great deal of archive newsreel material is incorporated, including footage of Dachau concentration camp. The film attempts to create a psychological history of the man. This program was broadcast on the "Armstrong Circle Theater" series.

Die Ermittlung
Director: Lothar Bellag, Ingrid Fausak Bellag. Screenplay: Peter Weiss. Production: Fernsehen der DDR, Akademie der Künste. Year: 1966. Country: GDR. Run time: 144 min. (cinema), 137 min. (TV). Fiction.

This film was a televised presentation of Peter Weiss's play, *Die Ermittlung* (*The Investigation*), which deals with the Frankfurt Auschwitz trial. The witnesses and accused were played by prominent East German actors.

Die Ermittlung
Director: Peter Schulze-Rohr. Screenplay: Peter Weiss. Production: Norddeutscher Rundfunk. Year: 1966. Country: FRG. Run time: 150 min. Fiction.

Another television presentation of the Peter Weiss play dealing with the Frankfurt Auschwitz trial. This is the West German version.

Insight: Edith Stein Story
Director: Jim Johnson. Production: CBS. Year: 1967. Country: USA. Run time: 26 min. Fiction.

An episode of the long-running American Family series "Insight." Edith Stein was born into a Jewish family but then converted to Catholicism in 1922 and became a nun. Nevertheless, she was deported to Auschwitz where she was murdered in 1944.

The World at War: Genocide: 1941–1945
Director: Michael Darlow. Production: Thames Television. Year: 1975. Country: UK. Run time: 50 min. Documentary.

The story of Hitler's Final Solution starting with anti-Semitism in Germany in the 1920s and ending in 1945 when the concentration camps were liberated. It contains interviews with Germans and Jewish survivors as well as archival footage.

Holocaust. The Story of the Family Weiss
Director: Marvin Chomsky. Screenplay: Gerald Green. Production: NBC. Year: 1978. Country: USA. Run time: 414 min. (4 parts). TV series, Fiction.

This film tells about the persecution of the Jews through the story of two very different families. The Weiss family are Jewish doctors and become the victims; the Dorf family, in which the parents are lawyers, become the persecutors. Mister Dorf is transformed from simply being a partisan of the Führer to becoming an active member of the Nazi party under Heydrich. The story spans the entire Nazi period, from the first persecutions to the deportations, the massacres, and finally the surrender of the Third Reich. This series played an important role in the collective realization of the extent of the Shoah tragedy, especially in the United States and Germany.

The Final Solution—Auschwitz. A World at War
Special
Director: Michael Darlow. Production: Thames Television for ITV. Year: 1979. Country: UK. Run time: 180 min. (4 parts). Documentary.

This was an expanded version of the Genocide episode from the series "The World at War," dealing with the entire history of the Nazi plans for the extermination of European Jews. It attempts to examine the theory and practice of genocide, as embodied in the Nazi doctrine. It analyzes the evolution of the growth of Nazi racial policies, and shows how, from 1939 to 1941, a conventional war became a systematic drive to murder civilians. It then describes the death factories and the extermination camps, and ends with a sequence trying to explain why the killing machine continued to function unhindered for so long.

Inside the Third Reich
Director: Marvin Chomsky. Screenplay: E. Jack Neuman from a book by Albert Speer. Production: Circle Films, American Broadcasting Company. Year: 1982. Country: USA. Run time: 250 min. Fiction.

An account of the relationship between Adolf Hitler and Albert Speer during the Third Reich. It examines Speer's rise from obscurity within the Nazi party ranks leading to his days of fame in the 1930s when he became responsible for building several Nazi monuments. The second portion of the film focuses on Speer's tenure as minister of armaments during World War II, when he became one of the primary motivators in keeping Hitler's war machine going.

Nazi-Hunter: The Beate Klarsfeld Story
Director: Michael Lindsay-Hogg. Screenplay: Frédéric Hunter. Production: Orion Television, William Kayden Productions. Year: 1986. Country: USA. Run time: 100 min. Fiction.

A portrait of lawyer Beate Klarsfeld, who, with the help of her (Jewish) husband, dedicated her life to tracking down war criminals. At great personal risk to herself, she travelled from Europe to South America to bring Klaus Barbie, the "Butcher of Lyon," to justice. While this film was being shot, the real Beate Klarsfeld was doing everything in her power to expose the war crimes committed by UN Secretary General Kurt Waldheim.

Die Geschwister Oppermanns
The Oppermanns

Director: Egon Monk. Screenplay: Egon Monk, from the novel by Lion Feuchtwanger. Production: Gyula Trebitsch Productions for Zweites Deutsches Fernsehen, Österreichischer Rundfunk, Schweizerische Radio- und Fernsehgesellschaft. Year: 1986. Country: FRG. Run time: 225 min. Fiction.

Based on the novel by Lion Feuchtwanger, this film tells the story of a wealthy and assimilated German Jewish family that was destroyed by Nazi ideology and their expropriation policies. One of the Oppermann brothers is portrayed as a naïve German who becomes the subject of Nazi tyranny. The film includes some documentary footage.

Lodz Ghetto

Director: Alan Adelson, Kate Taverna. Production: Jewish Heritage. Year: 1988. Country: USA. Run time: 103 min. Documentary.

Constructed as fiction and using a screenplay comprising a number of actual documents and reconstitutions, the film stages, as in a reality show, the forced labor that Polish and Czech Jews experienced in the Lodz ghetto until they were deported to the extermination camps in 1944. The film owes a great deal to its unusual blend of scrupulously reconstructed historical documents and a fiction-like dramatic structure. The ghetto story is told using one thousand still photographs made at great risk by ghetto dwellers, color slides taken by an unknown German photographer, and six minutes of authentic filmed images made in the ghetto by the Nazis. Excerpts from diaries are read in voiceover.

War and Remembrance

Director: Dan Curtis, Tommy Groszman. Production: ABC. Year: 1988. Country: USA. Run time: 1,620 min. Television series.

This gigantic series about World War II includes reconstructions of scenes about the extermination in the Nazi death camps that are as spectacular as they are objectionable.

Tsvi Nussbaum. A Boy from Warsaw
Director: Ilkka Ahjopalo. Screenplay: Matti-Juhani Karila. Production: MTV, Gamma TV. Year: 1990. Countries: Finland, France. Run time: 50 min. Documentary.

In a photograph we see a little boy, his arms raised in surrender, as a German soldier trains his machine gun on him. This very famous photo has come to symbolize the suffering of the entire Jewish people during the Shoah. Who was this little boy? Did he survive the war? Where was this photo taken and under what circumstances? This film about the life of Tsvi Nussbaum answers all these questions. He is now Dr. Nussbaum, a physician residing in New York State.

Mishpat Kastner
The Kastner Trial
Director: Uri Barbash. Screenplay: Motti Lerner. Production: Israel Broadcasting Authority. Year: 1995. Country: Israel. Run time: 180 min. (3 parts). Fiction.

Rudolf Kastner was a Hungarian Zionist leader, who, by negotiating with Adolf Eichmann, was able to save some 1,700 Jewish lives. Many of his friends and family were able to leave Budapest for Switzerland in August 1944 on "Kastner's Train." In 1953, Kastner ran for the Knesset and was accused of Nazi collaboration. He sued for libel.

The Lost Children of Berlin
Director: Elizabeth McIntyre. Production: Fogwood Films Ltd., Spielberg Survivors of the Shoah foundation. Year: 1997. Country: USA. Run time: 50 min. Documentary.

Fifty Holocaust survivors, students of the last Jewish school in Berlin before the Gestapo closed it in 1942, returned to the reopened school in 1996 to share their accounts of what Jewish life was like before, during, and after the brutal reign of the Third Reich. Anthony Hopkins hosts this emotional program.

Hitler's Holocaust
Part 1: Manhunt
Part 2: Decision
Part 3: Ghetto
Part 4: Murder Factory
Part 5: Resistance
Part 6: Liberation
Director: Maurice Philip Remy, Guido Knopp. Production: MPR Film und Fernseh Produktion GmbH, Zweites Deutsches Fernsehen, ARTE

G.E.I.E., Phoenix / History Channel, Channel Four TV, EO Television, Österreichischer Rundfunk, SBS. Year: 2000. Country: USA. Run time: 270 min. (6 parts). Documentary.

The series is divided into six episodes. It covers the Nazi invasion of the Soviet Union in 1941 and the cooperation of some Soviets, Hitler's rise to power, and the restrictions for Jews leading to their transportation to ghettos and deportation. One episode focuses on Auschwitz as the largest extermination camp. Resistance and uprisings in the ghettos or in camps are mentioned. In the last episode, the final year of World War II is discussed. Even when the Nazi empire was being invaded on two fronts, the mass murder of Jews and other "undesirables" continued. Throughout the series, most of the interviewees (both Jewish and non-Jewish) claim that they knew nothing, or at most they heard vague rumors, of the genocide until they saw overwhelming evidence.

Julius Streicher

Director: Michael Kloft. Production: Spiegel TV. Year: 2000. Country: Germany. Run time: 34 min. Documentary.

Although Julius Streicher was not acknowledged by high-ranking Nazis Joseph Goebbels and Hermann Goering, he was one of the most influential people in the Third Reich: Streicher was head of the anti-Semitic propaganda magazine *Der Stürmer* and was known for his very brutal and corrupt regime as Gauleiter of Franconia. To the Allies, he was the symbol of Nazi hatred against Jews. In 1946, he was sentenced to death at the Nuremberg trial. Archival footage, photographs, and documents complete this documentary.

Uprising

Director: Jon Avnet. Screenplay: Paul Brickman, Jon Avnet. Production: Avnet/Kerner Productions, Raffaella Productions. Year: 2001. Country: USA. Run time: 177 min. Fiction /TV Series.

Jon Avnet used restored archival documents of the Warsaw ghetto for this film. In this way, he reconstructs the story of Marek Edelman and his role in the rebellion of 1943. The film begins with the establishment of anti-Semitic laws in Poland, leading to the imprisonment of half a million Polish Jews in the ghetto. It shows the daily struggle against hunger and disease and the fear of German "deportations to the east"; and then focuses on the planning of the uprising and the uprising itself that began on April 19, 1943. The handful of fighters who had weapons took them to shelters constructed by the inhabitants, giving the uprising the advantage of defensive positions.

The Ninth Day
Der Neunte Tag
Director: Volker Schlöndorff. Screenplay: Eberhard Görner, Andreas Pflüger. Production: Provobis Film, Bayerischer Rundfunk, Videopress S.A., BeltFilm s.r.o., Arte Deutschland TV. Year: 2003–04. Countries: Germany and Luxembourg. Run time: 97 min.

In this film, the abbot of Luxembourg, Henri Kremer, has just been temporarily released from the Dachau concentration camp. Gebhardt, the fanatical Gestapo chief of Luxembourg, gives him the choice of either joining forces with the Nazis and remaining a free man or being thrown back into prison. For nine days, the Nazi and the priest carry out a fierce battle of ideologies.

Documents from the Period: Amateur Films and Unedited Footage

Aprilboykott und Bücherverbrennung 1933 in Deutschland
(possible title)
April Boycott and Book Burning 1933 in Germany
(possible title)
Production: Amateur film. Year: 1933. Country: Germany. Run time: 2 min. Documentary.

Joseph Goebbels, Reichsminister für Volksaufklärung und Propaganda, holds a speech at a mass rally in Berlin's Lustgarten for the Jewish boycott on April 1, 1933. It contains footage of the book burning on May 10, 1933.

Brand der Synagoge von Bühl Am 10. November 1938
(possible title)
Burning of the Bühl Synagogue on the 10th of November 1938
(possible title)
Production: Amateur film. Year: 1938. Country: Germany. Run time: 2 min. Documentary.

The synagogue in Bühl is burning and fire engines only prevent the spread of the fire to nearby houses.

Wien 1938 (possible title)
Vienna 1938 (possible title)
Production: Amateur film. Year: 1938. Country: USA. Run time: 2 min. Documentary.

Footage filmed by American doctor Monson during a visit to Vienna after the *Anschluss* in the summer of 1938. It shows swastikas and anti-Semitic graffiti in the city in color.

Ghetto Reichshof (possible title)
Production: Amateur film. Year: 1940. Country: Germany. Run time: 9 min. Documentary.

Ghetto Rzeszow (Reichshof) during the German occupation in Spring 1940. This documentary shows scenes of daily life in the ghetto: a boy begging, people passing by ruins, ghetto inhabitants wearing armbands, the marketplace. At the German administration building, employees have dinner and mock Jewish religious rituals, accompanied by a gypsy playing the violin.

Das Jüdische Ghetto im Regierungsbezirk Zichenau 1940
(possible title)
The Jewish Ghetto in the District of Zichenau 1940
(possible title)
Production: Amateur film. Year: 1940. Country: Germany. Run time: 8 min. Documentary.

Amateur film made in the ghetto of Zichenau in 1940, showing scenes from daily life: living conditions, work, people in the streets, and a funeral ceremony.

Konzentrationslager Posen (possible title)
Concentration Camp Posen (possible title)
Production: Amateur film. Year: 1940. Country: Germany. Documentary.

Amateur film showing the entrance to the transition camp for deportees at Zabikowo, near Posen. The prisoners themselves are not seen in this film.

Bruiloft van Kalken (possible title)
Van Kalken Wedding (possible title)
Production: Amateur film. Year: 1941. Country: The Netherlands. Run time: 1 min. Documentary.

Footage of the Van Kalken wedding. The couple descends from a car and enters a building accompanied by their guests. Anne Frank watches the scene from the window of her apartment at 37 Merwedeplein.

Judenexekution in Libau 1941 (possible title)
Execution of Jews in Libau 1941 (possible title)
Camera: Reinhard Wiener. Production: Amateur film. Year: 1941. Country: Germany. Run time: 2 min. Documentary.

Amateur film made by navy soldier Reinhard Wiener (Marine-Flak-Abt. 707) of mass executions of Jews in Libau in August 1941. Jews climb down from carts; Latvian minders force them toward a garbage dump where they are to be executed. Numerous Wehrmacht members are watching. The film was used in the trial against Rosenstock and others for assassination and other crimes in Hannover in 1965.

Judenpogrom am 1. Juli 1941 in Lemberg
(Originaldeutscher 8 MM. Film über Greuel Gegen Juden)
(possible title)
Original German Film of Atrocities Against Jews
(possible title)
Production: Amateur film. Year: 1941. Country: Germany. Run time: 2 min. Documentary.

Pogrom in Lemberg on July 1, 1941, showing mistreatment of individuals by the Gestapo and German military units apparently in the act of destroying the Jewish ghetto. German-made motion picture seized by U.S. forces from SS barracks near Augsburg. The film was used as evidence at the Nuremberg trial.

Ghetto on Kutno (possible title)
Ghetto pf Kutno (possible title)
Production: Amateur film. Year: 1941. Country: Germany. Run time: 16 min. Documentary.

Resettlement of Jews to the Kutno ghetto overseen by the SS.

Mogilew. Tötung von Menschen mit Motorabgasen im September 1941
(possible title)
Mogilew. Killing of People with Motor Exhausts in September 1941
(possible title)
Production: Amateur film. Year: 1941. Country: Germany. Run time: 1 min. Documentary.

This film shows the killing of prisoners with exhaust fumes from motorcars in September 1941 in Mogilew. At a 1967 trial in Stuttgart against Albert Widmann, which focused on the killing of prisoners with exhaust fumes, documents and eyewitness accounts confirmed what is shown in the film. This film was used in *Nuremberg and Its Lesson*.

Transport von Juden zum Krakauer Ghetto (possible title)
Transport of Jews to the Krakow Ghetto (possible title)
Production: Amateur film. Year: 1941. Country: Germany. Run time: 3 min. Documentary.

Jews from Krakow bring their belongings to the ghetto on horse-drawn carts or on their backs. We see people crossing the bridge over the Weichsel, school children carrying chairs, a girl scouring the garbage for anything useful. Passersby wear Star of David armbands. Signs on a streetcar read: "For Jews" and "For non-Jews."

Das Ghetto in Brzeziny (possible title)
The Ghetto of Brzeziny (possible title)
Production: Amateur film. Year: 1942. Country: Germany. Run time: 6 min. Documentary.

Shots of the ghetto in Brzeziny (Löwenstadt) in the Wartheland district of Reichsgau, during the winter. Poorly dressed people shiver, fetch water, crack the ice. We see the exterior of the ruined synagogue. Public executions of ten ghetto inhabitants for illegal kosher butchering in Welungen (Wielun). Others are forced to watch the scene, standing around the gibbet. Delinquents are directed to the gibbet by the Jewish patrol, where they are about to be hanged.

Ghetto in Dombrowa und Bedzin (possible title)
Ghetto w Dnbrowie Górniczej i Bedzinie (possible title)
Jews in Dombrova, Poland (possible title)
The Ghetto in Dombrowa and Bendzin (possible title)
Production: Amateur film. Year: 1942. Country: Poland. Run time: 9 min. Documentary.

Footage shot in the Dombrowa (Dombrowa Górnicza) and Bendzin (Bedzin) ghettos. Exteriors show faces, crowds, and Jews with stars on their clothes, while interior shots feature men at sewing machines and women sewing by hand.

Theresienstadt 1942 (possible title)
Director: Irena Dodalova. Year: 1942. Country: Germany. Documentary (fragment).

By order of the SS, prisoner Irena Dodalova was given the role of director on this film. Production took place in October and November 1942 in Theresienstadt and also partly in Prague. Besides Dodalova, at least a dozen Jewish prisoners were obliged to take part in the production. The film itself was lost, but some footage was found in 1994, containing scenes from the ghetto; it may have been shot for Dodalova's film. The scene shows daily life in the ghetto and includes appearances from famous prisoners, including Otto Neumann, Karel Svenk, and Kamila Rosenbaumova.

Warschau, Ghetto, März 1942
Production: Amateur film. Year: 1942. Country: Germany. Run time: 5 min. Documentary.

A shot of a wall with the inscription: "Quarantine. Restricted area. No trespassing." The camera tracks down the street. Members of the Jewish patrol open a gate, carts and rickshaws transporting ghetto inhabitants pass, peddlers sell used clothes.

Zusammenlegung der Letzten Juden aus Dresden on das
Lager am Hellerberg am 23. und 24. November 1942
(possible title)
Regroupment of the Last Jews of Dresden to the
Hellerberg Camp on the 23rd and 24th of November 1942
(possible title)
Director: Erich Höhne. Production: Zeiss-Ikon A.G. Year: 1942. Country: Germany. Run time: 22 min. Documentary.

Featuring narrated sequences from November 23 and 24, 1942, this documentary shows the eviction of Jews from Dresden's "Jew houses" under the supervision of Gestapo officers, the delousing and medical examinations in the "State Decontamination Institution," and the establishment of the Hellerberg camp in North Dresden. The Hellerberg Jew Camp was intended to provide forced labor for the Goehle factories of the Zeiss-Ikon Corporation. It also served as a collection camp for imminent deportations to Auschwitz.

Deportation von Juden aus dem Weissmeergebiet
(possible title)
Deportation of Jews from the Black Sea Area (possible title)
Production: Bulgarsko Selo for the Kommissariat für Judenfragen. Year: 1943. Countries: Germany, Belarus. Run time: 6 min. Documentary.

The deportation of twelve thousand Jews from Macedonia between March 4–22, 1943—first by truck to the port of Lom and then by ship.

Westerbork (possible title)
Production: Lagerkommandantur Westerbork. Year: 1944. Country: Germany. Run time: 55 min. Documentary.

Documentary film material made upon the order of the camp commander in the Dutch concentration camp of Westerbork. The film material, which is only available in unedited form, shows us daily life in the camp and the loading of prisoners into railroad carts for transportation to Theresienstadt and Auschwitz.

Zsidók Deportásá 1944 (possible title)
Judendeportation in Budapest (possible title)
Production: Oberkommando der Wehrmacht. Year: 1944. Country: Germany. Run time: 1 min. Documentary.

Carriage by carriage, a camera follows a deportation convoy of Hungarian Jews. On October 17 and 18, 1944, men, women, and children carrying the Star of David march through the streets with their arms raised. They are accompanied by Hungarian police as civilians look on, trams pass, and Hungarian soldiers and civilians sit on sacks in trailers pulled by tractors.

Bilder aus der Anstalt Meseritz-Obrawalde, den Konzentrationslagern Auschwitz, Majdanek u.a. nach Kriegsende 1945 (possible title)
Images of Meseritz-Obrawalde, of the Concentration Camps Auschwitz, Majdanek, and Others after the War (possible title)
Year: 1945. Country: Germany. Run time: 4 min. Documentary.

Compilation of documentary footage from the Meseritz-Obrawalde Institute and Majdanek and Auschwitz concentration camps after they were liberated in 1945.

Zachor
Director: Saul Goskind. Production: Amateur film. Year: 1946. Country: Poland. Run time: 8 min. Documentary.

Shots of the Warsaw ghetto in ruins, the cemeteries of Ansky, Kaminska, Zamenhof, and Ashkenas, the meeting of the Vaad Kihilot Kadoshot in Poland, Klausner handing a Torah scroll to a rabbi, an empty synagogue, a burnt Torah scroll, Nazi footage of deportation, people behind a concentration camp fence, the ruins of Warsaw, street signs standing amid the ruins, and memorial monuments.

Nazi Propaganda

Kaufmann, Nicht Händler
Director: Ernst Kochel. Production: Universum-Film AG for the Hauptamt für Handwerk und Handel der NSDAP. Year: 1933–36. Country: Germany. Run time: 23 min. Documentary (Nazi propaganda).

A recording of the speech by Theodor Adrian von Renteln, president of the chamber of commerce and head of the National Socialist Organization for Commerce, Craft, and Industry (*Nazionalsozialistischen Handels-, Handwerks- u. Gewerbeorganisation* or NS HAGO) at the meeting of the German Chamber of Commerce in Braunschweig on November 19, 1933. He talks about a "plague of locusts of Jews immigrating from Eastern Europe" who destroy commerce, rape German culture, blemish the sciences, and exploit the workers. The film includes anti-Semitic caricatures and short animations as well as archival footage. It ends with images from the Nuremberg party congress.

Erbkrank
The Hereditary Defective
Director: Herbert Gerdes. Production: NSDAP, Reichsleitung, Rassenpolitisches Amt. Year: 1936. Country: Germany. Run time: 23 min. Documentary (Nazi propaganda).

Nazi propaganda film promoting "Hereditary health." The narrative denounces "Jewish liberal ideas" that care more for the "Unuseful" than for healthy members of the German nation. The argument is illustrated with the bad living conditions of proletarian children and with scenes from mental hospitals. Intertitles claim that the percentage of Jews among the mentally ill is remarkably high.

Juden Ohne Maske
Directors: Walter Böttcher, Leo von der Schmiede. Screenplay: Leo de Laforgue. Production: NSDAP, Reichspropagandaleitung, Amtsleitung Film. Year: 1937. Country: Germany. Run time: 36 min. Documentary (Nazi propaganda).

This fragment of an anti-Semitic propaganda film features a voiceover agitating against the alleged Jewish influence on German film, which is said to glorify crime. "The Jews fight to destroy everything that is fine and good in this world." Scenes from such feature films as *Der Mörder Dimitri Karamasoff* by Fedor Ozep and *M* by Fritz Lang are used as "evidence" for this thesis.

Beseitigung der Brandruine der Dresdner Synagoge unter Mitwirkung der Technischen Nothilfe Dresden
Removal of the Ruins of the Dresden Synagogue with Help of Dresden's Emergency Service Organization
Production: Technische Nothilfe Dresden. Year: 1938. Country: Germany. Run time: 10 min. Documentary.

This film shows the preparation for the destruction of Dresden synagogue. Officers of the Wehrmacht watch the blasting of the staircase. A wagon is loaded with charred debris.

Synagoge in München (possible title)
Synagogue in Munich (possible title)
Production: NSDAP. Year: 1938. Country: Germany. Run time: 8 min.
Documentary.

Footage of the demolition of the Munich synagogue, built in 1887.
Demolition began on June 9, 1938. The film was produced after the first
blast and all shots are taken from the same angle.

Polenreise des Dr. Frank (possible title)
Dr. Frank's Tour of Poland (possible title)
Production: Deutsche Arbeitsfront, Propaganda-Amt, Abt. Film. Year: 1939.
Country: Germany. Run time: 15 min. Documentary (Nazi propaganda).

General Governor Hans Frank visits occupied Poland in
November 1939. The film contains shots of Krakow after the installa-
tion of the general government on November 7, 1939. Jewish citizens are
shown while the voiceover comments about Krakow being a German city
that had been "swamped by types from the East" who came to dominate
the town.

Der Ewige Jude
Director: Fritz Hippler. Production: Deutsche Filmherstellung und Ver-
wertung. Year: 1940. Country: Germany. Run time: 67 min. Documentary (Nazi propaganda).

This documentary, shown in different versions in the various occupied territories, was one of the main tools for spreading the anti-Semitic
stereotypes propagated by the Nazis: Poland as a "nesting place for Juda-
ism," the comparison of Jews with rats, the difference between Jews and
Aryans, the Jewish influence on the economy, culture, and politics, and a
detailed description of Jewish religious practice. Also included are clips
from Hitler's Reichstag speech on January 20, 1939, in which he promises the "annihilation of the Jewish race in Europe." It contains footage
from occupied Poland as well as extracts from newsreels, feature and
documentary films, and photographs.

Les Corrupteurs
Director: Pierre Ramelot. Production: Robert Muzard for the Institut
d'études des questions juives. Year: 1941. Country: France. Run time:
27 min. Fiction (Nazi propaganda).

A handful of stars of French cinema took part in this film, a rare
example of overt Nazi propaganda made in France. It aims to portray
the harmful influence of the Jews on society.

Riga nach der Einnahme durch Deutsche Truppen, Juli 1941
(possible title)
Riga after the Takeover by German Troops, July 1941 (possible title)
Production: Heeresfilmstelle. Year: 1941. Country: Germany. Run time: 14 min. Documentary (Nazi propaganda).

Anti-Semitic and anti-Bolshevik commentary. The film shows the citizens of Riga enthusiastically welcoming the invading German troops, while Jewish inhabitants are forced to clean up the city.

Aus Lodz wird Litzmannstadt
Year: 1941–42. Country: Germany. Run time: 26 min. Documentary (Nazi propaganda).

Fragment of a National Socialist propaganda film about "population development in Litzmannstadt," "redevelopment measures," and the resettlement of "ethnic Germans," following the annexation of Lodz (renamed Litzmannstadt by the Germans).

Juden, Läuse, Wanzen (possible title)
Jews, Lice, Bedbugs (possible title)
Production: Film- und Propagandamittel-Vertriebsgesellschaft GmbH. Year: 1941. Country: Germany. Run time: 11 min. Documentary (Nazi propaganda).

Anti-Semitic propaganda on living conditions in a Polish ghetto. It shows the crowded streets and houses, actions against lice, and shots of patients suffering from typhoid.

Jud Süss
Director: Veit Harlan. Screenplay adapted from the novel by Lion Feuchtwanger. Production: Terra-Filmkunst. Year: 1941. Country: Germany. Run time: 98 min. Fiction (Nazi propaganda).

A shameless hijacking of Lion Feuchtwanger's novel of the same name. This production supervised by Goebbels shows the seventeenth-century Jewish counselor to the Duke of Wurtemberg as greedy, salacious, and bloodthirsty. It was one of the Nazis' main propaganda tools, existing in different versions destined for the various occupied countries.

Im Warschauer Ghetto
Production: Amateur film. Year: 1942. Country: Germany. Run time: 10 min. Documentary (Nazi propaganda).

Color footage from the Warsaw ghetto in May 1942, focusing on poor and hungry children.

Das Warschauer Ghetto (possible title)
The Warsaw Ghetto (possible title)
Production: Amateur film. Year: 1942. Country: Poland. Run time: 8 min. Documentary (Nazi propaganda).

Nazi film on living conditions of Jews in the Warsaw ghetto. Contains some scenes also found in *Asien in Mitteleuropa.*

Kampf dem Fleckfieber!—Lehrfilm Nr. 347
Production: Heeresfilmstelle in cooperation with Forschungsgruppe der Militärärztlichen Akademie. Year: 1942. Country: Germany. Run time: 34 min. Documentary (Nazi propaganda).

Anti-Semitic Nazi propaganda film, "instructional film" No. 347, explaining methods to prevent the spread of typhoid. In the introduction of the film, the Polish Jewish population is accused of spreading the disease.

Asien in Mitteleuropa (possible title)
Das Warschauer Ghetto (possible title)
Asia in Central Europe (possible title)
Production: Amateur film. Year: 1942. Country: Germany. Run time: 63 min. Documentary (Nazi propaganda).

A propaganda film, which paints a crassly distorted picture of the worsening living conditions of the Jews in the Warsaw ghetto. The extravagant lives of a few Jews set aside from the majority of the poor are presented as a means of contrast. This fragment, an edited copy without sound, makes its message clear: a Jewish elite lives in luxury despite widespread poverty in the ghetto. The title *Asien in Mitteleuropa* is mentioned in *Azoi iz es gewen. Hurban Warsche* by Jonas Turkow, 1948.

Theresienstadt. Ein Dokumentarfilm aus dem Jüdischen Siedlungsgebiet
Der Führer Schenkt den Juden eine Stadt (working title)
The Führer Offers the Jews a City (working title)
Director: Kurt Gerron. Production: Aktualita Prag for Zentralamt zur Regelung der Judenfrage in Böhmen und Mähren. Year: 1944–45. Countries: Germany, Czechoslovakia. Run time: 95 min. (approx.). Documentary (Nazi propaganda, fragment).

A propaganda film commissioned by the SS and intended to give a false representation of the conditions in Theresienstadt concentration camp and to fool the outside world as to what was really happening to Europe's Jews. The prisoners wear civilian clothing, most of them with the stipulated Star of David, and are shown at work and at play. Many prominent prisoners make an appearance in order to prove to other countries that they are still alive. Nearly all the Jews who took part in the production were deported to Auschwitz and murdered after the film was finished. The film originally ran between ninety and ninety-five minutes, but only 25' 57" have survived.

"Cinematography of the Holocaust"

Documentation and Indexing of Film and Video Documents

RONNY LOEWY

THERE ARE MANY ARCHIVAL LOCATIONS dedicated to the Shoah, as well as others that include a large number of documents on the subject. Among them, the most significant are the Yad Vashem Museum (with the Spielberg Archives) in Jerusalem and the Holocaust Museum in Washington, DC. The Imperial War Museum in London and the Fortunoff Fund at Yale University also have extensive archives. In France, one can find many documents at the Mémorial de la Shoah, the Centre de Documentation Juive Contemporaine, the Musée d'Art et d'Histoire Juive, the Archives Nationales, the Institut d'Histoire du Temps Présent, the Bibliothèque de Documentation Internationale Contemporaine (Université de Nanterre), and, with regard to filmed documents, at the Service des Archives du Film, the Cinémathèque Française, the Cinémathèque de Toulouse, and the Service Cinématographique des Armées (ECPAD). Nevertheless, there is only one resource center that has an exhaustive scope with regard to audiovisual archives tied to the Shoah, and that is the "Cinematography of the Holocaust" program established by the Fritz Bauer Institute in Frankfurt. For this reason, and as a way of presenting fully the objectives and function of the project, we include here a text from 1999, when "Cinematography of the

Holocaust" was going online, and which is based on an original funding application and rationale from its creator Ronny Loewy.

J-M.F.

Translated from the French by Anna Harrison

Preface

In March 1992 the Fritz Bauer Institute[1] invited film directors, film historians, and film archivists from Israel, the United States, and the Federal Republic of Germany to an international expert discussion round. The sole topic was the establishment of the project "Cinematography of the Holocaust: Documentation and Record of Cinematic Documents." Starting point for the discussions during this meeting was the recognition of the growing, complementary role in academia, the media, and didactics played by film documents dealing with the Holocaust and the history of National Socialism. The participants acknowledged that neither in Germany nor elsewhere in Europe was a documentation center to be found that could be considered a central archive for film and video material on the history of the Holocaust. A task force was formed to work out suggestions for dealing with this deficit.

In the same year, and under the overall direction of the Fritz Bauer Institute, film archivists and historians and Holocaust researchers were collaborating with *CineGraph e.V., Hamburgisches Centrum für Filmforschung*, the *Deutsches Filminstitut—DIF*, in Frankfurt-am-Main, and the *Deutsches Filmmuseum* in Frankfurt-am-Main on the task of indexing and documenting films dealing with the history and impact of the Holocaust. A database of information on the respective film documents is being compiled within the framework of the "Cinematography of the Holocaust" project.

Since November 2000, a first comprehensive store of data has been published on the Internet. The information system of the "Cinematography of the Holocaust" then accessible to the public will have an infrastructure that is transparent for users with different interests; it will be at the disposal of both the general public and particular disciplines (contemporary history, film studies, film history, art history, literary science, psychology, Holocaust Studies) of filmmakers and television journalists, publicists, educators, and artists.

The Fritz Bauer Institute, founded in 1995, provided the necessary institutional and technical prerequisites for developing the project "Cinematography of the Holocaust." Research began in 1999, and since then a basic collection of data, information, and texts has been compiled. Since December 2000, the database can be accessed on the Internet.

Project Overview

The project "Cinematography of the Holocaust" records and indexes cinematic sources on the history and the impact of the Holocaust. Most of the pertinent information has been obtained from film archives in Germany, in the United States, in Israel, as well as in West and East European countries. Work on this wealth of data and research on its contents has consisted mainly in establishing an "electronic library" of filmographic and written source materials. Furthermore, films and film collections have been included that to date had been poorly or not at all archived and films that to date were not to be found in archives or, where included, were only rudimentarily documented.

Records collected in the database present an extremely heterogeneous and disparate body of material, assorted as to particular topics. All possible information and aspects relevant to research on film history and contemporary history are covered by the database: These include lists and collections of sources on the way films were received, reviewed, and put to use; information on copies, on showings, film reviews, propaganda material, stills, educational materials, censorship reports, and much more.

Data and text processing is being carried out in a relational database system providing links between film title, names of persons, institutional and company names, and bibliographic references. All of these data can be accessed via a subject catalogue and a thesaurus system and can be presented in differentiated combinations.

Establishing the database is at the core of the project and by far its most extensive element. Based on estimates of the amount of material and data in pertinent film archives in Germany and in Israel, and in selected film archives in the United States, database records for approximately eight thousand films should be created.

Project Goals

Academic Goals

In the past ten years, image memory and picture-storing media have become increasingly diversified and accordingly visual historical sources are assuming an ever greater social significance. A particularly precarious situation has evolved in the field of contemporary history, because the humanities traditionally give priority to written documents. Much is thus to be done to catch up on research on filmographic historical sources. The superior value of film documents for research on specific historical aspects is slowly but surely being recognized.

Neither in Germany proper nor elsewhere in Europe is there a documentation center to be found that could satisfy the growing need for visual source materials on the Holocaust and for the high level of source research needed. Researchers on visual sources pertaining to the Holocaust and its consequences have had to turn exclusively to the United States or to Israel. Information on previously unknown or inaccessible film sources will most probably provide an innovative impulse to academic, journalistic, educational, and political research on the Holocaust.

The complexity of the material mirrors the complexity of the subject. The perpetrators did not use cameras to record the brute fact itself, the murdering of people in the death camp gas chambers. Existing film sources thus must be thought of as concentric circles, focusing around the immediate deed, that is, the physical act of killing. The farther away from this focus film sources get, the more they contextualize the bureaucratic and societal processes behind the deeds, the accompanying propaganda, National Socialist disinformation, or, finally, the "working out and dealing with" direct and indirect consequences of the Holocaust until the present day.

Considering the Holocaust a focus by no means implies narrowing the scope of documentation. Rather, it provides a topical and interpretative point of reference for the enormous quantity of relevant materials. Moreover, the word *Holocaust* has established itself, beyond its etymological basis, as the sole internationally recognized term referring to the entire dimension of annihilation the National Socialists were striving for.

Public Access and Usage

"Cinematography of the Holocaust" offers important sources of information for both non-professional and professional researchers interested in film material on the Holocaust. The project's central purpose is to create a transparent infrastructure for a wide range of user interests. Such a database must be internationally accessible via the Internet and bilingual (German and English), and as such of interest to the general public as well as to various academic disciplines (film science, film history, contemporary history, Holocaust Studies).

"Cinematography of the Holocaust" addresses key researchers in the fields of academia, journalism, and education, and enables them to do research and gain information on films with the aid of a widely differentiated keyword system. The intention is to add substantially to the now widely accepted, but limited, collection of film materials on the Holocaust generally used by movie and television producers as well as by teachers.

Public access to the database and its publications must be assured. To this end, early on the project must begin to test and apply state of the art electronic means of distribution. This means, first and foremost, continually developing the configurations necessary for putting "Cinematography of the Holocaust" on the Internet. To date, the data structure applies to textual information only. With time it must be enlarged to include visual materials (stills, film sequences) as well.

Innovative Perspectives

The applicants are well aware of the fact that there exists a decisive criterion in evaluating a film's authenticity as a visual source: knowing where film materials come from and, if possible, having knowledge of how the film came to be made. Thus, a relational link system must be developed to allow researchers to trace back the generic process by which film takes are repeatedly used for compilation and even re-staged. The database's structure with its cross-references between film productions offers researchers primary data. Proof can be found on the one hand that a particular film document includes sequences taken from other films. On the other hand, it is possible to ascertain which film productions used one and the same sequence. Thus, the database also offers extensive information on exploitation and "erosion" of certain frequently used film documents. Detailed information on primary film sources also provides a tool for statistically determining multiple sequence usage and, ultimately, such sequences' "iconography."

The database will shed light on both genesis and previous usage of film traditions. Users will thus have guaranteed data at their disposal for their own further research on the "credibility" of film sequences and their subsequent interpretation.

Existing Material, Present Research Level, Preliminary Activities

Pertinent Film Stock and Collections, Research in German Film Archives

For historical reasons, German film archives have at their disposal mainly film collections on the history leading up to the Holocaust, on the propaganda context in National Socialist Germany and in occupied neighboring countries, and on the impact of the Holocaust in the Allied Zone, in the Federal Republic of Germany, and in the German Democratic Republic. These collections include all areas of film production: feature movies, short films, cinema newsreels (*Wochenschau*), amateur films, and film documentaries (military documentation and films taken during NS trials).

Filmographic and technical processing of the film collection to date has been neither uniform nor, in many cases, transparent. Some film archives have not yet finished computerizing their collections. Most film archives have concentrated on recording their collections for internal purposes only. This has meant indexing and recording contents and technical information, registering usage status, and storing, checking, securing, and working over film material.

The express purpose of the film archives makes it difficult or practically impossible to process film collections according to their contents in the interest of public usage. In accordance with its legal definition, for example, the (German) National Archives Film Archive (*Bundesarchiv*) must concentrate on collecting and securing films of German origin only. The National Archives Film Archive and a number of other film archives belong to the Cinematic Association (*Kinemathekenverband*). Each member has its own interests and preferences, which in turn result in splintered collections and individual archive nomenclature.

Publicly accessible collection lists include only such parts of collections that can be rented out, and these in turn represent but a small fraction of the total. For various reasons, academic researchers, journalists, and teachers find their possibilities for access and research starkly limited.

Film Stock and Collections and Research in Film Archives in the United States, in Israel, and in Other Countries

In addition to large, established film archives such as the National Archives (Washington DC) and Library of Congress (Washington DC) several film and video archives in the United States specialize in collecting and processing film sources on the Holocaust and put them at the public's disposal:

> United States Holocaust Memorial Museum, Washington, DC (videotheque and integrated database)
> Museum of Jewish Heritage, New York (integrated database)
> Jewish Museum, New York (integrated database)
> YIVO Institute for Jewish Research, New York (documentation and archive)
> National Center for Jewish Film, Waltham MA (archive and rentals)

Archives at the two large universities in Los Angeles, UCLA and USC, and the Library of Motion Picture Arts and Sciences keep extensive documentation on films about the end of World War II, liberation of concentration camps, and Displaced Persons' Camps. UCLA's film archive includes films on Allied liberation of concentration camps.

Collections records in U.S. archives vary considerably in technical, formal, and quantitative aspects. Some archives have only subject-card catalogues, others have extensive databases.

In Israel a number of museums, archives, and research institutions collect and record film sources on the history and impact of the Holocaust and put them at public disposal:

> Steven Spielberg Jewish Film Archive, Jerusalem (This archive has published a preliminary record of its own collections as well as of those at Yad Vashem and at other memorial institutions and archives.)
> Israel Film Archive/Jerusalem Cinematheque, Jerusalem
> Yad Vashem, Jerusalem

In addition, a number of European film archives have small specialized collections. Two examples are the Imperial War Museum in London and Národni Filmový Archiv in Prague.

Eastern European film archives in Poland, the Czech Republic, Hungary, Russia, and elsewhere have film materials on Holocaust history. Effective archival and contextual recording of these collections will have to take place within the framework of international cooperation. Good contact has been established with some of these archives and should lead to close cooperation.

Intensive cooperation already exists with the archives, museums, and institutions in Germany and abroad listed above. Partners in the United States and Israel offer their experience with their documentation systems, and data exchanges can easily be arranged.

Present Research Level

Very recently, it has been possible to gain valuable experience with an extensive filmography preserved on electronic data processing systems. The centennial Movie Film Jubilee in 1995 provided the impulse on a European level to coordinate and standardize records of entire national cinematographies. European film archives have since begun taking decisive steps to this end. In the Federal Republic of Germany, the editors of "CineGraph: Lexicon of German Language Film" (*CineGraph. Lexikon zum Deutschsprachigen Film*) and several members of the Cinematic Association have founded the German Filmographic Project (DEFI). Once basic records on all European films and all movies shown in Europe have been published, the basic research level will rise decisively. In addition to this project the authors of "CineGraph: Lexicon of German Language Film" have been collecting filmographic and cinematic data on German language film history for years. Since last year, the Project is collaborating closely with "filmportal.de," the central platform for free-of-charge information about German film, provided under the overall direction of the Deutsches Filminstitut—DIF in Frankfurt.

However, to date film archives in Germany have practically no topically indexed filmographies of contemporary history. Experience has shown that written sources (production information, production reports, film script records, film reviews, censorship documents, information on historical context, biographical documents) are of particular importance when processing film material relevant to Holocaust history. Many films no longer exist at all or exist only as fragments. But even existing film materials often possess a hidden meaning pertaining to the Holocaust that requires contextual knowledge in order to be ascertained. The (German) National Archives Film Archive and some of the state subsidized (öffentlich-rechtlich) television stations have begun to create annotated topical indices of their own audiovisual collections. The Hessian State Radio and Television (Hessischer Rundfunk), for example, has categorized topical films on "Jewish History," while the South West State Radio and Television (Südwestfunk) categorizes films on Holocaust and National Socialist history. Both have published their results, leading to a relevant overlap with "Cinematography of the Holocaust" as far as films go that the television stations produced themselves. In addition, Südwestfunk, Moses Mendelssohn Center in Potsdam, and National Archives Film Archive have begun to coordinate their topical research and publication planning with the Fritz Bauer Institute.

Archives in the United States, in Israel, and in Germany as well (the National Archives Film Archive, for example, inspired by its cooperation with the Fritz Bauer Institute) have commenced a certain amount of recording, which they gear logistically to the individual archive's own needs and interests. They have also begun using corresponding input systems. These archival surveys usually offer no more than a basic tracking system for the film materials in the archive itself. Nevertheless, an inventory extending beyond national borders which covers the many structural levels to be found in film material and which would make it possible to put the data into a thesaurus, has yet to be realized anywhere.

Preliminary Steps

In addition to task force conferences there have been several individual research projects and preliminary studies on various primary source materials. These include film material documenting the Holocaust survivors' situation in the DP camps (displaced persons' camps), Allied forces' films on concentration camp liberation, film documents on NS criminal trials, and film productions from the German Democratic Republic.

A filmography database has been developed based on the film lexicon CineGraph's tried and true standards and on preliminary research at Fritz Bauer Institute. The database will serve as a "blueprint" for the proposed research project.

The pilot study "Displaced Persons in Films" began in 1993. Information on approximately 1,200 film titles was sought and found in numerous archives in Germany and elsewhere. Six hundred of these titles have been recorded as records in the database.

Similar preliminary studies have been carried out on film documentation of National Socialist criminal trials. For years Fritz Bauer Institute has been cooperating with the Steven Spielberg Jewish Film Archive in Jerusalem on indexing the 250-hour-long video documents produced during the Eichmann trial.

The Fritz Bauer Institute's filmography and cinematography all in all includes 3,700 database records, chosen according to the aforementioned topics. This "pilot study," as it were, enables a realistic estimate of the work involved in in-depth recording and offers a representative cross-section of the huge quantity of material to be surveyed. The existing database records, some of them fragmentary, have to be worked over and set into relation to the overall growing body of film material. Some of the planned relational links will be optional, and only successively included. Further preliminary steps taken include the already existent infrastructure: office organization, basic electronic data processing equipment, library, text archive, video unit, and so forth.

The Body of Film Material

1. Film documents produced by the Germans before 1945 play a central role in the index: "firsthand" documents such as *Judenexekution in Libau* (1941), or *Die Zusammenlegung der letzten Juden aus Dresden in das Lager am Hellerberg* (1942), plus propaganda films such as *Der ewige Jude* (1940, Germany, Fritz Hippler), *Theresienstadt. Ein Dokumentarfilm aus dem jüdischen Siedlungsgebiet* (1944, Germany, Kurt Gerron).

2. An extensive selection of films from the preserved stocks of films by the U.S. Army Signal Corps and other film documents by the Allies are being indexed and documented. These films, which accompany the liberation of the death camps by the Allied soldiers and depict the life of the Holocaust survivors in the DP camps, represent one focal point

of the project. Some of these films were made by famous American film directors, such as, for example, George Stevens, who filmed the liberation of the Dachau concentration camp.

3. The main store of film material showing the National Socialists' annihilation of European Jewry consists, above all, of the films made by the U.S. Army Signal Corps immediately after liberation. The later compilation films, the numerous documentaries dealing with reports by eyewitnesses, and even the language of feature films, such as, for example, *Schindler's List*, have repeated recourse, directly or indirectly, to that footage taken by the Allies in 1945 in Bergen-Belsen, Buchenwald, Dachau, and other camps, while the takes by Russian cameramen in Auschwitz (some of them several weeks *after* liberation) only gained access to "cinema memory" at a later point in time.

4. Currently, around 150 anti-Nazi films—American feature films on the theme produced between 1939 and 1945—are being indexed. These will be followed by a further series of "anti-fascist" feature films produced in the USSR in the 1930s and 1940s.

5. Documentary films made after 1945. Whereas the different feature film genres were hesitant to address the theme of the Holocaust, as of 1945 the most varied documentary film forms played an important role in the reception of the crimes, from the weekly newsreels, and fundraising and reeducation films, to masterpieces by Claude Lanzmann, *Shoah*, and a rapidly increasing number of television reports.

6. Feature films made after 1945. American, European, and Israeli cinema addressed the theme of the Holocaust in numerous films, which document the extent and continuity of the debate and, above all, the way the approaches to the theme have altered in the course of time (keyword: fictionalization).

7. The task of this part of the overall project is to index the main store of those documentary and feature films produced in the English-speaking world from 1945 to today. These films show the—for Holocaust studies and the historiography of film—remarkable persistence of film images of the Holocaust. Furthermore, the significance for cultural memory since 1945 of the Holocaust, and the films that bear witness to it, is an important factor in the different historiographical and moral interpretations of the history and impact of the Holocaust on the present, and in most varied literary and artistic debates on the Holocaust.

8. In 2000, the DEFA Foundation subsidized another section of the project, entitled "The Persecution and Murder of European Jews 1933–1945 as a Theme in DEFA and Other German Film Productions," which indexed relevant documentary films from the GDR. Unlike in

West Germany, documentary film in the GDR focused at an early stage on National Socialism as a priority theme. The Holocaust was also a propaganda topic dealt with in a very indirect way for the specific purposes of the respective policy of that system. Only by way of exception, and then more covertly, did the DEFA films allow an undistorted view of the history of the murder of the European Jews. Comparative studies with the taboos, resistances, and distorted symbolizations in productions from the Federal Republic suggest themselves.

9. Extensive research was taking place on films and film material connected to the Frankfurt Auschwitz trial when the Fritz Bauer Institute presented its exhibition *"Auschwitz-Prozess. 4 Ks 2/63. Frankfurt am Main. Historisch-dokumentarische Ausstellung zum Frankfurter Auschwitz-Prozess."* This research was followed by documentation and indexing film and cinematic documents to other famous trials, such as IMT in Nuremberg, the Eichmann trial in Jerusalem, Majdanek trial in Düsseldorf, and the Barbie trial in Lyon.

10. Victims and perpetrators have not just been communicating their memories in front of the camera since the Shoah Foundation began large-scale recordings of interviews with contemporaries of the Holocaust. Such interviews have been part of documentaries for many years. These documentaries are an important part of our project in terms of the content of the memories and the form of the audio-visual representation of memories communicated by word of mouth.

11. Present research of the project is thoroughly surveying and documenting films and film documents presenting Jewish life in German and Austrian film, mainly from the years 1933 to 1945, but also from the previous periods—Kaiser Reich and Weimar Republic—as well as in postwar West and East Germany. The film collection is to include all forms: fiction films, documentaries, and television productions. The project focuses on the history of how Jewish life has been presented in German film with special reference to anti-Semitism, the Holocaust, and the history of National Socialism. This means dealing with visual material centering on stereotypical presentations of Jews, on anti-Semitic prejudice formation, and on visual fantasies of annihilating Jews. Other materials, however, will show Jewish self-representations in German film before 1933. Documentation on postwar German film in the Federal Republic of Germany and the German Democratic Republic concentrates on the one hand on material resulting from repression, transference, or philo-Semitic illusions. On the other hand it will include those films that discuss these psychological mechanisms, and those whose competent, empathic approach does justice to the victims.

Communication and Cooperation

The work group "Cinematography of the Holocaust" has been holding
annual seminars with international participants since 1992; the symposia are organized by the respective host partners of the group. So far,
these symposia have dealt with themes such as, in 1997 in Hamburg:
"Anti-Semitic Images—Anti-Semitism and the Image"; 1998 in Berlin:
"Home Movies and the Jewish Experience: The Example of the Lisa
Lewenz Film Collection in New York"; in 1999 in Frankfurt: "The Past
in the Present: Confrontations with the Holocaust in Feature Films in
Postwar German Society East and West"; 2001 in Hamburg: "The Role
of Trivial and Popular Media in Remembering the Holocaust"; 2002 in
München: "'Deutscher Wald, Deutsches Haus . . .' (German Woods and
German Home): The Nationalsocialist Documentary between Mystifica-
tion and 'Science'"; 2003 in Stuttgart: "Zwiespalt des Erinnerns: Opfer
und Täter des Holocaust in Film- und Fernsehdokumentationen er BRD
und DDR" (Dichotomy of Memory. Perpetrator, Victims and Holocaust
in Cinema and TV in West- and Eastern Germany); 2004 in Wien:
"Wien, Budapest, Prag"; 2005 in Berlin (Part 1) and 2006 in Frankfurt
(Part 2): "Nuremberg and Its Lesson: Der Nürnberger Hauptkriegs-
verbrecher-Prozess und die großen Prozesse gegen nationalsozialistische
Täter" (The Nuremburg Trial of the Major War Criminals and the Principal Trials Against the National Socialist Perpetrators).

Project Planning

Status and Significance for German Society

By establishing the project within the German archival landscape and by
including a task force with an international structure, the project takes
the following fact into consideration: archiving and registration, recording, and research on films documenting National Socialist politics of
destruction, focused on and in reference to the Holocaust's singularity,
has not yet taken place in Germany. Thus, the annual task force seminars on selected project issues must continue to bring together a circle
of international experts.

Reasons for the present situation are manifold and have to do with
the specific postwar German ways of dealing with National Socialist mass
murder. These have included social mechanisms of repression as well as
the previous actual historical experience on the part of the perpetrator
society with various disparate, contradictory steps in a process that ultimately led to European Jewry's almost complete annihilation. From the

viewpoint of a historiography based on the perspective of the perpetrators, the break with civilization caused by the Holocaust can only be grasped in a fragmentary way and is rooted in the perpetrators' contexts. As such it does not fit into the victims' universalistic perspectives on the Holocaust as a crime against humanity. Relevant film material is so extensive because the complexity of causes and effects of these processes in German society, in the countries to which survivors emigrated, and in the community of nations as a whole must be taken into consideration. After the two German states were unified, confronting the Holocaust in Germany became more and more important. In comparison to written and audio sources, visual sources are vivid and seemingly authentic and as such offer considerable educational possibilities. For the same reasons, however, visual sources carry risks and problems that must be taken into account as a subject for critical research on both the sources themselves and their subsequent impact.

Note

1. On January 15, 1995, fifty years after the National Socialist concentration and extermination camps were liberated, the State of Hesse, the City of Frankfurt-am-Main, and the Friends of the Fritz Bauer Institute Association founded the first German interdisciplinary center for the study and documentation of the history and the impact of the Holocaust. The Fritz Bauer Institute is trying to offer ideas and to sharpen our awareness of the way our society has developed since Auschwitz and of the ways we have confronted the consequences. Scientific reconstruction and a careful analysis of the means and limits to commemoration and representation are prerequisites to a better understanding of the significance and the effects of Auschwitz on our political culture. The Institute is named after Fritz Bauer, who in 1959, after becoming Hessian State Attorney General, had an essential part in the capture of Adolf Eichmann and set the stage for the Frankfurt Auschwitz Trial which took place 1963–65. For the first time in Germany, this trial evoked a wide public response and a readiness previously lacking to confront recent German history.

Contributors

Jean-Louis Comolli, the critic, filmmaker, essayist, and professor, is the author of *Arrêt sur histoire* (with Jacques Rancière) and *Voir et pouvoir*.

Hubert Damisch is an art historian and the author of *Ruptures-cultures*, *Le Jugement de Pâris*, and *Les Mots et les images*.

Arnaud Desplechin is a filmmaker and the director of *A Christmas Tale*, among other films.

Jean-Michel Frodon is the author of *L'Âge moderne du cinéma français*, *La Projection nationale*, and *Horizon cinéma*, and is the former managing editor of *Cahiers du Cinéma*.

Bill Krohn is a writer and critic, and the Los Angeles correspondent for *Cahiers du Cinéma*. He is the author of *Hitchcock at Work*, *Alfred Hitchcock*, and *Stanley Kubrick*.

Claude Lanzmann, the writer and filmmaker, is head of *Les Temps Modernes* and author of *Au sujet de Shoah* and *Le Lièvre de Patagonie*.

Stuart Liebman is a historian and professor at Queens College and CUNY Graduate Center, New York. He is the editor of *Claude Lanzmann's Shoah: Key Essays*.

Sylvie Lindeperg is a historian and professor at Université Paris 3. She is the author of *Clio de 5 à 7* and *Nuit et brouillard un film dans l'histoire*.

Ronny Loewy is a historian and director of the Cinema of the Holocaust project at Fritz Bauer Institute, Frankfurt.

Jacques Mandelbaum is a cinema critic and journalist for *Le Monde*. He is the author of *Jean-Luc Godard* and *Anatomie d'un film*.

Marie-José Mondzain is a philosopher and director of research, Centre National de la Recherche Scientifique, Paris, as well as the author of *Image, icône, économie, L'Image peut-elle tuer?*, and *Le Commerce des regards*.

Ariel Schweitzer is a cinema historian and critic, and professor in the Film and Television Department, Faculty of Arts, Tel Aviv University. He is the author of *Le cinéma israélien de la modernité*.

Annette Wieviorka is a historian and director of research, Centre National de la Recherche Scientifique, Paris. She is the author of *Déportation et genocide: Entre la mémoire et l'oubli, L'Ère du témoin* (in English as *The Era of the Witness*), and *Auschwitz*.

Index

Pages in italic denote photographs or photographic captions

379

PHOTO CREDITS

U.S. Army Signal Corps/U.S. Counsel for Prosecution of Axis Criminality, Washington DC: p. 268.

International Pictures (*The Stranger* by Orson Welles): p. 234.

Argos Films (*Night and Fog* by Alain Resnais): pp. 235, 238, 239.

Vides Cinematografica (*Kapò* by Gilles Pontecorvo): pp. 276–77.

Titus Productions Inc. (*Holocaust* by Marvin Chomsky): p. 242.

Harun Farocki Filmproduktion (*Images of the World and the Inscription of War* by Harun Farocki): p. 243.

Historia/Les Films Aleph/Ministère de la Culture de la République Française (*Shoah* by Claude Lanzmann): pp. 244, 245.

ABC Circle Films/American Broadcasting Company (ABC)/Dan Curtis Productions/ Jadran Films/Paramount Television ("War and Remembrance" by Dan Curtis and Tommy Groszman): p. 246.

Universal Pictures Inc./Amblin Entertainment (*Schindler's List* by Steven Spielberg): pp. 247, 248, 249.

Cecchi Gori Group Tiger Cinematografica/Melampo Cinematografica (*La Vita è bella* by Roberto Benigni): p. 250.

Amythos Productions (*The Specialist* by Eyal Sivan): p. 251.

Philippe Mesnard (photo of the poster for the Trust band in the Paris subway): p. 252.

Ken Lipper/June Beallor Productions/Shoah Foundation/Survivors of the Shoah Visual History Foundation (*The Last Days* by James Moll): p. 253.

REUTERS/Holocaust Memorial Museum: p. 254.